# Citizens Plus

 Brenda and David McLean
Canadian Studies Series

Other books in the series:
W.H. New, *Borderlands:
How We Talk about Canada* (1998).

Alan C. Cairns

# Citizens Plus: Aboriginal Peoples and the Canadian State

**UBC**Press · Vancouver · Toronto

Printed in Canada on acid-free paper ∞

ISBN 0-7748-0767-9 (hardcover)
ISBN 0-7748-0768-7 (paperback)

**Canadian Cataloguing in Publication Data**

Cairns, Alan C.
 Citizens plus

  Includes bibliographical references and index.
  ISBN 0-7748-0767-9 (bound); ISBN 0-7748-0768-7 (paperback)

  1. Native peoples — Canada — Government relations.* 2. Canada. Royal Commission on Aboriginal Peoples. 3. Indigenous peoples. I. Title
E92.C23 2000                    323.1'197071                    C99-911205-8

This book has been published with the help of a grant from the Humanities and Social Sciences Federation of Canada, using funds provided by the Social Sciences and Humanities Research Council of Canada.

UBC Press acknowledges the financial support of the Government of Canada through the Book Publishing Industry Development Program (BPIDP) for our publishing activities.

Canadä

We also gratefully acknowledge the support of the Canada Council for the Arts for our publishing program, as well as the support of the British Columbia Arts Council.

Set in Documenta and Citizen
Printed and bound in Canada by Friesens
Copy editor: Gail Copeland
Designer: George Vaitkunas
Indexer: Annette Lorek
Proofreader: Darlene Money

UBC Press
University of British Columbia
2029 West Mall
Vancouver, BC V6T 1Z2
(604) 822-5959
Fax: 1-800-668-0821
E-mail: info@ubcpress.ubc.ca
www.ubcpress.ubc.ca

# Contents

# Acknowledgments

I wish to thank Brenda and David McLean for their support for the Chair of Canadian Studies through their generous contribution to the University of British Columbia fundraising campaign. Allan Smith, Chair of the Program in Canadian Studies; Don Blake, Chair of the Political Science Department; and Richard Erickson, Principal of Green College, organized the presentation of preliminary versions of the first three chapters as public lectures at Green College in March 1995. They have my gratitude for giving me deadlines, audiences, and a venue to try out my ideas. I thank Nicola Malim Hall for arranging off-campus lectures to a downtown audience. Richard Cavell, successor to Allan Smith, encouraged and prodded me, in an appropriate mix, to leave some books unread if I was serious in my desire to contribute to the discussion of how Aboriginal peoples and other Canadians could fashion better relations with each other.

Tim Schouls, University of British Columbia; Christopher Adams, Queen's University; Andrew Staples, University of Toronto; and especially Russell Isinger, University of Saskatchewan, greatly eased my task by providing excellent research assistance. Peter Milroy, Director, and Jean Wilson, Senior Editor, at UBC Press concealed the impatience they must have felt about my snail-like progress behind a mask of professional civility. Emily Andrew, Acquisitions Editor, and her colleagues at UBC Press were very helpful in the closing stages of the publishing process.

Research funding was provided at various times by the Canada Council, the University of British Columbia, the Political Science Department and Faculty of Law at the University of Toronto, the School of Policy Studies, Queen's University, and for 1997-8 by the Law Foundation of Saskatchewan, as part of the support for the Law Foundation Chair that I held at the University of Saskatchewan.

Chapter 4, "The Constitutional Vision of the Royal Commission on Aboriginal Peoples," has benefited from the comments, often extensive, of Eric Bergbusch, Kathy Brock, David Cameron, Joyce Green, David Hawkes, Sam La Selva, Peter Meekison, Jim Miller, Paul Tennant, Jill Wherrett, and Norman Zlotkin. I am also very grateful to the three anonymous assessors of the manuscript for their suggestions.

My final heartfelt thanks go to the governments and citizens of Canada, and the universities they support, which make the life of a scholar possible. Within the university context, the day-to-day support comes from the departments and faculties. Don Blake, Chair of Political Science before I retired from the University of British Columbia in 1995, and Peter Mackinnon, Dean of Law for most of my two-year stay at the College of Law, University of Saskatchewan, 1997-8, were models of unobtrusive support and encouragement. I thank them warmly.

### Permissions Note
The quotation on pp. 22-3, from Georges Erasmus, "We the Dene," in *Dene Nation: The Colony Within*, ed. Mel Watkins (Toronto: University of Toronto Press, 1977), 178-9, is reproduced with permission. The quotation on p. 71 is from *In the Rapids: Navigating the Future of First Nations*, by Ovide Mercredi and Mary Ellen Turpel. Copyright © 1994 by Ovide Mercredi and Mary Ellen Turpel. Reprinted by permission of Penguin Books Canada Limited.

Citizens Plus

# Introduction

Within a span of 25 years,
Aboriginal peoples and their rights have emerged
from the shadows, to the sidelines,
to occupy centre stage.[1]

Public lectures, the genesis of the following chapters, are neither speeches nor orally delivered learned articles. When the speaker knows his words will later find their way onto the printed page, the ambiguity of the genre is compounded. Gesture and intonation will be lost. Hurrying on to the next thought – the lecturer's stratagem for concealing weak points in the analysis – can be frustrated by the attentive reader, who can press the "stop" button, and put arguments under the microscope.

Earlier versions of Chapters 1 to 3 were given as the Brenda and David McLean Lectures in Canadian Studies at the University of British Columbia in March 1995, under the title "Aboriginal Peoples in Canada: From Audience to Centre Stage." At the time, I thought (perhaps unwisely) that before I revised the lectures for publication – an obligation attached to the McLean Chair in Canadian Studies that I then held – it would make sense to delay any such changes until the *Report of the Royal Commission on Aboriginal Peoples* (hereinafter "the *Report*") appeared. It did not seem sensible to publish lectures on some of the issues that were central to the Commission's agenda without knowing its analysis and recommendations. Further, the possibility of adding an extra chapter dealing with the *Report* appealed to me.

The decision to delay, as it turned out, was made for me: the *Report* did not appear for another twenty-one months, by which time my relation to the original notes from which I spoke had become somewhat attenuated. Aboriginal issues had continued to evolve. The literature had proliferated. I was no longer who I had been. Then there was the *Report,* over 3,500 pages long, plus a mountain of research studies and hearings on a CD-ROM. Grasping the *Report*'s analysis and recommendations was not a task for one or even several weekends. At the various conferences on the *Report* that I have attended, I have not yet met anyone, other than Commission members, who has read it from front cover to distant back cover. This is one, admittedly minor, reason why the public response of governments to the *Report* has been so minimal.[2]

The appearance of the *Report* justified the addition of a fourth chapter to this book, which brings the interpretive framework of the earlier chapters to its analysis. The *Report* and its attendant research almost certainly qualify as the most exhaustive analysis ever undertaken of indigenous peoples in Canada, possibly in the world. It deserves more attention than it has thus far received.

The *Report* did convince me that one key theme of my original lectures was still useful. The many themes I could have addressed in the original lectures had shaken down to two, the second directly relevant to the Commission. The first chapter puts the Canadian situation into the global context of the rise and fall of empires, and argues that how Aboriginal/non-Aboriginal relations developed in Canada was and still is heavily influenced by changes in the international environment. We have been and still are responding as much to the messages about the changing relations among peoples that flow across our borders, as to purely domestic pressures. More accurately, the latter feed on the former, not to forget that for other countries we are part of their international environment. To look only at ourselves is to fail to see how we have become who we are. The second theme, for which the first is prologue, is the attempt to make sense of our intellectual and political grappling with the relations between Aboriginal and non-Aboriginal peoples in Canada. This is the focus, although there are occasional detours, of the remaining chapters. The key words and phrases here are assimilation, wardship, civilizing mission, inherent rights, treaty federalism, nation-to-nation, "citizens plus," partnership, First Nations, sovereignty, citizenship, and the two-row wampum – an illustrative, albeit not exhaustive list. These key words are central to the Commission's analysis, and to mine. Our assessments of their import and weighting, however, differ.

My point is not complicated. The language we employ – how we describe each other and our relationship – what we define as the goal toward which we are heading – is immensely significant. Who participates in developing the discourse, of course, influences its content. Thus the discourse of assimilation enjoyed a long hegemony largely because those who were opposed to it – especially the status Indian population – were silenced by their marginalization and by official policy. There was a potential debate throughout the assimilation era, but it was not joined. The majority society did not hear the other side. Aboriginal people, of course, knew that the majority view was not their own. They knew the other side – its weapons, its arguments, its power – and they knew, depending on the waxing and waning of their own resistance, the extent and nature of their silenced dissent.

The virtue of the contemporary period is that the debate about how we should relate to each other has opened up. We are closer to having an actual discussion than we have ever been. To say that there are imperfections would be an understatement. Aboriginal political organizations have shaky foundations, which weakens their representative role, and non-Aboriginals, in some cases, are subject to various cultural constraints that inhibit candour. The failure of the *Report of the Royal Commission on Aboriginal Peoples* to get a response from governments, except the belated and minimalist federal government response (discussed in Chapter 4 below), or to stimulate a more general public discussion, is disturbing and astonishing.

That said, relative to yesterday, there is now a debate under way, to which the following chapters are an intended contribution. My basic thesis is that the debate needs to be reformulated, that our language and our arguments are deficient from what I consider to be a central concern. What kind of country-wide Canadian political community are we aiming for? A viable constitutional vision, I argue, must address two facts: Aboriginal peoples and other Canadians differ from each other; our differences are not total. There is much overlap – and we share a common space. Are our future constitutional arrangements going to foster some version of common belonging so that we will feel responsible for each other, and will be eager to engage in some common enterprises, as well as accommodate our differences?

That large question is the focus of the following chapters. With the failed policy of assimilation behind us, but with the cleavages and suspicions that past policies have fostered still alive, can we construct a new complex Canadian people in which our differences are recognized, but do not monopolize our civic selves? Can we be, positively, more than what divides us? My thesis is that our present discourses have difficulty being simultaneously sensitive to our diversity and yet sympathetic to and supportive of a togetherness that is more than geographical.

I freely admit my limitations for my self-assigned task. The territory is an emotional minefield. The literature – legal, historical, political, sociological, anthropological, feminist, and more – is now unmanageable. The monopoly formerly enjoyed by white voices has been eroded. Aboriginal peoples now speak for themselves, in theatres, university lecture halls, academic journals, and public life, including in our constitutional discussions. The Aboriginal voice is plural, not single. "Aboriginal" covers not only the obvious diversity of Indian, Inuit and Métis, but multiple internal distinctions – men's voice and women's voice, modernizers and traditionalists, urban Aboriginals in Toronto and their relatives on isolated northern reserves.

Amidst all this diversity, there is common agreement that the present situation is unacceptable, and progress toward a better future cannot be delayed. Many Aboriginal voices are angry – the time for waiting, for talk, for research should be behind us. The implicit – often the explicit – message is that *now* is the time for action.

The question, however, remains – Behind what banner do we march? The Reform Party platform confirms the survival of the ancient assimilation policy. At the other end of the spectrum, a strain of separatism runs through some Aboriginal discourse. Perhaps the most frequent image of self-chosen Aboriginal futures is of parallelism – Aboriginal and non-Aboriginal communities travelling side by side, coexisting but not getting in each other's way.

As I see it, the present discussion is too polarized for our future health. There is insufficient attention to the middle ground. I am sufficiently old-fashioned to believe, even in a globalization era, that countries still matter, that those who share space together must share more than space. In one of the dimensions of their being, they need to share a sense of belonging to the same community for more than trivial purposes. My focus, therefore, is the whole. We have no lack of scholarship seeking to maximize Aboriginal self-government, especially from legal scholars. And we have some addressing questions of how it will all fit together,[3] which is where I locate these lectures.

How we define ourselves is not a trivial matter. A label is not a theory, but it constrains how we think about the subject matter the label encompasses. When the identification of francophone Quebeckers shifted from French Canadians to Québécois, the Canadian Constitution lost much of its former legitimacy. When Indians were labelled "wards," a host of behaviour-controlling assumptions automatically followed. When the "two nations" view of Canada appeared to be growing in legitimacy in the 1960s, those Canadians with other backgrounds who were left out of the charmed circle feared they were being reduced to second-class citizen status. When Indians successfully attached the label "First Nations" to their public recognition, and Inuit and Métis also spoke the language of nationhood, the traditional marginalized place of Aboriginal peoples in the constitutional order became anachronistic almost overnight. In other words, labels matter. At a minimum, they define a situation and sometimes they are vehicles for a social or political theory.

Thus the RCAP reiteration of nation-to-nation as the lens for viewing Aboriginal/non-Aboriginal relations inevitably conjures up images of a mini-international system and weakens the idea of a common citizenship. Academic and political support for a transformed federalism in which Aboriginal nations within Canada are defined by treaties – "treaty federalism" – drives us toward a view of Canada as a multinational polity in which we relate to each other through the separate nations we belong to – a lens that can only reduce our feelings of responsibility for each other and our willingness to share. Both treaty federalism and nation-to-nation are proud, dignifying, and status-raising rubrics for Aboriginal peoples, but this benefit comes at a price. They distance Aboriginal and non-Aboriginal peoples from each other. They also imply that our relations are community relations, not those of shared citizenship.

Many of the labels that now vie for our attention – treaty federalism, nation-to-nation, two-row wampum, third order of government,

Aboriginal rights, inherent right to self-government – reinforce the Aboriginal/non-Aboriginal cleavage. Often, that is their explicit intention.

We need to rethink and perhaps modify some of the descriptions and labels we apply to our present situation. Are the descriptions accurate? Do the labels have positive or negative consequences? Even though the RCAP terminology is later in time than the "citizens plus" language of the 1960s and 1970s – a phrase introduced to policy discussions by the *Hawthorn Report,*[4] and which stressed the virtues of a common citizenship as well as the reinforcement of difference – this does not make it superior. The fact that nationhood may have displaced, or weakened the support for Canadian citizenship in the arguments of some Aboriginal leaders and academic supporters of the maximum constitutional space for Aboriginal peoples says nothing about the long-run viability of their goals. The occasionally claimed incommensurability of Aboriginal and non-Aboriginal values, and the linked claim of profound cultural difference of Aboriginal from non-Aboriginal ways of life as a justification for self-government, sit uneasily with the profound interpenetration of Aboriginal and non-Aboriginal cultures.

We are impoverished by some of the contemporary labels and descriptions we employ. It is odd, possibly even bizarre, that the nation-to-nation label enjoys almost a conceptual hegemony at a time when the urban Aboriginal population – for which nation-to-nation has little meaning – is growing rapidly and already constitutes half of the Aboriginal peoples in Canada. It is unfortunate that citizenship as an encompassing label applying to both Aboriginals and non-Aboriginal peoples is in retreat in much policy advocacy at the very time when the former need and seek massive assistance from the latter. It is a dangerous exaggeration when the *Penner Report,*[5] Aboriginal leaders, and scholars describe the potential jurisdiction of Aboriginal governments, with their limited populations, in grandiose terms, and pay negligible attention to the continuing relation between members of Aboriginal nations and the federal and provincial governments. It is misleading when the massive effects of long and intensive cultural contacts are silently ignored in language that magnifies "otherness" in the service of separate treatment. In sum, to exaggerate our solitudes at the expense of a recognition of our moral and factual interdependence is a recipe for poor policy in the short run and profound regrets in the long run. The cultural differences of the past have diminished saliency. Intermarriage, urban living, the educational explosion among Aboriginal Canadians, and pervasive globalization pressures produce overlapping commonalities of belief and behaviour. Simultaneously, of course, the past identities that separated us from each other survive in memory and are reinforced by politics and policies that both feed on and provide sustenance to difference. The policy question we face is how to respond to these coexisting antithetical messages of where we are.

Neither a return to the goal of obliterating difference of the 1969 federal government White Paper,[6] nor the two-row wampum vision of separate societies on separate paths heading to separate destinations, which casts a blind eye on our interconnectedness, has much useful advice to offer. Both visions ignore significant realities. We are left, then, with the age-old task of restraining the imperialism of the homogenizers and simultaneously of persuading the disciples of difference and maximum exit that neither our togetherness nor our separateness can be escaped from, and that they can be most beneficially linked in symbolic tension if capped by a common citizenship. We may have taken the wrong turn in the road. C. Vann Woodward, writing of race relations in the American South, argued that between the end of the American Civil War and the vigorous introduction of Jim Crow legislation in the closing years of the nineteenth century, there was a period of improved race relations, of moves toward equality that were not aberrations, but that with fostering might have gained momentum. This, he laments, was "the forgotten alternative."[7] While the US post-Civil War situation and the Aboriginal policy evolution in Canada in the past forty years are scarcely parallels, the concept of "forgotten alternatives" may have merit. As argued in later chapters, "citizens plus" had a supportive consistency for a decade or more after it was introduced into the debates of the 1960s. Furthermore, it was the mobilizing label employed to defeat the 1969 White Paper.

"Citizens plus" could serve as the vehicle for a socio-political theory and as a simplifying label for public consumption that recognizes the Aboriginal difference fashioned by history and the continuing desire to resist submergence and also recognizes our need to feel that we belong to each other. The Hawthorn "citizens plus" suggestion, originally directed only to the status Indian population, but capable of extension to the Inuit and the Métis, was an earlier attempt to accommodate the apartness of Aboriginal peoples from, and their togetherness with the non-Aboriginal majority. The "plus" dimension spoke to Aboriginality; the "citizens" addressed togetherness in a way intended to underline our moral obligations to each other.[8]

"Citizens plus" appears to be a good description of the goals of Aboriginal peoples in Australia – "the status and privileges of *unequal* citizens ... that is, Aboriginal people of the 1990s want to be equal citizens *and* have the rights pertaining to their special status as 'indigenous peoples.'"[9] Henry Reynolds, also writing of Australia, argues that Aboriginal people will have a national loyalty to their Aboriginal first nation and a civic loyalty to the Australian state. He adds, "the paradox ... [is] that their commitment to the state may be enhanced by the fact that it alone can underwrite and protect indigenous nationalism and self-government from inimical forces both within Australia and without."[10]

"Citizens plus" may have had its day, and thus be incapable of revival in Canada, even although it can be argued that it is a better fit with our realities than the successors that have displaced it. It speaks easily to the urban Aboriginal in a way that nation-to-nation does not, and the plus aspect can be filled with a meaning appropriate to the urban setting. The "plus" aspect can accommodate the "nation" ambitions of the self-governing landed communities, and can help shape the emerging treaty regime. Both "treaty" and "nation" can be adapted to the positive constraints of the "citizens" label, which provides civic links with non-Aboriginal Canadians – a task for which the nation-to-nation paradigm is ill suited.

It is possible, therefore, that an updated and revised concept of citizens plus is a better recipe for a togetherness we cannot escape and for the preservation of an evolving Aboriginal difference that its bearers cherish than is the emergent and potentially hegemonic language of nations, treaties, and boundaries. Citizens plus or a differently labelled contemporary version is also better able than the former to encompass both the landless and the landed, and the urban and the rural. To go back to the concept, if not necessarily to the phrase, would be to agree with the Indian Tribes of Manitoba who stated in 1971 that "the rights of Indians must be protected, whether they are due to special status or as Canadian citizens,"[11] and with Harold Cardinal, whose criticism of the 1969 White Paper reminded Canadians that they "will have to accept and recognize that we are full citizens, but we also possess special rights."[12]

In preparing this material for publication, I have been acutely conscious of the pressures and cross-currents of this deeply conflicted policy area. The subject of Aboriginal/non-Aboriginal relations – its history, present situation, and future direction – does not lend itself to clinical detachment. The "isms" that mobilize emotions intrude at every turn. However, who among us could speak if pure detachment – absolute disinterestedness – were a criterion? Who would speak if a well-rounded competence, given the complexity of the issues and the mountains of literature available, were a requirement? And surely none would speak on this issue if potential disagreement were sufficient to deter them. We overcome these hesitations with the recognition that it is in the pooling of our separate, limited understandings that a democratic society increases the likelihood that future policy will have a better stock of intellectual capital at its disposal than past policies had.

A few personal comments may help the reader. We are all informed and shaped by our individual past experiences – informed and shaped, but of course, not controlled. For an academic, each new intellectual venture is simultaneously a continuity and a departure. In my case, the formative period to this project began with my D.Phil. thesis for Oxford University. In that study,[13] I immersed myself in the late nineteenth-century background to European, especially British, imperialism. This made me aware of the extent to which we are all caught up in the spirit of the times, which provides us with the ready-made paradigms we employ to make sense of our world.

The intellectual assumptions that supported imperialism were directly relevant to my first piece of sustained research after I joined the then Department of Economics and Political Science at the University of British Columbia in 1960. The *Hawthorn Report* of the mid-1960s was a federal government inquiry into the socio-economic, political, and constitutional conditions of status Indians, with the task of advising policy makers of the route to a better future for the Indian peoples of Canada. We were asked to examine the domestic, Canadian version of imperialism – the subordination of the Indian peoples of Canada, not at that time defined as nations. That report, for which I was one of the senior staff, responsible for research in the general area of broad constitutional policy, proposed that the Indians should be viewed, as already noted, as citizens plus. By that we meant to bring them fully into the category of

Canadian citizens, believing that much of the social malaise from which they suffered was a product of the neglect that had flowed from their historical post-Confederation status as wards.

Our proposal however, was not for citizenship pure and simple – which would have identified the *Hawthorn Report* as a precursor of the 1969 White Paper – but for "citizens plus." By "plus" we referred to ongoing entitlements, some of which flowed from existing treaties, while others were to be worked out in the political processes of the future, which would identify the Indian peoples as deserving possessors of an additional category of rights based on historical priority. In other words, we sought to preserve Indian "difference" while simultaneously supporting a common citizenship as a basis for empathy and solidarity between the Indian people and the majority population. "Citizens plus" was ignored, or to be blunt, repudiated by the federal government in its 1969 White Paper, which proposed an accelerated policy of assimilation. The idea was, however, positively received by many Indian organizations and leaders and was the rallying label employed to defeat the White Paper, with the vanguard role played by the Indian Association of Alberta.

My subsequent research is less directly germane to this monograph, focusing on federalism, the Constitution, constitutional reform, and the role of the courts in constitutional change. Nevertheless, that research involved me intellectually almost without interruption in the constitutional introspection of the past thirty years. This reinforced my beliefs in the importance of symbols in our collective life, of how we construct institutions that then shape conceptions of who we are, and that there is no resting point when our peoplehood is set for all time. We are not, therefore, prisoners of history, but neither do we have blank slates on which we can write as we will. My hope is that we can employ our limited manoeuvrability in the service of greater reciprocal empathy between Aboriginal and non-Aboriginal peoples in Canada. The pursuit of that objective is the driving force behind the chapters that follow. That being said, it is also true – indeed is reflective of a deeper belief – that the goal of an academic contribution to a public policy debate is not to vanquish the opposition but to have a debate. This does not preclude passionate advocacy. It should, however, preclude the arrogant belief that questions have been replaced by answers. Now, in my fourth decade of academic life, I am more than ever committed to the belief that we should argue passionately without forgetting our fallibility. In the last chapter, I repeat the strong support for the concept of citizens plus, which I first supported a third of a century ago. I hope that I am driven by more than nostalgia.

# Chapter One

# Empire

This bland assertion that First Nations and their governments
are represented by non-aboriginal politicians who have
no interest, demonstrated or latent, in advocating our rights is bogus
and without foundation in fact or action.[1]

## The Complex Problem of "Voice"

Nowhere is our cultural disorientation better captured, or the ambiguous transitional moment in which we find ourselves more clearly underlined, than in the complex issue of voice appropriation. The issue of who can speak for whom, and who can write about whom, is a major contemporary issue in the social sciences and humanities. There is, according to two recent authors, "a crisis of representation in the human sciences."[2] One version of that crisis has surfaced around the issue of who does and should speak for and about Aboriginal peoples. The resultant debate about Aboriginal "voice" takes place in the trenches of intellectual warfare in which the artist Emily Carr is accused of cultural appropriation,[3] and the novelist W.P. Kinsella's Hobbema stories are labelled "cultural theft, the theft of Voice," by Lenore Keeshig-Tobias.[4] A display of Native artifacts at the Glenbow Museum, "The Spirit Sings: Artistic Traditions of Canada's First Peoples," designed to "demonstrate the richness, diversity, and adaptability of indigenous peoples during the first years of contact with Europeans" was boycotted by the Lubicon Indians (who at the time were seeking support for a land claim), and as a result a number of museums refused to provide artworks to the show.[5]

These incidents, and many more that could be cited, reflect the profound paradigm shift now under way, but still incomplete, in how we converse with each other across the divides of a plural, heterogeneous society in politics, in everyday encounters, in academic disciplines, and in the creative arts. It is now almost a convention for a public speaker at an academic conference to have to establish his or her credentials if the subject of the lecture is an ethnic group, a national community, or a gender to which the speaker does not belong. In constitutional politics, the most telling critique of the Meech Lake Accord was to label it the product of eleven white able-bodied males meeting in secret – a description that undermined its legitimacy to a degree that former prime ministers from Macdonald to Mackenzie King would have found inconceivable. That an "A" can represent a "B" is now a controversial statement, rather than a taken-for-granted assumption of representative politics.

Universities are not immune from the "voice" debate. The explosion of programs in Native studies, women's studies, ethnic studies, gay and lesbian studies – overwhelmingly staffed whenever possible by "their own" – and the literature they produce, testify to the attractions of identity politics, to the incursions of particularisms into intellectual territory formerly blanketed, the critics argue, by a white male hegemony whose specious claims to universalism are now, appropriately, being unmasked.

The culture of authenticity, of speaking for oneself, of insisting on being directly represented at the bargaining table by one's own, unquestionably erodes the self-confidence of "outsiders" and changes their behaviour. Many non-Aboriginal commentators on Aboriginal issues, accordingly, tread carefully, and practice a restraint that diminishes candour. There is an unwillingness to conclude that some Aboriginal objectives might be undesirable or impractical, when to do so might raise questions about the author's motives. Gibbins and Jhappan observe that the "few scholars who have dared to express doubts about the appropriateness, and indeed authenticity, of aboriginal claims have been attacked and even ridiculed, regardless of the substance of their concerns."[6] A recent non-Aboriginal author felt compelled to defend himself in his preface against the charge that he was encroaching on Aboriginal territory, even although his thesis was obviously intended to be supportive of Aboriginal goals.[7] In other cases, non-Aboriginal scholars debate whether they should leave a field they view as excessively politicized.[8]

The analysis by an American anthropologist that two politically useful consciousness-raising Maori traditions – a belief about the manner of their arrival in New Zealand and about a creator god Io – could not be historically verified, generated a major debate about the propriety, not the rigour of, his interpretation.[9] *Pakeha* (white) scholars in New Zealand no longer study the 1841 Treaty of Waitangi, because their "conclusions ... would run counter to the political agenda and arguments that Maori organizations had been making."[10] Scattered evidence suggests that some Canadian politicians are subject to similar constraints in discussing controversial Aboriginal issues.[11] These difficulties of discussion are sociologically explicable in terms of the past treatment of Aboriginal peoples by the majority, and of how deep the Aboriginal/non-Aboriginal divide has become as a result.

The claim of the formerly silenced for "voice," for their turn on the stage, needs to be respected. In a heterogeneous democratic society whose multiple groups have separate identities, the argument that one has to be one to know one to speak for one is inevitable. The corollary, however, is sometimes forgotten – a conversation with the "other" will follow. There is no point in controlling "voice," in speaking for "A" to "B," particularly when the subject is the future relations between "A" and "B," unless it is assumed that "B" can understand and respond. The objective is to have a conversation, which not only informs each speaker about the other, but transforms the relationship between them and possibly, in addition, even modifies their self-understandings. When the issue is the past, present, and future relations between Aboriginal peoples and other Canadians, the participation of citizens and scholars from both backgrounds, therefore, is an irresistible requirement. Our present discontents are largely due to the past silencing of Aboriginal voices. The resolution of this set of circumstances can only occur if we talk to each other in a way that both articulates our differences and seeks with empathy to reconcile them in the search for at least a limited version of membership in a common community.

### History and Humility

The voice appropriation issue cannot be divorced from the delegitimation of dominant non-Aboriginal élites whose former policy monopoly has left us with a legacy of failed programs and with a litter of falsified predictions.

The recognition that the predictions and policy objectives of our non-Aboriginal parents and grandparents concerning future relations between Aboriginal peoples and the majority Euro-Canadian population were hopelessly wrong is appropriately chastening. What our non-Aboriginal forebears anticipated and worked for has been repudiated by Aboriginal peoples. The "Aboriginal peoples," a phrase only recently enshrined in the Constitution, did not fade away from the shock of foreign diseases and aggressive culture contact, nor have they assimilated into the surrounding society and thus given up their desire to survive as separate peoples, as our predecessors assumed would and should be their fate.

Their hopes and predictions ring with a staggering self-confidence. In 1887 John A. Macdonald asserted that "The great aim of our civilization has been to do away with the tribal system and assimilate the Indian people in all respects with the inhabitants of the Dominion, as speedily as they are fit for the change."[12] Macdonald's thesis was elaborated in 1920 by Duncan Campbell Scott, Deputy Superintendent General of Indian Affairs (1913-32) in a presentation to a House of Commons Committee to amend the Indian Act to give the Indian Department the power to enfranchise Indians compulsorily:

> I want to get rid of the Indian problem. I do not think as a matter of fact, that this country ought to continuously protect a class of people who are able to stand alone. That is my whole point. I do not want to pass into the citizens' class people who are paupers. This is not the intention of the Bill. But after one hundred years, after being in close contact with civilization it is enervating to the individual or to a band to continue in that state of tutelage, when he or they are able to take their position as British citizens or Canadian citizens, to support themselves, and stand alone. That has been the whole purpose of Indian education and advancement since the earliest times. One of the very earliest enactments was to provide for the enfranchisement of the Indian. So it is written in our law that the Indian was eventually to become enfranchised ...
>
> Our object is to continue until there is not a single Indian in Canada that has not been absorbed into the body politic and there is no Indian question, and no Indian Department, that is the whole object of this Bill.[13]

Similar views of the Indian future were reiterated again and again by Diamond Jenness (1886-1969), one of the leading anthropological students of Aboriginal issues, although without the hard edge of Scott. "Doubtless all the tribes will disappear," he wrote in 1932. "Some will endure only a few years longer, others like the Eskimo, may last several centuries."[14]

In 1950, Walter Harris, minister responsible for Indian Affairs, reiterated long-standing Indian policy: "Indeed, it may be said that ever since Confederation the underlying purpose of Indian administration has been to prepare the Indians for full citizenship with the same rights and responsibilities as enjoyed and accepted by other members of the community ... The ultimate goal of our Indian policy is the integration of the Indians into the general life and economy of the country."[15]

As recently as 1969, the federal government White Paper on Indian Policy recommended a form of shock treatment – the abolition of the Indian Act, the winding down of the Indian Affairs Branch, and the speedy assimilation of Indian peoples into the larger society.[16] The White Paper, in effect, was Trudeau's Durham Report for the Indian peoples of Canada. In both cases, the initial premise was that a culturally backward people – French Canadians or Indians – could only benefit from a more intimate and intensive encounter with the more progressive majority society. In both cases, the supporting premise was that cultures could be ranked, that in the last analysis it was impossible to escape a Darwinian competition among cultures, and that the higher would supplant the lower. It followed that individuals who ascended from lower to higher cultures, as a by-product of a competition they did not seek, would ultimately be grateful to those who guided them on their pilgrimage. In each case, however, although separated by more than a century, both the Francophone population (of what became Quebec) and the status Indian population rejected the thesis that their progress required their cultural assimilation.

The humility to which these episodes and predictions should lead springs from the chastening reminder that we may be as mistaken about the future we both anticipate and work for as were our predecessors. In some ways, this knowledge of our predecessors' fallibility generates a kind of perverse pride, for it underlines our freedom, our capacity to outwit and outsmart the plans our predecessors had for us. We are not simply pawns in the grand design of those of our ancestors who tried to steer us in a particular direction.

Of no group in Canadian society is this truer than of the Aboriginal peoples. They have defied the predictions and aspirations of the non-Aboriginal community and its political élites who, until recently, consigned them to the margins of Canadian society, and who defined their cultures as inferior, and necessarily destined for the graveyard. The move of Aboriginal peoples from audience to centre stage, from subjects to activists, the focus of these chapters, is their version of a theme previously applied to Canada as a whole in the evocative phrase *Colony to Nation* of the historian A.R.M. Lower.[17]

In Canada, a royal commission is often the chosen instrument to change the direction in which the momentum of the past is taking us and to raise the status or recognition of a people or a marginalized group. The Royal Commission on Bilingualism and Biculturalism[18] was clearly designed as a vehicle to elevate the position of French-speaking Canadians, and thus avert a looming constitutional crisis. The Royal Commission on the Status of Women[19] was an instrument to enhance the recognition and position of women in Canadian society. The task of RCAP,[20] which issued its massive Report in the autumn of 1996, was to enhance the recognition, status, and future prospects for the Aboriginal peoples of Canada.

The striking and subsequent reporting of such royal commissions on our Canadian peoplehood signals first, an understanding that yesterday's answers are just that, and second, that innovative thinking is necessary if we are to relax the grip of the past on our behaviour and improve our chances for a more harmonious, just society. Such commissions, if they succeed in their task, help us to redefine who we are and whom we would like to become. The mere existence of RCAP, therefore, signalled a paradigm breakdown in Aboriginal/non-Aboriginal relationships, and the search for a more positive successor paradigm.[21]

### Empire at Home and Abroad

The RCAP *Report* employs "colonial" again and again to describe the treatment of Aboriginal peoples in Canada. It is a standard term, coolly employed by scholars and passionately wielded by Aboriginal activists. By contrast, the majority society did not in the past and does not now see itself as an empire ruling over subject peoples. This discrepancy in perception complicates our analysis of where we have come from, where we are, and how we might move forward. The imperial-colonial analogy is, therefore, both fruitful and misleading. The disentangling of its ambiguities, and an assessment of its relevance is the purpose of this section.

Until fairly recently, Aboriginal peoples, in typical colonial fashion, were subjects of policy. Their possible participation in the discussions that led to Confederation was a non-issue. Their subsequent political influence was meagre. From 1927 to 1951 a person could be jailed for soliciting money from any Indian to pursue legal claims without the approval of the Superintendent General of Indian Affairs. Only thirteen of the 11,261 members of the House of Commons since Confederation (as of the 1993 federal election) have identified themselves as Aboriginal.[22] Status Indians, with few exceptions, did not get the federal vote until 1960. A study of party platforms from 1867 to 1960 revealed only one innocuous reference to Aboriginal peoples, in 1887, followed by silence until a 1958 Liberal Party endorsement of "voluntary integration of the Canadian Indians into our national life as full citizens." Following the 1960 vote extension, party platform references increased dramatically.[23]

Up until the 1960s, Inuit participation in the administration of their affairs was minimal, partly because administration itself was minimal. The federal government, as Prime Minister Louis St. Laurent admitted in 1953, had administered the north "in an almost continuing state of absence of mind."[24] *Canada and Our Eskimos* published in the same year by the new Department of Northern Affairs and National Resources, was the "first major statement by the Canadian government" of Inuit policy. It was presented as a take-charge policy to enable the Inuit "to share fully the national life of Canada."[25] The previous year, when the first meeting of a new Eskimo Affairs Committee took place, involving officials of the Hudson's Bay Company and church representatives, the absence of Eskimo participation was explained by the belief "that few, if any, of them have reached the stage where they could take a responsible part in such decisions." Their views, however, were represented by those who knew them well and had "their interests and welfare very much at heart."[26]

This well-meaning paternalism pervaded every aspect of a program relocating small numbers of Inuit to the High Arctic in the 1950s. The Inuit assumed they could not challenge the vision held out to them by southern Canadians, often RCMP officers, who explained what the government had in mind for them. They did not question what the authorities presented to them as an apparent choice, because "the feeling that whites inspire in Inuit is a kind of fear, a blend of awe and intimidation, the feeling you have about a person whose behaviour you can neither control nor predict, but who is perhaps going to be dangerous."[27] According to the RCAP *Report* that studied the Inuit relocation, their "needs and aspirations ... were routinely minimized,"[28] as a by-product of the "broader view that involved making what were considered to be the objectively right decisions for a people who could not make the right decision for themselves. It is implicit in their [government] view that the consent of those involved counted for very little."[29] The Inuit were treated "like children."[30]

Status Indians, the only Aboriginal people to have a separate branch of government devoted to their affairs, were an administered people. They were in a colonial situation. Indeed, the very language used to describe them for the first century after Confederation could equally have been used in the Gold Coast (now Ghana) and Ceylon (now Sri Lanka). They were described as wards, likened to children, and assumed to be unready for full citizenship.

Government policy for the Métis is best summed up in the labels "The Forgotten People"[31] and even "The Non-People."[32] The federal government denied that they were a federal government responsibility under s. 91(24) of the British North America Act (hereinafter BNA Act), and they did not have reserves.

When provincial government interest developed in the 1930s and 1940s in response to distressing socio-economic conditions among the Métis, the responses were highly paternalistic. The Ewing Royal Commission in Alberta, which reported in 1936, expressed pejorative attitudes to "half-breeds," concluded that Métis could not run their own affairs, and recommended the establishment of government-operated farm colonies to turn the impoverished Métis into farmers. Eight colonies were established by 1940, with negligible Métis input. Until the 1980s the settlements were paternalistically operated by the settlement superior – the functional equivalent of an Indian Agent – in an overall system characterized by "excessive government control."[33] Sawchuk refers to the "iron control" over the colonies, and the difficulty of appreciating "the absolute sway [of] the [Métis] Rehabilitation Branch" up to 1970."[34]

In Saskatchewan, the Cooperative Commonwealth Federation (hereinafter CCF) government, elected in 1944, building on initiatives of previous Liberal governments, established a number of Métis colonies in the south of the province. By the late 1940s, the population of the various colonies was about 2,500 Métis, which was about one-quarter of the provincial Métis population. Although the government's motivations were humanitarian – it was shocked by the anomie, poverty, and social disorganization of the Métis communities – its practice was highly paternalistic. It was policy from above that misread the Métis by falsely assuming a Métis propensity for cooperative activity. It was administered at the local level by "government functionaries ... [who] doubted the competence of the Métis people."[35] Government enthusiasm for the colonies evaporated by the end of the 1950s. The Métis, rather like the Inuit, were either left alone in depressing social conditions, or were paternalistically taken control of by the government who knew what was best for them.

To describe the relation of governments to Indian, Inuit, and Métis as colonial – when it was not simple neglect, as for long periods it was for Inuit and Métis – is factually correct, not a misapplied ideological construction. When Premier Robert Bourassa announced the Quebec government's massive James Bay hydro project, "no one in his entire government had even considered for a moment that there was an obligation – even if only out of politeness – to let the Crees know what the government had in mind for their land and rivers."[36] The experience of being colonized was graphically described by Georges Erasmus in 1977.

With the coming of the Europeans, our experience as a people changed. We experienced relationships in which we were made to feel inferior. We were treated as incompetent to make decisions for ourselves. Europeans would treat us in such a way as to make us feel that they knew, better than we ourselves, what was good for us. Those who presented themselves as "superior" began to define what was good for us. They began to define our world for us. They began to define us as well. Even physically, our communities and our landmarks were named in terms foreign to our understanding. We were no longer the actors – we were being acted upon. We were no longer naming the world – we were being named. We were named "Indian," we were being called "non-status and status Indians" or Métis ...

Traditionally, we acted; today we are acted upon ... We have been subjected to over fifty years of colonization, of forced assimilation. This experience has had a profound effect on us as a people. Whereas traditionally our laws were agreements we made amongst ourselves, today we see "laws" as something someone else imposes on us. Traditionally, we educated our own; today "education" is what someone else does to our children, often by forcibly removing them from their own families.[37]

In the academic world, Aboriginal peoples were, on the whole, subjects of studies undertaken by university-based scholars from the majority society. As late as the mid-1960s, when what became the Hawthorn team was being assembled as a federal government inquiry into the situation of status Indians, the federal Cabinet was concerned that the initial research team was insufficiently representative – not however of the Indian people – but of Canada's French-English duality at the time of the Quebec Quiet Revolution.[38]

Academics, especially anthropologists, along with journalists and other non-Aboriginal observers, supplemented by non-Aboriginal politicians, had a virtual monopoly in how Aboriginal peoples were represented to the larger society. There was no potent counter-image or counter-representation communicated to the dominant culture or to political decision makers that came directly from Aboriginal peoples. Aboriginal political organizations had great difficulty making themselves heard. Their leaders were routinely described as unrepresentative, as irresponsible agitators, and as selfishly seeking only their own personal goals.[39] In addition to the bias and misrepresentation that was the inevitable result of such one-sided portrayals, there is an inescapable indignity attached to always being an object of study by others.[40] It is rather like being a patient in a hospital who experiences never-ending examinations by one specialist after another, but is never discharged as "cured." By contrast, there was a different kind of indignity involved in four major texts in Canadian politics that came out from 1944 to 1947, texts that were viewed as a breakthrough in the Canadianization of the study of Canadian politics. Their comments on Aboriginal peoples in Canada were minuscule or non-existent.[41]

Earlier, on the premise that Aboriginal peoples were a dying race, their material cultures had been ransacked for artifacts that were removed by collectors to fill the display cases of museums around the world – to be preserved, it was thought, as perpetual reminders of ways of life too fragile and too impoverished to survive.[42] Diversity, to put it differently, was to be put on controlled display to satisfy non-Aboriginal curiosity, not accommodated in the world of everyday interactions between peoples of different backgrounds. Anthropologists analyzed the cultures and social systems of indigenous peoples in Canada and then reported back to the majority society, in the manner of Othello informing Desdemona of the wonders he had seen, of the lands where strange things happen.

We can now see that the Canadian situation was simply the local version of a global phenomenon in which a handful of European powers assumed the mastery of most of the non-European world – with Japan being a notable exception. The extensive European empires that spread over the planet – the British, French, Dutch, Portuguese, Belgian, and until the First World War, the German – gave an aura of naturalness to a situation in which skin colour and the presence or absence of power over others were highly correlated. When a handful of British ruled over millions in India, the overwhelming non-Aboriginal majority in Canada easily assumed that they should wield power over small indigenous populations – the latter not then graced with the status-giving label of nation. The Canadian situation was part of a global pattern in which, as Hedley Bull observed, "non-white peoples everywhere, whether as minority communities within ... white states, as majority communities ruled by minorities of whites, or as independent peoples dominated by white powers, suffered the stigma of inferior status."[43]

The Canadian policy of enfranchisement for individual Indians who had "advanced" to acceptable levels of civilization mimicked the policies of imperial powers. It was very close to the Portuguese concept of the "assimilado," the Spanish concept of "emancipados," the French concept of the "citoyen," subject to statutory law (rather than "sujet," subject to native customary law), and the Belgian concept of the indigenous person who had gone through the process of "immatriculation," and thus was no longer subject to native law. In each case the premise was that a given individual had advanced to a higher level of civilization, had left tribal practices behind, and was now worthy of a greater degree of, if not full, equality with the citizens of the imperial power.[44]

These European masters of the Third World were aptly labelled the *Lords of Human Kind* by Victor Kiernan.[45] As Kiernan's label suggests, imperial power was immensely gratifying to those who possessed it. Not surprisingly, the wielding of it over others deemed to be inferior led to exploitation and abuse, horrifically so in some cases, such as in the Belgian Congo. Nevertheless, there was always some attempt to clothe power in the garments of some noble purpose – such as Christianity, Civilization, and Commerce by the missionary explorer David Livingstone, or in Lord Lugard's idea of a dual mandate in tropical Africa, meaning both a responsibility to govern Native peoples in their evolutionary interest, and to develop the resources of the continent for the needs of humanity at large.[46] Article 22 of the Covenant of the League of Nations referred to a tutelary role "by advanced nations" over "peoples not yet able to stand by themselves under the strenuous conditions of the modern world."[47]

This tutelary relationship often implied the shedding of indigenous culture by subject peoples and their assimilation into the culture of the imperial power – a goal now seen as arrogant and illegitimate. We too easily forget, however, that historically the believers in assimilation were more likely to be thought of as optimists rather than as cultural imperialists. They held out the possibility of "progress," or cultural advance, as they defined it, for the subjects of empire. Many others, including most settlers in the colonies, considered such progress to be an unattainable goal for indigenous peoples placed no higher than on the first rung of the ladder of cultural achievement, which put European civilization on the top rung.

These global contexts may seem far removed from the relations between Aboriginals and newcomers in Canada, but they are not. It is simply naïve to believe that, in its broadest sense, Canadian policy toward Aboriginal peoples and the response of the latter were largely the product of domestic factors. Canadian policy as it was carried in the mentalities of those who devised and administered it and more vaguely as it was experienced by those who were on the receiving end, rose and fell as a side eddy of global trends in, first the rise, and subsequently the demise of empire. The latter not only transformed the international system, but also eroded the justification for viewing indigenous peoples at home as subject peoples. From Canada come these two examples: When

John Diefenbaker extended the franchise to status Indians in 1960, the desire to forestall criticism from the leaders of an increasingly multiracial Commonwealth, and at the United Nations (hereinafter UN), was at least as important as placating the Indian peoples, many of whom were suspicious of the suffrage gift.[48] Further, one of the strands that led to the 1969 White Paper proposing to abolish separate Indian status was the desire to overcome Canada's credibility gap at the UN over its Indian policy.[49] Similar fears of international public opinion, channelled through the UN, fuelled an early catalyst for more positive treatment by the Australian government of the Aborigines.[50]

The end of empire should not be thought of by Canadians, therefore, as a purely external phenomenon – as something that happened elsewhere, when the British "lost" India, the Belgians the Congo, the Dutch Indonesia, and the French Algeria – events in which Canadians were only vicariously involved because of their British links, or in the imperial era, were simply sitting in the audience while Europe subjected much of the globe to its dominion. Non-Aboriginal Canadians, although few would have used the label, were also imperialists, proudly taking part in the expansion of European civilization at home. More generally, they gained an unearned increment of pride from the reassuring message – reconfirmed every time they saw the checkerboard of imperial powers on the map of the world – that their civilization, their kind of people, represented the future.[51] In brief, although non-Aboriginal Canadians would not have described their relation to indigenous peoples in Canada as imperialist, they – if sometimes only unconsciously – had an imperial mentality. Unlike Africa and Asia, however, where the indigenous populations vastly outnumbered the European intruders – even in the settler colonies – the waves of European migrants in Canada quickly outdistanced the indigenous population. The end of the Canadian version of empire over Aboriginal peoples, accordingly, could not mean independence for the colonized or the departure of the colonizers.

In the Third World, empire's ending led to an explosion of newly independent peoples on the world stage. This transformed the international state system into a bewildering smorgasbord of cultural and racial diversity, capped by the high profiles accorded to the new Nkrumahs, Nehrus, and Sukarnos who challenged the formerly taken-for-granted hegemony of the European powers and their Cold War rivals.[52]

To end empire in Canada is not, unfortunately, as easy as in the former overseas colonies where power could be transferred to local élites claiming to speak for the vast majority of the colonized peoples. The dilemma of Aboriginal peoples is that although the Canadian state may lack legitimacy, they, unlike Quebec, cannot opt out of it. Although they have been subjected to colonial treatment, its natural resolution by independence is unavailable. While the Third World, note George Manuel and Michael Posluns, can seek and maintain its freedom, "the Aboriginal World is almost wholly dependent upon the good faith and morality of the nations of East and West within which it finds itself."[53]

In Canada, the majority is non-Aboriginal, and it cannot and will not go home, or give up power, as was the case when the independence flag was raised in colonies where white settlers were only a small minority. Nor is the Canadian case analogous to South Africa where a large and powerful European minority has to work out an accommodation with a black majority that outnumbers it six to one (blacks, Asians and coloureds outnumber whites seven to one). In Canada, decolonization applies to Aboriginal peoples who are now a small, divided minority (albeit growing), of under 3 percent of the overall Canadian population. This crucial fact that the Aboriginal nations will be in the minority in Canada even after the maximum degree of self-government has been realized, differentiates the Canadian – and the New Zealand, Australian, and American – and the situations of many Latin American countries – from the decolonization process in most of Africa and Asia. In no case does the relationship between the formerly imperialist and the formerly colonized completely end with independence, but the international coexistence with the formerly dominant that accompanies the winning of statehood is relatively straightforward compared to the complex domestic coexistence that has to be worked out within a single political community, as in Canada.

Future options for indigenous peoples in Canada are constrained by numbers, by their scattering throughout the larger society, and by their many internal divisions. Similar divisions were widespread in Africa and Asia, but they were partially masked by their location within the boundaries of a single colony. The attainable goal of independent statehood had a unifying effect on the anti-imperialist forces until independence was achieved. Aboriginal peoples in Canada lack the incentives for unity that the goal of independence can provide. Their fragmentation comes at a lesser price, which weakens the incentives to overcome it. To some extent, in fact, Canada's Aboriginal peoples are rivals – especially status Indians and Métis – for federal attention and federal largesse.

Although implementation of an inherent right to self-government has been the dominant aspiration of Aboriginal peoples in recent decades, its attainment will result in only a partial displacement of majority power. After self-government has been attained, Aboriginal Canadians will still be legally citizens of Canada and residents of provinces and territories from which many of the services they receive will come. They will remain entangled with the surrounding society. They will exist in the midst of their former colonizers. Indeed, for many Aboriginal Canadians, devoid of a land base, and living in urban areas, their relations with federal, provincial, and municipal governments may not differ greatly from those of their non-Aboriginal neighbours. Even for the fortunate, self-government will only be partial. The relevant goal, accordingly, is not an exit of Aboriginal peoples to independent statehood, but a coexistence that must include some element of common belonging and allegiance to a single polity by Aboriginal and non-Aboriginal peoples if it is to flourish.

Nevertheless, in spite of these qualifications that differentiate empire (and its ending) abroad from empire (and its ending) at home, the momentum of the last quarter century deserves the label revolutionary. Why and how?

Aboriginal peoples have firmly and successfully attached the label "nation" to their collective existence. This is one of the many efforts of Aboriginal peoples to take control of their own naming.[54] "Nation" distances them from the category of ethnic minorities, precludes their incorporation within the framework of multicultural policies, and places them in terms of status on a level with the two "founding" British and French peoples – hence the organizational label Assembly of First Nations (hereinafter AFN) for the main body that speaks for status Indians. The "nation" label, also used by Inuit and Métis, not only provides status, but presupposes political consequences. It now justifies, although not always without challenge, Aboriginal participation at the constitution-making table, and some move toward self-rule for Indians, Inuit, and Métis that is unavailable, for example, to Italian or Ukrainian

Canadians. And, although population figures are still low, their dramatic increase since the early years of the twentieth century reinforces the nation label. Thus, in contrast to the 1920s, when the indigenous population was about 110,000 status Indians,[55] and about 3,000 Inuit (then Eskimo),[56] and Métis were not considered an indigenous people, by 1996 the total Aboriginal identifying population, according to RCAP, was slightly over 800,000.[57] Seventy years ago, the Aboriginal population was smaller, politicization was minimal, and Métis had no constitutional recognition of their Aboriginality. Today, higher and growing numbers defining themselves as Indian, Inuit, and Métis nations challenge a status quo that insufficiently recognizes and empowers them.

### The Cultural Terrain over Which the Battle Is Fought

To treat one category of the population as wards (Indians), to marginalize another (Métis), and until the 1950s to pay negligible attention to a third (Inuit), and to regard all three, in different ways, as unfit for self-rule, is not simply a matter of exercising power. Power over others that is not accompanied by the consent of the governed is normally accompanied by a justifying ideology. Thus in the American South, the legacy of slavery, which treated blacks as property, was still influential when Gunnar Myrdal did his research for *An American Dilemma*[58] between 1938 and 1940. Blacks (then Negroes), viewed as racially inferior and unassimilable, were separated from whites by a fixed and permanent boundary that was sustained by legislation and customary social practices that routinized the inequalities that white beneficiaries viewed as the natural order. The ruling white majority subscribed to "whole systems of firmly entrenched popular beliefs" about blacks that served majority purposes, but that "are bluntly false."[59]

In apartheid South Africa, the theory of separate development justified the separation of the races so that each community – a "volk" – could develop according to its own inner logic. The dominating assumption was the impossibility of a common society and of a common citizenship. The Tomlinson Commission, which reported in 1955 as full-blown apartheid was implanted on the statute books, began with the premise "that there is little hope of evolutionary development" toward a common society, and "not the slightest ground for believing that the European population, either now or in the future, would be willing to sacrifice its character as a national entity and as a European racial group."[60]

More generally, in the belief structure of European imperialism, imperial rule was sustained by a cultural (and often racial) hierarchical world view that placed European civilization at the top, the cultures of Asia and the Middle East in the middle, and tribal peoples – often thought of as surviving examples of the childhood of the human race – at the base, and hence with the longest distance to travel before they could work their way to the top. The message transmitted to the subjects of empire was unambiguous – in a world of competing cultures and races, their way of life, cultural achievements, governing capacities, etcetera, were seriously deficient. Accordingly, they were to be taken care of, and administered by superior others. In many cases, cherished customs and practices were prohibited by the imperial administration. At the height of empire, just prior to the Second World War, subject peoples of empire constituted a majority of the non-European population of the world.

These ideologies, as Said brilliantly argued, permeate the whole culture of the imperial centre.[61] Their message of superiority is effortlessly imbibed by the rulers; its taken-for-granted quality ensures its assimilation and reproduction in literature, art, history, museum practices, the choice of statues on imperial thoroughfares, and the designation of heroes and traitors. In short, imperialism is a way of life both for those who exercise it and for those who are subjected to it.

The end of imperialism, accordingly, involves more than simply displacing foreign rule by local rule. It encompasses sweeping counterattacks on the imperial beliefs that denigrated subject peoples and attributed little value to their cultures, which were typically assumed to be anachronistic. In this sense, the formal ending of imperialism still leaves its former subjects with the decades-long task of overcoming its residues in the mentalities of its survivors – both of those who governed and those who were governed. The analysis of this complex task has spawned the massive and diffuse enterprise known as postcolonial theory.[62] Emma La Rocque, a Plains Cree Métis Native Studies professor, appropriately locates "Native scholars and writers in Canada [in] ... this non-Western international community" who challenge their non-Native colleagues to rethink the colonial assumptions they bring to their research.[63]

Empire's ending writ large is accompanied by critiques of Eurocentric views of the world – the view "that European civilization – 'The West' – has had some unique historical advantage, some special quality of race or culture or environment or mind or spirit, which gives this human community a permanent superiority over all other communities, at all times in history and down to the present."[64] Eurocentric assumptions generated ingenious explanations to show that such archaeological wonders as Zimbabwe could not have been built by Bantu, but were "proof of prehistoric white colonization in southern Africa," a belief congenial to the imperial mentality. The Ian Smith government of Southern Rhodesia, following its illegal declaration of independence in 1965, secretly ordered "that no official publications should indicate that Great Zimbabwe [which had become a cultural symbol for African nationalists] had been built by blacks."[65] Closer to home, there was for long an inability to believe that Maya temples and palaces were built by ancestors of the Maya Indians of today, and that their hieroglyphic texts were a phonetic writing system.[66]

The domestic Canadian version of a form of empire over Aboriginal peoples lacked the pomp and ceremony of the British raj, or the status-enhancing experience of a handful of officials ruling over millions in tropical Africa, Ceylon, or the Dutch East Indies. Nevertheless, we sent missionaries to Christianize, anthropologists to analyze, and Indian agents – our version of district officers – to administer. Indian children were taught wounding versions of history;[67] sacred practices and revered customs were forbidden or mocked; the use of Aboriginal languages was discouraged; customary forms of governance were bypassed; traditional healing arts were displaced; and treaties were accorded lesser significance by governments than by the descendants of the Indian leaders who had signed them. In general, Aboriginal ways of life, and thus their bearers, were stigmatized.

Not surprisingly, therefore, the Aboriginal nationalisms that seek, among other goals, implementation of an inherent right to self-government, simultaneously seek to undermine and transform the cultural assumptions and practices that supported Aboriginal marginalization and subordination. The fact that significant powers of self-government will not be available to half of the Aboriginal population that lacks a land base reinforces the need to struggle for positive recognition and acceptance from the society in the midst of which they live. This requires action on many fronts – across the whole range of culture.

History is one of the arenas in which struggles occur. Bruce Trigger suggested in 1985 that the enhanced status of Native peoples in Canada required more objective appraisals of their role in Canadian history. If so, that would finally overcome "the chronic failure of historians and anthropologists to regard native peoples as an integral part of Canadian society."[68] Yet although there were a few striking exceptions, he pessimistically concluded that "most historians continue to regard native peoples as peripheral to the mainstream of Canadian history."[69] Ten years later, he and Wilcomb Washburn positively noted the increasing number of Native researchers sharing responsibility for interpreting the past.[70] Although this was accompanied by some tension and ideological conflict, the positive results included a diminished ethnocentrism among non-Aboriginal researchers, greater appreciation of Native peoples as resourceful actors rather than as victims or simply background, and sound research revealing "the injustices, coercion, and hypocrisy that have pervaded relations between native peoples and Europeans."[71]

Historical debates are not trivial. When modified historical interpretations emanate from a source with high legitimacy they can, over time, shape our self-understandings. Thus the RCAP report, *Partners in Confederation,* argues for an inherent Aboriginal right of self-government in language designed to transform how we understand our past and, consequently, our present. By the "'inherent doctrine,' Aboriginal peoples are the bearers of ancient and enduring powers of government that they carried with them into Confederation and retain today ... Under ... [this] doctrine, Aboriginal governments provide the Constitution with its deepest and most resilient roots in the Canadian soil."[72] Aboriginal self-description as " First Nations" is employed for the same purpose – establishing historical priority, from which positive consequences are expected to follow.

Politicians get involved in a historical revisionism that seeks to replace imperial versions of the past with ones more supportive of Aboriginal dignity, and hence of the emancipatory goals of Aboriginal peoples. Joe Clark informed Canadians in 1991, when he was Minister Responsible for Constitutional Affairs, that Louis Riel was now "a Canadian hero."[73] Riel, in fact, has been transformed from a traitor to the status of a founding father of Manitoba. The Métis campaign to rehabilitate Riel culminated in a House of Commons resolution, also passed by the Senate, which "recognize[d] the unique and historic role of Louis Riel as a founder of Manitoba and his contribution in the development of Confederation."[74]

The Riel re-evaluation is part of a larger historical reassessment in which many of the cultural assumptions that formerly dominated the majority's historical narratives of contact are turned upside down. Micmac scholar Daniel N. Paul succinctly illustrates the countertrend, in a book appropriately titled *We Were Not the Savages,* research for which caused him "excruciating mental anguish."[75] His people, he wrote, "dignified, noble, courageous, and heroic ... for more than four centuries ... displayed a determination to survive the various hells on Earth created for them by Europeans with a tenacity that is unrivalled in the history of mankind."[76] "Real peace," he asserted, requires Canada to accept "responsibility for its past crimes against humanity and make ... amends to the Micmac and other Canadian Tribes for the indescribable horrors it subjected them to."[77] Paul makes extensive use of contrasts between Micmac virtues and European shortcomings from civilized standards, and recites a litany of observations about the iniquities of federal government policy – including his own experience of racism when he worked for the Department of Indian Affairs for fifteen years. He proudly reports the 1988 resolution of the American Congress that recognized the extent that the US Constitution and Bill of Rights "were modelled ... upon the constitutions and bills of rights of the Iroquoian Nations and other tribal groups."[78]

One of the most passionate recent examples of this use of revised history is *To the Source,* a ninety-three-page constitutional report issued in 1992 by the AFN as its story of the past.[79] *To the Source* is not a historical work in the technical sense, i.e., research intended to convince thesis committees of its validity. On the contrary, it is first and foremost a political document, designed to serve the constitutional objectives of its authors, a purpose that makes its message even more poignant, for it is an attempt to give legitimacy to an official indigenous counter-version of the past.

*To the Source* portrays an idyllic past in which the life Indians led "before the Europeans arrived was orderly, satisfying, serene; ... the people were healthy in body and mind; ... they were in harmony within themselves, between themselves, and with nature itself."[80] They had sophisticated governments, and "family, clan, and tribal systems that were in fact far more orderly – and more successful at justice and peace-keeping – than those of the incoming French, English, and Dutch."[81] Then came the Europeans, the oppressors, whose values of "individualization, materialism, sexism, authoritarianism" had a destructive impact.[82] They brought the "yoke of oppression, colonization, and assimilation."[83] In sum, Europeans "have left an ungodly mess, one that our people spoke about in pain and anger ... White values, white institutions half-killed us and are killing us now. We were a proud and independent people; we have been reduced, through Eurocanadian intervention, to poverty and massive social, familial, and personal distress."[84] These negative appraisals of the newcomers are underlined by a recurring resort to a litany of Aboriginal/non-Aboriginal contrasts – between, for example, "traditional values" that could "contribute greatly to the healing of Canadian society ... [and its] ideology of power-grabbing, money-grubbing, exploitation, and divisiveness [which] is bankrupt."[85] Then there is the contrast in governing practices, with the accompanying suggestion of the benefits to all Canadians if "governments adopted the principles by which our people historically governed ourselves; consensus, not conflict; inclusion, not exclusion; holism, not divisiveness; honour and trust, not politicking; generosity, not selfishness."[86]

Equally dramatic was the report's portrayal of the contrast in treatment and relative status of men and women, with "Aboriginal women ... viewed as equals, not inferiors ... They were no man's chattels."[87] The report includes ubiquitous references to "the earth our mother."[88] European attitudes to the environment that see "Mother Earth and her creatures as things to be used, lacking a soul, not fully alive" are contrasted with the "native tradition, in which all of these things – language, culture, spirituality, land, people, animals, plants, even the rocks themselves – form part of a seamless whole."[89] This contrast is heavily underlined. The European conquest of nature and material progress are turned into vices.[90] In the whole report of ninety-three pages, there is only one positive statement about Europeans – the admission that Indians have learned much from Europeans, "much of it good, some of it bad."[91]

*To the Source* is a classic, understandable response of a stigmatized people whose culture was assaulted by the Euro-Canadian majority. It is a counterattack – what recent authors described as *The Empire Writes Back*[92] – with its stress on the spirituality and moral superiority of traditional Aboriginal ways. The report is a consciousness-raising instrument for First Nations, designed to simultaneously probe the soft spots and fan the psychic insecurities of the majority society. *To the Source* may be thought of as the official status Indian equivalent of the report of the Royal Commission of Inquiry on Constitutional Problems (the *Tremblay Report*) that was presented to the Quebec government in the mid-1950s. That report contrasted the virtues of French, Catholic, spiritual, rural society with materialist, Protestant, acquisitive English Canada.[93] The dramatic political use of contrasts in Quebec nationalist social thought in that period was brilliantly summed up by Pierre Trudeau. "Our nationalism, to oppose a surrounding world that was English-speaking, Protestant, democratic, materialistic, commercial, and later industrial, created a system of defence which put a premium on all the contrary forces: the French language, Catholicism, idealism, rural life, and later the return to the land."[94] With suitable modifications, Trudeau's summation could apply to the social thought of *To the Source*.

The past, therefore, is contested territory, one consequence of which is unusually bitter and polemical scholarly controversy, driven by knowledge of the political consequences of historical interpretation.[95] The glorification of Columbus and his "discovery" in the quincentenary celebrations of 1492 inevitably stimulated a counterattack in which the subsequent 500 years are portrayed as a shameful blot in the annals of human interaction.[96] Historical controversy is especially heated over the size of the pre-Columbian Aboriginal population of North America. Estimates range from 1,148,000 in 1910 to 18 million in 1983. Although there is a marked tendency for higher population estimates from the 1960s to the 1980s, dramatic discrepancies remain.[97] While part of the explanation is methodological difficulty, other more political considerations are clearly relevant. Large populations assume more complex, more "advanced" Aboriginal societies, low estimates the reverse. Further, those who take a darker view of the coming of the Europeans, and hence of massive depopulation, find a larger pre-Columbian Aboriginal population. In general, "pro-Europeans" report small Aboriginal population figures, and "pro-nativists" report large figures.[98]

The politics of historical interpretation cannot be ignored, especially in courtrooms, where outcomes may depend on which version of history a judge believes. In these circumstances, "the adversarial imperative to present the best possible case"[99] is transmitted from lawyers to their expert witnesses from the disciplines of history and anthropology, who may face conflicting tugs from their disciplinary norms, their courtroom role, and their sympathies for one side or the other. For the historian, unfamiliar with the litigation process, the courtroom "experience may be very embarrassing, lonely, and devastating."[100] For the historian to become legally involved is to enter "what is in some respects a profoundly alien and, to some extent at least, hostile intellectual environment."[101]

Divergent interpretations of the past are central to the controversy over the 1991 ruling of British Columbia Chief Justice Allan McEachern in the Gitksan case,[102] subsequently overturned by the Supreme Court in 1997.[103] His judgment, which contained numerous negative evaluations of Gitksan and Wet'suwet'en culture, held that Aboriginal people had not been sovereign over the claimed territories, and held no Aboriginal title, but only limited-use rights. In addition to asserting they did not live in an organized society, he returned on a number of occasions to the absence of written language, the wheel, and the horse as proof of their backwardness.[104] As Robin Fisher notes, McEachern's dependence on written documents to interpret history, and his rejection of oral tradition has the effect of confirming "the hegemony of the colonizers."[105] According to Fisher, McEachern's understanding of historical research is amateurish, ethnocentric, and obsolete in that it is based on outdated assumptions that contemporary historians have rejected. The reaction of anthropologists – to whose views McEachern had given little credence, identifying them as advocates of the peoples whose cultures they studied – was, if anything, even more emphatic.[106] According to a reporter, the ruling "has so angered and disgusted many of Canada's leading anthropologists that they are considering legal action."[107] (McEachern's decision was overturned by the Supreme Court of Canada in a 1997 decision which, in effect, repudiated his negative assessments of pre-contact indigenous society).[108]

Even anthropology, however, the discipline historically most involved with indigenous peoples, is not immune to the criticisms of those who once were its subjects of study. The end of empire, and the assertiveness of the formerly studied, along with the growth of indigenous scholarship has triggered a profound introspection in the academic community of anthropologists. The recognition that their studies were a by-product of empire, or of the subordinate status of indigenous peoples generates reinterpretations of the history of the discipline.[109] In some cases, revered disciplinary founders are reassessed. In Canada, for example, Diamond Jenness has been accused by Peter Kulchyski of complicity for providing intellectual support for the Canadian state's policy toward Indian peoples.[110] His colleague Marius Barbeau is unflatteringly portrayed in a new biography. Barbeau's attitude to "half-breeds," a phrase he reiterated, was both paternal and pejorative. His treatment of William Beynon, a long-time Tsimshian interpreter and assistant, was often unfair, and his manner of purchasing totem poles and artifacts could be arrogant and aggressive. The author's judgment is perhaps revealed in his dedication: "To the women and men who conceived what Barbeau collected."[111]

The change of situation is pithily summed up in the aphorism that formerly anthropologists had their tribes, now tribes have their anthropologist. Clifford Geertz noted that anthropologists had to relinquish their role as intermediaries between the people they study and the audiences to which they reported their findings.[112] Geertz's own research was in the South Pacific and Morocco, but his interpretation of the crisis in anthropology caused by an aggressive effort by the formerly studied peoples to control their own portrayal clearly applies to the Canadian scene.

Noel Dyck reports antipathy to anthropologists by anthropologically trained Indian band members, partly based on resentment toward the attitude of some anthropologists "that they should have the freedom to do whatever they feel academic individuals should do – that no one should curtail their activities. We have no way of monitoring the accuracy of the information that they collect; they may get a very narrow perspective of a very complex situation in Native communities."[113] Elsewhere, Dyck notes that anthropologists no longer automatically "tell it like it is," when they return from their anthropological researches. They are constrained both by the public and by their own self-questioning of the reliability and authority that attaches to what they write about, and by the fear that the attainment of Aboriginal goals of self-government, which anthropologists generally support, might be jeopardized by revealing the degree of social breakdown, malaise, and abuses in a number of native communities.[114] Further, many Native communities will now only allow anthropologists to undertake community research with the approval of the community, on conditions dictated by the community, and permission is not always granted. Research considered unhelpful or unfavourable may get in the way of subsequent access to the community.[115]

The tension between Native peoples and those who formerly represented them spills over into the theory and practice of museums.[116] The issue, as Trigger summarizes it, is "who owns the Native past," with much of material history, including valued cultural artifacts, now resting in public museums.[117] Many of these materials were collected in ways that now appear ruthless and insensitive. For example, on the BC coast, "ritual objects were confiscated by the police as part of a suppression of Native religious rituals; while even cemeteries that were still in use were looted in order to collect skulls and artifacts buried with the dead." The distinguished anthropologist, Franz Boas, justified what he admitted was "repugnant work" as being "essential for the progress of anthropological research."[118] The ruthless collection of Native artifacts assumed the disappearance, either by assimilation or by disease, of the societies that had produced them. The belief that these societies had no future was interpreted to mean that they had minimum or no entitlement to possess what could not be transmitted to succeeding generations. The survival of Native societies undermines this colonialist logic. Museum collections acquired when Native peoples were believed to be dying out "must once again become part of the cultural heritage of their creators' descendants. Museums ... [are asked] ... to liquidate their colonial legacy."[119] Repatriation of Native, especially sacred, objects is a recurring item on the agenda of museums. Museums and anthropologists can no longer monopolize the task of interpreting indigenous peoples to the non-Aboriginal society. Archaeologists can no longer brandish "science" as justifying an unchallengeable right to dig up other people's pasts.[120] Professional archaeology associations now have to work out compromises, seek partnerships with, and accept the relevance of oral history of the Aboriginal peoples whose distant past they seek to explore.[121] Native deference can no longer be assumed.

The larger picture, of which the preceding are simply vignettes, should not be lost from view. The recognition that how one is portrayed depends on the portrayer, and that the resultant portrait influences the self-esteem of the studied and their status and treatment in the larger society lies behind the "voice appropriation" issue in literature, the social sciences, and history.[122] The tendency in the United States for "every group [to be] its own historian,"[123] with resulting challenges to outsiders to keep out, has an existence, admittedly weaker, in Canada that receives expression in Native Studies programs, associations, and conferences.[124] The acerbic exchanges that follow portrayals by outsiders that are judged to be detrimental to a group image or its political objectives underline both the politics of representation and the transitional era in which we exist. These exchanges, and the efforts to increase Aboriginal input are struggles over cultural power – over who will shape the images that condition how we treat each other.

Aboriginal and non-Aboriginal Canadians do not share a common, agreed-upon past, for the past was a setting for a confrontation between competing ways of life. The dominance of the newcomers over the original inhabitants, following an early period of nation-to-nation relations, is remembered – when it is thought about – as a triumph by the former and, much more viscerally, as a humiliation by the latter. Dissension over the past gets in the way of agreement on our future. Anne Norton is surely correct in observing that nationalist movements see history as disputed territory and "recognize the writing of history and the constitution of memory as means to political power."[125] They are reacting against the colonial reality in which "the criteria for being somebody and for belonging somewhere are defined by *someone else's historians, often located someplace else.*"[126]

History is more malleable if the colonized gain independence, for then they can take charge of their own history and the imperial version from which it differs can retreat to the imperial centre. However, when the imperialists remain in the guise of fellow citizens, and are also numerically dominant, the desirability of sustaining some common fellow-feeling among the members of the enlarged community of citizens may conflict with employing history as an instrument of self-assertiveness and pride among the formerly marginalized. One possible means to bridge the gulf – as in South Africa – is to get both sides – former victims and their oppressors – to confront the past openly, in the form of a truth commission, in the hope that guilt, confession, forgiveness, and rapprochement might follow.[127] This, however, is not easily achieved when Aboriginals are less than 3 percent of the population, the non-Aboriginal community is constantly reinforced by new immigrants with their own pasts, and the community they join has only mild feelings of guilt and responsibility for the plight of Aboriginal peoples.

In these circumstances, the best we can hope for is a continuing dialogue between competing versions of the past. While the former hegemony of non-Aboriginal versions is now appropriately challenged, this does not mean that the competing Aboriginal histories should be granted a hegemony equivalent to the ones they seek to displace. What we need is a continuing debate about our past in which alternative versions keep each other honest. In this debate, the Euro-Canadian majority's interpretation continues to enjoy a privileged place in our libraries, and in the mind-set of the non-Aboriginal population. Consequently, non-Aboriginal participants in the historical dialogue that Canadians need have a greater obligation to listen and to practice a self-restraint than do the Aboriginal participants. Self-restraint, however, is not a synonym for silence. No doubt, we will fall short of the civil dialogue we seek as we challenge each other's history, but if we do not accept the responsibility to both listen and speak to each other, history will continue to reinforce our inherited divisions.

### How Did We Get to Where We Are?

Let me try to bring the threads of this argument together. In the broadest sense, the dramatic contrast between the historic assumptions that formerly governed Aboriginal/non-Aboriginal relations in Canada and the contemporary paradigms struggling to the surface is triggered by the convergence of two broad macro trends.

First, the traditional beliefs that either Aboriginal peoples would die out or they would merge into and disappear in the majority population lost credibility. The Aboriginal population is now growing rapidly. Further, the growth in numbers is accompanied by a reinvigorated Aboriginal self-consciousness, a reassertion of cultural pride, and a desire to use governing powers to revitalize cultures that have been under sustained attack.

Second, by themselves, these domestic developments could not have brought us to where we now are without the support offered by the international environment. Indeed, Aboriginal nationalism, cultural pride, and the pursuit of self-government would all be much weaker in the absence of supportive messages from the international environment. Put simply, if somewhat exaggeratedly, the world turned over in the decades following the Second World War. The international racial hierarchy of European imperial rulers and subject peoples with darker skin came undone surprisingly quickly as the former lost nerve and colonial nationalism became increasingly aggressive and confrontational. The independence of dozens of former colonies in Africa and Asia eroded the close correlation between whiteness, or Europeanness, and imperial power that had long prevailed. In that former era, the message that tumbled across state borders in Canada and other Western countries made the subject, marginalized, and outsider status of Aboriginal peoples appear to be in the nature of things. Now, the nature of things outside our Canadian window is very different. A pale skin no longer carries with it an entitlement to rule over those whose skin colour is differently pigmented or whose cheekbones are differently shaped. Third World majorities in the UN have profoundly transformed the legal, intellectual, and moral climate of world politics in a "successful challenge to Western dominance," which has spilled over into domestic politics.[128] The normative beliefs behind the post-First World War mandates system of the League of Nations, which justified trusteeship over territories "inhabited by peoples not yet able to stand by themselves under the strenuous conditions of the modern world" were decisively repudiated by the UN General Assembly in 1960. Resolution 1514, Declaration on the Granting of Independence to Colonial Countries and Peoples, stated that "all peoples have the right to self-determination" and "inadequacy of political, economic, social and educational preparedness should never serve as a pretext for delaying independence." The vote in the General Assembly passed 89-0, with nine abstentions.[129] The move from fundamental norm to pretext took place in one generation. International law, which formerly "facilitate[d] empire building and colonization ... [now] provides grounds for remedying the contemporary manifestations of the oppressive past."[130]

It is easier to underestimate than to overestimate the impact of external developments on domestic politics, especially when we are dealing with attitudes, values, and implicit assumptions about the direction in which the world is moving. It is easy to track the movement of goods and peoples across frontiers – less easy to detect the influence of changes in the border-crossing messages we receive simply by being awake in a changed world. The Japanese victory in 1905 over Russia in the Russo-Japanese war – a victory of a non-Western over a Western people – was seen "as a victory, with global implications, of the Mongolian people over the European ... [an] event [which] shattered the myth of white invincibility."[131] Half a century later, when the British left India, and other imperial powers followed suit with their colonies, an essential support for Canada's past treatment of Aboriginal peoples crumbled. In our current search for a new, more egalitarian relationship between Aboriginal and non-Aboriginal Canadians we are responding not just to our insulated Canadian selves, for no such category exists, but to new internationally generated definitions of various ways of reconciling diversity with the requirements of unity in a society that is plural and democratic, and is emerging from a past in which Aboriginal/non-Aboriginal inequalities were state policy.[132]

Let me put the preceding into a different framework. Edward M. Bruner, an American anthropologist, has recently suggested that we understand the world and live our lives through stories, and that these stories are capable of sudden and dramatic change. One such story, which Bruner does not mention, would be the communist story of the coming triumph of the proletariat and the ultimate establishment of a classless society. Devout communists lived their lives in terms of that story, although they may have been unclear exactly where they were in the pilgrimage to the promised land. According to Bruner, we position ourselves in accordance with such stories, and we fit the events that impinge on our vision into them, until finally the discrepancy between story and reality becomes too great. Then the old story that once seemed eternal becomes an emperor with no clothes, incapable of accommodating a reality that can no longer be denied. According to Bruner, that is what happened in the 1960s and 1970s to the old story that formerly provided accepted interpretations of the past of the American Indian, their contemporary condition, and their likely future. He summed up the American stories, old and new, as follows: "In the 1930s and 1940s the dominant story constructed about Native American culture change saw the present as disorganization, the past as glorious, and the future as assimilation. Now, however, we have a new narrative: the present is viewed as a resistance movement, the past as exploitation, and the future as ethnic resurgence."[133]

According to Bruner, changes of story line can be relatively quick and complete. Successive stories may have little continuity, and a changed story line can have major consequences. Stories define the situation and distribute resources to actors in conflictual relations. The assimilation story easily became a mask for oppression by justifying the leadership of change agents with power over wards who needed to be taught. The resistance, ethnic resurgence story, by contrast, generates claims for redress for past exploitation, and turns yesterday's wards into activists for a cultural revival, a better future, and autonomy. Manuel and Posluns, writing in 1974, attributed the appearance of a Canadian Indian "awakening" to a new "climate of political, social, and economic forces [that] is allowing what was always beneath the surface to emerge into the light of day."[134]

In his own story-line terminology, Bruner agrees with the argument of this chapter that international factors importantly contributed to domestic change, which was driven by "the overthrow of colonialism, the emergence of new states, the civil rights movement, and a new conception of equality."[135] Australian experience confirms this interpretation. The emergence of "a new racial paradigm in Australia [in the 1960s] ... began in response to events overseas: black nationalism, decolonization, and opposition to apartheid in South Africa."[136] Because the emergence of minority indigenous nationalisms neither preceded nor coincided with, but followed the disintegration of the European empires, we can infer, though not prove, the causal priority of the latter. Before the Second World War, the community of sovereign states fell only slightly short of being a club of white states; with the end of empire most of the members are now non-white.

Not surprisingly, since global forces were the trigger, the Canadian story line also changed, although it was filtered through and adapted to various domestic realities, the most important of which was the 1969 White Paper, and the successful Indian resistance to its recommendations, discussed in the next chapter.

## Conclusion

We are in the midst of a major effort to overturn a historic pattern of inequality between Aboriginal peoples and other Canadians. The magnitude of the change is profound, both in terms of the goal – finding and implementing arrangements for coexistence and some degree of a common citizenship – and, compared to the past, the numbers involved, upward of three-quarters of a million Aboriginal people.

The transformations already under way are more than political, with a focus on self-government. They encompass virtually all of the ways in which we relate to each other. They extend across the humanities and social sciences – the disciplines of anthropology, archaeology, and history; literature, museum exhibits, and theatre – and the theory and practice of law. They are directed as well to our everyday encounters in social settings. We cannot escape from this re-evaluation of our life together, because we are carried on by global forces. The counterattack by the hitherto silenced against their historic marginalization has the support of contemporary norms – the rights revolution, identity politics, the ethnic and indigenous revival, and an erosion of the belief in the natural right of European peoples to be in charge that sustained empire abroad and domestic authority over indigenous peoples in Canada, Australia, and elsewhere.

That imperialism was a comprehensive way of life generates an equally comprehensive counterattack. RCAP explores one culture area after another in which recognition, respect, and fair representation are sought – education obviously, and history specifically,[137] and also all the other institutions of cultural expression and representation – Aboriginal languages, sacred sites, museums, research on Aboriginal peoples, radio, television, the press, literature, publishing, and the visual and performing arts.[138] Aboriginal efforts to control, or at least influence, their own representation are attempts not only to counter the misrepresentations that would otherwise prevail in the majority society, but also to counter the non-Aboriginal cultural bombardment they – especially youth – personally experience.[139] The search for respect and self-affirmation sometimes involves validating Aboriginal practices by positively linking them to the needs and practices of modernity, by the thesis that sustainable development is an ancient Aboriginal concept,[140] and by reports that some aspects of traditional healing and medicine are now validated by scientific research,[141] and that Aboriginal philosophy has much to offer to many branches of modern science.[142] This sweeping counterattack against the equally sweeping negativism that justified wardship reflects in part the holistic perspective that RCAP attributes to Aboriginal peoples. Although the changes toward which we are striving are clearly therefore more than political – involving vast areas of culture – political change remains central. Self-government is an instrument to make a statement about equality as well as to enhance the capacity of Aboriginal peoples to shape their own futures. Basing self-government on an inherent right strengthens the dignity of those who possess it.

We are ill prepared for this challenge. Long-standing Canadian policy assumed the erosion of Aboriginal difference on the road to homogeneity. Aboriginal cultures were transitional, not enduring. We were to be held together by citizenship after Aboriginal cultures had confirmed the premise of social Darwinism, and disappeared. That is not where we are today. History changed direction on us. We are like the new élites of Eastern and Central Europe and the countries of the former Soviet Union, whose bookshelves groan under the weight of tomes dealing with the transition from capitalism to communism but have very little on movement in the reverse direction – from communism to capitalism – which confronts and baffles them. The materials on our bookshelves also assumed a goal – assimilation – which we are moving away from toward a goal whose specifics are unclear, but which will combine difference and commonality in fruitful ways, if we are lucky.

Not surprisingly, the process of fashioning a new relationship is messy, untidy, chaotic, and unleashes considerable anger and resentment. Residues of past patterns of thought and behaviour persist, and impede the whole-hearted acceptance in Canada of our version of Bruner's new story line. "Ethnic resurgence" is with us, but its translation into positive social change lags behind. The tensions bred by our differences will not disappear in any future that need concern us. They are fashioned by competing versions of history, and sustained by politics that keep memories alive. Aboriginal and non-Aboriginal peoples live in different worlds, which fortunately have a degree of overlap that may be our salvation if we can nourish our commonalities.

Our present location between a world we have incompletely left behind and a future we have not fully worked out is dangerous intellectual and emotional territory, which cautions the politician or scholar to tread carefully. However, the temptation to avoid the cross-currents, intellectual tensions, and bitter exchanges of the emotional policy area encompassing future Aboriginal/non-Aboriginal relations should be resisted. To treat this policy area as taboo, because to enter it is threatening, is to court failure. Abstention increases the likelihood that we will make grievous errors of diagnosis and prescription, as we formerly did when Aboriginal peoples were relatively voiceless. The quality and permanence of the new relationship we seek to build requires mutual, civic discussion, which requires careful nurturing and candour.

# Assimilation

The central question in Aboriginal/non-Aboriginal relations in Canada following European settlement has always been "Is the goal a single society with one basic model of belonging, or is the goal a kind of parallelism – a side by side coexistence – or some intermediate position?" The same question has perplexed American policy makers. "A central policy issue in Indian affairs [in the United States] has always been whether Indian tribes should remain separate or whether they should be assimilated into the larger society."[1]

Historically, the Canadian debate has focused on status Indians. Since Confederation they have had a separate branch of government responsible for their affairs, a distinct legal status defined in federal legislation, and an Indian administration – the domestic version of a colonial service. Inuit and Métis, by contrast, were not subjected to the same or equivalent rigours of differential treatment or status. Distinct legislative responsibility for Indians meant that it was their future status that insistently called for attention and discussion. Accordingly, this chapter will focus primarily on the status Indian peoples. They were, par excellence, the targets of the official assimilation policy.

To use "assimilation" as a container for a century or more of government policy toward Indians strikes one observer as a contribution to confusion. To do so, according to Michael Posluns, is to make "assimilation" an "all-encompassing" term that huddles disparate meanings and policies under its too capacious rubric. Further, any suggestion that the "Government of Canada had a consistent policy for more than six months or from one agency to another will come as a surprise to many."[2] At the level of inter-agency differences of a decentralized administration, shifts over time, and fluctuations in optimism/pessimism over whether the policy could work, Posluns is correct. However, at the level of high policy, of official rhetoric, of the conventional wisdom, "assimilation" imposes order, consistency, and continuity on the government's view of its goal. To discard the word because of its ambiguities would do more harm than good to our understanding.

To simplify considerably, historically the post-Confederation reality was separation on reserves, but the goal was assimilation. The seeming contradiction was bridged by the premise that territorial separation was a preparation for assimilation. The reserve system was thought of as a protected training school in which Indians, sheltered from harsh contact, could be readied for membership in the larger society. The 1936 Ewing Commission, which recommended the establishment of Métis settlements in Alberta, employed the same logic. The choice for the Métis was disintegration or assimilation, and "segregation was a necessary step toward assimilation."[3] Hence, recognition of difference was not positive; nor was it intended to be permanent for Indians, or in Alberta for Métis.

Today, the goal of much official Aboriginal rhetoric, especially of Indians and Métis, appears to be an institutionalized parallelism at a time when overt cultural differences are much less than in the past. We have, thus, a kind of paradox. Formerly, when differences were greater, official policy was to eliminate difference. Now, when cultural differences are weaker, the direction of constitutional thought is to reinforce difference, or at a minimum to recognize it. A large part of the explanation for this change derives from who is generating policy. The elimination of difference was the official policy of the Canadian state at a time when Indian influence on that policy was negligible. The present drive to recognize and reinforce difference is a product of Aboriginal input. As noted in the concluding chapter, however, Aboriginal opinion is not homogeneous.

## Basic Assimilation Policy

In 1857, an "Act to encourage the gradual civilization of the Indian tribes in the Canadas" was passed by the legislature of the United Canadas, with the purpose of "the gradual removal of all legal distinctions between [the Indians of the province] and Her Majesty's other Canadian subjects."[4] Successive post-Confederation amendments of the Act, including the consolidated Indian Act of 1876, repeated the relevant provisions. As Arthur Meighen explained to the House of Commons in 1918, the Indian seeking enfranchisement "must have ceased to follow the Indian mode of life, and ... must satisfy the Superintendent General that he is self-supporting and fit to be enfranchised."[5] Frustration over the small numbers voluntarily seeking enfranchisement led to an amendment in 1920 that allowed compulsory enfranchisement. The provision was deleted in 1922 and reinstated in 1933, and remained in the Act until 1951. It does not appear to have ever been used.[6]

Until the late 1960s, basic government policies toward Aboriginal peoples minimized the long-run significance of cultural Aboriginality, and aimed for a common Canadianism. This melting-pot philosophy was especially clear for the Métis. They were treated as ordinary citizens, with minimal exceptions, who were intermingled with the larger society.[7] Similar treatment was accorded the Inuit, who were neither brought under the Indian Act nor provided with their own Inuit Act, in spite of a 1939 Supreme Court decision that they – then called Eskimo – were under federal jurisdiction, based on s. 91(24) of the British North America Act of 1867, "Indians, and Lands Reserved for the Indians."[8] Policy toward Métis could be called assimilation by neglect, which very frequently resulted in abject poverty, marginalization, and social disintegration. In Alberta, in 1936, four-fifths of Métis children were without schooling.[9] Although some Métis continued to make a reasonable living on the land up to the 1950s, as had previous generations, many of them, with good reason, were often envious of the treatment accorded their Indian neighbours.

Toward the Eskimo, policy was not assimilation by neglect, but simply neglect. Until the Second World War and the subsequent Cold War, which led to the construction of radar lines in the North, the federal government ruled with a light, almost nonexistent hand. Prior to the establishment of the Department of Northern Affairs and National

Resources in 1953, contact was mainly limited to the Royal Canadian Mounted Police, missionaries, whalers, the Hudson's Bay Company, and a few other traders. The feeble presence of government is evident from the chapter headings of Jenness's *Eskimo Administration: II Canada*: "Government Myopia (Pre-1903)," "Wards of the Police (1903-21)," "A Shackled Administration (1921-31)," and "Bureaucracy in Inaction (1931-40)." The 1950s fared little better, following the war and postwar flurry of activity in the 1940s, earning the chapter heading "Steering without a Compass."[10] Even when the Department of Northern Affairs and National Resources in effect became the department responsible for Inuit affairs in the 1950s, no Inuit Act emerged. Inuit were considered to be full citizens and any special federal responsibility was defined as "an extra service and not an alternative to normal citizenship."[11]

The relation of the Canadian government to the Indian people was almost a complete contrast to its historic neglect of the Inuit until the 1950s. The state presence for the former was long-established, firm, and with explicit policy goals. Clearly, Canada had no Aboriginal policy as such. Hence, the Inuit, Indians, and Métis arrived in the new 1982 constitutional category "Aboriginal Peoples of Canada"[12] by very different routes. This complicates the role of government in seeking to make policy sense of this constitutional grouping of peoples with very diverse backgrounds. It also, on occasion, makes the inhabitants of the category fractious partners.

The goal of a common Canadianism was explicitly and vigorously pursued for status Indians. Many of their cherished customs and rituals were banned – the potlatch on the West Coast in 1884 and the Sun Dance on the prairies in 1895.[13] Residential schools were designed as agents of assimilation – to remove children from the influence of their parents, punish them for speaking Indian languages, introduce Christianity, and inculcate negative attitudes to their own cultures.[14] The federal government in fact waged a cultural assault on the Indian peoples.[15] Noel Dyck's summary is apt: "From birth to death most Indians have been caught in a situation where they have had to listen to one unvarying and unceasing message – that they are unacceptable as they are and that to become worthwhile as individuals they must change in the particular manner advocated by their current tutelage agents."[16]

The previous chapter concluded with Bruner's thesis of the change of the story line that applied to American Indians – from seeing the "present as disorganization, the past as glorious, and the future as assimilation ... [to] a new narrative: the present ... as a resistance movement, the past as exploitation, and the future as ethnic resurgence."[17] In the Canadian case, the catalyst of change to a new story line was the defeat of the 1969 federal government White Paper by the organized resistance of the Indian people to proposals for their assimilation. The defeat put an official end to what had been the basic policy of the Canadian state from its inception, the ending of difference and the goal of assimilation. From the early 1970s then, some recognition of diversity, of particularity, would be on the Aboriginal policy agenda.

*The 1969 White Paper*

The White Paper was released in 1969.[18] Its basic philosophy was that the system of separate treatment and administration held Indians back. Separate treatment, originally conceived as a transitional arrangement preparing Indians for entry into the majority society, had backfired. By keeping Indians apart from other Canadians, it had kept them behind. The "road of different status ... has led to a blind alley of deprivation and frustration."[19] The remedy was "equality," essentially an undifferentiated citizenship. Accordingly, the legal distinction between Indian peoples and other Canadians was to be eliminated by repealing the Indian Act and amending the British North America Act to remove s. 91(24), which singled out Indian peoples for separate treatment. The federal Indian Affairs Branch was to be phased out, and services would in the future be provided for Indians by federal and provincial governments in the same way as they were for other Canadians. "There can be no argument about the principle of common services," the White Paper asserted. "It is right."[20] The significance of treaties was minimized. They were to "be equitably ended."[21] The bulk of the proposed policy was to be in effect in five years, and there were to be enriched programs for a transitional period.

Aside from the impatience the White Paper displayed toward the persistence of Indian separateness, the 1969 proposals fitted very comfortably into the basic policy toward Indians of the previous century. The assimilation paradigm was the common currency of policy makers and non-Aboriginal commentators up until the White Paper's appearance.

The White Paper's most striking feature was not its objective but its audacity. The analysis was replete with categorical statements, and virtually devoid of nuance or subtlety. It displayed a fundamental resistance to any permanent separate status. It repudiated the inherited separate reserve system for its failure to prepare Indians for assimilation. It unflinchingly focused on the Indian as simply an individual Canadian. If Indianness were to survive, it would be the result of unaided Indian efforts in the marketplace of competing lifestyles, not the product of government fostering, unwitting as the latter had been.

The guiding philosophy of the White Paper was supported by two of Prime Minister Trudeau's fundamental assumptions. He thought it "inconceivable ... that in a given society one section of the society [could] have a treaty with the other section of the society. We must all be equal under the laws and we must not sign treaties amongst ourselves."[22] For Trudeau, treaties undermined a common citizenship. Further, he resisted attempts to redress past injustices. A people, he argued, needs to forget many things, and "not try to undo ... the past."[23] He quoted President Kennedy favourably: "We will be just in our time. This is all we can do. We must be just today."[24]

Three other aspects of the White Paper deserve comment: First, although it was preceded by extensive consultation with Indian leaders, their input was completely ignored – a fact that helps explain the passionate opposition it aroused from Indian peoples, partly driven by a sense of betrayal.[25] Second, it was a major initiative, with the Prime Minister playing a leading role. Trudeau reported that he spent more time on Indian policy than on any other issue in his first year of office.[26] And third, it completely ignored – indeed it repudiated – the major policy thrust of the 1966-7 two-volume *Hawthorn Report*. That report rejected assimilation and the disappearance of separate Indian status as a goal. The past, it argued, could not be ignored. The historic presence of Indian peoples prior to the arrival of Europeans and their subsequent negative treatment – in spite of the treaties – justified, according to Hawthorn, a permanent positive recognition, labelled "citizens plus." This concept, later used by Indian leaders to fight the White Paper, challenged the Trudeau philosophy in two ways. Contrary to Trudeau, history mattered and justified special entitlements. Further, again in contrast to Trudeau, the *Hawthorn Report* supported asymmetrical citizen status. Indians were to be a bit more equal than other Canadians.[27]

It remains true, however, that the White Paper assimilation policy –

for all its audacity and simplifications – was not without antecedents and not without strong support in the intellectual climate of previous decades. It also fed on the American civil rights movement, and broader international trends. A few years prior to its release, Prime Minister Robert Menzies of Australia, in sentiments supported by both government and opposition, asserted in the Australian House of Representatives, "What should be aimed at ... is the integration of the Aboriginal in the general community, not a state of affairs in which he would be treated as a being of a race apart ... Should not our overall objective be to treat the Aboriginal as on the same footing as all the rest, with similar duties and similar rights? ... [The] best protection for Aborigines is to treat them, for all purposes, as Australian citizens."[28]

*Academic and Political Support*
A remarkably revealing glimpse of the prevailing assumptions of both Canadian and American students and administrators of Native policies was provided by a 1939 University of Toronto and Yale University seminar on *The North American Indian Today.*[29] With only minor qualifications, the conference papers described assimilation as inevitable and desirable. Professor Charles Loram, of Yale University's Race Relations Department, described "the Indian Problem [as] ... one of acculturation" and asserted that, "In the end, of course, the civilization of the white man must prevail ... The only question is the rate at which [Indian culture] ... should be eliminated or superseded or changed."[30] The only significant difference at the conference was over the timing and speed of the process. Those who advocated a little less haste, nevertheless "recogniz[ed] the inevitability of this assimilation."[31]

Assimilation was viewed, by the assembled officials, academics, and others, as a guided process, engineered by the relevant official change agents of the majority Canadian and American society. Non-Aboriginal policy makers, acting as agents of that society, thus had a paternal responsibility of "deliberately setting out to modify the indigenous culture of the Indians and to improve such cultural changes as have already been made."[32] The role of the anthropologist in Canada mirrored the thesis of A.P. Elkin, the leading Australian anthropologist between the two world wars: "Like all good members of a 'higher' and trustee race, [they] are concerned with the task of raising primitive races in the cultural scale."[33] Assimilation, therefore, was premised on an inequality of power relationships. It was also premised on a touching faith in social engineering by poorly qualified school teachers and a small cadre of untrained administrators working for a peripheral branch of government. The guiding belief was that the Indian peoples were to be the recipients of change, not the choosers. In standard colonial parlance they were variously described as wards or children. It was, however, colonialism with a difference, for the goal was not independence, but disappearance. The possibility that separate self-governing Indian communities might persist indefinitely was not seriously considered in non-Aboriginal society until the mid-1960s in the *Hawthorn Report*. As a consequence, there was no preparation for that outcome. The goal of the 1939 seminar was not to modernize or preserve Indian culture, but by pressure and inducements to progressively weaken it and detach individuals from it.

C.W.M. Hart, a University of Toronto sociologist, spelled out at the University of Toronto/Yale seminar the rationale for a policy that "consciously and deliberately" pursued the goal of full citizenship for Canadian and American Indians. The "modern world" leaves no alternative, given the role of industrialization in shaping society. Against this juggernaut "with its impersonal written law and its doctrine of individual responsibility" tribal ways were defenceless. Given "the prevailing conditions among the surrounding white population," tribal organization "is an anachronism."[34]

Diamond Jenness (1886-1969), unquestionably one of the leading Canadian anthropologists throughout his long professional career, was not only a whole-hearted believer in the policy of assimilation, but everywhere he saw evidence of cultural decay and social malaise. He was especially pessimistic about West Coast Indian peoples. Although they had intermarried with whites, he noted in 1935 that they are experiencing "a far greater decline than the tribes of eastern Canada who have been subjected to similar influences for four centuries ... Socially they are outcasts, economically they are inefficient and an encumbrance. Their old world has fallen in ruins, and, helpless in the face of a catastrophe they cannot understand, they vainly seek refuge in its shattered foundations. The end of this century, it seems safe to predict, will see very few survivors."[35] Jenness's pessimism blinded him to any possibility of a cultural revival or a separate nationhood for Indian peoples. He would have found such predictions or aspirations incomprehensible.

In 1947, Jenness proposed a plan to a parliamentary joint committee examining the Indian Act "to abolish, gradually but rapidly, the separate political and social status of the Indians (and Eskimos); to enfranchise them and merge them into the rest of the population on an equal footing." The plan was "for liquidating our whole Indian reserve system within a definite time limit, ... fixed, somewhat arbitrarily, at twenty-five years."[36] The plan was essentially a crash program of rapid social change by means of education. Jenness believed that the root of the "Indian problem" was the reserve system, which he likened to confinement camps. "We have made them pariahs and outcasts. In consequence, they have developed the warped mentality of world outcasts just like the occupants of the displaced persons camps in central Europe."[37] His proposals, he argued, would fulfil the pledges made to the Indians at the time of the treaties, "to train and educate ... [them] for citizenship so that they could become full citizens of the dominion. They put them on Indian reserves so they could be educated and trained and put on an economic basis equivalent to the whites around them."[38]

Jenness, who spent time in and wrote about the Arctic, was deeply concerned and pessimistic about the future of the Inuit. He saw little hope for more economic opportunity in the North, and feared the perpetuation of an unemployed, welfare dependent, demoralized people. Accordingly, he proposed that small colonies of Inuit should be established on the outskirts of a dozen or more cities in southern Canada where they could learn English and find jobs. He also advocated a special two-year program, initially to be operated by the armed services, to train Inuit youth in various marketable skills. Over time, he thought more and more Inuit would migrate to southern Canada for economic reasons. Why, he argued,

> should we confine our Eskimos to the Arctic? If nature now denies them a livelihood in their ancient homeland, why should they not migrate elsewhere ... They are citizens of Canada, and Canada is wide. Within its confines they may disappear as a separate people, as several tribes have disappeared before them: but surely it is preferable that they should succumb struggling for a better life in southern Canada than rotting away in

the Arctic on government doles ... Their descendants, one hopes, will inherit the race's buoyancy and self-confidence, and emerge as resourceful and enterprising as their ancestors.[39]

In the mid-1990s, when diversity and particularity are triumphant, it is easy to forget that for many non-Aboriginals, assimilation was thought of as a progressive policy. This is strikingly evident in the Indian policy of the Saskatchewan CCF government of Tommy Douglas and Woodrow Lloyd (1944-64).[40] CCF policy objectives were virtually identical to the later White Paper of the federal government. Overall, the CCF sought the ending of separate treatment, the ending of the reserve system, the demise of the treaty relationship, the elimination of the role of the Indian Affairs Branch, and the extension of all normal provincial services to Indians. The goal was to transform Indians into normal, taxpaying, service-receiving citizens of the province, indistinguishable from other provincial citizens, except presumably for fading memories of the bad old days when they were treated differently.

The CCF policy was not a response to Indian pressure. It was policy from above. In fact, two key components of the policy – the extension of the provincial franchise and the availability of liquor – were implemented despite strong Indian objections. Their objections were dismissed on the premise that Indian peoples were victims of their own false consciousness. They did not know what was good for them. The minister in charge of a Cabinet committee on Indian affairs, J.H. Sturdy, "compared Indians to children who needed guidance."[41] For the CCF, segregation was the problem, treaties were roadblocks that should be taken down, and integration was the solution. Reserves were likened to concentration camps, prisoner-of-war camps, and the gulag. The leading student of CCF Indian policy in this period, James M. Pitsula, succinctly summed up the CCF position: "The notion that Indians should constitute a distinct, self-governing entity separate from the rest of the population was completely alien to the Saskatchewan CCF."[42]

Ross Thatcher, Saskatchewan Liberal Premier (1964-71), was equally, if not more assimilationist than his CCF predecessors.[43] His goal was economic integration and cultural assimilation.[44] "Talk of Indian culture, treaty rights, and self-government left him cold."[45] He wanted the federal government to give up its special responsibilities for Indians, which should be taken over by the provincial government.[46] He supported the 1969 White Paper.[47] He knew what Indians needed, and thus could bypass the Federation of Saskatchewan Indians as a representative body. When his government was defeated in 1971, his bulldozing tactics left his successor with an "Indian policy [that] was in a shambles."[48] Thatcherite assimilation from above, however well intentioned, was a failure.

While Saskatchewan was exceptional in the enthusiasm behind its involvement with Aboriginal peoples after the Second World War, other provinces were moving, albeit less rapidly, in the same direction. British Columbia made policy changes to facilitate "integration," viewed as a less intrusive goal than "assimilation." Ontario established a legislative committee to examine the civil liberties and rights of Ontario Indians in 1953. The extension of services to Indians in Ontario was not designed to accommodate cultural difference or foster self-government, but simply to fit Indians into an ongoing provincial system of services the better to serve their social welfare and treat them equally. Both British Columbia (1947) and Ontario (1954) extended the provincial franchise to Indians, as did Manitoba (1952).[49]

In 1971, the Report of the Dorion Commission on the integrity of Quebec's territory referred favourably to the 1969 federal government White Paper and described the system of reserves and the Indian Act as "un aspect ségrégationniste et discriminatoire ... et constitue ... un anachronisme." The report advocated the municipalization of Indian reserves, and in general asserted that Indians and Inuit should relate to the federal and provincial governments in the same manner as other citizens. Although the report asserted that a "traitement privilégié" should continue, its overall thrust was directed to the normalization of relations between Indians (and Inuit) and the provincial government.[50]

From the perspective of the mid-1990s, the assimilationist policies of Trudeau, of the Saskatchewan CCF, of the Thatcher Liberal government, and of leading anthropologists and administrators appear not only as misguided but as culturally arrogant and insensitive – as the very opposite of the "politics of recognition"[51] that now symbolizes wise policy. Thus, the recent RCAP *Report* stresses the continuing Indian resistance to assimilation, reports the minuscule numbers who took advantage of the enfranchisement option in the Indian Act, and repeatedly underlines the contemporary desire of Aboriginal peoples for cultural revival.[52]

*Aboriginal Support*

The historical reality is more complex. There is at least fragmentary evidence attesting to some Aboriginal interest in assimilation, although some of the sources may be unreliable, confusing wishes with reality. Charles Loram, the co-editor of the previously cited 1939 Yale/University of Toronto conference proceedings, asserted that many people, "including paradoxically a large number of Indians," believe that "the sooner" Indians shed their inherited culture, join the "general citizenry," and participate "in the dominant culture of the North American continent, the better."[53] Diamond Jenness, writing in the early stages of the depression of the 1930s, though he saw little hope for many of the Indian peoples in terms of successful adaptation to white society, was impressed with the Iroquois, apparently because of their extensive intermingling with non-Aboriginal Canadians. "No small percentage," he reported, "has broken away from the reserves and merged successfully with the surrounding population, a few even attaining national fame."[54] Later, in 1947, Jenness cited a prominent member of the Six Nations who saw no reason why Indians should be classed as such, and separated from the "rest of Canada ... but as long as the government insists on keeping us as Indians we do not want to pay any taxes ... They should enfranchise us."[55]

In the late 1940s, A. Grenfell Price, an Australian student of comparative Aboriginal policies, not only identified the federal government goal as assimilation, but claimed that "assimilation is already far advanced over much of the country." He reported that at the Six Nations Brantford reserve, the Indians have become Christian, have improved their living standards, "and are assimilating with the whites." Similar developments were occurring on the British Columbia coast, where "the Indians have also adopted Christianity, and white industries, and are undergoing absorption." In his discussions with BC Indians, who "were intelligent people fully acquainted with, and anxious to discuss their racial difficulties," he reported that "they took the view that absorption was in full swing; that segregation was a mistake and that they should merge as quickly as possible in the white population." He concluded that the authorities were unanimous that "the ultimate fate of the Canadian Indian must be absorption."[56]

The mid-1950s study by Hawthorn et al., *The Indians of British Columbia,* with the subtitle *A Study of Contemporary Social Adjustment,* reported widespread evidence of acculturation. Their research took it as "axiomatic that the acculturative change of the Indian is irreversible and is going to continue, no matter what is done or desired by anyone. If present trends are maintained, change will go on to a final point of nearly complete cultural assimilation and racial amalgamation." They also concluded "that no customary actions, elements of belief or attitude, knowledge or techniques, have been transmitted from earlier generations to the present without major alteration." On the other hand, most individuals and most Indian communities were reported as still separate and different from non-Indians in multiple ways.[57]

Even the 1969 White Paper, now treated as a callous display of government arrogance, received some influential Indian support, according to Olive Dickason.[58] A 1969-70 study by Menno Boldt indicated that about a fifth of then "native Indian leaders" (84 percent of whom had reserve residence, and 81 percent who were registered Indians) favoured integration. Remarkably, "they proposed to do away with the present special status of Indians, eliminate all elements of separate political and legal administration and have Indians become as any other ethnic group."[59]

The contemporary intellectual, cultural climate is hostile to assimilation, and discourages efforts to assess its past frequency. The RCAP *Report,* although it almost systematically avoids any focus on the assimilated, nevertheless notes a sharp drop-off of more than one-third between the numbers reporting Aboriginal ancestry and those reporting an Aboriginal identity.[60] The gap was similar for the Métis.[61] The gap was greatest among the urbanized – only 15 percent of individuals with Aboriginal ancestry reported an Aboriginal identity in Montreal, and 18 percent in Halifax, contrasted with 86 percent in Regina (1991 figures).[62] Presumably some of those who gave up an Aboriginal identity had a positive evaluation of the host society, and voluntarily disappeared into it. In some cases, entry into mainstream society probably reflected the kind of choice that immigrants often make on behalf of their children. Other individuals passed for white to avoid the stigma that attached to Aboriginal identities.[63] Bruce Trigger's comment on urban Native persons without Indian status "who have sought to escape from domination through assimilation into Euro-Canadian society" probably has significant explanatory potential.[64] One student of the Métis reports that in the early decades of the twentieth century, "pride in being Métis was a luxury only the most independent or determined Métis could afford. For most Métis, the greatest gift they could have was that of being able to pass as a white person."[65]

No doubt, the preceding were minority positions, but their existence underlines the varied – as one would expect – Aboriginal response. Even in Australia, where the treatment of Aborigines was horrific, many of their leaders in the 1920s and 1930s vigorously pressed for full citizenship, incorporation into mainstream society, an end to segregation, and in some instances for racial amalgamation.[66] We badly need a serious major Canadian study that charts the diverse responses of the Aboriginal peoples throughout the period when assimilation was the prevailing policy – that explores responses ranging from rejection to ambivalence to positive enthusiasm for some aspects of the majority culture. Such a study should include the remarkably high enlistment patterns in both world wars, mostly voluntary in the First World War.[67] In wartime, Indian soldiers "had made white friends, had been wounded with them ... they all discovered that a person's race or religion seemed unimportant when they had to fight together to stay alive."[68]

No doubt such a study would be an exploration of "the multiplicity of aspirations," reported by Borrows, "that exist within native society."[69] He notes a recurring tension or uneasy coexistence – historical as well as contemporary – between what "can be very loosely classified as acculturation and segregation [which] have structured the articulation of native land interests until the present day." Sometimes this tension is transcended by indigenous peoples who simultaneously seek "the benefits of settler culture and the desire to remain apart," which may jeopardize the classical rationale for apartness – the "preservation of traditional ways of life."[70] A subtext of such a study should be to address the ambiguity from a late twentieth century perspective of the coexistence of "the emancipatory intentions ... of assimilation ... and the cultural arrogance [behind it] that looms large in indigenous memory." Tim Rowse, writing of Australian Aboriginal policy, argues that only by including both of these realities can we "do justice to the complexity of assimilation."[71]

To achieve its goal, such a study will have to go behind the tyranny of concepts – assimilation, acculturation, distinctive cultures – that both inform(ed) interpretations of present or past observers, and are/were also partly incorporated into self-understandings of Aboriginal people. Diamond Jenness and his contemporaries saw assimilation because that was the label provided by the spirit of the times. RCAP, reporting in 1996, reinterpreted or relabelled behaviour that Jenness would have interpreted as assimilation. Such a study, therefore, must explore the changing understanding of the link between culture and identity. To Jenness, culture change meant identity change. To RCAP, although there is some ambivalence in its analysis, cultural change can be an instrument of identity persistence.

We now understand what our predecessors were less likely to see, that identity persistence is perfectly compatible with pronounced cultural change for both individuals and communities. The labels used to describe what is happening are not only aids to interpretation, but are also instruments of domination or liberation. The hegemony of assimilation as an interpretive lens and its subsequent displacement by inherent rights, distinctive cultures, and nation parallels the move of Aboriginal peoples from being subjects of policy, to taking charge of their own self-labelling.

*Paternalism and the Culture of Leadership*
From the perspective of its authors and supporters the assimilationist policy had the support of numbers – the assumption that the relatively small Aboriginal population would simply be engulfed by the overwhelming non-Aboriginal majority. The American example next door seemed to suggest that the integration/assimilation of the black population was the almost unchallenged objective of progressive forces, including black leaders. More generally, the policy was fed by Darwinian theories about competition between cultures, and who the winners and losers would be. From a global perspective, especially in the period when empires were ascendant and gave at least lip service to preparing their colonial subjects for the rigours of the world outside, Westernization appeared to be the way the world was going. In the same way that Lenin saw the Communist party as the vanguard of the proletariat, and thus justified in imposing its rule on others afflicted with

false consciousness, the metropolitan centres of the global European empires saw themselves as in the vanguard, coercing, guiding, and preparing subject peoples for a future the latter could only dimly grasp. The same logic drove Indian administration in Canada. Assimilation policy was also supported by attributing imitative propensities to peoples considered to be at an earlier stage of civilization. Finally, there was a perhaps complacent paternalistic altruism – was not the majority diffusing its superior culture to less advanced people? Although this clearly reflected a cultural arrogance, it was not racist, as it presupposed that culture could be separated from race. The preceding supports for assimilation were reinforced by the belief that there were limits to the amount of diversity that was compatible with the theory of a normal nation-state.

From the perspective of the 1990s, the believers in assimilation of Indians are portrayed as arrogant, insensitive cultural imperialists. From a different perspective, however, they can be viewed as the optimists. Few held out hopes that Australian Aborigines, widely viewed as on the lowest rung of the ladder of cultural achievement, could be assimilated.[72] Blacks in South Africa in the apartheid era were considered unassimilable; a similar incapacity was widely attributed to blacks – now Afro-Americans – from the slavery era until the mid-twentieth century, a negative evaluation that still has supporters. Both regimes, the South African and the American, had difficulty defending their policies to the international community, which saw assimilation as a desirable goal in the United States, and sought the displacement of apartheid by a black majority democracy in South Africa. In Canada, the beliefs of the optimists were challenged by counter-beliefs, or at least doubts, about the capacity of the Indian people to meet the demands for full admission and equal participation in Canadian society. Perhaps, therefore, the believers in assimilation merit at least the faint half-cheer reserved for those whose ideals – however much they conflict with the contemporary *Zeitgeist* – were surely preferable to the beliefs of the pessimists and the doubters in the governing majority population.

Even half a cheer, however, may be too generous, for the policy was deeply flawed. The dominance of the assimilation paradigm did not reflect consensus among Indian people and the federal government with respect to its rightness. Rather, it reflected the limited possibility Indian peoples had to participate in defining their future. In the period between the two world wars the possibility of involving the Indian people in discussions of their future was either ignored or routinely rejected.[73] Indian agitation was dismissed as the product of "designing white men,"[74] or "the intrigues of smart Indians."[75] Indian political associations in the interwar period were viewed "as subversive organizations."[76] An accommodating, sympathetic response to impressive Indian leaders such as John Tootoosis (1897-1989) would surely have reduced the erosion of Aboriginal trust in non-Aboriginal politicians that is the legacy of the hostility so long visited by the majority society on Aboriginal politicians and their organizations in the assimilationist era.[77]

The right to make decisions for Indians without their input was repeatedly asserted. As Arthur Meighen stated in 1920, when asked to delay a bill allowing compulsory enfranchisement until Indian views were heard: "The department, through a long series of five decades, has known the views of the Indians, and it is in touch with them from day to day. If one were to deal with wards in the same way as he would deal with citizens, he would not be dealing with wards at all."[78]

Arthur Laing was equally explicit about the appropriate relation between the government, as leader, and its Indian clientele. "The prime condition in the progress of the Indian people," he asserted in 1963, "must be the development by themselves of a desire for the goals which we think they should want."[79] At the time Laing was Minister of Northern Affairs and National Resources.

It was the very essence of paternalism that the opinions of wards could be discounted. In the United States, writes the Indian legal scholar Rennard Strickland, "the 'Indian question' is a question most often viewed, in the final analysis, from a non-Indian perspective ... A recurring historical fact is that Indian policymakers have believed, or acted as if they believed, that Indians themselves could not know what was good Indian policy."[80] A similar paternalism prevailed in Australian Aboriginal policy until recently, "in so far as it attempted to engage people against their will in changes that did not have their interests at their base, with manifestly no control by the people themselves ... and on the basis of poorly estimated funding needs and imperfect understanding of social processes."[81] More generally, the mentality that justified empire in Africa and Asia and the marginalization of indigenous peoples in settler societies assumed that European civilization represented the destiny of humanity. What the imperial powers already were – in terms of culture, mastery of the planet, etcetera – was what the subjugated "they" might become if they were lucky. It logically followed that those in control had a better understanding of the future – since they embodied it – than their charges did, or could have.

Hence, to be in the vanguard was to have an entitlement to rule – to suppress customs viewed as retrograde – to channel subject peoples in a direction they would not have chosen for themselves – and to shape policy from above. A recent analyst of Indian policy summed up the situation: "As the discoverers and custodians of the means to progress, the non-native people in Canada regarded it as their task to lead the native people in the same direction ... In this context, self-determination did not make much sense. Similarly, dialogue would be largely pointless."[82] After detailing a host of oppressive policies inflicted on Indian peoples, Judge A.C. Hamilton noted that Indian opinion about their desirability was never sought. "The Aboriginal belief came to be that they were to have no say in matters affecting their lives." Policy decisions central to the way they lived were to be taken by "distant bureaucracy and the Government." As recently as 1995, in a report commissioned by the federal government, Judge Hamilton asserted that "a sense of paternalism continues to permeate the [comprehensive claims] policy and to poison relations between Canada and Aboriginal peoples."[83]

An inevitable by-product of the assimilation policy was what Edward Spicer called the "cultural blindness" that afflicts the dominant majority in such circumstances. They possess and wield power. They "do not have to adjust to others; they can require the subordinated peoples to adjust to them. Out of this springs their inability to bring the subordinated peoples into ordinary focus. The dominant people do not ordinarily experience any pressures to see the subordinated peoples as the subordinated peoples see themselves. Everything in the environment ... is conducive to the development and confirmation of an ethnocentric view of the world."[84] This ethnocentric world view justified a cultural assault on and a denigrating attitude toward – in the Canadian case – Aboriginal cultures destined to pass away. Given the inevitability of their disappearance and the assumed altruism behind the gift of a superior civilization that was offered, the dominant majority was for long incapable of seeing that its goals were not being achieved, and that Aboriginal peoples were surviving and retaining a sense of themselves as distinct, albeit evolving peoples.[85] Spicer's statement about the American experience is equally applicable to the Canadian case. "The colossal failure of this [assimilation] program for realizing cultural homogeneity must go down in history as the ultimate in products of cultural blindness."[86] The successful counterattack on that cultural blindness came with the political defeat of the 1969 White Paper by the organized resistance of the Indian people. Before discussing that defeat, we need to remember that the White Paper had some Indian support, and that, as already noted, hundreds of thousands of Canadians with Aboriginal ancestry do not identify themselves as Indian, Inuit or Métis. The differential weight, in terms of both power and numbers, of the interacting Aboriginal/non-Aboriginal societies almost inevitably means that a significant minority of the former, with intermarriage often being the bridge, will merge into the majority society.

*Significance of the White Paper Defeat*
The defeat of the White Paper dates from its withdrawal by the federal government in 1971, as a response to massive Indian opposition. Idiosyncratic factors help explain the failure – the élitism of the policy-making process, its timing when Indian leadership was getting stronger and more self-confident, faulty public relations, and other particulars that a microscopic analysis would no doubt divulge. In the longer run, however, its lack of success has deep historical roots in the interactions of the Indian people and the majority society and its agents throughout the assimilation era.

It is only a half-truth to assert that most Indian people rejected the assimilation they were offered. While the official policy of the Canadian state was assimilation, the unofficial policy of Canadian society was too often discrimination.[87] Insulted, humiliated, and rebuffed in their encounters with white society, Indians were unlikely to see assimilation as an escape from what they were told was a backward culture. The life stories of Aboriginal leaders underline the psychological impact of rejection and maltreatment – often by the Indian agent – in reinforcing their tenacious attachment to an Aboriginal identity.[88] In the 1950s in British Columbia, "band councillors and even chiefs were expected to stand hat in hand outside the Agent's office waiting for an audience. When the people went to town, they walked with their eyes downcast to avoid making eye contact with whites, not so much because they feared an attack ... but simply to avoid the insulting glance they would get in return."[89] A customary "Jim Crow" policy across the country kept Indians out of most hotels and restaurants and relegated them to the back rows of theatres.[90]

Psychologically, there was a fundamental contradiction at the very core of federal government policy, especially for treaty Indians. On the one hand, the treaties spoke the language of eternity – "as long as the sun shines and the rivers run." On the other hand, it was federal policy to detach the Indian people by assimilation from the communities that the treaties – from the Indian perspective – were supposed to nourish and protect. The banning of customs, the estrangement of children from their parents by the residential school experience, the attack on traditional ways of governing, and the demeaning experience of being treated as wards meant that protection was a code word for cultural aggression.

The assimilation policy, especially when implemented as an aggressive assault on Indian culture, only served to reinforce a stubborn sense of Indianness. Indian children ran away from residential schools, and were beaten when they were forcibly returned. Banned customs, such as the potlatch, were practised in secret. Indians, as Cole and Chaikin remind us, "were not supine victims of white legislation. That the [potlatch] law went largely unenforced was in great measure a result of native resistance, even defiance."[91] In general, as is typically the case in colonial situations, there was a gap between the public, visible behaviour of Indian people, and an underground life that constituted a kind of defiance of white rule and Indian subject status.[92] Jokes about the "white man" were another weapon employed to preserve self-respect.[93] Indian political activity, albeit confronted by official hostility and with Indians lacking the vote, was a constant factor in keeping alive the possibility of a different, better future.[94] In general, as Borrows observes, descriptions of Native society "written ... from a western perspective ... have often portrayed us in a way that does not capture the active and transformative role that we have played when reacting to settler institutions. We were not passive objects of colonial policy, but were active agents and creators of our own history." He confirms his thesis with an elaborate historical analysis of how the Chippewas of the Nawash, his ancestors, continually and successfully struggled "to maintain self-definition and self-government."[95]

The assimilation policy, therefore, was never the policy of the Indian people, although it had some support. It was white, majority, government policy. Its hegemony was always more apparent than real.[96] All along, there was an opposition party, disorganized, often covert by necessity, that could emerge if an appropriate catalyst surfaced. The White Paper was the catalyst.

The defeat of the White Paper was not just the defeat of a particular policy, of a bold initiative, it was a repudiation of the historic, basic, continuing policy of successive administrations since Confederation.[97] The defeat destroyed or rendered irrelevant much of our inherited intellectual capital in this policy area, for we were about to change direction. We had prepared for a future – assimilation – that did not happen – and thus were politically and intellectually unprepared for a future in which Aboriginal peoples – as peoples – were to have a permanent, recognized presence in Canada. If the old policy was to be pursued, it would have to be indirectly, by subterfuge.

The basic document in the Indian counterattack, the Red Paper, *Citizens Plus,*[98] a concept borrowed from the *Hawthorn Report,* was drafted by the Indian Association of Alberta, under Harold Cardinal's leadership, and it had the support of the National Indian Brotherhood.[99] It was presented to the federal Cabinet in the railway committee room. "In a scene that deserves to be preserved in oil paints on a giant canvas, Indian leaders stood majestically in feathered headdresses and white deerskin garb and presented the cabinet with an alternative *(Citizens Plus)*. It was an affirmation of faith in their Indian identity. After a century of being engulfed by a white tidal wave, they were still here, they were still different, and they were not about to let themselves be pushed into oblivion."[100]

*Citizens Plus,* by the Indian Chiefs of Alberta, accused the federal government of duplicity with its claim that the White Paper was a response to consultation with Indians. It opposed a policy that "will harm our people." It described the situation should the White Paper be implemented as one "whereby within a generation or shortly after the proposed Indian Lands Act expires our people would be left with no land and consequently the future generations would be condemned to the despair and ugly spectre of urban poverty in ghettos."[101]

The nationalism, or separatism, of the Red Paper was – by the standards of the 1990s – very mild. The psychological isolation of Indian communities should end by bringing the "entire [Indian] community into the mainstream of Canadian life."[102] Self-government ambitions were explicitly referred to in terms of local government.[103] The ultimate goal was for Indian peoples to "take their rightful place as full-fledged participants in the mosaic of the 'just society' as meaningful and contributing citizens of Canada."[104]

Harold Cardinal's *The Unjust Society*,[105] although it contains a vehement critique of the White Paper, nevertheless underlined the compatibility of Indianness with Canadian citizenship and Canadian identity,[106] and also expressed support for the idea of a Canadian cultural mosaic.[107] The Indian response to the White Paper, therefore, was surprisingly moderate. Although the language of nationhood was employed, so too was the language of Canadian citizenship. Dave Courchene, President of the Manitoba Indian Brotherhood, referred to Indians as "citizens of the province" of Manitoba, with a consequent right to provincial services.[108] The Manitoba Indian Brotherhood saw no incompatibility between being Indian and being Canadian;[109] referred to Indians contributing to the Canadian mosaic,[110] and to themselves as "Indians of Canada";[111] laid claim to full provincial citizenship,[112] clearly stated in the following words: "our relationships with the federal government may be unique, but they in no way interfere with our rights as provincial citizens," and vigorously asserted their rights as Canadian citizens, as well as rights flowing from special status.[113] The National Indian Brotherhood referred positively to the Hawthorn concept of citizens plus, which the federal government chose to ignore.[114] The philosophy, with its "plus" for special recognition of the Indian people, and its equally positive support for Canadian citizenship, was a recurring theme of the White Paper's opponents.

Following the White Paper's defeat, policy leadership no longer rested exclusively with the federal government. Its initiative had been rebuffed by those it had been intended to benefit, whose prior input in the consultation process had been ignored. The immediate legacy of the defeat was a policy vacuum, which came to be partly filled by Aboriginal élites and their political organizations, which the federal government commenced to fund generously in the 1970s.[115]

The post-White Paper uncertainty and ambiguity about future policy was further compounded by the Quebec-triggered constitutional crisis and the resultant debate about the future of Canada. The constitutional issue, by putting the fundamental question "Who are we as a people?" on the table, was a natural invitation for Aboriginal peoples to redefine their relationship to other Canadians. It not only gave them openings where they could bring effective leverage to bear, but encouraged them to couch their demands in constitutional terms. Between 1980 and 1982 they achieved a major constitutional breakthrough – which was, if anything, surpassed in the Aboriginal gains negotiated in the defeated Charlottetown Accord.[116]

The defeat of the White Paper opened up or at least kept alive the possibility of separate treatment and recognition for Inuit and Métis. If the White Paper had triumphed, which would have meant the end of differentiated treatment for the status Indian community, which was the largest and most nationalistic of the Aboriginal peoples, the Inuit and the Métis would have lacked both the power and justifying constitutional precedents or comparisons necessary to sustain their hopes for separate treatment. In a sense, therefore, the Inuit and Métis have ridden on the coattails of the status Indian population, which successfully fought the battle against the White Paper.

The new 1982 s. 35 constitutional category "Aboriginal peoples" – which includes Indian, Inuit, and Métis – both enlarges the indigenous population seeking separate treatment, and weakens whatever homogeneity it had when only Indians were a separate government responsibility. As a result, the category "Aboriginal" is much more diverse than was the former constitutional category "Indian," and has increased the officially recognized self-identifying Aboriginal population to about seven times the number of status Indians in pre-Second World War years. Also, the reinstatement by Bill C-31 (1985) of Indian legal status for Indian individuals has added slightly more than 100,000 people to the status Indian population, about one-seventh of the total.[117] The main provisions of the bill repealed a discriminatory section of the Indian Act that had deprived Indian women and their children of Indian status if they married a non-status person. Bill C-31 was necessary to bring the Indian Act into conformity with the Charter of Rights and Freedoms.

*Post-White Paper Aboriginal Constitutional Thought:*
*Preliminary Remarks*
Since the White Paper, constitutional thought has progressively departed from the assumptions of past governments.[118] The premise now is that there will be a permanent Aboriginal presence in Canada. Hence we now have to think about relationships between societies, rather than the disappearance of the smaller into the larger. Diversity and particularity, formerly the enemy, from the perspective of the Canadian state, are now to be sustained.

Instead of an assault on Aboriginal cultures, we now have the following philosophy behind the Aboriginal provisions in the Charlottetown Accord. The role of Aboriginal governments was "(a) to safeguard and develop their languages, cultures, economies, identities, institutions and traditions; and, (b) to develop, maintain and strengthen their relationship with their lands, waters and environment so as to determine and control their development as peoples according to their own values and priorities and ensure the integrity of their societies."[119] This, the complete antithesis of past policy, was agreed to by all governments in 1992.

Enhanced recognition is reinforced by the emergence of the potent descriptive label of "nation" – especially of the First Nations, with the assertion of priority that that label implies. As a corollary, there is increasing pressure to regulate relationships by treaty. Both "treaty" and "nation" symbolize an equality of status – and hence a heightened appreciation of the role of Aboriginal peoples in Confederation. Occasionally, the employment of these two terms appears to suggest relations within an international system.

Overall, the direction of much contemporary Aboriginal constitutional thought leans toward parallelism, toward a side-by-side relationship. This was true of the AFN under the leadership of Ovide Mercredi. It is true of the RCAP *Report,* which stresses coexistence, partnership, and a nation-to-nation relationship. Commission publications made constant references to "relations between Aboriginal peoples and Canada," suggesting they are separate entities. The RCAP *Report* refers frequently and positively to the two-row wampum, favourably described by Ovide Mercredi and Mary Ellen Turpel as follows:

> The First Nations view our relationship today as a continuation of the treaty relationship of mutuality where neither side can act unilaterally without consultation. This partnership is symbolized by the grandfather of all treaties, the Iroquois Confederacy ... two-row wampum between your ancestors and those of the Iroquois. The two-row wampum committed us to a relationship of peaceful coexistence where the First Nations and Europeans would travel in parallel paths down the symbolic river in their own vessels. The two-row wampum, which signifies "One River, Two Vessels," committed the newcomers to travel in their vessel and not attempt to interfere with our voyage. The two vessels would travel down the river of life in parallel courses and would never interfere with each other. It was a co-living agreement. The two-row wampum captures the original values that governed our relationship – equality, respect, dignity and a sharing of the river we travel on. This is how the First Nations still understand our relationship with Canadians.[120]

## Cross-currents

Several trends or events appear to suggest that a consensus has crystallized: the vigour of Aboriginal nationalism, the defeat of the 1969 White Paper, the constitutional breakthrough in 1982, and the publication of a massive royal commission report recommending a profound constitutional restructuring to accommodate Aboriginal peoples. If this is in fact the case, the next task would be the implementation of an agreed sense of direction. The reality, however, is otherwise. We have momentum, and we have roadblocks or complications – five of which will be briefly discussed below.

First, supporters of assimilation, of the 1969 White Paper approach, have not been vanquished.[121] The Nielsen Task Force of the new Mulroney government, given the assignment of eliminating waste and duplication in a time of retrenchment, identified Native programs as one of its policy areas for review. The Task Force report to Cabinet in April 1985[122] reflected Nielsen's philosophy. He saw little virtue in reserves where Indians "live in virtual quarantine in communities which have no real economic base and, in a number of instances, a disintegrating social and cultural fabric."[123] He denied the existence of "Aboriginality"[124] and consequently believed that Indians neither had nor should seek "cultural distinctiveness." "Rights," he thought, got in the way of Indian "absorption into society."[125] The Task Force proposals, a virtual repeat of the 1969 White Paper, proposed the dismantling of the Department of Indian Affairs and Northern Development and the devolution of Indian programs to the provinces.[126] While the recommendations were shelved in the face of strong Indian and other opposition, the seriousness with which they were proposed indicated that the philosophy of the White Paper was not dead. The mantle has now passed to the Reform Party.

According to Preston Manning in *The New Canada,* "special status in federal law" for Indians "has been an unmitigated disaster,"[127] a philosophy manifested in Reform Party policy. The Reform Party, now the official Opposition, supports the repeal of the Indian Act and the elimination of the Department of Indian Affairs, having powers of self-government delegated rather than constitutionally entrenched, and leaving the responsibility for preserving Aboriginal culture to Aboriginal individuals and groups. Although Reform agrees that treaties are to be respected, it is unsympathetic to their liberal and generous interpretation. Overall, the Reform position is driven by its adherence to what it views as the fundamental constitutional norm of equality of all citizens. While some encroachments on this principle are unavoidable due to the legacy of the past – particularly treaty and Aboriginal rights – they are clearly to be kept to a minimum.[128]

*Our Home or Native Land?* by Mel Smith, constitutional lawyer and former deputy minister in various British Columbia government departments over a long public service career, elaborates a position analogous to that of the Reform Party. Smith writes as a convinced supporter of the 1969 White Paper. His philosophy is summed up as follows: "A new native policy must be built on the twin principles of jurisdictional integration for natives within the mainstream of Canadian society, thus enhancing a sense of self-reliance and personal achievement, and on the principle of equality under the law consistent with the rule of law and the Constitution. Moreover, such a policy must be formulated and implemented absent any sense of collective guilt over what may have happened in times past. Until now, this sense of guilt has been allowed to hang like a pall over all efforts at native policy reform."[129] Not surprisingly, given its philosophy, the reception of *Our Home or Native Land?* has ranged from fulsome accolades to denunciation as a "divisive and Eurocentric book."[130]

The survival of support for assimilation is not surprising. That assimilation was official policy for more than a century after Confederation suggests that a certain naturalness for the majority attaches to its view of citizen-state relations. Its supporters have easy access to the symbolically potent rhetoric of equality. Further, in a society where assimilation has been the reality for immigrants, albeit now somewhat moderated by the multiculturalism policy, its application to Aboriginal peoples can be portrayed as logical and fair. Rowse's comments on Australia are pertinent to Canada. "Within Australian political culture, the notion of the simple equality of all Australians as individuals is unlikely to lose its appeal, so creating obstacles of rhetoric and principle for those who advocate various kinds of 'special treatment' – 'positive' discrimination, the affirmation of rights which are unique to Indigenous Australians." Further, he notes, "assimilation" is a simple concept with its postulate of a "single set of Australian norms," contrasting with the more complex concept of "'self-determination' [which] opens up the troubling possibility of normative plurality within the one nation."[131]

Canadian assimilationists of the 1990s differ from their pre-White Paper predecessors. Compared to the 1950s and the 1960s, assimilation has drifted from the liberal/left side of the ideological spectrum to the right – from T.C. Douglas to Preston Manning. Though related, its contemporary tone is harsher, defensive, and more strident. Its advocates may be convinced of the rightness of their position, but they are no longer convinced that history is on their side. Their opponents are organized and vocal, not marginalized as was the case until recent decades.

Second, there is now a large and growing urban Aboriginal population, almost half of the Aboriginal identifying population according to RCAP. Urban Aboriginal peoples do not fit comfortably into a view of Aboriginal/non-Aboriginal relations that sees the relationship in terms of parallelism, a third order of government, or the two-row wampum. They are intermingled with the non-Aboriginal population, frequently intermarried, and they lack the supportive cultural environment of land-based communities. In the urban environment, where the

Aboriginal population is itself very diverse, the self-government possibilities are severely truncated.

Third, it would be an exaggeration to say that the pursuit of Aboriginal self-government is a male activity. It would be simple truth, however, to report that apprehension about its possible implementation is much greater among Aboriginal women. The reasons are many and complex. At the most general level, they reflect the belief that power in Aboriginal communities is disproportionately held by males, that sexual and physical abuse is widespread,[132] and that the colonizers' patriarchal values have been taken over by Aboriginal men, which has undermined the pre-contact male and female roles and relations that accorded respect to women.[133] According to Emma La Rocque, fear prevents many Aboriginal women from speaking out against healing circles, which dispense a form of justice more sympathetic to the accused than to the (disproportionately female) victims of violence.[134] RCAP reported many instances of women who were afraid to speak out about abuse in their communities for fear of retaliation. They gave their testimony in private.[135]

Much of the debate has focused on the application of the Charter to Aboriginal self-government, a proposal passionately advocated by the Native Women's Association of Canada (NWAC). Male-female differences over the form of self-government and the Charter's application reflect in part the anomie and social disorganization that afflict many Aboriginal communities and that are manifest in violence against women. John Borrows, reporting on the exchanges that featured NWAC's insistence that the Charter apply to self-government, was struck by "the tremendous lack of confidence that some First Nations women had in Aboriginal governments."[136]

The restoration of legal Indian status to about 100,000 (mostly) women and children under Bill C-31 is an additional complication for Indian communities. Housing shortages and other impediments have prevented more than a handful from returning to their reserves, only 2 percent of those who wished to do so from 1985-90.[137] The opposition of the AFN to Bill C-31, and its subsequent opposition to the application of the Charter to Aboriginal self-government have reinforced women's fears that self-government may not be a blessing. In sum, internal divisions within Aboriginal communities are impediments to an easy transition to self-government.

Fourth, complete independence is not possible. Self-government will be limited. Even after self-government has been achieved and stretched to its maximum extent, Aboriginal peoples will still live in Canada. Aboriginal governments will not exhaust the state's authority over their Aboriginal citizens. The authority, legislation, services, coercions, etcetera, of the third order will be supplemented by those of the other two federal and provincial orders. For the smaller self-governing Aboriginal nations, the jurisdictions under their exclusive control will be dwarfed by the federal and provincial jurisdictions that will continue to apply to them.

Symbolically and psychologically, the Aboriginal governments will have a deeper hold than their federal and provincial counterparts on the identities of their members, but their authority will, nevertheless, apply to only part of their lives. Further, as individuals move across the boundaries of Aboriginal communities, they enter the traditional world of Canadian federalism, either as temporary visitors, or for longer, perhaps lifelong, residence.

Our constitutional thinking about Aboriginal futures cannot, therefore, restrict itself to the justification and elaboration of a third order of Aboriginal government. The excitement of carving out a sphere of Aboriginal self-government has appropriately attracted extensive scholarly and political attention. Aboriginal nationalism focuses on sovereignty, on the inherent right to self-government, and on maximizing the jurisdiction of the latter. However, the average Aboriginal nation, according to RCAP, with a population of 5,000 to 7,000 living on Aboriginal lands, will be dwarfed by even Prince Edward Island, with a population equivalent to fifteen or twenty Aboriginal nations.[138] Prince Edward Island's governing capacity and quality of service provision is significantly below the other provinces, Newfoundland possibly excepted. Further, of course, as already noted, about half of the Aboriginal population – those that lack a land base – will have limited opportunities to exercise even modest versions of self-government. The questions of how individual Aboriginal Canadians, both those within and those without self-governing communities, will relate as citizens to federal and provincial communities and their governments and how a third order of Aboriginal governments will mesh with the other two orders deserve a degree of attention they have not had.

Fifth, s. 35(2) of the 1982 Constitution Act declares that "in this Act, 'Aboriginal peoples of Canada' includes the Indian, Inuit and Métis peoples of Canada." While this clause is not a roadblock to constitutional change in the service of self-government, it is an impediment to clear thinking. To group Indian, Inuit, and Métis in a single category exerts pressure to apply similar policies to Native peoples with very dissimilar histories and contemporary situations. It tempts analysts and commentators to discuss Aboriginal peoples, but to draw almost all of their data from status Indians. The RCAP *Report,* for example, in spite of its "Aboriginal Peoples" mandate, overwhelmingly focused on status Indians. The conventional practice of putting "Aboriginal" in the title of a book, this one for example, and then focusing largely on status Indians is a widespread response to temptation.

The dominance of "Indian" in the "Aboriginal peoples" constitutional category reflects their numbers, the recent prominence of several of their national leaders – Ovide Mercredi and Phil Fontaine – the historic existence of a branch of government devoted to their affairs, and a Cabinet minister who represents their interests. In contrast, no one is responsible for "Aboriginal peoples" as such. The organizational response of governments to the constitutional recognition of the Métis has been minimal. By contrast, once Nunavut came into existence in 1999, most Inuit received quasi-provincial status. Although the Inuit are by far the numerically smallest of the "Aboriginal peoples" category, they have in Nunavut a degree of self-government and a public profile far beyond any self-government arrangement likely to be available to Indians and Métis. The Inuit already have significant achievements to their credit, including the division of the Northwest Territories, the development of three models of public government, the conclusion of two land claims negotiations, and the initiation of an Inuit television network.[139]

Nunavut changes the practical meaning of s. 35(2) by giving its Inuit citizens a unique degree of leverage to chart their own course. The much larger Métis population, by contrast – given its dispersal and its largely urban location – lacks the prerequisites for more than a modicum of what Nunavut Inuit receive. (Although the Alberta Métis have successfully gained a significant degree of local control from the provincial government over the eight Métis settlements in northern Alberta, the settlements encompass only a small minority of the overall Métis population.) The tension between the rubric "Aboriginal peoples of Canada," with its premise of commonality, and the centrifugal realities within the category will increase in the coming decades. By itself, this will generate instabilities in the relations among the Indian, Inuit, and Métis peoples, and in relations with governments, for it will encourage demands from the less favoured – drawing on the equality of Aboriginal peoples principle – for treatment similar to that of the most favoured, treatment that governments will be unable to provide.

## Conclusion

In a quarter of a century, the answer to the question "Is our goal a single society with one basic model of belonging, or is the goal a kind of side by side relation or some mixed solution?" has shifted from official endorsement of the single society model to a more complex set of answers in which supporters are lined up behind all three of the preceding versions of desirable futures: assimilation, parallelism, or something in between.

The long history of the policy of assimilation, which lasted for more than a century, is a remarkable example of a goal that survived from decade to decade in the face of limited evidence of success. The 1857 Act for the Gradual Civilization of the Indian Tribes in the Canadas "viewed enfranchisement as an honour for many Indians," and thus imposed penalties for Indians who tried falsely to pass as such.[140] Sixty years later, in 1920, an amendment to the Indian Act gave authority to the government for the compulsory enfranchisement of Indians who were not voluntarily accepting the honour in sufficient numbers.[141] Half a century later, the 1969 White Paper proposed applying the 1920 policy – abandoned in 1951 – to the entire status Indian population.

Throughout the period, prime ministers, the responsible ministers, senior officials, and concerned citizens reiterated the assimilation mantra as a self-evident truth. This remarkable survival of a goal that ever receded into the distance was made possible because the consistent objections of many of its proposed beneficiaries – the Indian people – were either not heard or were ignored, on the premise that as wards, or minors, or children, their views were irrelevant. They were held to suffer from a false consciousness that was a product of their backwardness, and that could only be overcome by the coercive introduction of enlightenment.

Psychologically, the official stigmatization of Indian culture by the Canadian state predisposed policy makers to treat as misguided any Indians who tried to defend the old ways. Further, the policy of assimilation, normally conceived in individual terms, could scarcely compromise with the logical alternative – the reinvigoration of the distinct Aboriginal communities that assimilation was supposed to eliminate.

The believers in assimilation were believers. Both Chrétien and Trudeau, for example, were taken aback by Indian repudiation of the White Paper.[142] They and their predecessors were, no doubt, arrogant, ethnocentric, paternalistic, and insensitive. However, in their time, the policies they supported were the common property of administrators, anthropologists, missionaries, progressive politicians, and some – how many we do not know – of what later was to become the Aboriginal peoples of Canada. Even now, although assimilation may be dead as an official policy, the impressively large numbers of Canadians with some Aboriginal ancestry who lack an Aboriginal identity suggests that considerable disappearance into the majority society has occurred.[143] Believers in the present emerging alternative paradigm – which has not yet sorted itself out, or conquered all opposition – are also convinced believers. Supporters include Aboriginal élites, especially males; the intelligentsia; some leading politicians (see the Charlottetown Accord), although their support is often pragmatic rather than enthusiastic; and in general, what are thought of as the progressive forces.

At the present time, we have a possible paradigm in-the-making – one that is not yet, however, a settled, routinized understanding. The momentum behind differing versions of parallelism, ranging from modest to some that verge on sovereignty association, comes overwhelmingly from Aboriginal, especially First Nation, élites. Important intellectual support comes from university law faculties across the country. The role of non-Aboriginal governments is defensive, reactive, pre-emptive, or reluctantly supportive. The "Canadian" constraints on the impressive Aboriginal constitutional gains – had the Charlottetown Accord been passed and implemented – gave the appearance of policy making on the run, rather than well-considered reflections of constitutional theory. The old assimilationist paradigm is in retreat and is no longer official policy. It has not, however, been vanquished. It has strong support in the Reform Party and from a number of authors and in segments of the public. This seriously limits the flexibility of governments.

There is still time and a need for discussion of basic questions, such as the following, which are addressed in the remaining chapters of this book.

- Constitutional arrangements can strengthen diversity or transcend it. What balance do we wish to strike?

- Is our goal to be a respectful side-by-side coexistence? Will this make us strangers to each other? If so, does it matter? Can we construct a workable constitutional arrangement from the concept of parallelism – the two-row wampum – with our relations governed by treaties among nations? Is parallelism a feasible model when the typical Aboriginal nation, even if we assume the unlikely realization of RCAP's ambitious hope for the regrouping of Indian communities, will have a basic population of 5,000 to 7,000 people, and may be as low as 2,000?

- How do the citizens of Aboriginal nations fit into federal and provincial communities if we try to constitutionalize parallelism? Many services relevant to their needs will be provided by federal and provincial governments.

- Even on the most optimistic assumption, nation-to-nation relations will be unavailable to about half – especially the urban component – of the Aboriginal population. Do we need a separate theory of Aboriginal citizen-state relations to apply to this situation?

# Chapter Three

# Choice

## A Time of Transition

We are at one of those rare moments when choices have to be made. We can, of course, simply drift into the future, in which case where we end up will be the result of inertia buffeted by ad hocery and circumstance. Such a wayward path risks repeating past failures when dialogue was absent, because Aboriginal voices were marginalized. The task is not to debate various Aboriginal futures as if we had a clean slate on which we could write as we wish. The beginning point for our discussion is here and now with the brooding presence of the past intruding on every conversation. Our real task, therefore, is to define relationships between Aboriginal and non-Aboriginal peoples. As we are not talking about relationships among prospective states in an international system north of the 49th parallel, we have to keep in mind that *one* of our essential tasks is to foster a sense of common belonging to a single political community, as well as the recognition of difference. If we achieve only the latter, our triumph will be pyrrhic, the creation of strangers indifferent to each other's well-being.

The assimilationist policies of the past are in disrepute. Aboriginal peoples have made major breakthroughs since the status Indian defeat of the 1969 White Paper. The 1982 Constitution Act gave the new category

"Aboriginal peoples" a degree of positive recognition[1] far surpassing the bare reference in the 1867 BNA Act of "Indians and lands reserved for the Indians." The latter clause was not really a positive recognition – Indians did not participate in its creation. It was simply a statement of who had jurisdiction over them. The 1982 Act was followed by four Aboriginal constitutional conferences that symbolized the nation-to-nation relationship, with the leaders of Aboriginal organizations sitting at the constitutional bargaining table with first ministers. Although the conferences failed in their major objective of giving substance to the inherent right of self-government, they nevertheless signalled the arrival of Aboriginal peoples as partners, in ways that have yet to be worked out, in a reconstituted Canada. One version of what that might mean was revealed in the Aboriginal components of the defeated Charlottetown Accord, which went a long way toward creating separate constitutional space for Aboriginal peoples. As the Accord was the last major constitutional statement directed to Aboriginal peoples prior to the RCAP *Report,* it deserves examination. It is often described as the starting point for a future constitutional round,[2] although this optimistic assessment possibly overlooks the particular constitutional conjunctions that facilitated the Aboriginal breakthrough – a conjuncture that may not return. Even so, the Accord merits examination as a relatively coherent constitutional vision that received a remarkable degree of support before failing to get over the final hurdle of the 1992 constitutional referendum.

The Charlottetown Accord proposed extensive changes in the relationship of Aboriginal peoples to the constitutional order. What was formerly rejected was now accepted – the constitutional recognition of the inherent right to self-government; the inclusion of Métis, under s. 91(24), as being in federal jurisdiction; and, building on the 1983-7 Aboriginal constitutional conferences, the acceptance of nation-to-nation bargaining in the executive federalism negotiating process that produced the Accord, with its subtle implication that non-Aboriginal governments do not speak for Aboriginal peoples in their electorates. Although the Charlottetown Accord was thin on details, the overall direction was clear and consistent.[3]

The Accord proposed constitutionally entrenching a third order of Aboriginal government based on an inherent right of self-government. Aboriginal peoples, accordingly, would be removed from the jurisdiction of federal and provincial governments to the extent they assumed jurisdiction over themselves.

Separate Aboriginal representation in the House of Commons was supported, with details to be proposed by a House of Commons committee reacting to the recommendations of the Royal Commission on Electoral Reform and Party Financing.

Aboriginal peoples were to have guaranteed Senate representation. As their Senate seats were to be in addition to provincial seats, the clear implication was that Aboriginal peoples were not considered part of the provincial communities. Aboriginal senators might be given a "double majority power in relation to certain matters materially affecting Aboriginal peoples."

Aboriginal peoples were to have a limited role in the preparation of lists of candidates for Supreme Court appointment and could offer advice on candidates proposed by provincial and territorial governments. Consideration was to be given to a proposed Aboriginal Council of Elders that could make submissions to the Supreme Court when it considered Aboriginal issues. In general, the Aboriginal role relating to the Supreme Court was to be on the agenda of a future first ministers' conference and was to be recorded in a political accord.

Aboriginal consent would be required for constitutional amendments directly referring to Aboriginal peoples, by a mechanism to be determined.

Aboriginal representatives were entitled to participate on any agenda item at first ministers' conferences "that directly affects the Aboriginal peoples."

The Métis people were to be brought under the federal jurisdiction of s. 91(24), a goal for which they had long striven.

A Métis Nation Accord was being prepared by the federal government, the five most westerly provinces (Ontario to British Columbia), and the Métis National Council, which would commit governments to negotiate various issues related to Métis self-government. Further, the Métis were to be defined and members of the Métis nation were to be enumerated and registered.

Aboriginal exemption from the Charter, already provided for in s. 25, was significantly extended by new language ensuring that nothing in the Charter "abrogates or derogates from ... in particular any rights or freedoms relating to the exercise or protection of their languages, cultures or traditions."

Aboriginal governments were specifically exempted from the Charter's democratic rights, which gave every citizen "the right to vote in an election of members ... and to be qualified for membership" in federal and provincial legislatures, an exemption to allow traditional Aboriginal practices of leadership selection for Aboriginal governments that would otherwise violate the Charter.

The Charlottetown Accord proposed four first ministers' conferences on Aboriginal constitutional matters commencing no later than 1996 and following at two-year intervals.

The philosophy lying behind the above-noted Aboriginal proposals was expressed in the *Consensus Report*'s description of Aboriginal governments' authority within their jurisdiction as being "(a) to safeguard and develop their languages, cultures, economies, identities, institutions and traditions; and, (b) to develop, maintain and strengthen their relationship with their lands, waters and environment so as to determine and control their development as peoples according to their own values and priorities and ensure the integrity of their societies."[4]

The Accord's Aboriginal clauses elicited astonishment and enthusiasm from students of Aboriginal issues. Recognition of self-government as an inherent right "was a major step toward the decolonization of the Canadian Constitution."[5] Virtually every major institution of the Canadian state would in future have a distinctive Aboriginal input or presence – Senate, House of Commons, Supreme Court (tentatively), first ministers' conferences, and amending formula. The Charter, a crucial symbol of citizenship to many Canadians, would have a greatly weakened application to Aboriginal peoples; further, depending on the jurisdiction of Aboriginal governments, their peoples would have an attenuated relationship to either or both of the two traditional orders of Canadian government, federal and provincial. One of the implicit paradoxes of the Accord was the tension between its proposals to reduce the federal Parliament's jurisdiction over Aboriginal peoples by implementing self-government while simultaneously advocating an enhanced and explicit Aboriginal representation in both houses of Parliament.[6]

The Accord's political theory was parallelism. Its clauses, when regrouped into a single package, amounted to no less than a separate mini-constitution for Aboriginal peoples. Parallelism is further elabo-rated in the RCAP *Report,* which defines Canadians – Aboriginal and non-Aboriginal – as members of separate nations to be linked by treaties. It can be assumed, although some compromise obviously occurred, that the Charlottetown Accord and RCAP reflected extensive Aboriginal input, the Accord because Aboriginal organizations contributed to its formation, and the search for a constitutional compromise with Quebec could not be jeopardized by Aboriginal opposition, as happened to the earlier Meech Lake Accord, and the RCAP *Report* because more than half of the commis-sioners were Aboriginal, and the Commission's task was to give expres-sion to Aboriginal constitutional ambitions.[7] Both the Accord and RCAP build on the arguments of the 1983 *Penner Report* that "self-government would mean that virtually the entire range of law-making, policy, pro-gram delivery, law enforcement and adjudication powers would be available to an Indian First Nation government within its territory."[8]

A year later, a leading constitutional lawyer, in a study that pushed Aboriginal self-government to the limit, asserted: "Their [Aboriginals'] primary allegiance will be to native communities and governments. Since neither the federal nor provincial government reflects their com-munities, they will enjoy special, separate rights in all matters where cultural values count ... To the extent that they will look to their own governments to make decisions and provide services, aboriginal peoples will have no need to participate in other governments, either by way of voting or running for office."[9] David Ahenakew, National Chief of the AFN, informed the Special Committee on Indian Self-Government that "we expect that First Nations will retain and exercise most rights and jurisdictions which provinces now have within Canada, and some oth-ers which are the special rights of the First Nations."[10] In 1984, the AFN stated that Indian government would mean that "the laws governing land, social services, cultural development, education, taxes, economic development – all aspects of life – would be directed by the needs of the people enacting them."[11] In the late 1980s, the AFN asserted that the "federal government's relationship is to First Nations as collectivities, not to our citizens as individuals." This led Cassidy and Bish to observe that "from this perspective, Indian people are, first and foremost, citi-zens in their First Nations. Their primary relationship with the federal government, with Canada, is as part of these First Nations."[12] In this scenario, First Nation governments would have extraordinary power and influence over their citizenry, who would have minimal citizen links with federal and provincial governments.

The preceding proposals – Charlottetown, Penner, AFN, RCAP – go beyond tinkering to a fundamental reconceptualization of the Canadian community and of the constitutional arrangements for its governance from an Aboriginal perspective. Unfortunately, the federal government's response to the recent constitutional proposals of RCAP was belated and limited – an exercise in symbolic politics (see Chapter 4 of this book). The Chrétien government appears to prefer action to discussion and pragmatism to constitutional theory. It is engaged in an extensive devolution of responsibility to Indian communities by non-constitutional means.

We cannot, however, avoid a major constitutional debate on our future. Another Quebec referendum may occur in the next few years, which will reopen the constitutional issue. If it passes, the reconstitution of Canada without Quebec, including the place of Aboriginal peoples, will be on our agenda, as well as the question of the future of Aboriginal nations within Quebec. More generally, the gulf between the emerging Aboriginal constitutional philosophy since the 1982 Constitution Act and where we are now is, in many ways, too profound for silence to be an acceptable response.

We do not have a choice. There is no worthwhile alternative to open discussion. Our past failures, whose depressing legacy haunts us, were caused by misguided theory, and the belief that successful policy could be devised without real discussion with Aboriginal peoples, with the latter myopia contributing to ill-formed theory. Such was the genesis of the 1969 White Paper, whose crushing failure left the formal assimilation policy in ruins.

Accordingly, this chapter and the two that follow are intended as a contribution to a debate that Aboriginal and non-Aboriginal people in Canada have had great difficulty in joining. I hope to frame the discussion in a way that avoids the present volatile combination of sporadic violence, pent-up Aboriginal demands, supportive contributions from the academic (especially legal) community, and an unhelpful reticence from the rest of the non-Aboriginal community, except for strident interjections from surviving supporters of the philosophy of the 1969 White Paper. The latter are no longer found on the liberal/democratic left side of the ideological spectrum, but on the neo-conservative, market-oriented right. What is missing, or inadequately represented, is analysis of the middle ground that simultaneously recognizes both Aboriginal difference *and* the need for connection to, involvement with, and participation in the Canadian community. How can Aboriginal peoples be Canadian, and how can Canadians be Aboriginal? The task is to recognize two overlapping communities and identities. At base, the issue is citizenship.

To participate in the debate, given its politicization and the sensitivities involved, is to risk being misunderstood. To keep silent is to guarantee that one will *not* be understood. If we talk, we all might learn.

### The Influence of the Past

We do not meet as strangers, confronting each other for the first time, with no encumbrances from the past. We are conditioned by the histories of all our previous encounters. Aboriginal and non-Aboriginal peoples in Canada are trying to escape from a past pattern of relationships viewed as counterproductive. However, the past cannot be easily discarded. Those who seek to shape the future have been made what they are by history.

We do not meet as common members of a single society sharing citizenship, common memories, and mutual pride in past achievements. History divides us. Its overcoming, at least to the extent that we can take pride in each other's presence in our common country, is a goal toward which we must steadily work. Reaching it will not be easy.

The postcontact past for Aboriginal peoples – after an early period of nation-to-nation relations – is an unhappy record of negative, often stigmatizing interactions with the majority society. The contemporary politics of Aboriginal national assertiveness, combined with the strategy of making claims that employ past injustice as a political resource, keeps memories of past injustice alive. These memories are inevitably divisive. The RCAP *Report* functions almost as a truth commission in its historical sections as it takes the reader on a pilgrimage through abuses – residential schools, relocation of Inuit and other Aboriginal peoples, shabby treatment of veterans, and the coercions of the Indian Act – inflicted on Aboriginal peoples. The *Report* seeks a reconciliation and healing based on an admission of guilt and acceptance of responsibility by non-Aboriginal Canadians and their governments.

For Aboriginal peoples, the colonial past is experienced as a violent discontinuity. Their subjection and displacement disrupted the ongoing narratives through which they lived their lives. For the colonized, "colonial rule ... severed the ties that bound the present and the future to the past."[13] Suddenly, they belonged to someone else's future, carried along, in the Canadian case, by the majority society's momentum, driven by its own inner logic and sense of destiny. The contemporary positive Aboriginal portrayals of the pre-contact past, and the lead role attributed to the elders in the recovery of tradition are efforts to re-establish historical linkages, to employ the past as a support for identities that have been uprooted. The phrase First Nations has the same purpose. No major Aboriginal constitutional demand or legal challenge can be fully understood if history – and how it is remembered – is kept out of the interpretation. This is especially pronounced in land claims cases, where Aboriginal claims are founded on versions of history and historical episodes that are deeply embedded in their memories and identities.

History lives in the social malaise and anomie of many Aboriginal communities, which are the legacy that self-government is to overcome. The apparently widespread contemporary sexual abuse is, in many cases, a repetition of abuse previously suffered by the perpetrators, often in residential schools. For many young Aboriginal males, imprisonment is their most frequent encounter with the Canadian state. The relative unwillingness of many status Indians to identify themselves as Canadian citizens harkens back to past policies when citizenship was equated with assimilation and the loss of Indian status. The "ambivalence and resistance that First Nations display toward Canadian citizenship"[14] helps explain the recurrently low voting turnout at elections, and the physical prevention of voting on several (mainly western) reserves in the Charlottetown Accord referendum.[15] As Rick Ponting observes, the foremost theme in Indian discourse is "the 'untrustworthiness of government.' The federal government ... was repeatedly portrayed as betraying trust, being deceitful, lying, not dealing in good faith, and being insincere or hypocritical."[16] The context of suspicion that permeates the search for a different constitutional future drives much Aboriginal constitutional theorizing in the direction of maximizing autonomy and maximizing guarantees.

More generally, the history of treatment as a separate people (status Indians), the geographical isolation of the Inuit and the recent nature of their more intense interactions with the larger society, and the Métis perception that they were the forgotten people – all foster a sense of difference, of otherness, in Aboriginal peoples. This is reinforced by memories of the recent past when their cultures were viewed as inferior, and when, for status Indians, the Canadian state engaged in a sustained attempt to eradicate Indianness.

Difference is fostered by Aboriginal organizations that see its stimulation and recognition as a valuable political resource. This is especially the case in constitutional politics, where the justification for self-government is partly based on a claim for recognition of diversity. Jockeying for position occurs within the Aboriginal community as well. Métis leaders are ever alert to assert their singularity from status Indians and the consequent need for separate Métis arrangements when, for example, the possibility of common services for urban Aboriginal peoples is mooted. The purposive fostering of Aboriginal difference replicates the provincial government practice of rhetorically employing difference and uniqueness claims – of whatever kind – in the service of provincial jurisdictional enhancement.

The intrusion of historical complexity into our efforts to find policy solutions to the unsatisfactory relationships between Aboriginal and non-Aboriginal Canadians is not confined to the history of long ago. The repercussions flowing from the addition to the Constitution in 1982 of the phrase "Aboriginal peoples of Canada," defined as including Indian, Inuit, and Métis, are immense.

To bring Inuit and Métis into the new 1982 constitutional category "Aboriginal peoples of Canada" with Indians, is to group different histories and identities under a common label. This generates a subtle intellectual pressure to rearrange the past so that it accords with the new reality. The new "Aboriginal peoples" rubric also induces us in some circumstances to think of policy in terms of an omnibus, abstract label removed from the different realities grouped under it. When we do so, the greater availability of information about status Indians as a particular and historic clientele of the state, plus their greater numbers, and the relatively high profile of the AFN, lead to the widespread practice of discussing generalized Aboriginal policy on the basis of realities and examples that are overwhelmingly Indian. This is an understandable, simplifying, and economizing strategy. However, in certain circumstances – the constitutional arena being one – when we are looking for "Aboriginal" answers, this strategy will bias the response toward insensitive, homogenizing policy. Pressures toward common treatment also emerge from competitive comparisons within the "Aboriginal" category. Thus the Métis seek to enhance their recognition and treatment by employing the phrase "levelling the playing field," which means bringing them into the same constitutional and policy relationship with the federal government under s. 91(24) that is enjoyed by status Indians, and thus gaining the leverage to achieve the benefits available to the latter. The common treatment syndrome stimulated by the "Aboriginal peoples" constitutional category contributed greatly to the diffusion of the status Indian reserve-based self-government goal to Métis and other off-reserve landless Aboriginal peoples, many of them in urban centres, for whom its applicability is problematic. Without the vanguard role of the AFN speaking for territorially based Indian peoples, it is unlikely that as much intellectual and political attention would have been devoted to self-government possibilities in urban settings.

The past also lives among the non-Aboriginal population, although the steady stream of new immigrants dilutes its hold on a growing proportion of the population. For the remainder, the residue of an imperial mentality still lingers, albeit complemented by a shallow goodwill. The sense of guilt for past injustices is weak. Knowledge and appreciation of early nation-to-nation contacts probably verges on the infinitesimal. Where conflict with Native claims is direct – when control of land or access to resources is in dispute – sympathy tends to be overpowered by self-interested fears. The second major party in the country, Reform, is hostile to any form of special treatment.

Overall, then, this is not a hopeful context for a great act of public reconciliation. It is, however, more favourable for such action than at any previous time in our post-Confederation history. We should not forget that the leaders of all governments and apparently a majority of the electorate supported the Aboriginal provisions of the Charlottetown Accord. There is no guarantee that the future will provide us with a more auspicious time to sort out our relations with each other. When we direct ourselves to the search for a rapprochement, which cannot be long delayed, we need to know the requirements of good Aboriginal constitutional policy.

### The Requirements of Good Aboriginal Constitutional Policy

Aboriginal constitutional policy needs to be sensitive to two fundamental facts. First, it applies to a particular category of peoples whose previous history has set them apart and generated, in the contemporary era, varying degrees of nationalist self-consciousness and particularistic identities. Some response to the specificity of Aboriginal peoples – including some degree of recognition, and where appropriate some self-governing powers – is essential. Aboriginal peoples of the future, accordingly, will not be standard Canadians, although individuals may choose to be so if they wish.

Second, the future of Aboriginal peoples lies inside, not outside the Canadian state. Independence is not a realistically available option. Hence, the policy response to Aboriginal peoples must include some conception of a common citizenship – some way in which we relate to each other as more than strangers. The creation of a third order of Aboriginal government will take us only halfway to our goal. In addition to their Aboriginal identities – and where feasible, their membership in self-governing Aboriginal communities – individuals should also relate as citizens to both federal and provincial governments. The task, therefore, is to devise institutional incentives that over time will encourage the normal divided identities of federalism as well as an Aboriginal identity. This will not be easy, as many nationalist élites at this breakthrough time are more concerned with maximizing self-government and settling claims (both of which reflect and reinforce Aboriginality) than focusing on the non-Aboriginal Canadian and provincial dimensions of their future existence. As already noted, many status Indians are uneasy about provincial involvement, seeing it as a threat to their unique relationship to the central government. Others, given their histories, understandably attach little meaning to their Canadian citizenship. Nevertheless, the constitutional strategy should *not* be – as primarily it was in the Charlottetown Accord, and largely is in the RCAP proposals – to ensure that the maximum possible interactions with the state reflect an Aboriginal perspective. Aboriginal people are not only Aboriginal, and should not be constitutionally treated as if they were. If our political community has meaning, we need also to meet and treat with each other as Manitobans and Canadians. This will take time, but we should not throttle the possibility by the institutional arrangements we initially put in place.

Responding positively to Aboriginal difference – and simultaneously reinforcing the pan-Canadian community of citizen membership – does not, on the surface, appear to be an unattainable goal. However, we have managed to put many impediments in the way of reaching it. Whether we move or do not move in the "right" direction depends on the lens we employ as we think about our future.

### Assimilation versus Parallelism: Warring Paradigms

Historically, our two main policy paradigms – traditional assimilationist and emerging parallelism – have focused on either the first or the second of the preceding requirements – not simultaneously on both. The assimilationist paradigm, dominant for the first century after Confederation, focused entirely on the state's long-run concern for an inclusive community of standardized citizens, but had no sympathy for any enduring positive recognition of Aboriginality.

There were two versions of the assimilation policy: The official, and most obvious, was the statutory policy directed by official federal change agents to assimilate the status Indian population. The original official policy recognition of difference by the reserve system, the Indian Act and a separate branch of government to administer it, was negative, not positive. Difference was something to be overcome on the road to homogeneity. Until that goal was reached one was kept outside, to be invited into full membership when certain criteria were met. As we now know, the policy was counterproductive. It fostered the difference it was supposed to transcend, and it gave status Indians an extraordinarily strong attachment to the federal government – and to the Crown, the by-product of which was a distancing and alienation from the provinces. In other words, the policy was almost classically ill suited to achieve its long-run objective – the placing of its clientele in a normal relationship with both orders of government.

The second version of assimilation policy was the absence of any specific administrative and policy regime for Inuit and Métis. This non-recognition policy was underlined in 1939 when the Supreme Court decided that Inuit were caught up in s. 91(24), but the federal government did not respond with a distinct policy regime. The premise was that natural forces would suffice for the assimilation of the Inuit and the Métis. In terms of explicit policy, therefore, the state accorded them neither positive nor negative recognition.[17]

Overall, there was no deliberate positive reinforcement of the identity of any Aboriginal people by the state in its assimilation policy – version one or two. The weakness of the assimilation policy in both its versions – in terms of the criteria identified earlier – was its failure to respond positively to culturally reinforced separate identities cherished by their possessors, a failure that contributed to the alienation of Aboriginal peoples from the Canadian political community. Post-Second World War Australian policy toward Aborigines earned similar criticism. On the one hand, "there was an heroic (and mistaken) simplicity in the normative pretensions of 'assimilation.' 'They' would eventually be like 'us,' and little more need be said, because this conviction manifested an egalitarianism which no reasonable Australian could question." On the other hand, this goal of "a magnificent departure from certain kinds of colonial racism, this emphasis on 'equality' proved to be racist in a different way – its failure to acknowledge the right to be different."[18]

The emerging paradigm, still in the making, which I call the parallelism paradigm, displays considerable sensitivity to the desire of Aboriginal peoples for some positive recognition, including self-governing powers, but pays lesser attention to what holds us together, to what prevents us from being strangers. The parallelism proposals – of Penner, Charlottetown, and RCAP – display little concern, should their proposals be implemented, for whether the nature of community in the country as a whole will induce us to feel responsible for each other. The two-row wampum model so frequently proposed as the arrangement that will fit our needs, stresses the permanence of difference. As an image it postulates parallel paths that never converge. The image is of coexistence with little traffic between the solitudes. It does not suggest shared endeavours for a common purpose. Further, of course, parallelism has little to offer the growing urban Aboriginal population, jumbled up with other Canadians. Its vision is of distinct peoples coexisting in a side-by-side relationship – friendly, perhaps, but with little appetite for common endeavours. Parallelism – the two-row wampum – does not address the reality of our interdependence, and of our intermingling. It speaks, therefore, to only part of who we are. It can justify a third order of Aboriginal government, but it provides little justification for a central government or a country-wide community of citizens. It is a contemporary version of the compact theory of Confederation. That theory was designed to stress the priority of the provincial parts over the Canadian whole, to prevent the centre from using its spending power to strengthen a sense of Canadianism, and thus weaken provincial identifications.

Parallelism has many faces. The stress on nation-to-nation relationships and treaties as the instrument to regulate them; the AFN argument that the Charter should not apply to self-governing Indian First Nations, thus distancing subjects of First Nations from a fundamental symbol of Canadian citizenship; the bypassing of parliamentary theories of representation when Aboriginal élites bargain directly with first ministers at the constitutional table (understandable, but the inference is that there is no positive relationship between Aboriginal voters and their elected representatives); and the separatist strain that runs through much Aboriginal constitutional theorizing – these are all examples of parallelism. Admittedly, there is often a reassuring statement by advocates of parallelism that complete independence is not sought, but the area excluded from self-government is often treated with brevity and limited enthusiasm. This is the area, of course, where a common Canadianism should exist, where Aboriginal peoples will be directly linked to the federal and provincial governments that will provide services outside the jurisdiction of Aboriginal governments. These services, given the capacity limitations of small populations, will not be marginal. For at least half of the Aboriginal population living outside of self-governing communities, parallelism will have little meaning. Their links will be overwhelmingly to federal, provincial and, in many cases, municipal governments. As discussed in the next chapter, RCAP candidly and revealingly admits that it devoted negligible attention to participation in the sharing, Canadian dimension of the country's ongoing existence, except as a recipient.

The now almost conventional application of the label "nation" to Aboriginal peoples – RCAP proposes sixty to eighty self-governing Aboriginal nations in Canada – induces respect and a greater degree of equality in Aboriginal/non-Aboriginal relations. "Nation," however, may come at a price. It has a distancing effect. It reduces the likelihood that those outside the "nation" will treat those inside it as fellow citizens. In at least a limited sense, it internationalizes domestic relations. Treaties, as the preferred instrument for regulating relationships between nations, generate perceptions of "otherness" between the parties to the treaty. Treaties create obligations but they also presuppose and create boundaries. (Nevertheless, treaty federalism, as it is called by James [sákéj] Youngblood Henderson,[19] has strong intellectual roots in the historical treaties, and potentially a strong contemporary resonance for the members of Aboriginal nations. The future it postulates is so radically different from the assumptions of my argument that I have left its discussion to the concluding chapter).

Some colleagues inform me that I exaggerate the significance of "nation" as a label, remind me of its historical roots in the early contact period, and suggest that those who employ the label know full well that it is not intended to be a vehicle for independent statehood. It is, I am told, essentially a status-raising term, meaning little more than a linguistic or cultural community with a historical identity. These reminders would be more convincing if those who used "nation" simultaneously paid serious attention to the federal and provincial dimension of Aboriginal citizenship and membership in non-Aboriginal communities. However, key policy documents, such as the Penner and RCAP *Reports* systematically employ "nation" *and* pay negligible attention to the civic relation of Aboriginal peoples and individuals to federal and provincial communities and their governments. It is difficult to believe that the stress on the former does not contribute to the neglect of the latter. "Nation" tends to crowd out other civic identities by encouraging their definition as competing, rather than complementary.

Further, the nation label for Aboriginal communities lies behind the emerging tendency to describe Canada as a multinational community inadequately encompassed in a territorial federalism. This in turn leads to an implicit false equivalence of individual Aboriginal nations (prospectively sixty to eighty according to RCAP) with the Quebec nation: false equivalence because the potential consequences of Quebec nationhood, including independence, are unavailable to Aboriginal nations whose average population size – using RCAP estimates again – would be less than one-thousandth of Quebec's population.

Parallelism, the "nation" concept, and the treaty instrument positively recognize the distinct peoplehood of Indians, Inuit, and Métis and symbolize an ongoing nation-to-nation relationship that reflects and supports equality. While these are positive consequences, we need to ask how much of a common citizenship is compatible with nation-to-nation relationships, regulated by treaty, and modelled on the parallelism of the two-row wampum. Equality among nations is not the same as equality among citizens. It is not easy to have both at the same time. If the absence of a vital common citizenship is the price tag of parallelism, what will provide the empathy that makes us feel responsible for one another? If there is no equally potent functional alternative to citizenship, is this a known, predictable cost that advocates of parallelism are willing to pay?

My argument, then, is that each of the two main models – the assimilation model of the past and the emerging parallelism paradigm – have been and are one-sided. The bias of the assimilation model against sensitive recognition of Aboriginality, and for the supremacy of the existing non-Aboriginal Canadian community was a natural bias for a policy process that heard no Aboriginal voices and did not wish to. Hence a concern for the whole, easily equated with the dominant society, was natural for those who supported the assimilation policy.

The bias in the emerging parallelism paradigm toward strong recognition of Aboriginality and minimal recognition of the integration requirements of the political system reflects the pressures on many Aboriginal élites to behave as apostles of difference. Their goal is to achieve a modified exit, one rationale for which is their dissimilarity from the majority. In pursuing this goal, it is not their task to stress what they hold in common with other Canadians, which too easily gets redefined as a revival of the assimilation policy. They are not trying to break in. They are trying to break out. The adversarial politics of constitutional change – the rhetoric that appears to be necessary to carve out some distinct constitutional space for one's people – puts a premium on the identification of difference.

Difference becomes the justification for distinctive constitutional recognition and perhaps jurisdictions, and the latter in turn are to be vehicles for reinforcing difference.[20] Cultural difference, and the superiority of Native cultures, are also stressed as ways of restoring pride for peoples whose way of life was stigmatized as a justification for their past subordination.[21] The circular sequence of a claim to a past or surviving cultural difference as justification for the future reinforcing of cultural difference is most likely when past treatment of the minority has been stigmatic, has in fact been culturally punitive, as was particularly the case with Indian peoples. Further, this stress on difference is most likely to be strongest at the time of making claims for separate treatment, for the establishment of Aboriginal governments. The strategy requirements for exit, even partial exit, for breaking out, are the reverse of the requirements for breaking in, for becoming a normal citizen with standard rights and duties. To seek the latter is to stress similarity, common membership, and the treatment that flows from being like everybody else. To maximize the claim for exit is to weaken the claim for standard belonging.

Formerly, the non-Aboriginal majority recognized Aboriginal difference, pronounced it inferior, and either ignored it or attempted to extinguish it in pursuit of an undifferentiated citizenry. Now, the Aboriginal nations recognize their own difference, seek to have it validated, and in the strongest political version minimize what their peoples have in common with Euro-Canadian society. Neither of these is a workable starting point to establish an enduring pattern of relationships based on a recognition of sufficient similarity and an acceptance of common community so that we can profit from the differences that survive our interdependence and our proximity to each other.

Neither the assimilationist paradigm, nor the parallelism paradigm is capable of handling difference and similarity simultaneously. Neither, therefore, is an adequate recipe for a future constitutional order that needs to recognize difference and also recognize or reinforce similarity. The assimilationist paradigm says to Aboriginal peoples, "You can only become full members of Canadian society by ceasing to be yourself." The parallelism paradigm says to non-Aboriginal Canadians, "You cannot expect to share a strong sense of citizenship with Aboriginal peoples, for you and they are not travelling together." Clearly we can no longer deny our differences, but if this is all we have, and if we are unable or unwilling to try to transcend them in part, we have no basis for trying to reconstruct a common country.

The language, or more grandiosely, the constitutional theory we need must simultaneously support "breaking out" by self-government, and "breaking in" to the federal and provincial dimensions of what it means to belong to a complex constitutional order that requires multiple identities and memberships for successful functioning. If our rhetoric is geared only to "breaking out" or "breaking in" we will fail. The simplifiers, the polarizers, and the advocates of either/or are enemies of the subtlety that is the servant of wise policy in an area where booby traps await us at every turn.

Accordingly, we need a vocabulary and a constitutional theory that reduces the distance between Aboriginal nationhood and Canadian citizenship. The "nation" label and identity for Aboriginal people will not disappear in any future we need concern ourselves with. "Nation," however, is not enough. It needs to be blended and supplemented with the concept and identity of being a Canadian citizen. It may be that Aboriginal nation/Canadian citizenship will appear as a constitutional oxymoron to true believers on both sides of the divide we have inherited. Nevertheless, to the extent it remains an oxymoron, the grounds for optimism erode.

### How We See Ourselves: The Discourse of Contrast

The choice of discourse – how we describe where we are and how we got here – has a major effect on what we define as problems and the kind of solutions we seek. This and the following section discuss two discourses – one based on contrasts, the descriptive underpinnings of parallelism, and an alternative less fully developed that I have labelled a modernizing Aboriginality. The first, the discourse of contrasts, is most appropriate when Aboriginal and non-Aboriginal Canadians are geographically separated, and have little intercultural contact. As cultural exchanges increase in frequency, as we increasingly intermingle with each other in urban centres, as intermarriage becomes more frequent, as more Aboriginal peoples graduate from high schools and universities and take up successful professional careers, a descriptive language of contrasts that defines Aboriginal and non-Aboriginal peoples in terms of "otherness" becomes progressively detached from reality. It applies to a diminishing proportion of the Aboriginal population, and thus has diminishing relevance for how we might structure our future lives together. Nevertheless, a discourse of contrast is pervasive – which suggests that it is deeply rooted in Aboriginal experience. According to Keith Basso, "it appears to be the case that in all Indian cultures the 'White man' serves as a conspicuous vehicle for conceptions that define and characterize what 'the Indian' is not."[22] Contrast is also functionally related to claims for special treatment, which are sustained by the contrasting presence of traditional ways of life. "Once tradition has gone as a basis for claims, then people will not be as willing to settle past wrongs with a society that appears to be much like itself."[23]

Justifications for a separate Aboriginal justice system are couched in terms of contrasting Native (healing) and white (retributive) approaches that, according to one Aboriginal critic, romanticize the Aboriginal view of justice and are simply historically inaccurate. In many instances, "Aboriginal societies lived with the biblical dictum: An eye for an eye. Traditionally, there was swift justice for [major] transgressions ... indicating that 'healing' was not the means of dealing with criminals."[24]

The ideology of parallelism, as noted in the previous example, is sustained by a rhetoric that constantly stresses the contrasts between Aboriginal and non-Aboriginal culture, values, and lifestyles. Thus Aboriginal women advocates of the Charter's applicability to Aboriginal self-government were informed by the AFN that the Charter was a "foreign" document, and that the restoration of Aboriginal tradition would give them more power, status, and respect "than their female white sisters."[25] Another Charter supporter was "labelled ... a dupe of the colonizing society."[26] Two supporters of a separate Aboriginal justice system claimed that "Aboriginal peoples, [who are] ... both different and separate, simply cannot be considered as part of Canadian society ... We are ... set apart by our cultures, languages, distance and histories." These differences justified special constitutional status.[27] As noted earlier, the AFN constitutional document *To The Source* is a veritable catalogue of contrasts between status Indians and the majority society.[28] According to one Native Studies professor, "the strident insistence by the Native leadership on our cultural differences has pushed Aboriginal people to the extreme margins. We have given the message that we are so fathomlessly different as to be hardly human ... as if we do not require basic human rights that other Canadian citizens expect."[29] The same point was made more pithily by Phil Lujan, an American Indian lawyer: "If we Indians aren't careful we'll *unique* ourselves out of existence."[30]

The rhetoric of contrast between Aboriginal and non-Aboriginal peoples has a double effect. It puts the two sets of peoples into separate camps, and normally accords the moral high ground to Aboriginal peoples. The roots of this rhetoric, in reality a counterattack, are simply the past tendency of the Euro-Canadian majority to do the same, with good and bad and the moral high ground reversed, of course. It responds to a profound "hunger within the Native community for an identity separate from the Canadian mainstream."[31] Formerly, the majority society's rationale for negative, stigmatizing treatment of Aboriginal peoples was their "otherness." That message has been digested, stood on its head by its recipients, and employed for what is hoped to be a positive differentiation. A stress on "otherness," however, hampers the making of wise policy.[32]

Such contrasts construct ideological walls around cultures, minimize points of cultural convergence, tend to look to the past for guidance, and have difficulty accommodating change. Contrast provides a basis for a separate Aboriginal sphere, or for complete independence, but it provides no rationale for togetherness. To read *To the Source,* the AFN constitutional document, is to ask why would First Nations people wish to live with and share citizenship with the non-Aboriginal community they so unflatteringly portray? Joe Carens argues that it is "regrettable necessity ... the need for ongoing transfers of resources," coupled with the small size of Aboriginal communities that keeps Aboriginal peoples in Canada. The reasoning is instrumental rather than reflective of "a fundamental identity or attachment."[33] A purely instrumental Aboriginal reply, however – "we can't go it alone" – may generate instrumental reasoning by the non-Aboriginal majority.

The rhetoric of contrast, especially if coupled with maximum opting-out by self-government, may induce the non-Aboriginal partner to say they (Aboriginal peoples) – by their own admission – are not part of us and should not therefore be treated as if they were. Or, it may put the burden of nurturing and defending a common citizenship and an overarching community on the non-Aboriginal partners, which may then induce Aboriginal peoples to see a common citizenship as an act of cultural imperialism.

The stress on contrast, as Macklem argues, underestimates the extent to which the "boundaries of culture are ... porous," and thus overlooks the coexistence of both difference from and similarity to the dominant culture in circumstances where there are "intersecting and competing structures of belief [and] ... conflicting or overlapping cultural affiliations." Later he underlines the reality of multiple identities, observing that to be Indian need not be antithetical to being Canadian.[34]

Another impediment to realistic self-understanding are portraits of our condition that attribute wholeness, uniqueness, and separateness to both Aboriginal and non-Aboriginal societies. They distort reality. Such language has become an inescapable component of our thinking, and we cannot entirely escape its influence for it is heavily laden with symbolism. We should not, however, forget that references to the integrity of societies, or to distinct societies with unique cultures, get in the way of clear vision. When the Charlottetown Accord said that Aboriginal governments had the authority and responsibility "to determine and control their development as peoples according to their own values and priorities and ensure the integrity of their societies" it was assigning them an impossible task. Even the most powerful of contemporary states is massively penetrated by external forces. Neither the totalitarian Soviet Union nor the South African apartheid regime could resist the global pressures that defined their versions of peoplehood and citizen-state relations as anachronistic. From this perspective, the distinctiveness of Quebec's distinct society is a minor variation in a pattern of interdependence and interchange with the world outside its borders. The smaller, dependent, local Aboriginal societies are also caught up in contemporary globalizing economic pressures and outside cultural and lifestyle influences. Intermarriage rates dramatically underline the degree of intercultural contact. In their 1992 report, Clatworthy and Smith estimate an overall out-marriage rate of 34 percent for status Indians. For off-reserve status Indians, they estimate this figure to be as high as 62 percent; for the on-reserve population they estimate a more modest rate of 25 percent.[35] Another study, prepared for the Department of Indian Affairs and Northern Development, reported that approximately 50 percent of status Indians married non-status persons between 1965 and 1985.[36] In the United States in 1990, 59 percent of married Indians (of all ages) had non-Indian partners; for those Indians under the age of twenty-five the rate rises to 65 percent. These figures reflect the reality that "most Indians enter marriage markets predominantly composed of non-Indians."[37] Both Canadian and American figures are even more remarkable when contrasted with interracial marriage by African Americans, which, although rapidly rising, was only 12.1 percent in 1993.[38]

These intermarriage rates suggest high levels of cultural exchange, and weaken assertions of ineffable cultural differences or basic incommensurability between Aboriginal and non-Aboriginal values. Few groups surpass the Native Women's Association of Canada in avid support for the Charter of Rights. Even a nationalistic document such as *To the Source* reports that "native youth, like young people everywhere, want the best of both worlds: the formal training to succeed in the white world, and education in their own language, culture, and traditions."[39] A report in the late 1980s noted "an abandonment of the aboriginal life style" among the Inuit and the loss of the "Inuit language, culture and traditional land skills ... at an alarming rate."[40]

Aboriginal societies, like all other societies, therefore, are penetrated societies. Their members live in many worlds at once, and relate to more than one community. Aboriginal societies, as is also true of Quebec and Canadian society, are partial societies. They do not exhaust the identities or community senses of their members, although their primary identity may be Aboriginal. They should not, therefore, be viewed as if they were whole societies with only minimal relations with the Canadian society. Carol La Prairie argues that many values are shared with non-Aboriginal society, that "differences between Aboriginal and non-Aboriginal values are disappearing and there may be as much plurality of value systems within Aboriginal cultures themselves as between Aboriginal and non-Aboriginal cultures."[41] The reality for Aboriginal, as for non-Aboriginal peoples, is the interdependent, cosmopolitan reality in which all of humanity now lives, albeit the pace and degree of our incorporation varies. "The contents of a citizen's mind are ... increasingly composed of elements not exclusive to a country, ethnic group or religion. Thus no firm separatism within the internal cultural world of an individual, is objectively possible, or viable in a real sense in today's world ... in today's world, multiple selves and multiple identities are necessary to function in any viable society, including one that has declared sovereign separation. No single subculture has exclusive access to an individual mind, no one culture owns it exclusively ... This is the contemporary modern self."[42]

One of the leading students of Aboriginal history, Bruce Trigger, states that "treating native peoples as members of autonomous groups denies the realities of life for most Indians over the last several centuries. If many of them have valiantly resisted European domination and fought to preserve what they could of their freedom and way of life, they have all been forced into increasingly narrow spheres of action and had to adapt to these straightened [sic] conditions."[43] Jeremy Webber reinforces Trigger's reminder in an analysis of early contact between Indians and the incoming Europeans, by documenting the emergence of a "framework [that] provided moral constraints and stable expectations" on both sides. This framework, which he labelled a "normative community," regulated intercommunal relations in such key areas of potential intercultural conflict as murder and land disputes.[44]

The pervasive connections with the surrounding society and the ineradicable heterogeneity of values and identities they foster in Aboriginal peoples are inescapable facts to which the theory and practice of future self-government must sensitively respond. Future policy for the Métis, intermingled with Euro-Canadian society, and for non-reserve-based Indians (both status and non-status) must also be sensitive to the demographic and cultural considerations that affect their reality even more profoundly. Conceptions of contemporary Aboriginality, therefore, must accommodate the non-Aboriginal influences that help to shape it.[45]

The argument that Aboriginal societies are penetrated societies, or partial societies whose members are linked in multiple ways to the "outside" world does not mean that the goal of self-government is a mistake, but only that its limitations, which apply to all governments,[46] should be recognized now – which will reduce the disillusion that will follow if inappropriate utopian hopes are pinned on its achievement. Self-government will give some leverage, some control to Aboriginal peoples, and that is justification enough to implement it.

### An Alternative Vision: A Modernizing Aboriginality

The stimulation of "otherness" in the service of redemptive nationalism denies what other analysts see as a pervasive contemporary reality – the extent to which we are all involved with each other in the making of cultures that intermingle and fuse. Three quotations, by a Ghanaian – now an African American – a Palestinian, and a lapsed Muslim reveal and revel in a counter-definition of where and who we now are. They are not, of course, talking specifically of Canada or of Aboriginal peoples, but of the contemporary world, of globalization, of the end of empire and of the movement of peoples. All three live outside their country of origin.

Kwame Anthony Appiah, the Ghanaian, said: "If there is a lesson in the broad shape of this circulation of cultures, it is surely that we are all already contaminated by each other, that there is no longer a fully autochthonous pure-African culture awaiting salvage by our artists (just as there is, of course, no American culture without African roots). And there is a clear sense in some postcolonial writing that the postulation of a unitary Africa over against a monolithic West – the binarization of Self and Other – is the last of the shibboleths of the modernizers that we must learn to live without."[47]

Palestinian scholar Edward Said remarked that "all cultures are involved in one another; none is single and pure, all are hybrid, heterogeneous, extraordinarily differentiated, and unmonolithic." And: "We have never been as aware as we now are of how oddly hybrid historical and cultural experiences are, of how they partake of many often contradictory experiences and domains, cross national boundaries, defy the *police* action of simple dogma and loud patriotism. Far from being unitary or monolithic or autonomous things, cultures actually assume more 'foreign' elements, alterities, differences, than they consciously exclude."[48]

Salman Rushdie, who has until recently been under a *fatwa,* or religious death sentence, describes the book that provoked it: "Those who oppose [*The Satanic Verses*] most vociferously today are of the opinion that intermingling with a different culture will inevitably weaken and ruin their own. I am of the opposite opinion. *The Satanic Verses* celebrates hybridity, impurity, intermingling, the transformation that comes of new and unexpected combinations of human beings, cultures, ideas, politics, movies, songs. It rejoices in mongrelization and fears the absolutism of the Pure. *Mélange,* hotchpotch, a bit of this and a bit of that is *how newness enters the world ... The Satanic Verses* is for change-by-fusion, change-by-conjoining. It is a love-song to our mongrel selves."[49]

While the views of Appiah, Said, and Rushdie may have little appeal to nationalists – Aboriginal, Québécois, or otherwise – they capture a crucial reality of the contemporary condition. Further, they link up with a view of Aboriginality that does not depend on contrast. That view, earlier labelled a modernizing Aboriginality, builds on the changed story line of ethnic resurgence, identified by Bruner,[50] that captures the present situation. It is, however, ethnic resurgence with a difference.

In the assimilation era Aboriginal practices that approximated white, majority behaviour – clothing, jobs, lifestyle, foods, etcetera – were called assimilation or acculturation. Now, with the new story line, going for a Big Mac, or becoming a lawyer, are simply contemporary ways of being Aboriginal. From this perspective, being Indian, Inuit, or Métis is not defined by fidelity to past cultural practices. Aboriginality is not frozen, but rather is evolving, adapting, and choosing. Sally Weaver explains the new paradigm thinking as follows: "Old paradigm thinking sees culture in some quantum sense in which 'traditional' or 'real' Indian culture diminishes under the forces of acculturation to the point that it disappears. Thus the Cree can not eat pizza and remain 'real Cree.' Under the new paradigm, First Nations cultures continue to be reconstructed into the distant future, as all cultures are, and some 500 years from now there will be First Nations chiefs and Cree culture in existence in Canada. New paradigm thinking does not reify 'traditional' culture as a state which the First Nations seek to freeze in some form. Rather it sees First Nations groups as continuing to adapt to the changes in their natural, social and political environment and thus maintain the current diversity they display today."[51] This understanding is naturally more congenial to Aboriginal peoples than the assimilation interpretation, for it means that cultural change is normal rather than threatening.

In a sense, it is not that the process of cultural transformation has changed, but that we now think of it differently. Driving a car, watching television, drinking Pepsi, going to university, are no longer thought of as signs of assimilation, but as responding to a changing environment, as simply indicating contemporary ways of being Aboriginal. Again, part of the change is who is doing the labelling – when the process was described by non-Aboriginals in the past, it was assimilation or acculturation; as described by Aboriginal persons today, it is simply a modernized version of Aboriginality; paradoxically, then, ethnic resurgence not only means a recovery of the past – some of which is captured in the Ranger and Hobsbawm phrase "the invention of tradition"[52] – but also an enhanced openness to change stimulated by self-confidence.

Further, acculturation or assimilation privileges the assimilating culture, and attributes at a minimum a superior attractive power to it. Conversely, when cultural change derived from cultural contact is relabelled cultural growth, it gives priority to the choosing, incorporating

Aboriginal person, community, or nation. The move from being assimilated to that of an agent transforming one's own culture or one's individual personality by incorporating outside influences, as everyone else is doing, is from being a vessel filled by others to an in-charge actor scanning the options.

Most overt changes of behaviour and of norms can be brought under either the label of assimilation or of an adaptable Aboriginality. That we have moved from one to the other is powerful testimony to the positive changes, from an Aboriginal perspective, in the cultural/intellectual/political climate. Formerly, assimilation/acculturation was seen as a progressive erosion of Aboriginal values and behaviour, which were displaced by majority values and behaviour. This meant that culture change constantly enlarged the majority and reduced the minority Aboriginal population. Aboriginal peoples were rather like immigrants, expected to leave their past behind after a transition period. The overt indicators of this process would be bungalows rather than igloos, and snowmobiles rather than snowshoes. Indianness, viewed through this lens, was how Indians used to live, and similarly for Inuit and Métis.

When viewed from a modernizing perspective, Aboriginality is no longer defined in terms of an authenticity with roots in the distant past. Rather, its redefinition presupposes a constant, selective, adaptive, and incorporative behaviour as individuals and communities remake themselves by choosing from the options at hand. Borrows observes that for his ancestors, the Chippewa, the "Christian religion, farming, and education [were instruments to] ... provide the strength necessary to retain much of what they already enjoyed as self-governing peoples."[53] To assume new practices and values is simply to be open to change. Indianness and Aboriginality are now capacious concepts no longer confined to historical ways of life. Aboriginality now incorporates non-traditional beliefs, practices, and values from outside without ceasing to be Aboriginality. Dara Culhane, describing Gitksan and Wet'suwet'en society, agreed that change followed contact, but denied that this meant "transforming from the status of 'truly Aboriginal' peoples to that of ones 'not truly Aboriginal.'"[54] Borrows' summary is apposite: "Aboriginal peoples are traditional, modern and post-modern."[55]

When Aboriginality and change are no longer viewed as being in contradiction, it follows that museums will be castigated if they portray

Native peoples as they were when Columbus arrived, rather than as a people who are adaptable, contemporary members of the global human community.[56]

### A Basis for Living Apart and Together

This version of Aboriginality is incompatible with the previously mentioned polarizing discourse of contrasts between Euro-Canadian (bad) and Indian/Aboriginal (good) that is widely used politically. The emphasis on the absorptive capacity of Aboriginal peoples does not deny cultural change, does not even deny that much of the impetus to change comes from outside, but denies that it signals the end of Aboriginality. Thus RCAP, while it stresses traditions and the role of elders, and is passionately concerned with the continuity and survival of Aboriginal culture, simultaneously underlines that culture's adaptability and its positive, selective incorporation of values, customs, and technologies of the majority society.[57] Although culture contact can produce "alienation from Aboriginal culture,"[58] the *Report* stresses that Aboriginal identity is perfectly compatible with "telephones, snowmobiles, or video games."[59] From this perspective, RCAP both reports and supports a modernizing Aboriginality.

In the discourse of contrast, Aboriginal and non-Aboriginal identities are clothed in vastly different cultural forms – they are cultural solitudes. In the discourse of an evolving Aboriginality, the identity differences are retained, while overt cultural differences decline. This version of identity is perfectly compatible with a high degree of overlapping cultural values, practices, etcetera, with non-Aboriginal Canadians. In the same way, Canadian identity is compatible with holding many values in common with Americans. This version of identity also cautions us not to assume that pervasive cultural differences are necessary to support deeply felt identity differences.

We are less prone than formerly to assume that identity changes follow quickly, easily, and automatically as by-products of overt lifestyle changes. Identity is a more frugal phenomenon than we once thought – a sparer, more adaptable phenomenon that does not have to be moored in particular and unchanging cultural patterns. This, of course, is one of the lessons of the Quiet Revolution in Quebec, which brought Canadians closer together in terms of our values and lifestyles, but not in terms of our identities.

If the reality is that we are all – Aboriginal and non-Aboriginal alike – massively shaped by cultural and other forces outside our immediate local culture, and if we nevertheless retain separate identities while sharing common values and experiences, we then have a basis for living together and living apart at the same time. If both partners – Aboriginal and non-Aboriginal – are imbibing from and contributing to a battery of overlapping and interpenetrating cultures, the source of which is often external, then a degree of togetherness and sharing is less threatening than when they belong to cultures that are believed to contradict each other fundamentally. Identity by contrast produces coexisting solitudes with no reason for sharing the same space except the accident of history. An absorptive Aboriginality transmits a different message. It makes contact with the non-Aboriginal society, which is also subject to external influences; it suggests overlapping concerns and values; it denies incommensurability. Yet it does not imply the disappearance of Aboriginal identity, and since it suggests a selective incorporation of values, goods, and practices from the outside it presupposes some continuing cultural differentiation. It also, however, provides a basis for building a Canadian community that combines some value congruity with respect for identity difference. Thus, although the RCAP *Report* describes "culture as the whole way of life of a people,"[60] it nevertheless notes that language is not necessary to identity, and its loss does not imply assimilation.[61] Further, the contemporary reality it describes is of a modernizing Aboriginality. It reports that 500 years of encounter have produced "an intercultural common ground ... where attitudes and expectations of the various parties are familiar to one another."[62]

If we are to think clearly about our situation, we need to complicate further the previous discussion with the reminder that we all carry multiple identities, and that they are constantly being reshaped. We can be Métis and Manitoban, Cree and Albertan, Inuit and Canadian. The coexistence in our lives of membership in more than one community, and the accompanying reality of multiple identities reflect that we live in many worlds at once, each of which calls forth a modified version of who we are. Individuals can and do juggle multiple identities. We would be paralyzed if that were not the case. To proclaim only one identity is to cease to be a social being.

Of course, particular identities can fade and disappear. So we should not be surprised that the population with *some* Aboriginal ancestry is larger than the population with *an* Aboriginal identity. The vast movement of peoples around the world, the culture contact that follows, plus intermarriage and the interaction of choice and drift guarantee that identity loss and gain is never ending. This can only be denied by denying individual freedom.

Students of American Indian demography note both the flexibility and the ambiguity of identity. The very rapid growth of the American Indian population from 1960 to 1990 was triggered by dramatic increases in self-identification as Indians; three-fifths of the growth during the period 1970-80 can be attributed to that factor.[63] One explanation for this trend is that a general ethnic assertiveness, combined with Native American political mobilization "may have removed some of the stigma attached to a Native American racial identity," which would encourage persons of mixed ancestry to proclaim an identity they formerly concealed.[64]

These identity changes reflect the ambiguity of identity when intermarriage rates are high. Distinctions between Native and other Americans lose their clarity as cultural change and exogamy suggest that individuals may identify as American Indian in one setting, but not in another.[65] There is no reason to doubt the existence of a Canadian version of flexibility and ambiguity in Aboriginal identity.

This process of the transformation of identities, however, does not mean that we need to accept a social Darwinian free-for-all. We can and do decide politically to provide supports for cultures and identities that are threatened, yet still cherished.[66] We distribute governing power to provide leverage for a people to strengthen their abilities to adapt to incoming pressures in ways that preserve continuity with the past. We also support multiple identities by the cues we transmit to each other. Thus the Canadian Constitution and the policies that flow from it reinforce the multiple realities of being Canadian, Albertan, Aboriginal, male, female, young, old, employed, retired, gay, and lesbian.

The transmission of cues from public authorities and from our daily interactions with each other may, of course, ignore or even stigmatize some identities. This unquestionably happened in the past with status Indians who were told they could either be Indian or could be standard Canadian citizens if they met the criteria for enfranchisement, but they could not be both at the same time. Further, the special federal government administrative regime that governed their affairs inevitably estranged them from the provinces. They existed in a unitary regime in the midst of federalism. This historical legacy of differentiated treatment greatly complicates the task of simultaneously fitting Indian peoples into a federal system that reinforces Canadian, provincial, and territorial senses of identity and community and one that now must expand to reinforce Cree, Mohawk, and Indian identities. With slight modifications the previous sentences could apply to Inuit and Métis.

The choice we face is what mix of multiple identities do we wish to support in the future. The answer depends both on our starting point and on our assessment of the consequences of different choices. My argument, which is the connecting thread of these chapters, is that we can have it both ways – that multiple identities are both possible and desirable, and that they can and should include one of several possible Aboriginal identities and an identity as a Canadian. Further, if we do not succeed in recognizing and reinforcing both of these identities and making them compatible with each other we will have failed in the task of creating a workable constitutional order. If we do not affirm Aboriginality, there will be little Aboriginal support for membership and participation in the Canadian community. However, if Aboriginal and non-Aboriginal Canadians do not feel that they belong, in one of the ways of their being, to the Canadian community of citizens, we will have made us strangers to each other with minimal feelings of mutuality and solidarity. Not only is such an outcome a denial of our massive interdependence, but it is a repeat of past mistakes in which the de facto and de jure (for Indians) exclusion of Aboriginal peoples was an instrument for the anomie and social problems we now seek to resolve.

The great German sociologist Georg Simmel is a helpful guide to the complexities of our situation. The "practical significance of men for one another," he asserted, is determined both by similarities and differences among them. "Similarity ... is no less important than difference. In the most varied forms, both are the great principles of all external and internal development. In fact, the cultural history of mankind can be conceived as the history of the struggles and conciliatory attempts between the two." He went on to note that for the individual and for the group engaged in competitive struggles with other groups, there is an overpowering tendency to differentiate oneself or one's group from rival groups. Such difference, of course, is usually dressed in the language of moral superiority. For both individual and group, morally superior difference is the essence of their identity. Simmel argues that "the interest in differentiation in fact is so great that in practice it produces differences where there is no objective basis for them." He added, however, that "similarity ... provides the indispensable condition for any developing action whatever."[67]

Simmel translates rather easily into the constitutional language of federalism. The giving of breathing space to difference is why we have provinces, why Nunavut has emerged, and why some version of a third order of Aboriginal government is on our agenda. At the moment, for obvious historical reasons, the political and moral pressure is toward maximizing the exit of Aboriginal peoples via self-government from majorities they can only influence at the margins. The stress on difference recognition is also a kind of natural pendulum reaction to the previous stress on assimilation. On the other hand, we need to have commonality as well as difference. We need to be more than coexisting strangers. A federal system is more than provinces. A third order of government presupposes two other orders, one of which is the government for all Canadians. Aboriginal citizens in the third order will also live in the first and second orders. Their province or territory of residence and the country-wide community of citizens should be important components of their civic identity. For urban Aboriginals, who will not live in a third order of government, their membership and participation in the provincial and Canadian communities will be their primary citizen relationship to the political order. Their situation should not be overlooked simply because their self-government opportunities are limited. In the future, given present rates of educational achievement, many more people with Aboriginal backgrounds will live successful lives in urban centres.

Shared civic identities may be a project for the future. The same, however, could have been said of the Canadian identity in 1867. Conceptions of who we are are not immutable; they are not simply inheritances. Collectively, we are the subjects of our own creativity.

### Self-Government Is Only Half an Answer
Given the concept and practice of a modernizing Aboriginality, Simmel's analysis of the symbiotic complementarity of similarity and difference, the differential availability of self-government, and other

relevant considerations, what is the role of self-government in the future of Aboriginal peoples in Canada?

*Self-government is a response to the failure of past policies.* The explicit guided change applied to Indian peoples has clearly failed. The Métis, whose experience is more appropriately summed up as neglect, cannot be seen as a success story – as confirming that when the heavy hand of government is absent, the natural forces of social change will produce a steady improvement in their condition. A recent report on the Inuit paints a bleak portrait of their condition – in terms of education, employment skills, and survival of their culture.[68] In large part, therefore, self-government was seized on because the obvious rival was an indefensible status quo, relentlessly attacked by Aboriginal nationalists who believed that Aboriginal peoples could do a better job of governing themselves.

*Self-government is neither a gift, nor a delegation, but an inherent right.* Although important differences of interpretation remain, this is now recognized by RCAP, by the leading Aboriginal organizations, by the federal government, and by legal scholars. Policy discussion, accordingly, is no longer about whether it should be a goal, but about how it should be achieved.

*Self-government has the potential to give dignity to those who live it and practise it.* It is a powerful symbolic indication of equality. It contributes to self-reliance by supporting the thesis that responsibility begins at home. Presumably it will erode the powerful tendency of dependent peoples to blame others for their misfortunes and to expect others to be their salvation.

*The inherited context for its exercise, however, is not always favourable.* The social consequences of past policies (or non-policies) that often failed or were counterproductive – and whose failure provides a key rationale for self-government – do not provide auspicious circumstances for a thriving democracy. Many communities are poor, anomic, and characterized by social breakdown and malaise. According to RCAP, "in too many Aboriginal communities, or among subgroups within Aboriginal communities, violence has become so pervasive that there is a danger of it coming to be seen as normal."[69] In some cases, the "sense of [community] cohesion [has been eroded] to an extent that can be described as collective trauma."[70] Many women, in particular, are fearful that self-government will not reduce the high incidence of sexual and physical abuse that now prevails in many communities.[71] Many of the citizens of the self-governing nations of the future are burdened with "a depression of spirit resulting from 200 or more years of damage to their cultures, languages, identities and self-respect."[72] The inheritance of deplorable conditions that self-government is to solve will get in the way of their attempted resolution. In her discussion of sentencing circles, Carol La Prairie notes that their advocates often falsely assume "a consensus in values and the widespread acceptance of traditional norms" in Aboriginal communities, when the reality is, citing R.F. McDonnell, "complex sorts of mayhem that now pervade virtually all Native communities."[73] At a minimum, these conditions suggest caution in assuming such communities can balance the rights of victims and accused in a judicious way that contributes to community healing.[74]

Self-government will lay bare the internal complexity and heterogeneity of many status Indian communities. According to a recent report, Indian communities are riven with cleavages between status and non-status residents, and between those who are and those who are not members – a different distinction.[75] Further, the significance of kinship combined with the importance of the public sector as a source of employment and benefits – including housing – will strain against universalistic standards.[76]

Vaclav Havel returns again and again to the crippling effects of history on the peoples of the former Czechoslovakia. The corrupting effects of decades of communist rule have produced a civic immorality that is infertile soil for responsible citizenship.[77] Nelson Mandela confronted a similar problem – how to find the moral, spiritual, and civic resources among a brutalized black population to transform that same population. Basil Davidson, surveying the wreckage of his earlier hopes for the independent states of tropical Africa, lays much of the blame on the fact that the "colonial intrusion and its monstrous coercions ... wrecked ... [the] moral order" of African societies.[78]

*There will be failures as well as successes.* Social movements typically generate unrealistic expectations of the progress and improvements that will accompany their triumph. When these expectations are not realized, anger may be directed at the leaders who have failed to deliver the goods, even if such failure is largely attributable to a multitude of appalling community conditions.

*Self-government has limited application to non-land-based Aboriginals.* It has most meaning for land-based communities – and hence for the reserve-based residents of status Indian communities – and for the Inuit in Nunavut, and a handful of others (a special form of self-government for the Métis is optimistically canvassed in RCAP). This still leaves out well over half of the Aboriginal population. Some approximation of democratic involvement in such service areas as health, welfare, and education may emerge for Aboriginal peoples scattered throughout the non-Aboriginal society. Nevertheless, most of their relations with governments will continue to be with the traditional federal, provincial, and municipal governments. For the growing class of successful urban Aboriginals – many of them intermarried – their way of life and civic expectations may over time come to differ little from their non-Aboriginal neighbours.

By one estimate, by the year 2000, 30 percent of the population of Regina, Saskatoon, and Prince Albert will be Aboriginal. Since not all of them will have adapted successfully to urban life, the possible emergence of an Aboriginal underclass – indicators of which are now present – cannot be ignored.[79] Large urban cities of the future may become Canadian versions of American cities – with a successful black middle class and black ghettos duplicated in Canada by an Aboriginal middle class and Aboriginal ghettos. While local empowerment may have much to offer, it is unrealistic to believe such social breakdown can be alleviated without massive support from non-Aboriginal municipal, provincial, and federal governments.

*Self-government will be partial, not total.* Even where the maximum of self-government is possible, it will fall far short of total independence. The small size of all Aboriginal nations limits the jurisdiction they can wield. The citizens of self-governing nations will continue to be intimately linked to federal and provincial governments for services, funds, and so on. Part of the Aboriginal future then resides in their civic relations to the non-Aboriginal governments of the federation.

Because we cannot escape from each other, because independence is not an option, and because the possibilities for parallelism are limited, we must employ our interdependence as the vehicle for recognizing our similarities and appreciating that, following Simmel, they "provide the indispensable condition for any developing action whatever."[80]

*Self-government will not absolve the Euro-Canadian society of some residual responsibility for its performance.* Disaffected individuals protesting their maltreatment where self-government has fallen short of hopes will appeal to the federal government and to the consciences of non-Aboriginal Canadians for redress. Further, the international community will not consider Canada blameless where self-government does not produce socio-economic improvement.

*Exit is always a choice for the individual Aboriginal person.* Exit to the non-Aboriginal community is an available option for individuals dissatisfied with local conditions, political or otherwise. For the off-reserve Aboriginal, the shedding of an Aboriginal identity will be an available option for some. Self-government, therefore, will introduce some redistribution of the Aboriginal population. Where legal status is involved, as for the Indian people, self-government will modify the incentives to retain, or quietly drop legal status. The successful experiments in self-government will attract some returnees to the nation community. The unsuccessful will have the reverse effect. This is already under way in advance of significant powers of self-government. "Canadian cities are full of urban refugees from the neglect, domestic violence, and sexual abuse of community life in many Aboriginal settlements."[81] Several generations of off-reserve living, especially if accompanied by intermarriages, will weaken Aboriginal identity, and in some cases lead to its disappearance. This is unavoidable.

In spite of the qualifications just discussed, self-government will properly remain the most significant goal for Aboriginal peoples. Nothing else can equal the enhancement of dignity it offers when its responsibilities are well handled. In a globalizing world, where external influences are massive, it offers not only refuge, but it can be the site for a cultural adaptation that sustains an evolving Aboriginality. Simply by its existence, as an instrument of popular rule, it at least holds out the possibility of reinforcing a sense of community.

## Conclusion

The creation of a viable, equitable relationship between Aboriginal and non-Aboriginal Canadians will not emerge from the implementation of a single constitutional recipe. Assimilation is not available as an encompassing policy goal, although some individuals will continue to choose that option. A thoroughgoing parallelism – two-row wampum solution – is also unworkable. It would lack staying power as its sensitivity to Aboriginal difference is not matched by an equal concern for the cohesion of the Canadian community. We need to strike a balance.

The diversity within the category "Aboriginal" also strains against a single response that rides roughshod over difference. Métis, Inuit, and status Indians have different histories, live in different locales, do or do not have a land base, and have different urban-rural distributions. No single recipe can do justice to these diversities. Any comprehensive package must not only respect the varying circumstances of Aboriginal peoples – that is the sensitivity component – but also must nourish civic bonds that will sustain the degree of empathy and solidarity that will allow us to engage in common enterprises, and to feel responsible for each other. For now, the latter requirement means, at a minimum, trying to ensure that the wealthy, powerful, overwhelmingly dominant majority society – thirty or forty to one – takes for granted that Aboriginal peoples belong to the same community of citizens as the majority. We have seen the destructive effects visited on Aboriginal peoples in the past, when they were shoved to the margins of society and either culturally assaulted (Indians), treated with withering indifference (Métis), or benignly neglected until the mid-twentieth century (Inuit). Even an apparently positive and supportive recognition of Aboriginal difference will probably be counterproductive if, over time, it is not accompanied by or does not lead to a Canadian solidarity firmly based on a common, shared, equally valued citizenship. That is not where we are. It is where we should go.

It was to answer these and other concerns that the Royal Commission on Aboriginal Peoples was established. Its report is discussed in the following chapter.

# The Constitutional Vision of the Royal Commission on Aboriginal Peoples

The final *Report of the Royal Commission on Aboriginal Peoples*[1] was released on 21 November 1996, slightly more than five years after the Commission was announced. The Commission was co-chaired by the Honourable René Dussault, Justice of the Quebec Court of Appeal and former Quebec Deputy Minister of Justice (1977-80) and Georges Erasmus, former president of the Dene Nation (1976-83) and National Chief of the Assembly of First Nations (1985-91). As summarized by Commissioner Peter Meekison, the Commission met 100 times, had 178 days of hearings, recorded 76,000 pages of transcript, generated 356 research studies, published four special reports – on Justice; Land Claims and Extinguishment; Suicide; and Relocation of Inuit to the High Arctic – two commentaries on self-government, and a five-volume, 3,500 page *Report*.[2]

The *Report* provides the most thorough Aboriginal constitutional vision to have appeared since the defeat of the 1969 White Paper. Although we do not know the inner workings of the Commission, we may reasonably assume that the *Report* reflects an Aboriginal perspective, as four of the seven commissioners, including the co-chair, were Aboriginal. Further, the basic thrust of the *Report* clearly builds on the prior parallelism thinking of Aboriginal nationalists. Finally, the *Report* has a supplementary significance in that it had to grapple with the composite category "Aboriginal Peoples of Canada" introduced into the Constitution in 1982.

### A Many-Splendoured but Problematic Report

A report of this magnitude needs to be approached cautiously, and the many faces it presents to the reader need to be examined before one decides what kind of analysis to undertake. Six perspectives on the *Report,* which reveal its complexity and its richness, are suggested as a preliminary to this chapter's focus on the *Report*'s constitutional vision.

First, for years to come, the *Report* and the accompanying publications, along with the many (mostly, and regrettably, unpublished) research studies, will inform public debate, academic research, and Aboriginal claims. In this sense, the simple fact of the Commission's existence and its legacy will transform the political and intellectual context of future discussions on Aboriginal/non-Aboriginal relations in Canada. The massive presence of the Commission's output, most notably the *Report,* will not, of course, vanquish competing interpretations and policy prescriptions, but the latter will have to come to grips with the Commission's legacy.

Second, in an indirect way, the Commission is a Canadian version of a truth commission, confronting the majority society with the unhappy past of its treatment of Aboriginal peoples, with particular attention paid to residential schools, the relocation of Aboriginal communities, the inequitable treatment of Aboriginal veterans of both world wars, and the cultural aggression of the Indian Act. To read the relevant chapters is an emotionally wrenching experience as the dark side of Canadian history is methodically explored. The chapter "Relocation of Aboriginal Communities" concludes, appropriately, that "some past grievances are too great to ignore."[3] One of the relocations studied by the Commission – the move of the Sayisi Dene to Churchill and North Knife River[4] – received fuller attention in the book *Night Spirits.* It includes graphic testimonies by the relocated of the almost unimaginable horrors this hopelessly bungled operation brought in its wake. The story of suffering, social breakdown, and the insensitivity of the Indian Affairs Branch is a devastating account of the consequences of irresponsible paternalism.[5]

The past is a historical storehouse of maltreatment, duplicity, arrogance, coercion, and abuses of power by the majority society. Beyond the particulars, the majority non-Aboriginal society is castigated for its disrespect, insensitivity, and systematic disregard of Aboriginal interests and ambitions. The Indian Affairs Branch is singled out for a scathing denunciation of its mismanagement, complacent paternalism, and failure to fulfil its trusteeship responsibility for its "wards."[6] Reconciliation and rapprochement based on a "great cleansing of the wounds of the past"[7] can only come from public acceptance by government of responsibility for past misdeeds. This necessary act of contrition in a new Royal Proclamation will contribute to healing, and thus allow a new beginning.[8]

Third, the *Report* provides a historical analysis of the pre-contact setting of "Separate Worlds," followed by three contact stages – "Contact and Co-operation," "Displacement and Assimilation," and the contemporary period, "Negotiation and Renewal," which dates from the defeat of the 1969 White Paper. The stage three "Displacement and Assimilation" chapter documents the theory and practice of constitutional stigmatization – the relegation of Aboriginal peoples to the sidelines. In area after area the *Report* portrays a self-centred majority society inflicting both deliberate and inadvertent harm on Aboriginal peoples, encroaching on their way of life and disregarding their ambitions. Lands reserved for status Indians were whittled down, and rights they thought they had in sacred treaties were disregarded or trivialized.

Fourth, in addition to the general purposes of producing a more equitable version of history and shaking the majority society's belief in its own virtue, the resort to history has two specific purposes: to find out why an initial nation-to-nation relationship of equality became a colonial relationship of power and subordination; and to find in the past a model for a renewed relationship based on mutual recognition, mutual respect, sharing, and mutual responsibility.

Fifth, the *Report* is a forum for Aboriginal voices, for letting the people speak. Presumably as a response to and as compensation for the past silencing of Aboriginal peoples – for the period when they were spoken for by others – the *Report* cites extensively from the hearings. For the non-Aboriginal reader, this generates an immediacy, effectively communicates Aboriginal perspectives forged by history, and provides an often emotional human dimension to the analysis.

Sixth, the preceding are servants of the recommendations of the *Report,* which cover more than a hundred pages, and are designed to institute a "renewed relationship between Aboriginal and non-Aboriginal people in Canada."[9] Building on its generous mandate, the Commission's objective was massively to transform the position of Aboriginal peoples and nations in Canada. Virtually every institution of the majority society – education, medicine, the media, state symbols, the justice system, municipal governments, the organization of the federal bureaucracy, the constitutional order (especially federalism and parliament) – was to contribute to the new relationship (which was to be based on the four key principles of mutual recognition, mutual respect, sharing, and mutual responsibility) and to the new regimes for access to lands and resources, and much more. Indeed, the *Report* was encyclopedic in its coverage.

A new Royal Proclamation, acknowledging past injustices, recognizing the inherent right of Aboriginal nations to self-government, and establishing the principles of the new relationship and its institutional components would inaugurate the new era. A combination of legislation, treaty commissions, an Aboriginal Lands and Treaties Tribunal, an Aboriginal Nations Recognition Act, and an Aboriginal Peoples Review Commission to monitor progress, and other bodies would give momentum to a process that would take decades to complete.

The hoped-for result in the middle-range future was sixty to eighty self-governing Aboriginal nations with an enlarged land base, assured external funding, strengthened Aboriginal cultures, significant declines in the indicators of social breakdown, more employment, and higher incomes. Urban settings would be more sensitive to Aboriginal culture, and there would be Aboriginal control and administration of some basic urban services. An Aboriginal House of First Peoples representing Aboriginal nations – the legislative counterpart in the federal government of the new third order of Aboriginal government – would represent and protect Aboriginal interests. From an Aboriginal perspective, when the new regime had settled into place, Canada would have become a multinational federation.

Justification for this massive program came from five sources: (1) the tragedy of the status quo; (2) the ethical responsibility of the majority society and its governments to redress past injustices; (3) the thesis that in the long run the heavy transitional expenditures would pay for themselves as the anomic condition of many Aboriginal peoples was replaced by healthy communities; (4) the fact that this vision of the future and the proposals to implement it emerged from the most massive investigation ever undertaken in Canada of the situation of Aboriginal peoples and their interdependent relationship with the majority society; and (5) the logic that the inherent right of self-government would lack substance if it were unaccompanied by sufficient resources, including land, to make it meaningful.

It is difficult not to be overwhelmed by the *Report*. If the hundreds of recommendations are viewed as a multitude of particulars from which a selection is to be made, the sympathetic reader will nod positively again and again. A more difficult, demanding, and indeed elusive task is to step back and ask larger questions – of the philosophy that holds the *Report* together, of the rhetoric it employs to convince the reader, and of its vision of the nature of the Canada of the future if the *Report* were to be implemented. This is where the real debate has to take place, and for it to be successful many voices need to be heard, for it is only by viewing the *Report* from various angles that our understanding of its strengths and weaknesses can be refined. We need to remember three things in undertaking this task – that all royal commissions are massive mobilizations of facts and analysis in a particular direction; that a unanimous report, such as that of RCAP, is the product of compromises that the royal commission version of cabinet solidarity prevents the commissioners from divulging; and that the issues at stake – the hope for a better future for Aboriginal peoples and for a healing rapprochement between Aboriginal peoples and other Canadians – all push in the same direction; that is, to the need for discussion in the service of better future policy. The *Report*'s constitutional vision provides the normative framework that gives coherence to hundreds of recommendations. That constitutional vision is the focus of this chapter.

What constitutional vision of a future Canada does the *Report* hold out in which the wounds of the past have been healed, and Aboriginal and non-Aboriginal Canadians share a fruitful interdependent coexistence? Is the Commission's portrait of our future plausible, and if implemented would it be viable? These are big questions, any attempted answers to which are bound to be controversial. Even if so, they may at least contribute to the debate we so badly need.

Before proceeding to a detailed analysis of the *Report*'s constitutional vision, it is necessary to make two preliminary observations.

It would be reassuring to inform readers that their interpretation of the *Report* can be aided by reading a sophisticated federal government response to the *Report*'s constitutional vision. We are not so blessed. It took more than a year for the federal government to issue *Gathering Strength: Canada's Aboriginal Action Plan*,[10] which included a statement of reconciliation. Credit for the appearance of *Gathering Strength* is generally attributed to Jane Stewart, Minister of Indian Affairs and Northern Development, who prodded the federal government out of its embarrassing silence, and also worked closely with Phil Fontaine, National Chief of the Assembly of First Nations, to ensure a favourable reaction from the largest Aboriginal organization. The regrettable absence of the prime minister from the ceremonial release of the federal government response muted the symbolism appropriate to such an occasion.

In terms of engaging the debate that the most expensive royal commission in Canadian history merits, the federal response is evasive. The *Report*'s constitutional vision is ignored. Proposals for restructuring federal institutions are bypassed with the promise that the federal government is "open to further discussions."[11] The vast, ambitious, and expensive twenty-year program to generate a new partnership and rebuild Aboriginal communities is not mentioned. There is no response to hundreds of specific proposals. *Gathering Strength* is a welcome plea for a new partnership, supplemented by expressions of regret for past actions, recognition of the inappropriateness of assimilation policies, and "we are deeply sorry" for the sexual and physical abuse experienced in residential schools.[12] The latter was accompanied by a commitment of $350 million to facilitate healing.

The general direction of *Gathering Strength* is a litany of support for good causes rhetorically described. There is, however, neither agreement nor disagreement with RCAP's constitutional vision of the future relations of Aboriginal and non-Aboriginal peoples. The responsibility of government to educate the Canadian people about a basic fault line in Canadian society is not assumed. This federal government failure is reinforced by the fact that the *Report* has not been sent to committees of either the House of Commons or the Senate. That the commission did not receive funding to publish hundreds of peer-reviewed research studies further underlines the capacity of the federal government to thwart the debate and discussion it should have facilitated. The federal government's response to the Erasmus-Dussault commission is an embarrassment.

As is noted below, the overwhelming policy focus of the Commission is on self-rule, especially for land-based communities, based on the inherent right of self-government. The elaboration of the conditions necessary for attaining meaningful self-rule is undoubtedly the legacy for which the commission will be remembered. Recognition and implementation of an Aboriginal right of self-government have been the central objective of Aboriginal nationalism in the last quarter of a century. Its achievement is not only desirable because the colonial-type administration, especially of status Indians, has manifestly failed, but because the activity of self-governing can be ennobling and dignifying to those who practise it. It can provide some capacity, even in the context of globalization, to give its possessors some control over their fate. Hence, as Patrick Macklem convincingly argues in two impressive articles, there are strong intellectual and moral justifications for both formal and substantive equality that argue powerfully for self-government as an instrument to recognize the equality of peoples.[13] This strength of the *Report,* however, contrasts with the absence of a larger Canadian constitutional vision that goes beyond self-government to confront and answer the Canadian question of what will hold the system together – what will provide enduring bonds of empathy. The following pages focusing on those concerns are not intended to negate the *Report*'s advocacy of self-government, but simply to suggest that a third order of self-governing Aboriginal nations takes us only part of the way toward a viable constitutional vision for the country as a whole.

### The Constitutional Vision of RCAP

RCAP, whose massive terms of reference[14] reflected the gravity of the problems affecting Aboriginal peoples, needed an organizing framework to make its task manageable. Three working premises set boundaries to the Commission's task: a preference for the landed Aboriginal nation over the urban Aboriginal community, manifested in a relative neglect of the latter; the exclusion from the analysis of persons of Aboriginal ancestry who did not have an Aboriginal identity; and a policy choice for collective cultural renewal over economic opportunity where they appeared to conflict.

*Relative Neglect of the Urban Dimension*

In one of its voices, the Commission embraces modernity. Aboriginal communities have joined the "world culture" of the information revolution,[15] must be equipped to "reach out and participate in global society"[16] and "in a global economy."[17] Further, their living standards should be brought "up to the level enjoyed by other Canadians,"[18] and they should enjoy "the same quality of life as other Canadians."[19] Most emphatically of all, the Commission foresees a future where Aboriginal people are proportionally represented in all the prestigious professions, "doctors, ... biotechnologists ... computer specialists ... professors, archeologists and other careers."[20]

Modernity, however, is not to be approached from an urban setting, but from one that ensures that "Aboriginal cultures have support to preserve and transmit the core of language, beliefs, traditions and knowledge that is uniquely Aboriginal."[21] The appropriate setting, given the priority of cultural goals, is the non-urban nation-government with, on the average, a resident population of 5,000 to 7,000.

The Commission's organizing nation-to-nation theme, allied with "nation-government" on a land base as the locus of its hopes for the reinvigoration of Aboriginal culture, inevitably marginalized urban Aboriginals – 45 percent of the Aboriginal population[22] – as well as many of the additional 20 percent off-reserve rural Aboriginal population.[23] "Nation-government," the Commission's preferred self-governing instrumentality, is not available to the non-landed Aboriginal peoples, because the conditions for its exercise are absent. This excludes the 60 percent of the registered Indian population in southern Canada that is non-reserve based.[24] Those who fall outside the ambit of "nation-government" or who do not identify with an Aboriginal people are also marginalized by the *Report*'s recommendations for representation in central government institutions, which is to be by "nation [or] people."

The Commission links cultural survival directly to a land base. The "full exercise of Aboriginal nationhood" requires a "territorial anchor."[25] In the context of arguing the importance of a rural land base for the Métis nation, the *Report* suggests that a few rural communities with high Métis concentrations "may well hold the key to preserving and perpetuating Métis culture for the future."[26] They also note that the retention of Aboriginal languages is gravely hampered by the absence of a "territorial base."[27] The centrality of land to culture and identity is a lead-ing theme of Part 2 of the second volume, *Restructuring the Relation-ship.*[28] Land is the "heartland of [Aboriginal] culture."[29] Accordingly, sufficient land must be made available for cultural autonomy, as well as political autonomy and economic self-reliance.[30] Further, economic development should not be understood in narrow economic terms of "maximiz[ing] incomes," which would privilege the urban setting, but in terms of "maintaining and developing culture and identity" and other non-economic goals where the advantage lies with the rural landed community.[31] Given this analysis, it was inevitable that hopes for cul-tural survival would be directed to the self-governing landed communi-ties of the future, not to the cities with their threatening capacity to "undermine a positive cultural identity."[32]

The lesser importance to the Commission of "Aboriginal groups without any form of land base" was systematic, not accidental. It was indicated in its early 1993 publication, *Partners in Confederation: Aboriginal Peoples, Self-Government and the Constitution,* which stated that their situation "poses a range of complex problems that cannot be dealt with here."[33] It was evident in the contrast between the massive treaty research undertaken by the commission[34] – "The Commission undertook historical and legal research on the treaties on a scale unprecedented in our country's history"[35] – and limited research on urban issues.[36] Jeffrey Simpson, who devoted four columns to the report in the *Globe and Mail,* noted that the "recommendations for urban Aboriginals ... [were] distressingly thin."[37] According to David Newhouse, Native Studies professor at Trent University, it was difficult to "get urban aboriginals on the agenda" of commissioners who were "more interested in traditional native life and problems."[38] Their agree-ment, when it came, was reluctant and limited.[39] When co-chairs Erasmus and Dussault presented and explained the *Report*'s analysis and recommendations to the Standing Senate Committee on Aboriginal Peoples they focused almost entirely on Aboriginal nations, govern-ment-to-government relations, and the proposed third order of Aboriginal nation-governments.[40] Academic and journalistic assess-ments of the published *Report* contribute to the neglect of the urban dimension by concentrating overwhelmingly on the main thrust of the *Report* – self-government on a land base.[41]

The relative inattention paid to the urban Aboriginal population flows directly from the Commission's decision to focus not on the several positive indicators of the urban experience, but "on the survival and maintenance of Aboriginal cultural identities in urban society."[42] From this perspective, the urban setting has little to offer. Intermarriage rates are high, projected at 62 percent for off-reserve status Indians.[43] Knowledge of Aboriginal languages erodes, especially among the young;[44] the link to the Aboriginal nation of origin is attenuated, especially among youth and women who have become estranged from their nation, and often think of themselves in terms of their city;[45] or identification with a particular nation is replaced by a diffuse Aboriginal identity; the link between Aboriginal ancestry and Aboriginal self-identity is very weak in some major metropolitan centres;[46] further, the urban Aboriginal population is very heterogeneous.[47] In sum, the survival of cultural Aboriginality in the urban setting is problematic from the Commission's perspective compared to the more favourable situation of territorially bounded communities.

Not only do urban Aboriginal peoples lacking a land base not meet the conditions necessary for inclusion under the nation self-government rubric on which the Commission pins its hopes for the cultural reinvigoration of Aboriginal peoples, but the very relevance of nation declines in the urban setting.[48] The Commission departs from its nation focus with its recommendation that "services to Aboriginal people in urban areas generally be delivered without regard to legal or treaty status."[49] The urban population itself disappears from view in the crucial chapter on "The Principles of a Renewed Relationship,"[50] which focuses exclusively on the principles to govern relationships between societies. The fact that nearly half of the Aboriginal population is urban, most of whom do not fit comfortably into principles designed to govern the relationship between collectivities is overlooked. As noted below, the *Report*'s treatment of the Métis, nearly two-thirds of whom live in cities, is a partial exception to this paragraph's generalizations.[51]

Although the Commission's hopes for flourishing Aboriginal cultures are invested in the self-governing landed communities, it nevertheless recommends various arrangements to enhance the sensitivity of urban policies to Aboriginal peoples. The suggestions include guaranteed Aboriginal representation on various urban commissions, the establishment by municipal governments of Aboriginal Affairs committees, and what are called "community of interest arrangements." These would involve a voluntary association of urban Aboriginal peoples who would take responsibility for the provision of one or more functions, such as health, education, child welfare, etcetera. None of these service-providing community of interest arrangements qualify as nation-governments, and their powers would be delegated. They would not be part of a third order of Aboriginal government.[52] Urban Aboriginal residents are not the hope of the future. That status is reserved for their kinfolk on a land base.

*Ancestry versus Identity*

Identity "is in the blood, the heart and the mind, Aboriginal people told us; you carry it with you wherever you go."[53] Nevertheless, there is a dramatic discrepancy between those who report an Aboriginal ancestry and those who report an Aboriginal identity.

Overall, in an Aboriginal ancestry population of just under 1,100,000, the Aboriginal identity population is 720,000, and the non-identifying population is 375,000.[54] In five of eleven metropolitan census areas, less than half of the individuals with an Aboriginal ancestry declared an Aboriginal identity – ranging from 15.2 percent in Montreal and 17.7 percent in Halifax to 43.4 percent in Victoria. The highest percentages reporting Aboriginal identity were in the Prairie provinces, especially Saskatchewan – 86.3 percent in Regina and 83.8 percent in Saskatoon.[55] More than one-third with Métis origins lack a Métis identity. In five of eight provinces and in the Yukon, excluding Prince Edward Island and Newfoundland because of the non-existence or ambiguity of the data, less than one-half of the Métis origin population reported a Métis identity.[56]

These dramatic figures are reported but not analyzed. The Commission's lack of interest in the non-identifying population simply reflects its dominant concern with Aboriginal culture and identity. Those who no longer have or profess either, have, in a sense, emigrated from the constituency that concerns the Commission, those capable of maintaining a continuing Aboriginal cultural presence in Canada. Individuals whose Aboriginal ancestry does not translate into an Aboriginal identity have personally repudiated the Commission's nation-to-nation organizing theme. They are not candidates for self-government, not even for its limited expression in urban centres. They have, one might say, gone over to the "other side," a choice the commissioners could neither approve nor, apparently, examine. The issue is not the Commission's political neglect of this large ancestry without identity group, which is both understandable and defensible, but its analytical neglect.

This analytical neglect is shortsighted. We would know more about how identity is retained if we knew more about how it is lost. Who are the 375,000 individuals whose Aboriginal ancestry does not translate into an Aboriginal identity? Are they individuals who have "passed" for white? Are they, at the individual level, success stories? Are they examples of assimilation? If this *Report* had been written in the 1950s, or earlier, would they have been positively highlighted as proof of cultural convergence? The *Report* provides no answers. It downplays indications of what formerly would have been called assimilation. It stresses resistance to and the failure of federal assimilation policies.

No information is provided on this non-identifying group, beyond a casual footnote reporting "some evidence that [they have] socio-economic characteristics quite similar to those of Canadians as a whole, while those who do identify as Aboriginals have quite different socio-economic characteristics."[57] The failure to explore why and when Aboriginal ancestry does not generate an Aboriginal identity has the unfortunate effect that the *Report*'s reiteration of the almost universal desire of the Aboriginal identifying population to retain Aboriginal identity is misleading, as it has excluded from its database the more than one-third of the Aboriginal ancestry population who have apparently already made a different non-identifying decision. The absence in the *Report* of any data on or analysis of intermarriage compounds the reader's difficulty in understanding the factors influencing the process of identity choice and change. There is no discussion of intermarriage rates, or their cultural consequences in the chapter on "Urban Perspectives," nor in the "Women's Perspectives" chapter, even though much of the chapter deals with Bill C-31 returnees who lost Indian status by marrying out.[58] Discussion of the non-status or non-Aboriginal partners in marriage – not necessarily the same – is systematically avoided. The Commission is, of course, aware that many individuals have a mixed Aboriginal/non-Aboriginal ancestry, and then "choose" their identity.[59] Further, the *Report* notes the emergence in urban settings of a "bicultural identity," in which individuals are rooted in their Aboriginal background, and skilled in functioning in urban society.[60] The possible link between this composite identity and intermarriage is not discussed. Given the high rates of intermarriage,[61] the large numbers who have lost their Aboriginal identity, and the Commission's central theme of cultural survival, the absence of attention in the *Report* to intermarriage is puzzling, especially given the Commission's massive research program.[62]

I am not claiming that the *Report* should have had a policy concern for individuals who, in spite of some Aboriginal ancestry, have no Aboriginal identity, that, for example, it should have made policy recommendations to facilitate "passing." My point is simply the common sense one that if the *Report*'s basic concern was cultural survival and the conditions necessary to secure it, the deliberate exclusion from its analysis of why more than one-third of the ancestry population came to lack an Aboriginal identity is extraordinary. The analogy would be a report, backed by massive research, whose goal was to preserve the institution of marriage, but excluded divorce from its analysis.

*Cultural Survival versus Economic Opportunity*
Though this theme overlaps with the neglect of the urban dimension previously discussed, its centrality in structuring the *Report* justifies its separate treatment in this section.

Although the Commissioners did not and would not phrase it this way, one of their crucial decisions was whether to stress the economic and other benefits of urban existence for Aboriginal peoples, or whether to stress the contributions of self-governing land-based communities to cultural survival.[63] The Commissioners' data clearly indicate various positive features of the urban experience compared to the on-reserve experience.[64] The projected growth of jobs is much more favourable in urban locations.[65] Incomes are significantly higher, educational attainment is superior,[66] labour participation rates are higher and unemployment rates are lower,[67] the likelihood of holding a full-time job is higher,[68] the population of social assistance recipients is much lower.[69] Indian people in urban settings have the highest life expectancy among Aboriginal peoples.[70] Various indicators of social breakdown – family violence, suicide, sexual abuse, rape, alcohol and drug abuse – are markedly higher for the on-reserve Indian population over the non-reserve population.[71] On the other hand, cultural retention is weaker for the latter, participation in traditional activities diminishes,[72] language loss is greater,[73] intermarriage rates are much higher, and fewer persons with Aboriginal ancestry retain Aboriginal identity.

The commissioners, therefore, faced two realities as they drafted their *Report:* land-based communities, where the possibility of cultural survival was superior but economic opportunities were weaker; and urban settings, where the possibility of cultural survival was weaker but economic opportunities were better. The commissioners sought the best of both worlds – increased economic opportunities in landed communities by economic development, and by the allocation of more land and other resources, and also increased cultural survival possibilities in urban settings by instituting the limited forms of self-government and other culture-supporting institutions that the urban setting allows. However, they strongly leaned to the former, given the Commission's operating premise that its "major focus is the cultural identity of Aboriginal peoples."[74] The "Urban Perspectives" chapter accordingly did not focus on jobs, income, or prospective career opportunities for the emerging Aboriginal university graduates, but "on the survival and maintenance of Aboriginal cultural identities in urban society."[75]

The Commission's decision to opt for "nation" as the *Report*'s key organizing concept sprang from the priority it attached to the goal of cultural survival and the nation's right of self-determination to achieve it. The focus on nation, the necessary social base for Aboriginal governments, which were to be the key levers to reinforce Aboriginal culture and identity, necessarily made the urban setting a less attractive location, in spite of its economic and other attractions, for nations in general lacked an urban presence. Had the Commission stressed economic and other objectives for which the urban setting appeared superior, and as a necessary consequence allocated a lesser priority to cultural factors, it would have written a very different *Report* – one that might have seen migration to the cities more in terms of its economic and other advantages than of its cultural disadvantages. The numerous indicators of Aboriginal urban experience that were superior to the reserve situation were discounted in two ways: First, by repeatedly stressing that Aboriginal people in the city did less well than their non-Aboriginal urban counterparts in terms of income and other criteria,[76] and second, by emphasizing that urban Aboriginals did less well in the threatening city in terms of cultural and identity survival than did their landed kin.[77] The *Report* contrasted its optimistic vision of the future of "healthy, sustainable communities that create the conditions for a rounded life ... [with] forced emigration to the margins of an essentially alien urban environment. Even if such communities have to be subsidized in the long term to give their citizens access to standards of health and education equivalent to those of other Canadians, the costs, both social and financial, are likely to be significantly less than those occasioned by a rootless urban existence."[78] Nowhere does the *Report* employ the positive indicators of the urban experience that it cites as an argument in favour of migration to the city.

Given the priority the *Report* attaches to culture, the denigration of the urban experience flows directly from the brutal logic of the Commission's chosen priority value. This logic can be challenged either by postulating more flexible meanings to cultural survival in urban settings (see argument following the next two paragraphs), or by supplementing the hegemony the Commission accords to culture with other goals that lie behind the migration to the city. The latter would weaken the implicit stigmatization of Aboriginals opting for the city.

The Commission could have argued that for the future there are two versions of success stories – one land-based, culture-sustaining, self-governing communities, and the other, more individualistic success stories in urban settings where success is measured in terms of lifestyles and incomes closer to the urban norm. The Commission could have given its support to a different balance between economic and cultural goals in urban settings and in the land-based self-governing nation communities – with a different, but equally legitimate mix of goals applicable to the different contexts. This would have legitimated and dignified the experience of the successful urban Aboriginal person, even if the cost was a weakening of Aboriginal identity and some cultural erosion. To the Commission, however, the city was not seen positively as a site of economic and other opportunities, but negatively as a vehicle for a "constant barrage of non-Aboriginal values and experiences."[79] By concentrating on the landed nation, and denigrating the urban experience, the Commission risked placing itself on the wrong side of history. A balanced support for both routes to the future would have better reflected emerging realities.

The negative evaluation of the urban setting was inevitable given the restricted criteria the Commission adopted to judge the quality of the urban Aboriginal experience – the survival of Aboriginal culture and identity in urban settings.[80] This perspective precluded acceptance of a weaker Aboriginal cultural identity as an acceptable cost of economic and other advantages of the urban environment.[81] It ruled out even more emphatically any possibility even of discussing, let alone of viewing positively those who lost or gave up their Aboriginal identity in the city. Unfortunately, we do not know whether the new non-Aboriginal identity of the latter was positive, for the Commission was not interested in their situation, their experience, or their own judgment of the quality of the "choice" they had made. They are lost souls.

There is another possibility. The loss of identity, especially in the heterogeneous urban setting, may be because "evidence" of identity has been too narrowly defined in terms of yesterday's criteria. The retention of Aboriginal identity would be facilitated by generous, open-ended definitions appropriate to the realities of Toronto and Vancouver. From this perspective, the Commission could be faulted for linking cultural survival and identity persistence too tightly to a land base, and as a corollary, putting impediments in the way of alternative Aboriginal identities and cultural continuities appropriate to the urban setting. In other words, if the right materials for identity reconstructions are at hand, identity loss might be reduced by expanding the acceptable ways of expressing it.[82]

These three fundamental choices – first, the landed community over the urban setting; second, the exclusive focus on the Aboriginal-identifying population and the lack of interest in the very large constituency whose Aboriginal ancestry no longer translates into an Aboriginal identity (a serious analytical shortcoming that weakened the *Report*'s capacity to explain the sources of identity survival in the population that was its main concern); and third, the priority given to cultural resurgence – are all different versions of the prior master choice, the preserving and reinforcing of Aboriginality, variously expressed as culture or identity. These choices structured and gave coherence to the *Report,* but the price was high – from my perspective the disappearance of a more balanced *Report* that would not have forced the commissioners to choose between the self-governing landed communities and the urban experience, and to accord superior virtue to the former. The positive acceptance of alternative routes to the future would have been one more example of the appreciation of diversity that is a recurring RCAP theme.

## The Centrality of Nation

In a sense, the very structure of the Commission anticipated its focus on "nation" as its central organizing concept. Thus the co-chairs Erasmus and Dussault respectively represented, at least symbolically, the Aboriginal and the Canadian dimension. Commissioners Paul Chartrand,[83] Viola Robinson, and Mary Sillett were connected with the Métis, non-status, and Inuit communities respectively. The other two commissioners, the Honourable Bertha Wilson and Peter Meekison (who replaced Allan Blakeney) gave the Commission an overall distribution of four Aboriginal and three non-Aboriginal commissioners – four men and three women. The Commission had two research directors (both of whom were academics): an Aboriginal woman, Marlene Brant Castellano, and a non-Aboriginal male, David Hawkes. Wherever possible, research studies were assessed by an Aboriginal and a non-Aboriginal person.[84] The Commission practised the parallelism that it subsequently embodied in its *Report.*

The centrality of nation meant that the Commission was self-consciously pioneering a contemporary version of a multinational Canadian federalism, one in which the self-governing Aboriginal nation – "the core around which the Commission's recommendations are built"[85] – was to be the vanguard actor in the revitalization of Aboriginal cultures. Aboriginal peoples are to be part of a "multinational federalism" that practises a "multinational citizenship."[86] Canada's "true vision," accordingly, is a partnership of nations, held together by civic allegiance to the separate nations.[87] This vision has little room for a common Canadian citizenship grounded in individual allegiance, or for the idea of a common Canadian community that is more than the sum of its parts. Nations were the key actors in the past, and should equally be so in the future. The future key relationship, therefore, is nation-to-nation, based on some sixty to eighty nations on the Aboriginal side. Consequently, negotiation is the preferred route to the future, rather than judicial solutions, because it "mirrors the nation-to-nation relationship."[88]

The commissioners did not, accordingly, see their task as incorporating Aboriginal individuals into the Canadian community of citizens, but as incorporating self-governing Aboriginal nations through their governments into the Canadian system of governments. It is "through the nation – the traditional historical unit of self-governing power, recognized as such by imperial and later Canadian governments in the treaty-making process – and through nation-to-nation relationships, that Aboriginal people must recover and express their personal and collective autonomy."[89] The primary institutional vehicle for this proposed accommodation is to be a constitutionally entrenched third order of government, comprising Aboriginal governments representing Aboriginal nations, and given the task of fostering the cultural survival of their peoples.

The goal of creating constitutional space for an Aboriginal order of nation-governments raises several basic questions. Federalism, as conventionally understood, is a system of communities and citizens, as well as of governments. What theory of federalism does the *Report* express? In particular, how do Aboriginal nations and individuals relate to the federal and provincial communities and their governments? Although the Commission's rhetoric sometimes appears to suggest otherwise, a nation-to-nation relationship will not remove the citizens of Aboriginal nations from the reach of federal and provincial governments. High state policies of foreign relations and international trade will not be handled by Aboriginal governments. The federal budget will not be a matter of indifference and the capacity limitations of small populations will require frequent resort to provincial governments for health and education services that can benefit from economies of scale. Does the Commission believe in the divided civic identities normally associated with federalism to which it proposes to add an additional constitutional identity reinforced by a new third order of government? How does the *Report* propose to handle the increased complexity of intergovernmental relations that is a necessary consequence of a new third order of government comprising sixty to eighty nations? How does the *Report* handle the fact that its governing nation-to-nation paradigm leading to nation-governments is – on its own admission – inapplicable to about half of the Aboriginal population? Most important, what kind of overall Canadian political community does the Commission visualize? Will it be viable?

*The Nation-to-Nation Approach*

The nation-to-nation approach overwhelms the citizen-state relationship, and in some cases renders it almost invisible. The nation-to-nation relationship, structured by treaties, might help us to become neighbours,[90] facilitate coexistence – a repeated phrase[91] – or contribute to a partnership – another recurring phrase.[92] That relationship is, however, if not hostile, at least unfriendly to the idea of a community of citizens.

That the key relationship is to be between nations – and hence a political relationship between organized communities – necessarily privileges governments. Aboriginal governments with appropriately enhanced powers would symbolize the reinstatement of the past equalities of the early contact period, and would be the vehicles for the cultural revival of Aboriginal nations. The solution of enhancing governing powers is also driven by the *Report*'s employment of a colonialist analysis of the past treatment of Aboriginal peoples – escape from which in classic imperialist situations is by independence, reduced in the Canadian case to the maximum possible exit via self-government.[93] Self-government has been at the centre of Aboriginal élite ambitions for several decades and, in the modern era, it is the obvious vehicle for respect and recognition. The *Report* concludes that "in every sector of public life there is an urgent need to liberate Aboriginal initiative by making room for Aboriginal institutions."[94]

The next stage in the chain of reasoning is that self-government is the necessary vehicle to address the multitudinous socio-economic problems facing Aboriginal communities. Accordingly, the *Report* is an advocate of strong, activist government. The statist language is reminiscent of the Quebec "Quiet Revolution." The Aboriginal state is to be the vanguard, catalyst, shaper, and leader of the Aboriginal nation.

As cultural survival is integrally linked to a land base (see above), and nation-government is impossible without one, the Commission repeatedly underlines the land/self-government connection, and consequently the need for an allocation of more land and resources to Aboriginal nations.[95] They need "enough territory to foster economic self-reliance and cultural and political autonomy."[96] Achieving this goal "will be the work of a generation."[97]

The centrality of the nation concept privileges treaties as the instrument to regulate the relationship between Aboriginal and non-Aboriginal peoples. They should be available to all Aboriginal nations.[98] They have the virtue of being nation-to-nation, sacred and enduring, and are "practical arrangements for coexistence."[99] Treaty relationships with the Crown are in fact relationships with both the people and governments of Canada.[100] They are preferred by Aboriginal peoples as they reflect the basic principles of nation-to-nation equality.[101] Historically, they have been the vehicle for formalizing "relationships between Aboriginal and non-Aboriginal people [and] are the key to the future of these relationships as well."[102] Treaties will include "governance, lands and resources, and economic issues."[103] The jurisdiction of an Aboriginal government outside its core area will be regulated by treaty,[104] as will its entitlement to fiscal transfers.[105] In general, the treaty process will define the functioning of treaty nations as a third order of government.[106] Canada in this proposed treaty regime becomes the setting for a domestic version of a mini-international system. It is impossible to exaggerate the importance of the treaty process to the commissioners. The summary volume, *People to People, Nation to Nation,* states that "an agreed treaty process can be the mechanism for implementing virtually all the recommendations in our report – indeed, it may be the only legitimate way to do so."[107]

The nation-to-nation treaty relationship is a modern version of the compact theory, with the corollary that the parts are superior to the whole, and an autonomous role for the central government is logically problematic.[108] Treaties are "sacred compacts,"[109] and the commissioners compare them to the "terms of union whereby former British colonies entered Confederation as provinces."[110] "Treaty federalism," linking Aboriginal peoples and the Crown, therefore, "is [already] an integral part of the Canadian constitution."[111]

The Confederation analogy, however, is imperfect – the makers of Confederation brought the formerly separate colonies together in order to create a new people, a pan-Canadian community (or as Cartier phrased it, a Canadian political nationality based on fraternity), as well as to protect the territorial diversities, whose existence dictated the choice of federalism.[112] The pan-Canadian objective of the original Confederation settlement – the creation of a new people – has no counterpart in the Commission's support for treaty federalism.[113]

The nation-to-nation approach is to be both the negotiating vehicle

for the new relationship and its end product, Aboriginal nations constitutionally entrenched in a third order of government – the Aboriginal
component of a multinational federation, or at least a decisive step in
that direction.

*A Third Order of Aboriginal Government*
RCAP displays little interest in Parliament, the monarchy, the Charter,
and Canadian citizenship, in brief, the Canadian dimension. Some
attention is given to the courts, but they receive no separate treatment,
although paradoxically in its concluding volume the *Report* proposes –
in four sentences – Aboriginal representation on the Supreme Court that
is neither supported nor discussed elsewhere in the text.[114] The institution that attracts the Commission's attention is federalism.

RCAP, while noting that some Aboriginal peoples do not consider
themselves to be Canadian, is nevertheless adamant that Aboriginal
governments are to be "within Canada,"[115] constitutionally entrenched
in a third order of government. Federalism is seen positively as a facili-
tating and appropriate institutional arrangement for several reasons.
First, the government-to-government relations characteristic of federalism translate comfortably into the nation-to-nation relation that is at
the centre of the *Report*'s recommendations. Second, one of federalism's
virtues, its protection and nourishment of diversity, is viewed as especially appropriate for Aboriginal nations seeking to reinvigorate their
cultures. Third, Canadian federalism has a well-developed theory and
practice of revenue sharing. The s. 36(2) equalization clause of the 1982
Constitution Act is singled out as a key vehicle for providing financial
support for Aboriginal governments that, at least for the immediate
future, will lack adequate sources of domestic financing.[116]

Self-rule for the nation participants in the third order of government is justified by the indisputable failures of past colonial administration. It is supported by the moral dignity it can provide for those who
practise it. It provides support for cultural pluralism against homogenizing pressures. Because non-Aboriginal Canadians have their own versions of self-rule its denial to Aboriginal peoples cannot be justified
in an anti-colonial era. These practical and moral justifications for
self-rule, independent of legal justifications based on an inherent
right to self-government, are irrefutable. Nevertheless, the exercise of

self-rule has to be accommodated, as the Commission recognizes, to various realities.

The participants in the third order of government are Aboriginal nations. They include the historic Indian nations that have been fractured by their fragmentation into bands by the Indian Act, the main Métis nation in the Canadian West, smaller Métis nations elsewhere, and possibly the Inuit, unless their choice of public government disqualifies them. Indian bands, with their small populations, lack the capacity for the governing functions necessary for the revival of indigenous cultures. They will have to pool their resources to create politically viable nations.[117] The *Report* excludes Aboriginal peoples without a land base from the category of nations capable of exercising self-government – with the exception of the Métis, who are treated separately (see following paragraph). RCAP recommends the allocation of additional lands to prospective self-governing nations in order to enhance their economic prospects. The necessity of a land base is linked not only with economic opportunity, but with the traditional idea of sovereignty being exercised on a defined territory, and with the logical assumption that the preservation of culture is facilitated by the more frequent and intense interactions possible in a territorially bounded community.

The special circumstances of the Métis require and receive special treatment. They are an appropriate candidate for nation-to-nation treatment,[118] in spite of their heavy urban concentration (65 percent of Métis).[119] The Commission distinguishes between the "Métis Nation members who trace their roots to the western fur trade"[120] and other Métis. It notes that the special position of the Métis may generate "agreements that have little resemblance to treaties made by First Nations."[121]

Métis constitutional thought differs profoundly from that of First Nations. Proposed Métis governing structures are to mirror the federal system – in what is described as a layered approach – with Canada-wide Métis Nation government, and provincial Métis governments, possibly including provincial Métis legislative assemblies, delegating authority to Métis locals who would provide services to their peoples both off and on a land base. Off a land base, Métis citizenship will be voluntary.[122] Although most of the Métis Nation will not live on a land base, the *Report* argues the need for "a relatively small number of exclusive Métis land bases scattered throughout the homeland" – including an urban land component – to "nurture the culture that makes self-government worthwhile."[123] The Métis Nation proposals are complex, innovative, and experimental. The Commission presents them but, somewhat curiously for a royal commission, does not judge their workability. "It would be inappropriate," according to the *Report,* "for the Commission to suggest the form or forms that Métis self-government should take."[124] Why such self-denial is appropriate for a royal commission whose terms of reference include "the recognition and affirmation of Aboriginal self-government; its origins, content and a strategy for progressive implementation"[125] is not explained. It is also indefensible when the workability of such a complex proposal is the first question that springs to mind for any student of government. Apart from the special Métis situation, and the public government chosen by the Inuit, the third order of Aboriginal government will differ from the second provincial order in numerous ways.[126] The cumulative effect of the differences discussed below underlines the extent of the constitutional transformation that the Commission proposes.

The third order of government differs from the second in the sheer number of units it will contain. Its establishment will produce a major increase in the complexity of Canadian public life, with sixty to eighty nation-governments enmeshed in a network of intergovernmental agreements with their federal and provincial government neighbours. The existing executive federalism process, which brings federal and provincial governments together to manage their interdependence, cannot accommodate a six- to eight-fold increase in the number of actors. Unless some way of aggregating their positions is developed, the participation of Aboriginal governments in the overall management of the new three-order federalism will be limited. The complexity of intergovernmental relations will be further compounded because the third order of government, unlike the second order, will not comprise relatively similar governments with similar jurisdictions performing similar tasks.

Small populations averaging 5,000 to 7,000, the Commission's estimate of the average size of an Aboriginal nation living on Aboriginal lands,[127] with a lower limit of about 2,000,[128] will severely limit the capacity of Aboriginal governments.[129] Further, in many cases even these low figures will only be reached after a difficult process of consolidating Indian communities has been successfully completed. In the absence of this regrouping the typical self-governing Indian community will have a population of less than 1,000 – which does not meet the Commission's population criterion for "nation" viability. Prince Edward Island, with twenty times the population of the average Aboriginal nation proposed by the Commission and a developed infrastructure of government, has difficulty keeping up with the other provinces. While the bureaucracy of a nation-government will probably be large relative to its population, partly because of the significance of the public sector, much of its energy will be directed to managing relations with other governments – federal, provincial, and municipal – in the intergovernmental arena. The nation-government necessity of purchasing many of the services for its citizens from non-Aboriginal governments will clash with democratic responsiveness to its own citizenry. In general, the policy-making autonomy of Aboriginal nation-governments will be constrained by their capacity limits and the intergovernmental networks in which they will be caught. The *Report,* while it understands these limitations, is not intimidated by them, and goes on to recommend major responsibilities and large tasks for what in reality will be small governments. It argues that Aboriginal nations should have "the same range of law-making authority available to the provinces."[130] Co-chair Georges Erasmus informed the Standing Senate Committee on Aboriginal Peoples that there would be "small provincial-type governments all across the country."[131] "The core of Aboriginal jurisdiction includes all matters that are of vital concern to the life and welfare of a particular Aboriginal people, its culture and identity; that do not have a major impact on adjacent jurisdictions; and that otherwise are not the object of transcendent federal or provincial concern."[132]

A partial list of an Aboriginal nation's core jurisdiction on an exclusive territory would include the authority "to draw up a constitution, set up basic governmental institutions, establish courts, lay down citizenship criteria and procedures, run its own schools, maintain its own health and social services, deal with family matters, regulate many economic activities, foster and protect its language, culture and identity, regulate the use of its lands, waters and resources, levy taxes, deal with aspects of criminal law and procedure, and generally maintain peace and security within the territory," plus the regulation of some protected Aboriginal and treaty rights.[133] Although, as previously noted, the

*Report* suggests that some smaller bands and communities will have to pool their resources, the average nation-government population figures (5,000-7,000) sit uneasily with the potent language of jurisdictional powers – equal to that of a province – that the *Report* suggests should be available to such governments. The Commission responds to this reality by devoting considerable attention to the issue of governing capacities.[134] Overall, however, it presents an extraordinarily optimistic view of what very small populations can accomplish through government.[135]

This optimism is, however, qualified when the *Report* discusses the range of choices dictated by various necessities that the differently circumstanced nations will encounter. Unlike the provincial governments in the second order, whose jurisdictional powers vary little, and are now constrained by the principle of equality of the provinces, the jurisdictional powers of the Aboriginal governments in the third order will vary markedly. The *Report* repeatedly repudiates the idea that Aboriginal governments should possess a standard set of responsibilities. Variations in size, capacity, location, and ambition will generate different responses to the core package of jurisdictional responsibilities. Further, each nation-government can proceed at its own pace in assuming core powers. This jurisdictional asymmetry means that the relations of Aboriginal nation citizens with federal and provincial governments will vary from nation to nation depending on the relative significance of the latter governments for them. (The Commission displays a striking lack of keenness for direct individual connection with federal and provincial governments by the members of self-governing nations.)

Aboriginal nation-governments will not be miniature institutional replicas of their federal and provincial counterparts. They will not be constitutional monarchies. Some will be internally federal. They may not be electoral democracies, as they may choose their leaders in traditional ways. Both their goals and the legislative and executive means employed in their pursuit will be influenced by traditional values.

One of the instruments available to nation-governments to meet their responsibilities to preserve and nourish Aboriginal cultures, identities, lifestyles, etcetera, will be the definition and control of their own citizenship, criteria for which are proposed by the Commission.[136] Aboriginal nations, therefore, unlike provincial societies, are not open societies that can be entered and joined by non-Aboriginal Canadian citizens at will, although there will be some non-citizen residents who "should have some means of participating in the decision making of Aboriginal governments."[137] The closed citizenship nature of Aboriginal nations elevates the significance of boundaries between Aboriginal and non-Aboriginal peoples and thus will inhibit feelings of fraternity between citizens and non-citizens within the nation territory, as well as between nation citizens and Canadians outside the nation territory.[138] The treatment of non-citizens by Native governments will inevitably be a concern of Canadians elsewhere.[139]

The constitutional status of each nation-government, including its jurisdictional responsibilities outside of core areas, will not flow from a uniform grant of jurisdiction to all nation-governments in the third order, but from separately newly negotiated and updated treaties, which will vary from nation to nation.[140] Since their own treaty will have high symbolic value for Aboriginal citizens, its separate individual application to each nation will reinforce the latter's particularistic identity. This will set the nation apart not only from the surrounding Canadian community of citizens, but from other Aboriginal nations.

Nation-governments will depend heavily on external funding for a lengthy transitional period. Even if external funding is unconditional, a small polity largely sustained by external fiscal resources is unhealthy. Although nation-governments will have the authority to levy taxes, in many cases this will produce little revenue in the mid-range future. The limited relationship between revenues from self-taxation and government expenditures discourages responsible citizenship.

In summary, the third order of government, the nations that comprise it, and the citizenry that belongs to them will not repeat the normal constitutional categories of province and citizen in the second order. While the Charter will apply,[141] the cumulative effect of the special characteristics of the third Aboriginal order of government if implemented as proposed will be to institutionalize a profound degree of civic distance between Aboriginal and non-Aboriginal Canadians. The *Report*'s overwhelming focus on self-rule, the limited attention paid to shared rule (see below), and the ambitious jurisdictions to be made available to Aboriginal governments confirm that the Commission goal was to maximize exit from subordinate status and from arenas for common action with the majority, and to seek a form of coexistence in which Aboriginal nations enjoyed the largest degree of constitutional autonomy that was possible.

The third order of government is the Commission's elaborate response to the autonomy side of the position of Aboriginal nations in Canadian federalism. Nations are generously defined by the Commission. They are intended to be encompassing, inclusive communities that will bridge for Indians the status/non-status divide created by federal policy. Also, in selected policy areas the Commission sees possibilities of extending the landed nation's jurisdiction to off-reserve urban members of the nation, although this raises major questions of feasibility. This generous definition of the Aboriginal nation and its citizenship is one of the most positive features of the *Report*. It is intended not only to enhance policy capacity by increasing population size, but also to reach out to the broader conceptions of nation and community that were fragmented by the Indian Act's fostering of more than 600 band governments with small populations.

*Law, Not Politics*

The Commission's reiterated goal is a return to the principles of the nation-to-nation contact of the early period when treaties regulated relations between Aboriginal nations and the newcomers.[142] That rough equality of treatment was sustained by economic interdependence from which both sides benefited, military alliances at a time when Aboriginal nations were an important factor in the balance of power, and population ratios that precluded the coercive policies that lay in the future when numbers changed.[143]

The special conditions of that early period are gone. The population ratios of the eighteenth century, which sustained a working equality and reciprocity based on mutual interdependence, no longer exist. Economic interdependence diminished with the decline of the fur trade at a time when the role of Aboriginal people "as friends and military allies" was in retreat.[144] Instead of mutual dependence based on a rough equality of power, Aboriginal peoples now have only a "very limited" capacity "to affect Canada's interests," contrasted with the massive power of Canada to do the reverse.[145] Coexistence in a mini-international system in the eighteenth century in which cross-cultural exchanges and communications were focused and limited has evolved into a relationship in which the formerly separate societies are knit together in innumerable ways, and there is a massive flow of influence from the larger to the smaller Aboriginal societies. Finally, the contemporary nation-to-nation relationship is not international but is to be "within Canada." The goal is for the Aboriginal nation to be a functioning partner in a contemporary state that is parliamentary, federal, monarchical, and endowed with a Charter of Rights and Freedoms. This makes nation-to-nation a somewhat misleading description, for the Canadian nation encompasses the Aboriginal nation with which it is negotiating. The latter is part of the former.

If a future nation-to-nation relationship will not emerge from the contemporary distribution of power, from mutual economic interdependence, or from military necessity, the crucial question then is "What is to sustain it in contemporary conditions drastically different from those of the early contact period?" The Commission's answer emerges in the contrast between its antipathy toward majoritarian democratic politics and its consistent espousal of a regime of rights coupled with monitoring and enforcement mechanisms distanced from government and from the ebb and flow of public opinion. What is missing in the *Report,* or perhaps more accurately, rejected, is an analysis followed by proposals for the participation of Aboriginal individuals and nations in the competitive politics of Canadian society – the world of voters, political parties, elections, and in general of participatory citizenship in federal and provincial political arenas. The same omission surfaces in the Commission's discussion of Aboriginal peoples in urban settings. Although the need to make urban policy more sensitive to Aboriginality is recognized – for which various proposals are offered – political participation by voting or running for office is not mentioned.

A major Commission premise is that Aboriginal peoples, at least those in nation-governments, can and should be insulated from the ups and downs of democratic politics; their protection and guarantees for future treatment are to be sustained by a regime of rights and a battery of supportive institutions. The preference for law over politics feeds on Aboriginal, especially First Nation, distrust of Canadian governments and the majority society.[146] This leads to distrust of majoritarian politics, to a weak sense of common citizenship, and to an unwillingness to accord credibility to a possible civic empathy reaching across the divides of a fractured society. The *Report* speaks of the "inherent ineffectiveness of the democratic political relationship as seen by Aboriginal peoples. There has been a profound absence of representation for Aboriginal peoples in Canadian democratic institutions. But more important, such representation, when cast in terms of conventional democracy, is itself regarded as illegitimate. Aboriginal peoples seek nation-to-nation political relations, and these cannot be achieved simply by representation in Canadian political institutions."[147] For some, distrust feeds on a lack of identification with Canada. "In many cases," Aboriginal nations deny that Canada's sovereignty extends to them.[148] Aboriginal peoples have been ruled for 400 years by "foreign powers," French, British, and Canadian, devoid of legitimate authority over them.[149]

The Commission's solution to the recovery in contemporary conditions of the historic equalities of the early contact period is, therefore, to gain recognition for a regime of rights and institutions that will keep the everyday politics of democracy at bay. The starting point for this recognition is the thesis that Aboriginal peoples possess an inherent right of self-government. They "are the bearers of ancient and enduring powers of government that they carried with them into Confederation and retain today."[150] In light of this history, the Commission proposes a new Royal Proclamation that will, among other things, acknowledge past injustice and declare a new beginning based on the foundational principles that Aboriginal peoples are "nations with an inherent right of self-government."[151] The Proclamation will also elaborate rationales for and descriptions of a future regime of treaties, rights, a constitutionally entrenched third order of government, and a battery of tribunals, treaty commissioners, and monitoring agencies to bring the new regime into existence and to sustain its future operation. Ensuring that the new regime is "honoured, [must be treated as] a continuing responsibility, one that cannot be left to governments alone, pulled as they are by the tides of events and fleeting priorities. The establishment of institutions to formalize and implement a renewed relationship will [produce] stability."[152]

Thus new agreements bargained nation-to-nation and reflecting a parity of representation would reflect "the fundamental rights – and not necessarily the economic and demographic power – of each party."[153] Elsewhere, the Commission contrasts the uncertainties and lack of "staying power" of ad hoc and crisis responses with the stability of "regimes created by new treaties."[154] "If treaty making and land allocation are to become effective means of defining the new relationship, applicable policies and procedures must be subject to the discipline of legislation and to the effective operation of the treaty commissions and the Aboriginal lands and treaties tribunal, which, while appointed by governments, will operate at arm's length from them."[155] The proposed Aboriginal Lands and Treaties Tribunal would have authority to issue binding orders on provincial governments if negotiations fail.[156] The Commissioners also propose an Aboriginal Peoples Review Commission, modelled on the Office of the Commissioner of Official Languages, to monitor the progress and well-being of Aboriginal people and to report annually to Parliament.[157]

The Commission's preference for an enforceable legal regime over resort to the competitive political process to advance and protect Aboriginal interests is an attempt to duplicate in the modern era relationships that were functional several hundred years ago, and that developed in response to realities of power, numbers, mutual economic interdependence, and military necessity that no longer prevail. In other words, the treaties of the past were not self-enforcing. They did not create nation-to-nation equality. They reflected it. Treaties were ratifications of existing power distributions. Further, intercultural contact in that earlier era was relatively limited compared to the massive transformation of Aboriginal society that subsequently occurred.

The past supports for nation-to-nation relationships have vanished. The conventional contemporary democratic process is distrusted. The fundamental bond of citizenship receives only passing attention. The non-landed population, half the total population, is largely excluded by the nation-to-nation paradigm that is at the heart of the Commission's analysis. The long-run viability of the proposed regime, should it be implemented, and its capacity to enforce the necessary flow of financial and other support for decades is dubious. The credibility of the apolitical infrastructure that is to support the Commission's constitutional vision is problematic. The *Report* lacks a workable political theory to support the institutional scaffolding that it proposes to both insulate Aboriginal nations from the vicissitudes of democratic politics, and simultaneously to guarantee them long-run, positive differential treatment by the majority society.

This weakness, based on the Commission's preference for law over politics, is further revealed by the *Report*'s cursory discussion of "Representation in the Institutions of Canadian Federalism."

*Representation at the Centre*

Although the Commission's terms of reference included "the representation of Aboriginal people in Canadian political institutions,"[158] they paid negligible attention to the subject. This minimal coverage complicates the task of the reader. Elsewhere in the *Report,* the reader is overwhelmed by the lengthy, detailed coverage of, say, treaties. Here, the reader has to speculate where the too cryptic text offers only limited guidance. As a result, my attempt to interpret this section of the *Report* is less grounded than I would like. What was not said, but simply left out, rivals the importance of what was said as the raw material for interpreting the Commission's position on "Representation in the Institutions of Canadian Federalism." Discussion with senior Commission staff has been helpful, although not without contradiction.

There is no discussion of a role by Aboriginal nations or individuals in terms of voting, standing as candidates, or serving as elected representatives in provincial politics. The provincial exclusion is unfortunate and surprising, as Commission research by Professor Kathy Brock on Aboriginal/government relations in Manitoba clearly indicated that the Aboriginal presence in the legislature of six of fifty-seven MLAs (at the time of writing) helped to keep the government responsible.[159] In recent years, one-fifth of NDP caucus members in Manitoba have been Aboriginal.[160] Elijah Harper's role in blocking the Meech Lake Accord suggests that in some circumstances a single individual, reflecting strongly held Aboriginal opinions, can have a decisive effect. The Aboriginal presence can only increase in legislatures across the country, given projections of Aboriginal population growth. As noted below in the concluding chapter, the Federation of Saskatchewan Indian Nations, probably the most impressive provincial Aboriginal political organization in the country, advocates vigorous Aboriginal participation in provincial politics. Nunavut's legislature is overwhelmingly Inuit. The Legislative Assembly of the Northwest Territories has had an Aboriginal majority since it became fully elected in 1975. In 1996, two-thirds of its members were Aboriginal.[161]

There is an additional surprising omission. Although the terms of reference included "the role of native women in political institutions ... in non-native society,"[162] the subject was ignored. The limited attention to representation was confined to a short section "Representation in the Institutions of Canadian Federalism,"[163] where the commissioners observe that federalism involves shared rule, as well as self-rule.[164] However, they go on to assert that their attention has focused on a third order of Aboriginal government, the site of self-rule, as "the area of governance in which the Commission can make the greatest contribution."[165] Off the record discussions with knowledgeable insiders indicate that this short section was hastily and belatedly drafted as the recognition sank in that something had to be said on the subject of shared rule at the centre. The low priority attached to Aboriginal participation in central government institutions is confirmed in the Commission's 149-page summary report, which devotes only two sentences to the subject.[166] This lack of attention, one might even say of interest, is extraordinary given that other students of treaty federalism, a variant of which RCAP proposes, assert that adequate representation in the central government is "by far the most critical objective,"[167] essential as a counterweight to self-government that "can reinforce ... political segregation."[168]

The *Report* underlines the historic reality that the "lack of participation by Aboriginal people in Canadian institutions has been a growing problem in Canadian federalism and undermines the legitimacy of our system of government."[169] Accordingly, it asserts the necessity for more effective Aboriginal representation and fuller participation "in the institutions of Canadian federalism ... to build the moral and political legitimacy of such institutions in the eyes of Aboriginal people."[170] That fuller participation, however, has to respect the primacy of the nation-to-nation relationship.

The *Report* discusses and rejects two proposals for guaranteed Aboriginal representation, one for the House of Commons – proposed by the Royal Commission on Electoral Reform – and one for the Senate – proposed in the Charlottetown Accord. Both proposals are seen as a threat to the integrity of the Aboriginal nation. Their rejection cogently expresses the *Report*'s philosophy: "We are concerned that efforts to reform the Senate and the House of Commons may not be compatible with the foundations for a renewed relationship built upon the inherent right of Aboriginal self-government and nation-to-nation government relations. Three orders of government imply the existence of representative institutions that provide for some degree of majority control, not minority or supplementary status."[171]

The commissioners' strategy is to subject shared rule in the representative institutions of the federal government to the requirements of the nation-to-nation relationship. Accordingly, they recommend a House of First Peoples representing Aboriginal peoples/nations as their long-run goal, which could only be instituted by a constitutional amendment. The House would be able to initiate legislation, "and to require a majority vote [by the House of First Peoples?] in matters crucial to the lives of Aboriginal peoples."[172]

In the interim, the *Report* advocates an Aboriginal parliament to advise the House of Commons and Senate "on legislation and constitutional matters relating to Aboriginal peoples."[173] The Aboriginal parliament would also have review and oversight responsibilities with respect to reports from treaty commissioners and other matters, plus a fact-finding and investigation capacity, including sitting on relevant joint Senate and House Committees. More generally, the Aboriginal parliament could "review all legislation" from an Aboriginal perspective.[174] Its overall role is best described as a watchdog, rather than as a participant in shared Canadian enterprises.

Representation in the new Aboriginal parliament should be from each Aboriginal nation, or people, with a total representation of between 75 to 100 members. This manner of representation is especially desirable, because it would reinforce "what we consider to be a fundamental value of the new relationship between Aboriginal and non-Aboriginal people – that it is a nation-to-nation relationship within Canada,"[175] a relationship "at the centre of our proposal."[176]

The minimal attention paid to representation in central government institutions, its nature, and its omissions suggest the following. First, the overwhelming priority of self-rule over shared rule defined the Commission's task as maximizing Aboriginal autonomy and separateness by means of a third order of self-governing Aboriginal nations. Participation in central government institutions, the site of shared rule, was of lesser importance. The stress on self-rule also limited the attention paid to Canadian citizenship. Equally plausibly, the limited attention paid to and interest in Canadian citizenship discouraged concern for shared rule.[177] The Commission failed to confront the challenge identified by Schouls, "to provide a counterweight to the divisionist proclivities of Aboriginal self-government initiatives."[178]

Second, the form of participation recommended was designed to strengthen the view that Aboriginal persons should be linked to Canada through their membership in distinct nations or peoples. Aboriginal citizens of separate Aboriginal nations or peoples are to vote for Aboriginal members of an Aboriginal parliament to protect Aboriginal interests. This inward-looking orientation is also evident in the *Report*'s recommendation for a consultation process to establish the new Aboriginal parliament. Although the process would involve the federal government and representatives of national Aboriginal peoples' organizations, the *Report* makes the remarkable proposal that "major decisions respecting the design, structure and functions of the Aboriginal parliament would rest with the Aboriginal peoples' representatives."[179] No justification is offered for this proposed unilateralism, nor is there any explanation of why the federal government would agree to the denial of a significant role for itself in a major reshaping of federal institutions.

Third, the election and subsequent roles of representatives of Aboriginal nations and peoples in an Aboriginal parliament are not vehicles for participating as fellow citizens in Canada-wide concerns, but focus on the representation and protection of Aboriginal interests.

Fourth, the dominant parallelism theme – third order of government, Aboriginal parliament – perhaps explains the absence of discussion of how the Aboriginal population not connected to a self-governing Aboriginal nation or to a people is to be represented. Presumably, they will continue as ordinary voters in their constituencies, but this "Representation" section ignores their existence. Whether Aboriginal voters for the new Aboriginal parliament, and subsequently for the House of First Peoples, would also vote for ordinary members of the House of Commons – in other words, whether the territory of a self-governing Aboriginal nation would be a part of a regular federal constituency – is unclear in the text. According to senior Commission staff members, ongoing Aboriginal voting in federal constituencies was assumed. That it was not discussed reveals the haste and confusion that attended the writing of this section. The only indication that it was intended is a phrase elsewhere in the *Report* that the Aboriginal parliament "supplements representation in the House of Commons," with no further explanation offered.[180]

To overlook, or implicitly dismiss the role of Aboriginal voters in selectively influencing federal policy via their MPs weakens the *Report*'s analysis. The pathbreaking 1983 *Penner Report* (House of Commons Special Committee on Indian Self-Government) was produced by a handful of MPs from ridings with significant Indian populations. According to Tennant, the *Penner Report*'s strong self-government recommendation reflected the knowledge and sensitivity derived from the citizen-MP relationship. He doubted that MPs not so situated could have produced such a report.[181] The *Penner Report*'s proposals, and even the striking of such a committee, would have been completely unthinkable prior to the extension of the franchise to Indians in 1960. More generally, it is surely more than a coincidence that more positive attention was paid to the Indian peoples after they gained the franchise than before. The franchise gave them voice, however limited, and increased the obligation of the majority society, especially its politicians, to listen. Indian associations could not have employed the label "citizens plus" to fight the 1969 federal government White Paper had Indians lacked the franchise and thus the positive civic identities that accompanied its possession. The Commission's analysis is weakened by its neglect of the benefits of standard membership in the community of the individually enfranchised. Its symbolic and hence practical importance is underlined by observing that the reaction to the removal of the franchise would produce an outraged counterattack far greater than the mobilization against the White Paper.

Fifth, "citizenship" is more likely to be employed as a claim for services than as a vehicle for participation with other Canadians in the citizen politics of federal and provincial democracy. As noted above, neither in this section, nor elsewhere, does the *Report* discuss the representation of Aboriginal individuals or nations in provincial politics. However, although no mention is made of a positive civic participatory role for Aboriginal individuals who are not in a land-based nation-government, they are to be considered full provincial citizens as recipients of provincial services.[182] Citizenship also emerges as a positive concept in the chapter on "Urban Perspectives," where the goal of equitable treatment for Aboriginal peoples is supported by the obligation of federal and provincial governments to respect "the equal citizenship rights of all Canadians."[183] Citizenship emerges as a claim for fair treatment as a recipient of services, albeit unaccompanied by any mention of a democratic civic participation role, where nation-government is not possible. Even this limited, seemingly strategic mention of citizenship virtually disappears when nation-government, the Commission's vastly preferred option, is possible.

For example, the *Report* notes that where provincial services are provided to citizens of Aboriginal nations, payment should be made by the Aboriginal nation-government directly to the provincial government.[184] There is to be no direct taxpayer link between the Aboriginal nation citizen and the provincial government.[185] Whether there is to be a voting link is ignored. This deliberate fiscal isolation (and possibly voting isolation) would limit the development of a competing civic attachment of Aboriginal nation citizens to the provincial community and the provincial government. A direct taxpayer link via personal and corporate income tax with the federal government would also be lacking, as the Commission proposes that all such taxes should be paid to the Aboriginal government.[186] There is an undercurrent in the *Report* of indifference or antipathy to individual citizen links with federal, provincial, and municipal governments by such traditional means as paying taxes, voting, or standing as a candidate for elected public office. For example, in the short section "Reform of Urban Governments and Public Authorities," the *Report* advocates guaranteed Aboriginal representation on appointed local agencies, boards, and commissions, and the establishment of Aboriginal affairs committees at the municipal level with appointed Aboriginal members.[187] Here, as elsewhere, the *Report* seeks to bypass the normal democratic politics of voting, etcetera.

The commissioners' philosophy appears to be summed up in a position held by "many treaty nations people," that they positively report, that the relationship with the provinces is "government-to-government ... [and] nation-to-nation" with the Crown in right of Canada.[188] Perhaps this explains the absence in the *Report* of any interest in the citizen role of individuals in the Canadian and provincial worlds of politics – of voters, candidates, political parties, and elections. Canada is seen as a community of governments, or nations, or peoples, and only secondarily of citizens. The Commission appears to see the citizen politics of democracy as a threat, not as an ally.

## Conclusion

Concern for the "other," for the larger Canadian constitutional order, is limited. The *Report* gives minimal attention to or analysis of the non-Aboriginal partner. The ubiquitous use of the rubric "non-Aboriginal" contributes to a binary view of Canada as two societies and conceals the heterogeneity of the Canadian majority population.[189] The contemporary majority society, to which the appeal for major change is directed, is not examined.[190] This contrasts with Gunnar Myrdal's approach in *An American Dilemma*,[191] which took as its starting point the impossibility of understanding the position of blacks in American society without an exhaustive analysis of the power-holding dominant white majority. Although the *Report's* vision is of a future multinational Canadian federalism, there is no analysis of the other national partners, or even who they are, or of how such a system would work. Is Canada a national partner? Is English Canada? If so, who speaks for it? The move from a provincial federalism to a multinational federalism is not an easy transition as the paralyzing debate over Quebec's distinct society confirms.[192]

That same lack of concern lies behind the only cursory attention paid to Aboriginal participation in the institutions of the federal government – the site of "shared rule." The attention that is paid focuses almost without exception on representation, protection, and enhancement of Aboriginal interests. The idea of voting and legislative participation as Canadians for the advancement of common Canadian interests is neglected, although it is possibly assumed. A related neglect of the Canadian dimension is evident in the negligible attention paid to the management of the increased intergovernmental complexity that will be a direct consequence of inserting a constitutionally entrenched third order of government into the existing system.

The *Report* does not appreciate that the legitimacy of the s. 36 equalization payments that are to be provided to Aboriginal governments in response to the principle of sharing (one of its four principles for a renewed relationship) derives directly from the common base of Canadian citizenship of the provincial residents of the receiving have-not provinces. Although the payments are made to governments, the federalist theory and morality that sustains them is the thesis that Canadian citizens in the poorer provinces should not be penalized by receiving inferior provincial services simply because of provincial poverty.

British Columbians contribute through federal taxation to the equalization grants payable to Newfoundland because Newfoundlanders share a common Canadian citizenship. The *Report,* by contrast, justifies equalization for Aboriginal governments on the much weaker rationale that the "Canadian economy is a shared enterprise."[193] For the Aboriginal governments that require extensive flows of funds from the majority society, it is a high-risk strategy for the *Report* to assume that the dilution of the Canadian citizenship component of Aboriginal civic identity will have no effect on service provision and financial transfers that presuppose a common citizenship. A nation-to-nation relationship only minimally sustained by a common citizenship will not have the same positive fraternity effect.

The stress on the nation-to-nation treaty relationship underlines the primacy of nation membership and leaves little room for a Canadian citizenship that encompasses both Aboriginal and non-Aboriginal individuals.[194] Aboriginal people "form distinct political communities, collectives with a continuing political relationship with the Canadian state. That is the central reality that Canadians must recognize if we are to reconstruct the relationship."[195] The occasional references to Canadian citizenship are, accordingly, mostly perfunctory or strategic, rather than enthusiastic.[196] The Commission has difficulty with the divided civic identities that are natural to a standard federal system. The *Report* does not appear to view Aboriginal peoples living under nation-governments as having an independent status as individual provincial or federal citizens. That status, if it exists, is not easily detected in the *Report.* Its philosophical underpinnings are close to the Charles Taylor "deep diversity" thesis, in which membership in and identification with the overall Canadian community is mediated through the Québécois or Aboriginal nation.[197]

Given the constitutional logic of the *Report* as a whole, this appears to be the proper interpretation of the recommendation that Aboriginal people be recognized as having "a unique form of dual citizenship ... as citizens of an Aboriginal nation and citizens of Canada," and that Canadian passports recognize this duality and identify the relevant Aboriginal nation.[198]

The RCAP *Report* has a clear and consistent constitutional message. Its primary focus is on sixty to eighty Aboriginal nations, with separate

treaty relations with Canada, whose governments are to be constitutionally entrenched in a third order of Aboriginal government. These governments are to occupy the maximum constitutional space possible
within what are called core and peripheral areas of jurisdiction. The
Aboriginal nation is to be the primary membership community for its
citizens. It is a closed community in that the criteria for and admission
to membership are controlled by the Aboriginal government. The
Aboriginal nation or people is the appropriate unit for representation in
an Aboriginal parliament, and, after constitutional amendment, in a
House of First Peoples, with the primary goal of representing Aboriginal
interests. Whether nation-based Aboriginal individuals or those identifying with an Aboriginal people would vote as individual citizens in
provincial elections is not discussed. The Commission does not discuss
whether they would vote as individuals in federal constituencies for
members of the House of Commons, as well as for representatives for
the House of First Peoples, although it appears to be assumed.[199] The
role of individuals in federal and provincial elections who belong to neither a nation nor a people is not discussed. What is clear is that the
Commission has little enthusiasm for a direct individual citizen link
with federal or provincial political authorities. In general, the nation,
through its government or its representatives, is to be the intermediary
between the nation-based Aboriginal individual and the other two
orders of government. For example, the vehicle for "negotiating adapta-
tions in mainstream institutions that serve Aboriginal citizens" is neither Parliament nor provincial legislatures responding to voters and
legislators, but self-government, which is the "reinstatement of a
nation-to-nation relationship."[200]

Both the virtues and the possible problems that attach to this
nation-government constitutional vision have a reduced practical significance because it only applies in its entirety to less than half of the
Aboriginal population.[201] On-reserve First Nations people and Inuit
accounted for only 42 percent of the 1996 Aboriginal population.[202] The
Report's preferred arrangement excludes the non-reserve-based registered Indian populations of southern Canada – 60 percent of the registered total. From a different perspective, it excludes most urban
Aboriginals, although some urban Métis will be included in an adapted
version of Métis nation-government; it has diminished relevance for

Inuit, who have opted for public government, and who see themselves as a people rather than a nation (although the nation terminology is sometimes used).[203] In spite of these limitations, nation-government is unquestionably the commissioners' preferred constitutional future, the subject on which they lavish the most attention, and that most clearly reveals their constitutional philosophy. Their nation-driven constitutional vision is most likely to garner support from the reserve-based status Indian community, assuming individual bands can be persuaded to collectively aggregate their numbers to reach nation size.

The Commission's constitutional vision raises one fundamental question. Assuming its implementation, what will sustain our feelings of responsibility for each other? Historically, it was the marginalization and stigmatization of Aboriginal peoples and the silencing of their voices that largely explains the majority society's indifference to their fate, or, for status Indians that facilitated a coercive onslaught on their culture. In the past, the reserves were enclaves that separated Indians and the surrounding society from each other.[204] Indians did not benefit from federal and provincial social security programs until the Second World War. They were excluded from the Old Age Pension Act, 1927-51, but included in the 1951 Old Age Security Act, which paid universal pensions at age seventy. As recently as 1966, Indian women were included in the mothers' allowance programs of only three provinces.[205] During the depression of the 1930s, provinces and municipalities felt no responsibility for reserve Indian peoples who were "seen as being outside local society."[206] Even now there is a sense of isolation from surrounding regions.[207] Succinctly, when non-Aboriginal Canadians in the past said "we," there was an almost automatic exclusion of Aboriginal peoples. They were not, in an effective sense, full members of the Canadian community of citizenship. Their voices were not heard. They were, as the Métis described themselves, the "forgotten people." Thus they, especially status Indians, were often deprived of many of the social benefits of citizenship. The same exclusion from social benefits applied to Aboriginal people in Australia until the 1940s.[208]

Citizenship is the core concept of the democratic welfare state. In 1949, the British sociologist T.H. Marshall explained the evolution of social rights as the progressive amplification of the rights of citizenship. He defined citizenship as "a status bestowed on those who are full members of a community. All who possess the status are equal with respect to the rights and duties with which the status is endowed."[209] Social rights, for Marshall, encompassed the positive rights to a standard of care, security, and income normally associated with the welfare state. They were justified by the prior possession of citizenship, and as an elaboration of its practical meaning. Banting's definitive analysis of the emergence of the Canadian welfare state confirms Marshall's analysis, particularly in the income security field, by documenting how the pressures to progressively expand the welfare state and the rhetoric employed to justify that expansion were based on an appeal to a common Canadian citizenship that transcended the provincial divisions of Canadian federalism.[210]

The original Rowell-Sirois proposals for what later became the equalization program of unconditional grants to "have-not" provincial governments were inspired by the civic morality that the accident of provincial location in a "have-not" province imposing an average level of taxation should not deprive the Canadian citizens living there of an average level of provincial services for matters under provincial jurisdiction. This civic morality is sustained by a common citizenship that defines the boundaries of a sharing community, belonging to which justifies the unconditional equalization payments that, for example, recently amounted to more than a quarter of the annual revenues available to the government of Newfoundland.[211]

The 1982 Charter of Rights was driven by Prime Minister Trudeau's desire to strengthen Canadian citizenship against centrifugal provincialism by confronting provincial policies with a Canadian floor of rights they could not encroach on, unless the provincial government employed the notwithstanding clause with its attendant possibilities of a hostile public reaction. The policy diversities that naturally flow from federalism and that indeed are part of its raison d'être, now are limited by the Charter rights of Canadian citizens. When Bourassa used the notwithstanding clause to impose legislation discriminating against the use of English on signs, the negative reaction outside Quebec was not triggered simply by the perception that English-speaking residents of Quebec were being unfairly treated, but because their rights as Canadian citizens in Quebec were being violated. What in pre-Charter days would have been a provincial matter was elevated to a Canadian matter because the rights infringed were Canadian and thus Canadians outside Quebec could come to their defence. Our feelings of responsibility for each other flow directly from our shared possession of rights and a common citizenship.

Historically, the marginalization of the status Indian peoples and their explicit exclusion from the category "citizen" turned their special constitutional status into "a millstone."[212] Subsequently, it was the availability of Charter rights that gave Native women the constitutional support, as Canadian citizens, to obtain the removal of s. 12(1)(b) of the Indian Act that deprived them of their Indian legal status when they married non-Indians.

The RCAP proposals do not, of course, reject the application of the Charter to Aboriginal governments,[213] although the AFN strongly opposed it. However, the overall thrust of the *Report* – building on the concept of nation, the instrument of treaties, and the reinforcement of difference – gives the residents of self-governing Aboriginal nations a weak and attenuated relation to Canadian citizenship. Citizenship, however, provides the necessary justification for "universal, comprehensive as of 'right' social services." In standard welfare state theory, individual claims on their fellow citizens are based on solidarity sentiments, "which enjoin that their wants be recognized and met."[214] In a federal system, such claims are based on the common, country-wide citizenship that transcends provincial boundaries. For the commissioners, however, the attraction of federalism lies in provincialism, which provides the model for a limited exit, for a third order of Aboriginal government.[215] Canadian citizenship, and membership in the coast-to-coast Canadian community – the other face of federalism – are almost ignored in the Commission's constitutional vision.

The *Report*'s theory of federalism is idiosyncratic. The commissioners apparently thought they could sever their self-rule third order of government proposals from the shared-rule dimension of federalism, that is, from a discussion of the Canadian and provincial arenas in which we do things together. Thus they spell out self-rule in elaborate detail. Their argument for its expansive recognition is strong and convincing as a stand-alone claim. However, their analysis of the political and constitutional context into which it will fit, of what will provide enduring support – moral and financial – for the third order of government from the majority society for decades to come is weak and unconvincing. Shared rule appears as an afterthought. Thus the *Report* lacks a vision of a common society, of a community of citizenship that reflects part of the identity of each of us, of the divided civic identity of a federal people. The Commission has responded to our diversities, but diversities alone are insufficient to sustain a meaningful togetherness. Canada was born not only to protect our differences, but to create a new country that would transcend differences without destroying them in a pan-Canadian dimension where we undertook common tasks together. The *Report* pays limited attention to what holds the overall political community together. Its stress on diversity is unaccompanied by a countervailing stress on unity. The Commission rarely thought of governance in terms of the overall system of government and peoples that is visualized for the Canada of the future. By defining their task largely as finding a place for Aboriginal nations in the constitutional order to exercise self-rule, the commissioners overlooked the connectedness of the system.

The Commission's gamble is that a constitutionalized treaty relationship between nations is a substitute for or a viable alternative to a community of citizens. This might be plausible if the Aboriginal nation-governments could autonomously flourish with minimal dependence on external governments and their electorates. However, this is far from the Commission's view. The Commission's goal was not only to revamp the Canadian constitutional order with a third order of government composed of Aboriginal nations, but to do so in such a way that a massive flow of emotional, practical, and financial support will be provided for at least a lengthy transitional period. Can a nation-to-nation relationship, even given the proposed infrastructure of treaties, tribunals, enforcement mechanisms, and rights, generate the necessary civic empathy to sustain the long-term commitment that is required?

When the Commission departs from its ambitious yet incomplete constitutional vision, and focuses on the practicalities of service provision and public administration, the image of parallelism, of the two-row wampum, disappears. The stress on nation and treaties and the image of coexisting solitudes has a much weaker presence in *Gathering Strength,* the third volume of the *Report,* which deals with health, education, social policy, housing, and cultural institutions. In these areas, there is an explicit recognition of an important continuing role for federal and provincial governments, and for the institutions of mainstream society. This will be the case even after the fullest implementation of self-government.[216] The chapter "Health and Healing" advocates dialogue and collaboration,[217] and cross-cultural communication[218] between "Two Great Traditions of Health and Healing."[219] Aboriginal institutions "cannot operate in isolation from the mainstream."[220] Limitations of capacity will require resort to specialized mainstream institutions in some cases; in other instances, institutions of the majority society will be the preferred choice of Aboriginal individuals.[221] At times, this volume appears almost as a catalogue of the necessity of positive relations with and responses by a host of mainstream institutions – CBC, CRTC, museums, universities, professional associations, and other agencies of federal and provincial governments.[222]

The overall picture in *Gathering Strength* is not of boundaries or of wary partners maximizing social distance but of interdependence, intermeshing, collaboration, and mutual endeavours. The work grapples with the practicalities of resources, of economies of scale, of trained personnel, and of Aboriginal persons opting for mainstream institutions. The grassroots reality of this volume portrays massive interdependence, which for Aboriginal nations means massive and unavoidable dependence. The image of a domestic version of an international system in an attempt to recapture the nation-to-nation relationship of the eighteenth century has virtually disappeared.[223] The Commission's large constitutional nation-to-nation vision clashes with its separate analyses elsewhere of the realities of interdependence in numerous concrete policy areas at the local level. The *Report*'s macro- and micro-perspectives appear to be driven by different logics that do not meet.

There is an unavoidable tension, possibly even a contradiction, between the Commission's constitutional vision, which distances Aboriginal nations from the majority community and minimizes any shared-rule pursuit of common endeavours in the common Canadian government, and the innumerable cooperative endeavours that it recommends at the local level. This tension between the local and the pan-Canadian raises the larger question of whether the philosophy of parallelism that underlies the commissioners' constitutional analysis would reduce the willingness of the majority society to share at the national level and act as a good cooperative partner at the local level. If it does, can this be overcome by a legal regime of tribunals, intergovernmental agreements, and so forth? The Commission's assumption appears to be that a new regime, invigorated by a new Royal Proclamation, characterized by treaties between nations that spell out jurisdictional and fiscal obligations, treaties whose emergence has been facilitated by a new federal Department of Aboriginal Relations assisted by a new Lands and Treaties Tribunal, is a viable alternative to the bonds of citizenship.

When the assumption is rephrased as a question, the answer is not self-evident. Rights employed in the service of difference, with little concern for solidarity or fraternity, may generate "otherness" on both sides of the divide inherited from the past, and provide little of the sustenance and fellow-feeling that the carrying out of the task of healing and rapprochement requires. The Commission, therefore, provides us with an answer which, on analysis, turns out to be a question.

# The Choice Revisited

I cannot emphasize too strongly that we are in a new ball game.

The old approaches are out. We've been allowed to delude ourselves

about the situation for a long time because of a basic

lack of political power in native communities.

This is no longer the case and there is no way that the

newly emerging political and legal power of native people is

likely to diminish. We must face the situation squarely as a

political fact of life, but more importantly, as a fundamental point

of honour and fairness. We do, indeed, have a significant piece

of unfinished business that lies at the foundation of this country.[1]

### An Early Vision: Citizens Plus

In 1971, H.B. Hawthorn wrote an article titled "The Survival of Small Societies," which focused on Indian peoples, in a special issue of *Anthropologica,* "In Memory of [the anthropologist] Diamond Jenness."[2] Jenness had written extensively on Hawthorn's topic, often with a pessimistic forecast of the cultural future of the communities he observed. He spoke for his generation of anthropologists. His policy proposals for Canadian Indians in 1947 and later for Inuit were basically arguments for crash programs in assimilation.[3]

Hawthorn, by contrast, was the leading academic and research organizer of the project in the mid-1960s that advocated the "citizens plus" label as the appropriate status for the Indian peoples under federal jurisdiction. "Indians," the *Hawthorn Report* asserted, "should be regarded as 'Citizens Plus.' In addition to the normal rights and duties of citizenship, Indians possess certain additional rights as charter members of the

Canadian community."[4] (I was involved in the research and writing of the *Hawthorn Report,* and in the discussions that led to the citizens plus recommendation. Accordingly, the reader is warned that my initial commitment to the concept survives, whether as a naïve unwillingness to let go of my own past, or as a laudable allegiance to a concept that merits resurrection, and is supported later in this chapter).

The *Hawthorn Report* was the first major post-Second World War, Canada-wide inquiry to assert that assimilation was neither an unquestioned goal nor an appropriate policy. Indians, the *Report* argued, should be given the educational and other tools they need to make meaningful choices of how they wished to live. It was assumed that sufficient numbers would choose a contemporary version of Indianness that Indian communities would persist into the indefinite future. This understanding was consistent with an earlier Hawthorn study, *The Indians of British Columbia,* co-authored with C.S. Belshaw and S.M. Jamieson, which viewed "reserves as being with us in perpetuity," partly because of the "material and psychological security" they offered to Indians. That earlier 1958 volume had possibly anticipated "citizens plus" with its recommendation that Indians were entitled to retain their special taxation privileges in perpetuity, which makes them "a special class of Canadian citizens."[5]

Hawthorn, then, was clearly one of the earliest non-Aboriginal policy advisors to both anticipate and advocate a future in which there would be a continuing distinctive Indian presence in Canada. However, as the very title suggested – "The Survival of Small Societies" – he was not making big claims. He saw villages, not nations. The people whose future he assessed, lived in "the small and comparatively powerless communities associated with Indian reserves."[6] He asserted that what he called the "cultural flow" was primarily from the larger society to the smaller.[7] He wrote of the "Europeanization" of the Indian people,[8] not of course their complete Europeanization, but certainly a major tendency. Further, he knew, as his own inquiry of a few years earlier had reported, that a vast migration to the cities was under way, and that some of the migrants who had acquired the skills for successful urban living would disappear into the urban society and leave Indianness behind.[9]

Hawthorn and his colleagues saw the move to the city as inevitable given Indian aspirations for a North American standard of living, and the limited possibilities that could be achieved on many reserves. The appropriate strategy, therefore, was both a massive economic development program for reserve communities and policies to ease the adjustment to urban living. The Hawthorn strategy rested on the twin premises that acculturation would continue and that an autonomous development path was neither desirable nor available.

The *Hawthorn Report* was struck by the small size of Indian communities "scattered over a vast land in tiny groupings of the hamlet or village category."[10] According to their data, 77 percent of Indian bands had less than 500 population, and 42 percent had less than 200.[11] Although the *Report* strongly supported giving the maximum decision-making power to Indian communities, their small size and limited resources precluded the optimistic assessments that characterized the academic and political support for Indian nationhood in the 1980s and 1990s. The caution of Hawthorn and his colleagues also reflected what in retrospect can be seen as their underestimation of the practical significance of existing treaties, and of the future satisfaction of Indian claims by new treaties.[12] The latter issue was not examined on the premise that the establishment of an Indian Claims Commission was imminent.

When Hawthorn wrote his 1971 article, the 1969 federal White Paper advocating the ending of Indian status was on the ropes, under an impressive counterattack by Indian organizations. The attack was led by the Indian Chiefs of Alberta speaking for the Indian Association of Alberta, based on a powerfully argued brief entitled *Citizens Plus*.[13] From the vantage point of the 1990s, the relative moderation of the Alberta presentation strikes the reader. The language of nationalism is weak. The Indian Chiefs of Alberta supported the Hawthorn recommendation that the Indian Affairs Branch had a continuing role to play as a national conscience on behalf of the Indian people.[14] They advocated bringing "not just individual residents, but the entire community, into the mainstream of Canadian life."[15] The "rightful place" for Indians of the future was to be "full-fledged participants in the mosaic of the "Just Society" ... meaningful and contributing citizens of Canada."[16] Indian youth had to be prepared "to compete successfully with their fellow citizens of Canada for the rewards of the modern affluent dominant society."[17] This was far from the language of nationalism of the future. Indeed, the Alberta chiefs spoke of their political future in the limited terms of local government.[18] Harold Cardinal, who orchestrated the attack on the White Paper, stated shortly after its release that Canadians "will have to accept and recognize that we are full citizens, but we also possess special rights."[19]

The tenor of the Indian Chiefs of Alberta's *Citizens Plus* was not idiosyncratic. *Wahbung: Our Tomorrows,* a 1971 publication of the Indian Tribes of Manitoba, commenced with a reminder that Indian rights come from "our sovereignty as a nation of people."[20] However, *Wahbung* went on to define a complementary dual identity as Indians and Canadians,[21] referred to the contribution of "Canadian Indian culture" to the Canadian mosaic in Manitoba,[22] described Indians as "registered Indian Canadians,"[23] referred positively to their status as citizens of Canada[24] and insisted on their status as "full provincial citizens"[25] of Manitoba, a status entirely compatible with a unique relationship with the federal government.

In 1976, the Nisga'a Tribal Council published the Declaration of their claims under the title *Citizens Plus*.[26] They reported their agreement with the Hawthorn citizens plus proposal, and noted their earlier agreement with the 1969 White Paper principle that "true equality presupposes that the Indian people have the right to full and equal participation in the cultural, social, economic and political life of Canada."[27] Subsequently, the citizens plus thesis was favourably noted in the Pepin-Roberts Task Force on Canadian Unity.[28]

None of the preceding proposals that offered support to the citizens plus concept denied Indian difference, or argued that their distinctive presence in Canada was only a way-station on the road to assimilation. On the contrary, they all proudly, defiantly, or both, insisted on the right of Indian communities to maintain a separate existence, while recognizing their interdependence with the majority society. Further, they did not see what they hoped to become as being incompatible with Canadian citizenship. Canadian citizenship was a positive phrase, and self-identification as a Canadian was frequent. Although they noted the impediments that racism, discrimination, their colonial situation, and the absence of many modern skills among their people put in the way of their full enjoyment of citizenship, they did not see Canadian citizenship as the imposition of an unwanted status. Further, they often referred positively to mainstream society and to their desire to share in its benefits and participate in its undertakings. The self-description of what they would like to become is summed up in the phrase I employed earlier – a modernizing Aboriginality. In sum, the language of nationalism was weak, and the two-row wampum image was absent. The White Paper was defeated by angry moderates.[29]

The contest between the White Paper and the concept of citizens plus was won by the latter. Of course, the federal government did not adopt the "citizens plus" designation. It never received official support. When the suggestion of a Royal Commission on Indian policy was raised in the late 1960s by Gordon Robertson, the Clerk of the Privy Council, Jim Davey, a key Trudeau advisor, and Trudeau himself feared "that Natives might argue convincingly that they be regarded as 'citizens plus.'" As Davey reported to Trudeau, "I shudder to think that any royal commission might bring about such a [recommendation]."[30] In a defence of the White Paper in 1969, Jean Chrétien responded to a request that the government consider enshrining Aboriginal rights in the Constitution by observing, "To suggest that we should have in the constitution a provision to make the Indian citizens of Canada something other than full citizens is wrong."[31]

"Citizens plus" languishes in the pages of a mid-1960s report, in the language of a few academics, and for a time was employed in the rhetoric of Indian leaders. Had it been institutionalized by federal government support, it might have become the policy paradigm for Indian peoples for several decades. In that case, the discourse might or would have focused on the practical meaning of shared membership in the category "citizen" and the nature and extent of the "plus" category, rather than on the very different nation-to-nation terminology that pays little attention to our commonalities. In the absence of institutionalization, political and academic trends leading to new labels and perspectives would inevitably displace it. This may have been a missed opportunity.

### Aboriginal Rights and Aboriginal Nations
The defeat of the White Paper was more than the defeat of a policy. Psychologically and politically it signalled the official ending of paternalism. The undisputed policy leadership role of the federal government and the Indian Affairs Branch, heavily influenced by the views of the non-Aboriginal majority, passed into history. The era of what later was called "voice appropriation" was over. Further, the new and vigorous federal policy of subsidizing Native organizations – Inuit and Métis as

well as Indian – along with the White Paper defeat injected articulate Aboriginal voices into the debate over Aboriginal futures and the Aboriginal/non-Aboriginal relationship. Core funding, "undoubtedly the most significant event in the history of Native organizations," transformed Native politics. It fostered the emergence of the full-time, professional, salaried political leader, a career now followed by "hundreds of Natives."[32] From this time onward, Aboriginal policy discussions became a public dialogue, which, simply by existing and with all its admitted imperfections, symbolized an emerging equality that had to be worked out.

Although the politics of subsequent decades were transformed by the Aboriginal presence, many of the underlying realities to which policy had to respond were little altered. In spite of population growth, the small societies of which Hawthorn wrote in 1971, and that informed the earlier *Hawthorn Report*'s recommendations, are still relatively small in the 1990s, although many of them have added "nation" to their band name. By the late 1970s, support for "citizens plus" as an organizing label began to fade, to be replaced by Aboriginal rights as the tempo of constitutional discussion picked up following the Parti Québécois 1976 election victory.[33] "Nation" received a powerful boost with the Dene Declaration of Nationhood in 1975 – "We the Dene of the Northwest Territories insist on the right to be regarded by ourselves and the world as a nation."[34] According to Sawchuk, the 1982 patriation of the Constitution with its s. 35 recognition of Aboriginal rights generated intense pressure on Aboriginal leaders to define their "political activities ... in terms of nationhood rather than in terms of accommodation to the Canadian state. [This changed] ... negotiations and the whole structure of the language surrounding negotiations (even the whole idea of 'nation')."[35] By 1983, the *Penner Report* could employ a painting of the two-row wampum on the front cover and a two-row wampum statement on the back cover of its recommendations for Indian self-government.[36]

"Citizens plus" had disappeared, indeed citizenship was absent from the *Penner Report.* The relevant unit was the Indian band, relabelled nation, situated in a constitutionally entrenched third order of government, wielding the maximum possible degree of self-government, and engaged in government-to-government relations with the federal and provincial governments. Penner, in part reflecting the focus of its mandate on Indian self-government, which, in turn, reflected the unwillingness of the federal government and its administrative arm, the Department of Indian Affairs and Northern Development, to extend its writ outside the reserves, paid only passing attention to the growing off-reserve status Indian population. Thus, federal policy indirectly stimulated the nation terminology by its failure to follow the growing migration to the city where "nation" lost much of its meaning. This federal government bias was reinforced by the leading advocacy role of the Assembly of First Nations, which represents reserve-based communities, specifically the governing band council élite. That "nation" would be a privileged term in the dialogue between these two actors, and that the urban Aboriginal population would receive minimal attention are not surprising. The locus of "nation," however, was, and is, not clear. The federal government, when it employs "nation," tends to locate it at the level of the band, while the AFN – as of 1995 – lacked a clear position, but felt that in most cases it was not at the band level.[37] Support for the concept of an encompassing Canadian citizenship is much more likely to come from the federal (and provincial) government(s) in Aboriginal/non-Aboriginal constitutional dialogues, than from Aboriginal leaders – Inuit and urban leaders excepted.

From an Indian First Nations perspective, "citizenship," in a sense, belongs to the federal government against whom they are battling. It appears as a claim for a rival allegiance. Citizenship is part of the "they" against which the First Nations "we" seeks to make headway. Further, First Nations' chiefs and AFN leaders speak for collectivities – their nations, peoples, communities – on whose behalf they seek more power. The "nation" basis of their claim clashes with, or at least does not facilitate an easy simultaneous allegiance to, the concept of the individual Canadian citizen. This tension between the Aboriginal "nation" collectivity and the concept of citizen is exacerbated in land claims controversies, when the stakes are high, and Aboriginal and non-Aboriginal governments are pitted against each other as adversaries. We know "that feelings run high between First Nations and non-aboriginal governments, especially when they face off in litigation."[38] Further, claims for land, sovereignty, or compensation for malperformance of the federal government trusteeship role are not based upon an appeal to a common citizenship, but on histories of maltreatment, non-recognition, absence of treaties, and so on. The Aboriginal parties in land claims negotiations, and those seeking a third order of government, base their claims on their historical nationhood, not on their contemporary citizenship. As Joyce Green observes, the superficially positive terms "citizenship" and "equality" were traditionally employed "by the federal government to package its racist assimilative policies until 1969. Therefore, it is not only the Indian Act but Canadian citizenship and the language of equality that is suspect for many Indian people, for 'equality' can be read as 'become the same as' and 'citizenship' can be read as acceptance of the legitimacy of the oppression state. Allegiance to the oppressor state is problematic for many indigenous people."[39] The Métis, of course, seek a partial escape from the common citizenship they now enjoy, to a status analogous to Indian First Nations.

Yet after the claims have been settled and the third order of government has been established, Aboriginal peoples will still be Canadian citizens. They will still live in Canada and in a province or territory. Their nation will not be the only community deserving their allegiance. For the non-landed half of the population, nation will have a much lesser, possibly no, meaning. For them, the rights of citizenship will be crucially important. These realities should not be forgotten.

The influence of structure on policy, on how we see ourselves, was beautifully illustrated when, at the same time as the Penner Committee was exploring Indian self-government linked to the legislative responsibilities of the federal government under s. 91(24), the federal and provincial governments were engaged in a constitutional dialogue based on s. 37 of the Constitution Act that led to four Aboriginal constitutional conferences – with Aboriginal organizations representing Indians, Inuit and Métis, and urban Aboriginals. The legislative arena – s. 91(24) – responded to Indians; the constitutional arena – s. 37 – responded to Aboriginals.

By the 1990s, the language of nationalism, of inherent right, of nation-to-nation equality was widespread. By 1996, the RCAP *Report* could refer dismissively to the citizens plus idea that Aboriginal peoples "are ... citizens with a slightly expanded set of rights based on their descent from the original inhabitants."[40] On the contrary, they are nations, "distinct political communities, collectives with a continuing political relationship with the Canadian state," whose "nationhood" must be accommodated.[41] Rhetorically, the move from citizenship (the citizens plus version) to nationhood occurred relatively quickly. RCAP is a massive embodiment of the nation-to-nation orientation, although a draft Assembly of First Nations' discussion paper on the *Report* criticized it for its timidity.[42]

The transition to a new language commenced in the 1960s. Harold Cardinal reports that he first heard the phrase "aboriginal rights" as a student at Carleton University in the mid-1960s. Simultaneously, the Plains Indians were assimilating the concept, previously so unfamiliar to them that they developed a Cree equivalent to aid their understanding.[43] The 1969 authors of the federal government Statement on Indian Policy, including Prime Minister Trudeau, clearly accorded negligible significance to the concept of Aboriginal rights. However, between 1969 and 1971 Indian leaders and Indian organizations began to discuss Aboriginal title, and published various position papers defending its existence and importance.[44] The concept was adopted by the National Indian Brotherhood in 1971, and subsequently presented to a standing House of Commons Committee on Indian Affairs.[45] The issue of Aboriginal title surfaced briefly in the 1972 federal election campaign, with the Tories supporting recognition, and Trudeau doubtful of its legal validity.[46]

Aboriginal rights entered the legal mainstream with the 1970 publication of the report of the Research Committee on Treaty and Aboriginal Rights of Canadian Indians and Eskimos by the Indian-Eskimo Association of Canada.[47] The second, revised edition of *Native Rights in Canada,* by Peter A. Cumming and Neil H. Mickenberg, described as "substantially a new book," appeared in 1972.[48] It was "the indispensable textbook of native law in this country," according to Flanagan, writing in the mid-1980s.[49] Further, observes Flanagan, "considering how many of Canada's experts in native law had a hand in composing this work, it represents a collective adoption of the concept of Aboriginal rights by the legal profession."[50] Ten years after *Native Rights in Canada,* "Aboriginal rights" were constitutionalized and protected in the 1982 Constitution Act.[51]

Both editions were strongly supportive of Aboriginal rights; indeed their purpose was to raise their profile. They provide the reader with a far from flattering portrayal of the casual attitude to Aboriginal rights historically displayed by the majority society and its governments. Their appearance signals the emergence of the academic legal community to prominence as advocates and defenders of Aboriginal peoples and the diminishing role of anthropologists as intermediaries. But these two volumes were very timid compared to articles in the legal periodicals in the 1990s.

Although the successive editions of *Native Rights in Canada* transformed the Aboriginal policy dialogue – doing for Aboriginal peoples in a limited way what the 1982 Charter was later to do for all Canadians – by elevating the language of rights at the expense of a pragmatism that historically had served majority interests, they only partly anticipated the future to which they contributed. Neither "nation" nor the "inherent right to self-government" graced the pages of either edition, although both were intended to be comprehensive, if pioneering treatises on Aboriginal rights. The concerns were traditional – hunting, fishing, land, mineral rights, and extending treaties to areas and populations not under treaty. The second edition defined Aboriginal rights as "those rights which native people retain as a result of their original possession of the soil. We have defined Aboriginal rights as those property rights which inure to native peoples by virtue of their occupation upon certain lands from time immemorial."[52] There is no intimation that two decades later, Aboriginal "nations" would be an important justification – in addition to Quebec nationalism – for describing Canada as a multinational country. Indeed, the 1970 edition, after noting US Chief Justice Marshall's description of American tribes as "domestic dependent nations" (an appropriate term given their extensive "internal legislative autonomy"), concluded that the absence of the latter capacity in Canada meant that "the term 'nation' seem[ed] less appropriate here."[53] "Nation" was for the future. There was no self-reference to "nation" in the presentations of Aboriginal organizations to the 1970-2 joint Senate-House of Commons committee on the constitution.[54]

*The Opening Up of the Debate*
The subsequent evolution of constitutional thought outside of government on Aboriginal issues was heavily influenced by four phenomena.

First, in 1973, the Supreme Court of Canada divided on the question of whether the Nisga'a, who lived in the Nass Valley in British Columbia, had Aboriginal title and, if so, whether it had been extinguished. Three judges on the seven-person court asserted that Aboriginal title had existed, but had been extinguished. Justice Pigeon dismissed the appeal on a technicality, and gave no opinion on the substantive issue. Justice Hall's dissent, concurred in by Laskin and Spence, supported the existence of Aboriginal title, asserted that its extinguishment would have had to be "clear and plain," and concluded that such had not been proved. Accordingly, Aboriginal title still existed.

Although the Nisga'a did not win their case, the fact that six of seven Supreme Court judges had agreed that Aboriginal title had existed, and three judges asserted it had not been extinguished, gave Indian land claims a credibility they had previously lacked. In 1973 the federal government, which in its 1969 White Paper had dismissed "Aboriginal claims," now admitted the existence of Aboriginal title. Thus began the comprehensive land claims policy of the federal government and the subsequent settlement of major land claims in the Yukon and the Northwest Territories and (northern) Quebec. In British Columbia, a plethora of land claims is under negotiation, settlement of which is facilitated by the British Columbia Treaty Commission.

The Nisga'a case, and its successors, gave to Indian peoples not under treaty a marked enhancement of their bargaining power with governments, leverage in the judicial arena, and, equally important, a recognition that they had lived in organized societies prior to the coming of the Europeans. They would no longer be referred to as they had been in earlier court decisions as "wholly without cohesion, laws or culture, in effect a subhuman species."[55]

Second, the opening up of the Constitution to respond to the Quebec-Canada crisis following the 1976 Parti Québécois victory gave Aboriginal peoples the opportunity and incentive to couch their demands in constitutional terms. This unquestionably stimulated constitutional introspection and, especially following the 1982 Constitution Act with its commitment to a constitutional conference on Aboriginal rights, reinforced a nation-to-nation definition of the situation.

The "nation-to-nation" premise was bolstered because the Aboriginal representatives spoke for the Indian people, the Métis people, the Inuit people, and not for particular interests within each people, such as education or housing. Given the prominence of "nation" in Quebec sovereigntist discourse, the pressure on Aboriginal élites to employ the language of nationalism was irresistible.[56]

The *Penner Report* systematically used the phrase "Indian First Nations" in deference to the language of the witnesses before the Committee and to acquaint the Canadian community with the term.[57] As one Aboriginal constitutional conference expanded to four in the mid-1980s, with the leaders of the major Aboriginal organizations bargaining with federal and provincial first ministers, a major premise that was never formally articulated – that the first ministers of the federal and provincial governments did not represent or speak for the Aboriginal constituents in their electorates – was implicitly accepted. Instead, they were seen as representing non-Aboriginal Canada. The Aboriginal organizations spoke for Aboriginal nations. This implicitly removed Aboriginal individuals from the standard citizen category, spoken for by the federal and provincial governments. Carried to its logical conclusion, this structuring of constitutional bargaining at least intimated that the Aboriginal peoples on whose behalf the Aboriginal organizations spoke were not standard Canadian citizens, possibly might not be Canadian citizens at all.

This apparently logical conclusion is, however, illogical. The backdrop to this nation-to-nation image is the minimal Aboriginal representation in Parliament, a product of the small Aboriginal population and its scattered distribution. This results in a representation gap filled by Native organizations, which see their role in nation-to-nation terms. This image, however, subtly misleads if it induces us to overlook the possession of the franchise by Aboriginal peoples. The reality, which the composition of Parliament conceals, is that the recognition of Aboriginal organizations as advocates for their peoples is both because of the limited overt presence of indigenous Canadians in Parliament *and* their status as voting citizens, which symbolizes their inclusion. Status Indians did not bargain nation-to-nation when they lacked the franchise.

The Aboriginal constitutional process took place during the period 1983-7 and consisted of four separate constitutional conferences, which contributed to the emerging definition of Canada as a multinational polity that now coexists uneasily with the historic federal-provincial division of who we are. The candour of the discussions was hampered by a constraint on the non-Aboriginal participants – an unwillingness to raise the critical questions about self-government that privately troubled them.[58] The representatives of the governments of the federal system held the trump card of power, but on this issue they had only a weak legitimacy. The Aboriginal/non-Aboriginal divide in these and subsequent constitutional discussions was reinforced by the absence of an Aboriginal "Trudeau" on the federal side, capable of authoritatively representing and speaking for the Canadian dimension of Aboriginality. The relative weakness of an overt Aboriginal presence in legislatures discourages the emergence of the divided identities normal to federalism – the coexistence of a provincial and Canadian sense of civic self – supplementing Aboriginal nation membership. An additional impediment, of course, explicitly underlined in the RCAP *Report,* is the desire to accord overwhelming priority to the nation-to-nation relationship, for which citizen links to federal and provincial governments are seen as rivals.

Speculation is only that, but it is possible that the timing of the Aboriginal emergence on the constitutional policy agenda is an important explanation for the consolidation of demands behind nationalism and self-government. Population increase will enhance Aboriginal representation in legislatures, especially in several provinces. Further, twenty years from now, given the dramatic increase in the number of Aboriginal students in postsecondary institutions, there will almost certainly be a large, successful urban Aboriginal community. Their successful urban presence in and of itself will be evidence of an alternative route for individuals. Also, and here of course the speculation grows, their policy interests will focus on general adaptation to urban society. To the extent that their careers and lifestyles are satisfactory, they may become defenders of the society they have joined. At that time, an Aboriginal counterpart to Trudeau may emerge.

Third, the 1982 Constitution Act, which constitutionalized the phrase "Aboriginal rights," also recognized a new constitutional category, the "Aboriginal peoples of Canada," defined to include Indian, Inuit, and Métis. The latter had momentous consequences. It enlarged and diversified the indigenous population for which the state had special responsibilities, of those who were more than standard Canadians. Section 35(1), which declared that "the existing aboriginal and treaty rights of the aboriginal peoples of Canada are hereby recognized and affirmed," dramatically enhanced the status, recognition, and bargaining power of Aboriginal peoples. Judge A.C. Hamilton said that he could not "overemphasize the importance of this substantial reversal of government policy towards

Aboriginal peoples. It officially and finally changed Canada's approach to the Indigenous peoples of this land."[59]

Fourth, the Aboriginal constitutional breakthrough in the 1982 Constitution Act, the four inconclusive constitutional conferences on Aboriginal issues, the recurring bouts of subsequent constitutional activity (i.e., the failed Meech Lake and Charlottetown accords) and, most important, the lack of agreement on what had been gained in the 1982 Constitution Act (i.e., the recognition of rights in s. 35, but no specification of what they were) created a constitutional vacuum. A segment of the academic community, especially in the law faculties, took on the obligation of providing the meanings the Constitution had not spelled out. The involvement of academic lawyers in legal research on Aboriginal, especially Indian, issues, was a departure from their previous lack of interest. In *Sparrow*, the Supreme Court of Canada observed the long history of ignoring "the rights of the Indians to their aboriginal lands ... For fifty years after the publication of Clement's *The Law of the Canadian Constitution* (3rd ed., 1916), there was a virtual absence of discussion of any kind of Indian rights to land even in academic literature."[60] In the mid-1960s, Ken Lysyk, who subsequently did much to change the situation he deplored, indicated his distress at the insignificant attention paid by Canadian legal scholarship "to the fascinating complexities of the legal status of this growing minority group." In this respect, the Canadian situation at that time compared unfavourably with the American.[61] By the 1970s, Lysyk's lament had lost much of its relevance. It is clear from Peter Hogg that how law related to Aboriginal peoples is no longer a backwater. Writing in 1997, Hogg refers to "a vast literature on Aboriginal rights."[62] In his first edition in 1977, he devoted eight pages to "Indians and Indian Lands," a division of powers focus.[63] In 1997, he allocated forty-one pages to what had become a much more significant constitutional policy area under the heading "Aboriginal Peoples," a constitutional category that did not exist before the 1982 Constitution Act.[64] In the 1950s and 1960s when constitutional law was little more than the "division of powers," s. 91(24) received scant attention, only two pages in the 1960 edition of Laskin's *Canadian Constitutional Law*.[65] This inattention began to erode in the 1970s[66] and was vanquished with the passage of the Constitution Act, 1982, and the accompanying high drama constitutional politics of the next decade and a half. Section 35 of the Constitution Act, s. 25 of the Charter, an awakened legal community (both academic and practising), reinforced by and reinforcing the growing rights consciousness of Aboriginal peoples, have generated a proliferation of court cases, law journal articles, and commentaries on judicial decisions.

Specialist law practices have emerged to handle Aboriginal legal issues. There is now a "land claims industry," which for some of its practitioners can be very lucrative.[67] Most law faculties now have court watchers who monitor Aboriginal decisions and who, in general, are supportive of expansive judicial interpretations of Aboriginal and treaty rights. Several Aboriginal law professors bring "insider" knowledge and experience to their contributions to the understanding of the past and prospective relations between Aboriginal and non-Aboriginal peoples.[68] Legal scholarship on Aboriginal issues is now a growth industry. Academic interest accompanied and influenced a succession of high-profile cases that has fleshed out Aboriginal constitutional doctrine since the passing of the 1982 Constitution Act.[69] The impact of legal scholarship on Aboriginal constitutional discourse is so important that it requires elaboration.

*Academic Activism and Legal Scholarship*
The contemporary role of legal scholarship in fleshing out Aboriginal rights, in searching for and finding constitutional space for the future exercise of a third order of Aboriginal government, in elaborating the historic rationale for a special place for Aboriginal peoples in Canada – where Brian Slattery has made major contributions[70] – and in general seeking to put law at the service of Aboriginal aspirations can scarcely be exaggerated.[71] The leading role of anthropology as the interpretive community through which Aboriginal realities had been filtered has been ceded to the law faculties, although there is still a significant anthropological presence,[72] and philosophy in the person of Will Kymlicka[73] makes a seminal contribution. Anthropology played the role of interpretive intermediary at a time when Native peoples had limited opportunities to speak for themselves. Up to the 1950s, academic (including anthropological) scholarship focused on the long-run goal of a single society, or simply presupposed its emergence and the disappearance of a separate Aboriginal existence.[74] Anthropologists sought to ease the

process of transition, but they did not try to thwart it. The contemporary goal that scholarship serves is the preservation of an enduring Aboriginal distinctiveness by maximizing self-government, for the achievement of which rights are potent weapons.

The contribution of legal scholarship to sociopolitical movements is a tradition, not a novelty. Legal scholarship from the 1880s – from the contribution of Thomas-Jean-Jacques Loranger – to the present has provided powerful intellectual support to Quebec provincial autonomy, and more recently to Quebec nationalism and independence. McGill law professor Frank Scott and his colleagues were major intellectual players in Canada's evolution from colony to nation. In many cases, they also operated as allies of the central government against the expansive or protective strategies of provincial governments. The vanguard role of legal scholarship in providing roadmaps to a better future for Aboriginal people is both unsurprising and positive – although not without some negative side effects. The goal is to help Aboriginal peoples to manoeuvre through the legal labyrinth of an ancient constitutional order guarded by an establishment of governments, endowed with a Constitution that was not designed to foster Aboriginality, and that is enforced by a judiciary whose flexibility is limited by the mindset of its members and the role of precedent.

The titles of three recent articles indicate the general thrust of recent legal scholarship on behalf of Aboriginal peoples: Kent McNeil, "Envisaging Constitutional Space for Aboriginal Governments"; Bruce Ryder, "The Demise and Rise of the Classical Paradigm in Canadian Federalism: Promoting Autonomy for the Provinces and First Nations"; and Patrick Macklem, "First Nations Self-Government and the Borders of the Canadian Legal Imagination."[75] Macklem himself correctly notes that "Canadian academic scholarship has been as creative as its American counterpart in providing arguments for the creation of constitutional spaces in which Indian forms of government can take root and flourish."[76]

The 1997 Supreme Court decision in *Delgamuukw* v. *B.C.*[77] confirms Macklem's observation by citing Macklem and McNeil, especially the latter, and other legal scholars, in its landmark decision that overturned the earlier decision of the trial judge, BC Chief Justice Allan McEachern, which had denied the existence of Aboriginal title.[78] The decision also argued that oral histories had to be "placed on an equal footing with the types of historical evidence that courts are familiar with,"[79] a further disagreement with the trial judge. Supreme Court Chief Justice Lamer indicated that he had "profited greatly from Professor McNeil's article 'The Meaning of Aboriginal Title.'"[80] The role of the academic legal community is clearly part of the company in "Court and Company" that in complementary fashion generate court decisions.

In order to minimize the likelihood that my subsequent observations will be misunderstood, I hereby underline the fact that I applaud legal scholarship supportive of a better future for Aboriginal peoples by self-government, recognition of Aboriginal title, etcetera. My objective is simply to note that the pursuit of those noble goals tends to be accompanied by a lack of concern for, or attention to what we will share, what moral ties will hold us together. These highly relevant Canadian concerns, when noted at all, are found in asides, in *obiter dicta* that are not germane to the main argument.

Macklem argued for a constitutional imagination that would carve out a sphere of Aboriginal self-government that would not be constrained by the logic of the division of powers, by the conventions of Crown sovereignty, or by parliamentary supremacy. Ryder viewed "autonomy for First Nations people [as] a hidden constitutional value whose injection into interpretive practices is long overdue."[81] Kent McNeil's purpose was to "decolonize Canadian constitutional law"[82] by an expansive interpretation of s. 35 as the constitutional space for Aboriginal peoples to exercise their inherent powers of self-government.

The purpose that drove these authors is summarized by Macklem's statement that he sought "to place native self-government at the centre of the law governing Canada's First Nations."[83] They share additional characteristics. Their goals are ambitious, and focus on the advancement of Indian/Aboriginal peoples. They write not as judges or mediators reconciling opposing parties, but as advocates. They display little or no concern for Canadian citizenship, or for the fact that after the maximum self-government has been implemented, Aboriginal peoples will still be linked to federal and provincial governments. Although the extent and significance of the latter may be noted, it is not examined. Macklem, for example, asserts that "federal laws and provincial laws of general application that do not bear on matters relating to cultural self-definition could continue to apply to native people without threatening forms of self-government."[84] However, he indicated his priorities with the statement that questions about the relationship between self-government and Canadian citizenship should be addressed later, "preferably once institutional structures of native self-government are in place."[85] His notion of that self-government is imprecise, but certainly ambitious. It straddles political autonomy within the Canadian state and "self-determination as a form of political autonomy ... outside" existing state structures – although he preferred the achievement of self-government "through domestic, as opposed to international law."[86] Perhaps understandably, this uncertainty about the ultimate destination of self-determination relegates discussion of citizenship to another day.

Kent McNeil recommends that Aboriginal peoples "fill [the] constitutional space [of s. 35(1)] with Aboriginal laws," space that probably encompasses "all aspects of Aboriginal life."[87] His purpose was to facilitate the step-by-step emergence of a third order of Aboriginal government without the necessity of "constitutional haggling."[88] This would effectively preclude the application of federal and provincial laws that infringed Aboriginal and treaty rights. Ryder argues that federal legislation based on s. 91(24) should apply to Indians only with their consent.[89] This would deprive Parliament of any discretionary capacity to enact laws on a subject matter historically considered to be under federal jurisdiction. In effect, it would create a separate legal regime for First Nations people that would remove First Nations policy issues from the electoral and legislative agenda of non-Aboriginal Canadians. Macklem concurs, advocating that legislation based on s. 91(24), and which affects s. 35(1) rights should require Native participation and consent as "a precondition of constitutionality."[90] The implementation of Native consent and participation is not discussed. Ryder also proposes that First Nations people off reserves should be insulated from provincial legislation that touches "matters at the core of their individual or collective identities as members of First Nations."[91] Ryder, Macklem, and McNeil had the same goal – to maximize the autonomy of First Nations, particularly land-based communities, by devising innovative constitutional doctrine, and to minimize the impact of federal and provincial legislation that affected the core of Indianness. To what extent Indian people had Canadian and provincial identities in addition to their Aboriginal identities is unclear in all three articles. In general, the almost exclusive focus is on Aboriginal identity.

The issue raised by this genre of scholarship is not that its logic is weak, or that its focus on Aboriginal autonomy is somehow improper – which would be a ridiculous allegation – but rather its unremitting focus on one of the communities that make up Canada and an indifference, or at least lack of attention to, the Canada of which Aboriginal peoples are a part. The retort that there is a division of labour in the legal academy and individual authors can leave the task of gap-filling, or balancing, to their colleagues is, in the abstract, legitimate. The reality, however, is that the scholars focusing on Aboriginal issues are more akin to an intellectual social movement than participants in a broad-ranging debate with checks and balances.

The underlying purpose and philosophy of these articles is repeated in countless companion pieces. In an "unapologetic critique" of the Charter, Mary Ellen Turpel questioned its applicability to Aboriginal peoples, given "the collective or communal basis of Aboriginal life," for the "conceptions of law [of the two societies] are simply incommensurable." She cites Ruth Benedict's assertion that "[Aboriginal] cultures are oriented as wholes in different directions. They are travelling along different roads in pursuit of different ends, and these ends and these means in one society cannot be judged in terms of those of another society because essentially they are incommensurable."[92] Taken literally, Benedict's view would have very little support from contemporary anthropologists.[93]

A distinct category of articles espousing treaty federalism differs only in the instrumentality – a regime of treaties between Aboriginal nations and the Canadian state – employed to achieve similar goals. Treaty federalism is most prominently identified with the writings of James [sákéj] Youngblood Henderson.[94] Treaty federalism proposes a parallel treaty federal order alongside the existing provincial order.[95] From a First Nations perspective, the existing constitutional regime is illegitimate because s. 91(24), "Indians, and lands reserved for the Indians," should not have been interpreted to give the federal government a general power to impose legislation on Indian peoples that was not authorized or commanded by the treaties.[96] The Indian Act, which should have been a vehicle for meeting treaty obligations, was illegitimately transformed into a weapon for the subordination of Indian peoples and for an assault on their cultures.[97] The treaties were nation-to-nation agreements establishing relationships "often called treaty federalism."[98] Further, they were made with the imperial Crown under the authority of the Royal prerogative.[99] In that sense, the treaty relationships placed the treaty nations outside the Canadian constitutional order, as conventionally understood.[100]

Further, neither federal nor provincial governments had any legitimate jurisdiction over First Nations lacking a treaty relationship. The factual post-Confederation subordination of Indian nations, accordingly, reflects both a misunderstanding and a violation of the relationship the treaties were intended to serve, and derivatively is based on an illegitimate use of federal and provincial authority to undermine Native autonomy, culture, and identity independently of the existence or non-existence of a treaty relationship.

The resolution of the contradiction seen by Henderson in the existing constitutional order requires the recognition of First Nations as autonomous, wielding all the jurisdictions they have not given up by treaty as an expression of their collective right to self-determination.[101] It further requires the direct representation of First Nations as such in federal and provincial legislatures. The borders of Aboriginal electoral districts "should conform to the existing treaty areas as well as to Aboriginal communities."[102] The participation of "Treaty Delegates" in legislatures is necessary to end the "political apartheid" of past exclusions, and to supplement self-government, which, by itself, "can reinforce ... political segregation."[103]

Henderson's analysis is supported by Mary Ellen Turpel, who stresses the necessity of direct Aboriginal participation in legislatures to influence the policies – and the public opinion on which they rest – that are required for Aboriginal self-determination and autonomy. Indigenous peoples must be represented directly as such. Simply voting for non-Aboriginal politicians is insufficient, for the party system is geared to the representation of French and English, not Aboriginal peoples. "It may be helpful [in thinking about direct Aboriginal participation in legislatures]," she writes, "to conceptualize special indigenous representatives as ambassadors or international representatives of indigenous communities with a quasi-diplomatic function. This model helps to dispel the impression that indigenous peoples are seeking assimilation into dominant institutions."[104]

Treaty federalism rejects any version of one person-one vote that is not based on Aboriginal electoral districts. The 1960 extension of the federal franchise to status Indians was a federal attempt to justify "the oppressive extension of ... [its] powers over Aboriginal peoples."[105] For Henderson, the leading representative role of the major Aboriginal organizations in constitutional reform arenas is also illegitimate, for they occupy seats at the bargaining table that properly should be occupied by Indian nations.[106]

Treaty federalism is not simply an expanded version of existing federalism, but a transformation. It postulates two distinct federal orders, provincial federalism and treaty federalism. In Henderson's analysis, the treaty order differs from the provincial order in its apparent rejection of the idea of a separate individual citizenship to be held by Indians in their capacity as Canadians. Accordingly, it has no or little place for the normal divided identities of traditional federalism. Further, if read correctly, it is directed primarily, if not exclusively, to territorially bounded Indian political communities.[107] Treaty federalism, as proposed by Henderson, is based on rigorous historical research about the original nature of the treaties, the unsurrendered governing powers they leave with Indian nations, the imperialist distortion of their meaning by the Canadian government, and the possibilities their reinvigoration would hold out for a reconstituted constitutional order that would finally have shed its colonial legacy.

Henderson underlines that he is writing from an "Aboriginal perspective" that some other legal thinkers will consider "unacceptable" but is "no cause for alarm." Aboriginal contributions to the discussions on Aboriginal/non-Aboriginal future relations are "only now being heard in Canada in a climate that is not mired in racial discrimination and hostility to our very presence."[108]

His discussion begins with First Nations in a treaty relationship with the British Crown and ends with a domesticated treaty federalism in a revamped Canadian constitutional order. The Aboriginal identities of individuals living within First Nation communities in a treaty federalism relationship will be reinforced, and a Canadian identity will be attenuated. This would appear to be the case, even given his insistence on representation at the centre, described in *The Road* as "by far the most crucial objective,"[109] for that representation is to be by tribe or nation. The electoral participation of individual Indians in heterogeneous constituencies is dismissed as an attempt to legitimate the illegitimate – the legislative intrusion by the federal or provincial governments in matters reserved to Indian governments.

Given this perspective, treaty federalism is hostile to the concept of citizens plus, with the "plus" criticized as a trivial difference compared to the expansive governing possibilities opened up by treaty federalism for First Nations as they progressively assume control over the rights and powers that the treaties did not extinguish.[110] This criticism may be somewhat unfair as the *Hawthorn Report,* which contributed the phrase to public discussion, deliberately declined to spell out the "plus" aspects, which it argued should appropriately be left to the political debates of the future.

For treaty federalism and the other legal scholarship described earlier, the relationship of Aboriginal nations with the inherited constitutional order and the Canadian community emerges as a by-product of the author's views of the maximum rights-based autonomy available for future self-governing Aboriginal nations. "Citizens plus," by contrast, had the goal of bringing Indian peoples into the Canadian community of citizenship as well as supporting self-government for the expression and protection of diversity. (At that time, in the 1960s, self-government was conceived in much more modest terms than its present-day successors.) The difference between "citizens plus" and treaty federalism and the goals of the previously cited legal scholarship is not simply a dispute over the best means to an end, but a difference in the ends themselves. Admittedly, the choice of ends is conditioned by disagreement over what goals are realistically available. Political scientists, as noted below, tend to argue the necessity for a strong common bond, morally located in a common citizenship, as an essential support for positive responses to the alleviation of the ills that afflict too many Aboriginal communities.

"Citizens plus" presupposed that a common citizenship that included all of us in some Canadian version of our being was desirable. This recommendation was informed by the belief that the denial of citizenship to Indians in the past was a crucial factor in their immiseration. A degree of common connection between Aboriginal and non-Aboriginal Canadians was considered a necessary support for the empathy that would make us feel responsible for each other. Treaty federalism, by contrast, explains the historical record of maltreatment as an arrogant and wilful violation of the treaties, and of the rights of those not yet under treaty. The counterargument would be that if the members of First Nations with treaties had also been citizens, respect for their treaties would have been greater.

No consensus is possible on this historical might-have-been. It is raised simply to suggest that the issue of how, and to what extent, and in what capacities we are to relate to each other – as members of nations, as citizens, or some combination, and with what consequences – underlies every future constitutional change that we make. Treaty federalism, for the Aboriginal peoples it will encompass, stresses nation and minimizes a common citizenship. "Citizens plus" tilts in a different direction, although the "plus" component has expansive possibilities.

We never have a clean slate on which to write. We do, however, have some manoeuvrability. Our choice of a future is informed by debates that straddle law and politics, and are informed by rival constitutional visions. James [sákéj] Youngblood Henderson, frequently in collaboration with Russel Lawrence Barsh, has been a seminal contributor. They have been joined by numerous legal academics. My goal here is to contribute to that debate. Different choices will produce different future costs and benefits, although their precise nature will only be known when they emerge. In our present transitional stage, the one choice for which the costs will clearly outweigh the benefits would be the choice not to have the public presentation of alternative futures.

The valuable objective of all these legal analyses – replacing the sins of the past when law and the Constitution were instruments of suppression, with revised legal, institutional, and constitutional arrangements that will serve Aboriginal liberation – is pursued with minimal attention to various non-trivial ancillary concerns (Henderson's treaty federalism proposals being somewhat of an exception). It is possible to read dozens of articles that come close to ignoring the reality that Aboriginal peoples will still be part of the provincial and Canadian communities in which they live, even after the maximum of self-government has been achieved.[111] A pervasive tendency in this literature is to undervalue, underestimate, or overlook the continuing links of the members of self-governing nations with the federal and provincial governments on which they will continue to depend for many services. Although the bonds of citizenship and moral connection with the surrounding

Canadian society are ignored or downplayed,[112] its governments are expected to undertake "an all-encompassing set of parallel reforms" responding to Aboriginal concerns across virtually the entire range of policy areas of the modern state.[113] As noted earlier, this is very close to RCAP's view.

Several concerns emerge from a reading of this literature. There is an overwhelming focus on the landed Aboriginal communities – particularly the reserve-based status Indian community. Although Indian and Aboriginal are often employed interchangeably in this literature, Inuit and Métis receive scant attention. The focus on the landed community means that negligible attention is paid to the urban off-reserve population, a not inconsiderable exclusion for they constitute about half of the total Aboriginal population. This focus builds on the model of the *Penner Report,* which also ignored the off-reserve population. The latter, of course, as RCAP noted, are not candidates for significant powers of self-government, and their Aboriginal culture and identity often weakens in the urban setting. Nevertheless, the systematic overlooking of their concerns reveals the tendency for legal scholarship to be attracted to the big themes of decolonization and cultural diversity at the expense of the more practical problems of urban living where the individual Aboriginal person is much more clearly a member of three non-Aboriginal communities – urban, provincial, and national – on which that person depends for various services. Further, some of the neglected half presumably have made positive decisions to enter the majority society and succeed on its terms.

The basic issue here is the relationship between the homeland and the diaspora, the Aboriginal version of the tension between French Canada and the province-controlling francophone majority in Quebec. Once the state comes to be seen as the agency for protection, for cultural nourishment, and as a powerful symbol of status recognition – as happened in Quebec's "quiet revolution" of the 1960s – nationalist élites emerge who vest their hopes in strengthening the homeland. Those in the diaspora may then be seen as lost souls, or if perchance they should thrive, as a reproach to the homeland they left in search of better opportunities.

Law professors are not alone in their focus on landed communities and inattention to urban Aboriginal issues. Sawchuk claims there has been "a total lack of scholarly interest in urban Native issues since the 1970s."

Scholarly indifference parallels the failure of Aboriginal organizations to represent the urban population. "Almost all the effort and plans the [Aboriginal] organizations are making for self-government, land claims, or economic development, are aimed at rural populations."[114]

Clearly, if the vehicle is nationalism, the instrument is self-government, and the goal is the preservation or enhancement of culture, then attention will focus almost exclusively on the territorially based community. This concentration, however, comes at a very heavy price. It implicitly undervalues the choice of half of the Aboriginal population – even if for many the choice is dictated by necessity. It may be on the wrong side of history, if urbanization trends continue. Even the most generous allocation of more land to Aboriginal nations is unlikely to stem the flow of migrants to the cities. Ours is an urban civilization. Few Aboriginal homelands are likely to have Quebec's capacity to stand out as beacons of language survival, of cultural invigoration, of power and prestige within Canada, as home to major cities, and as possessors of a modern economy. Disregard for the (relatively far larger) Aboriginal (than francophone) diaspora is unwise. Aboriginal homelands will be unable to absorb the growing population of postsecondary graduates, who will end up in cities. In 1969, 800 First Nations people pursued postsecondary education. The number increased to 26,800 in 1994.[115] A vibrant urban middle class of Aboriginal background is a distinct possibility. It may be the catalyst for an Aboriginal cultural revival sensitive to the cosmopolitan realities of major metropolitan centres. The relative status of homeland and diaspora for Aboriginal peoples is unlikely, therefore, to duplicate the Quebec homeland/francophone diaspora distribution of power and status. Future generations may look back with sympathy and understanding at the Aboriginal migrants who pioneered successful urban living and an urban Aboriginality whose content we cannot anticipate, especially if the contrast is with (what may be) the spotty success stories of self-governing small Aboriginal nations facing daunting odds.

Even within its focus on the self-governing Aboriginal nation, legal scholarship is curiously inattentive to the governing capacity of the Aboriginal nations whose interests it seeks to advance. While there are obvious variations in capacity depending on resources, population size, and community morality, the inescapable reality is that these will be small governments incapable of handling many of the activities of contemporary statehood. Legal analysis sometimes appears to confuse legal/constitutional capacity with effective governing capacity. The same shortcoming pervades the *Penner Report,* whose ringing advocacy of self-government for Indian bands – the equivalent of provincial powers, if not more – gives short shrift to the problems of capacity for governments whose population base is several hundred people. According to Ponting, using 1993 data, 282 of 609 Indian bands have populations of less than 500, and only 59 have more than 2,000, two-fifths of whom live off-reserve (1996 figures).[116] Even the Inuit, the largest concentrated Aboriginal community in Canada (84 percent of the estimated 1995 population of Nunavut – 24,900 – had some Inuit origins[117]), now in possession of quasi-provincial powers in Nunavut, face formidable difficulties.[118] While implementation of the RCAP proposals would increase the average nation size to 5,000-7,000, and treaty federalism might be based on even larger communities, population figures will probably still be below that of the smallest province. The geographic dispersal of the Métis and their heavy urban concentration makes the devising of workable self-government arrangements a challenge to institutional ingenuity. RCAP, after describing Métis self-governing proposals, excused itself from the task of judging their workability.

The 1982 addition of a Charter and Aboriginal rights to the Canadian Constitution has obviously heightened the significance of courts as policy arenas. Interest groups and social movements, supported by sympathetic lawyers, employ the courts to protect and expand their rights. Morton and Knopff have labelled the combination of social interests and the legal activists that support them the "Court Party." With the assistance of a steady stream of legal scholarship supportive of judicial interpretations favourable to the groups concerned, the separate components of the Court Party attempt to influence judicial decisions in preferred directions.[119]

Although Morton and Knopff do not explicitly focus on Aboriginal interests linked to Aboriginal clauses in the Charter and the Constitution Act, it is clear that law faculties' role in generating scholarship supportive of Aboriginal claims is analogous to the flood of Charter-supporting scholarship. Legal writings have fleshed out the initially unspecified meanings of the Aboriginal clauses in the 1982 Constitution

Act, challenged the traditional interpretation of s. 91(24) as giving legislative power over Indians to the federal government, and have greatly enhanced the significance of treaties in the constitutional order.

The contribution of legal scholarship to the advancement of Aboriginal peoples in the contemporary era is undeniable. That on the whole it has been an instrument of Aboriginal liberation will be the judgment of future historians. Yet legal scholarship by an intellectual vanguard in the service of a social movement has defects that are by-products of its virtues.[120]

Although legal scholarship does not speak with a single voice, diversity is not its strong point.[121] It verges on the monolithic in its focus on and support for maximum autonomy for self-governing Aboriginal nations. It displays minimal interest in Canadian citizenship, or in the more general question of what kind of overall Canadian community will coexist with Aboriginal self-government. What holds us together – why we should feel obligations to each other – is not on its agenda.[122] What is also overlooked are terribly important practical problems of what is possible for small populations to achieve even if financial and other support from the larger society is very generous. The legal approach, with its stress on rights and its search for maximum constitutional space for Aboriginal peoples pays little attention to the governing capacity of the nations its analysis serves. Furthermore, legal scholarship overwhelmingly focuses on territorially bounded, landed populations and shows minimal interest in urban populations with negligible possibilities of self-government. This, in turn, means that there is limited interest in Aboriginal peoples engaged in the most intense cultural interaction with the larger society – which will increasingly include growing numbers of the best educated. Finally, it is not self-evident that the focus on self-government, on breaking out, on maximizing constitutional space for Aboriginal peoples is realistic unless the appropriate relationship of mutuality is established with the majority society whose support is essential.

Peter Russell's summary is apposite:

> Even for those Aboriginal people who seek to recover and maintain a more autonomous condition, a very high degree of political and economic integration is inescapable. For the autonomy they seek is, of necessity, limited and conditional ... The self-governing communities they seek, in

order to satisfy material expectations ... will need large fiscal transfers from other orders of government especially in the early rebuilding stages. They cannot expect to receive this support and maintain a fruitful and mutually beneficial political association with the larger society unless they participate in the governing institutions of that society as active citizens rather than abrasive foreigners.[123]

The view of Canada that lies behind published research and policy advocacy depends on the question that is asked. The fundamental question for RCAP, as noted above, was how to maximize the autonomy of Aboriginal nations with a land base, the better to serve the goal of cultural rejuvenation. A similar question, with minor variations, drives much legal research. This introspective focus postulates maximum autonomy as the preferred goal. Although the saving clause "within Canada," is typically noted, relations with Canada are often described in instrumental terms. A pan-Canadian community engaged in common tasks, a coast-to-coast shared citizenship that knits us together in one of our dimensions as a single political people exists at best as a shadowy background reality with little substance. In much of this literature there is a deep, if implicit strain of separatism.

*Land Claims, Treaty Negotiations, Self-Government, and Citizenship*
The literature on these subjects is vast, daunting – and growing. It is impossible in a few pages to do more than highlight the major issues, tensions, and ambiguities that are constants as we try to come to grips with the surfacing complexities of how we are to live together. The broad perspective that is my goal will, no doubt, leave nuance behind, but the gain may be a surer grasp of the whole.

The prominence of land claims is a by-product of the 1973 Calder decision in which the Supreme Court held that the Nisga'a had had Aboriginal rights, which three of seven judges held had not been extinguished, leading the federal government to reverse its former denial that such rights existed (see above, pp. 170-1). Such rights were strengthened by s. 35(1) of the Constitution Act, 1982, which declared that "the existing aboriginal and treaty rights of the aboriginal peoples of Canada are hereby recognized and affirmed." As vast areas of Canada were not under treaty, particularly in British Columbia, the Yukon and the Northwest

Territories, Quebec, and Atlantic Canada, the federal government incrementally developed comprehensive land claims policy, punctuated by periodic inquiries that reported, usually negatively, on its adequacy.

There is close to unanimity among serious analysts that the federal goal of extinguishment of Aboriginal title is counterproductive. Aboriginal peoples oppose it because it strikes at their very identity. Its pursuit as a federal goal makes an already difficult process even more adversarial, and it does not generate the certainty that is its justification, as it leaves the Aboriginal party resentful.[124] Aboriginal criticism of the process and the federal criteria has been a constant. A fundamental process criticism was that the federal government had a conflict of interest in that it was simultaneously a party, and, supposedly, capable of objectively determining whether a claim should proceed, and determining the criteria for its resolution. By November 1997, twelve comprehensive claims had been resolved in Quebec and the Yukon and Northwest Territories. Various other negotiations were under way. In British Columbia, a unique British Columbia Treaty Commission to facilitate negotiations had emerged.

Recognition of the inherent right of self-government, and its implementation, has been the major policy goal of Aboriginal organizations since the 1970s. Four constitutional conferences tried and failed to reach agreement (1983-7) on the content of the right. Its recognition and implementation in a constitutionally entrenched third order of Aboriginal government was the central recommendation of RCAP (see Chapter 4 of this book). Its prominence springs from the colonialism analogy applied to the past treatment of Aboriginal peoples, escape from which is by self-government, given the unavailability of independence. It derives additional support from the pervasive beliefs that self-government gives dignity to those who possess it, and that the past policies that denied it have left a legacy, especially for status Indians, of which no one can be proud.

An examination of several of the key documents and academic analysis in these two key policy areas gives us a window on the developing constitutional theory applicable to the position of Aboriginal peoples in Canadian society.

I will avoid a well-trodden path in these discussions – the one that leads travellers to basic questions about whether land claims agreements should aim to extinguish Aboriginal rights, whether the negotiation process is fair, whether self-government is or is not an inherent right, and if so with what consequences. These are significant questions that deserve the debate they have engendered, and I do not mean to slight their importance by raising different ones that I believe to be equally important, although receiving lesser attention.

The settlement of comprehensive land claims and the implementation of an inherent right to self-government are unquestionably major constitutional developments. This is particularly so if, as is now possible under federal policy, self-government is included in comprehensive land claims. My question, writ large, is what constitutional theory underlies the discourse on land claims and self-government in some of the major official and unofficial contributions to policy discussion? In particular, what view emerges of how Aboriginal nations, and the individuals who belong to them, will fit into the Canadian constitutional framework? My particular concern is citizenship.

It would be reassuring if analysis of the discourse on land claims and on self-government uncovered something akin to a constitutional theory that gives direction to our endeavours. We are not so blessed. The federal government has signalled its unwillingness or inability to do constitutional thinking in public by its failure to respond intellectually to the RCAP *Report*, which, as argued in the previous chapter, falls short of adequacy. Perhaps, for the federal government, the humiliating retreat from the 1969 White Paper episode has confirmed the virtue of caution, of incrementalism (clearly the preferred strategy of Prime Minister Chrétien), of having theory emerge as a by-product of practice. Its preference for the concrete over the abstract is explicit in its approach to Aboriginal self-government. In a 1995 policy paper, it proposes "setting aside legal and constitutional debates that have stymied progress toward Aboriginal self-government and instead working out practical arrangements through negotiated agreements."[125] This is discussed below.

Two RCAP publications, *Treaty Making in the Spirit of Co-existence*[126] and *Partners in Confederation*,[127] reveal an Aboriginal perspective, given their genesis, on the meaning and purpose of land claims agreements and on self-government. Both publications, I argue, have serious shortcomings.

The main purpose of *Treaty Making* was to argue against the then federal policy that required extinguishment of undefined Aboriginal rights in return for specified treaty rights. The report argues compellingly that, given their spiritual relationship with the land, extinguishment produces a loss of identity for Aboriginal peoples.[128] The Commission then argues that the certainty and clarity that Ottawa seeks can be achieved without extinguishment. The Commission's proposals are reasonable and deserve serious consideration.

The premise of *Treaty Making,* so obvious as not to require discussion, is that there are two separate parties, the Aboriginal nation or band on the one side, and the Crown, represented by the federal government, on the other side. If, however, the Crown is assumed to be representing the interests of all Canadian citizens, there is a fundamental ambiguity or slippage in the dichotomous description of the parties. In the modern era, the federal government consistently claims that Aboriginal individuals are part of the Canadian community of citizens. They are citizens of Canada, and members of provincial/territorial communities. This differentiates modern treaty making from treaty making in the early decades of contact when the negotiating parties clearly were separate actors, and from the post-Confederation nineteenth-century treaties when status Indians were clearly not members of the Canadian civic community. Now, however, they are.

Aboriginal people, therefore, are represented on both sides of the table, respectively in their Aboriginal capacity, which *Treaty Making* addresses, and also in their Canadian capacity, for which the Crown speaks, and which *Treaty Making* overlooks. This is not the argument that the Crown has an obligation "to act in a fiduciary capacity with respect to aboriginal peoples,"[129] but that the Canadianness of Aboriginal peoples is to be represented and spoken for by the Crown. Even if the extreme argument is adopted that citizenship for Aboriginal peoples only emerges after a comprehensive agreement is in effect, the Crown nevertheless is responsible for speaking on behalf of the pending Canadian citizenship of the Aboriginal people who are negotiating a claim. The two parties negotiating, therefore, are much more complex than the initial image suggests, for they shade into each other.

*Partners in Confederation,* another RCAP publication, makes the case that s. 35 includes the right to self-government, and argues cogently that the s. 35 recognition of Aboriginal and treaty rights transformed the constitutional order by recognizing Aboriginal peoples as constitutional actors with protected rights deriving from their existence as organized self-governing societies when the European newcomers arrived. *Partners in Confederation* makes it clear that self-government is to be within Canada, and that Aboriginal peoples and governments are now part of a complex system of federal and provincial governments. Accordingly, the inherent Aboriginal right of self-government "involves *circumscribed* rather than *unlimited* powers."[130] The report adds that "whereas Aboriginal peoples were once like trees growing in relative isolation on an open plain, they are now more like trees in a grove, co-existing with others in a complex ecological system. So, while the ancient pine of Aboriginal governance is still rooted in the same soil, from which it draws its sustenance, it is now linked in various intricate ways with neighbouring governments."[131]

Although *Partners in Confederation* indicates that self-government can mean many things, "including participating more actively in new or existing institutions of public government at the federal, provincial, regional or territorial levels,"[132] the overwhelming focus is on relationships between separate parties. Hence it sees and privileges relationships among governments, not citizens.

Accordingly, both *Partners in Confederation* and *Treaty Making*, which deal, respectively, with the inherent right to self-government and the negotiation of comprehensive land claims, structure the discussion in such a way that they cannot or will not, or in any case do not, in more than a cursory way, face the reality that the citizens of Aboriginal nations are also part of the Canadian and provincial communities. This is implicitly admitted, simply by accepting "within Canada" or "*circumscribed ...* powers," but not confronted. To do so would require dropping the image of discrete actors and admitting that we all share citizenship in the Canadian and provincial communities. This is not a small difference. To accept it transforms our understanding of what we are doing, and changes our understanding of who we are. To deny it is to ask if "within Canada" means anything, and to ask if Aboriginal people negotiating a land claim or self-government are to be thought of as having citizen links with the federal and provincial governments that are the agents circumscribing First Nation governing powers.

We badly misperceive what is happening if the picture in our mind's eye is one of two separate actors, each distinct from the other, bargaining the terms of their future relationship – the connections they will construct to link their prior solitudes together. They will meet at the bargaining table nation-to-nation and they will leave with a nation-to-nation agreement that governs their future interactions. This image of separate actors who have struck a deal in which each sacrifices some independence of action for the benefits of a rule-governed interdependence misleads us. Yet versions of it are common.

A recent rigorous analysis of the comprehensive claims process by two leading scholars supportive of Aboriginal positions shares with RCAP publications the view of separate actors striking an agreement.[133] The policy proposal of Michael Asch and Norman Zlotkin is to restructure the claims negotiating process so that the federal government gives up its goal of extinguishing Aboriginal title in exchange for defined treaty rights, and accepts the desirability of affirming Aboriginal title. This view, which verges on being a developing conventional wisdom among critics of existing federal policy, is seen as better suited to produce the certainty and stability sought by the federal government than is the existing policy it aims to replace.

The objective of claims policy is variously described by Asch and Zlotkin as "mutual accommodation,"[134] and a "mutually legitimating partnership among equals."[135] The Aboriginal perspective, which they support, is to establish "ongoing political and legal relationships between Aboriginal collectivities and the Crown,"[136] "to shape a relationship between Aboriginal people and the newcomers based upon sharing, ... [to clarify] how Aboriginal people and non-Aboriginal people will accommodate each other."[137] Asch and Zlotkin sympathetically describe the above-noted mutual accommodation goals of negotiation for Aboriginal people as being "the same as it has always been, since the time of the first historic treaty."[138] This "sameness," however, is unattainable. The original treaties were between separate actors in a mini-international system. Contemporary treaties are situated in a federal system in which Aboriginal peoples are also part of the very communities with whom they are bargaining. The goal is not to readjust relations in an international system, but to rearrange domestic relations in a common country to which we all belong.

This analysis, which presupposes separate actors working out the nature of their future relationship, leaves out other realities. After the resolution of land claims, the Aboriginal beneficiaries will also be citizen members of territorial/provincial and Canadian communities. Indeed, they are part of those communities while they are negotiating a new relationship. In constitutional terms, Aboriginal nations negotiating land claims agreements are not simply rearranging their relations with an external other, not simply deciding what kind of neighbours they should be. They are rearranging the extent and nature of their ongoing membership in provincial or territorial communities and the nature of their citizenship in the Canadian community and their civic links to the federal government. The issue is not relations with an external "other" but a new pattern of involvement with three communities, each of which responds to one segment of what it means to be an Aboriginal individual – the federal, provincial/territorial, and land claims community. While this may be implicitly understood by the Aboriginal nation while it is in negotiation, and by scholars who seek a fairer and more workable set of criteria for resolving claims, its explicit understanding would give us a better grasp of what we are really doing in reaching land claims agreements.

Thus the RCAP has company in having difficulty in handling the complex reality of multiple civic identities in a federal system that is generating yet another level of civic identity by constitutionally entrenched land claims agreements and recognition of the inherent right of Aboriginal self-government. Much of the academic and some of the official discussion of comprehensive land claims treats the bargaining process and the goal of an agreement as a self-contained world in isolation from the larger Canadian constitutional context. The report of the Honourable A.C. Hamilton dealing with the issue of extinguishment in land claims agreements repeatedly refers to the goal of establishing an ongoing relationship between two or more peoples.[139] This image of separate actors, each with a distinct existence, once again distracts our attention from the political and constitutional reality that federal and provincial governments do not speak only for non-Aboriginal Canadians and that the spokespeople for the individual Aboriginal nation or party do not monopolize the entire identity of those they represent.

There are many reasons why this reality is concealed. The "nation-to-nation" image does not help us to see that the parties shade into each other. While it may not preclude, it certainly does not reinforce the idea that the negotiators share a common citizenship, especially when nego-tiations are difficult and stretch over years. Land claims negotiations generate solidarities on both sides, which make it difficult to remember that there is or will be a common shared civic identity. Justice Hamilton repeatedly stressed the deep suspicion and distrust, well founded in his estimation, that Aboriginal peoples bring to negotiations.[140] The Department of Indian Affairs and the federal government are viewed "as adversaries, who look after the needs and demands of others."[141] These sentiments generate little inclination to see the federal and provincial governments as representing different aspects of the overall identity of Aboriginal peoples in negotiations that are inherently adversarial. Even if the federal and provincial governments on the other side of the table are fairly representing the total membership of their own societies, political majoritarianism makes it difficult for them not to be cast by their opponents in a non-Aboriginal image.

The natural tendency to see federal and provincial governments as representing only non-Aboriginal Canadians is reinforced by the weak Aboriginal representation in federal and provincial legislatures and cabi-nets. The francophone Québécois observing negotiations between Quebec and Ottawa can scarcely be unaware that they are simultaneously repre-sented by both parties. Aboriginal peoples are not so circumstanced. Further, and most important, the Aboriginal allegiance to and identifica-tion with their own nation and its government are almost certainly stronger than allegiance to and identification with their federal and provincial counterparts. Nevertheless, since neither the purpose nor the outcome of land claims agreements is to produce an independent Abo-riginal nation-state, the consequence of that fact should not be ignored. Completed land claims agreements, particularly if self-government is part of the agreements, are statements about the mix of Aboriginal, provincial/territorial, and Canadian identities – prospective if initially only weakly present in the Aboriginal citizens enjoying a new land claims agreement. Admittedly, the Canadian and provincial dimensions of the future status of members of self-governing land claims communities are vigorously inserted into the debate by federal and provincial govern-ments. Their approach, however, has its own, if different, shortcomings, as noted below in a discussion of the treaty-making and self-government policies of British Columbia and the federal government, respectively.

The position of the government of British Columbia, virtually all of which is without treaty, fits prospective treaties firmly into the Canadian and provincial framework.[142] Treaties will not create separate countries or justice systems. Treaty settlement land will be part of British Columbia and Canada. The British Columbia position paper on self-government consistently refers to "all British Columbians" as an inclusive category. It notes that the Charter will apply, and goes on to elaborate a lengthy list of subject matters where "the province will ensure the maintenance of Province-wide standards ... [including] education, social services, labour laws, consumer protection, health and safety, motor vehicle licensing and traffic regulation, housing, environmental protection and assessment, fish and wildlife management and land-use planning and zoning." The pre-eminent concern of the British Columbia government in land claims negotiations is to "maintain the ability to govern the province to the limits of its constitutional jurisdiction." The authority of an Aboriginal government is not to extend beyond its land base and is to be "circumscribed by provincial standards."[143] In another position paper, the British Columbia Ministry of Aboriginal Affairs asserted that after treaties had been implemented, the s. 87 Indian Act tax exemption for Indians would be "phased out" and First Nations members will pay taxes to both the province and Canada.[144] In yet another position paper, the British Columbia Ministry of Aboriginal Affairs indicated that sovereignty was not negotiable, that treaty settlement land will be "only a small part of the traditional territory" and that British Columbia has no interest in "recreating the past," or in basing contemporary treaties "solely on evidence from the past."[145] The British Columbia position will be further discussed immediately following a short presentation of the federal government policy on self-government.

A comprehensive examination of the federal role in extending self-government would include various sectoral moves, including transferring education jurisdiction to the Micmac in Nova Scotia; the dismantling of the Department of Indian Affairs and Northern Development in Manitoba and the transfer of responsibilities to Manitoba First Nations; and earlier moves to self-government for the Cree, Naskapi, and Inuit in northern Quebec under provincial local government legislation as part of the James Bay and Quebec agreements. The complexities of the overall position are too great for detailed discussion in this short section.[146]

The basic federal government position is elaborated in Ronald Irwin's 1995 policy statement *Aboriginal Self-Government*. Its position is no less emphatic than that of British Columbia in insisting that its recognition of the inherent right of self-government requires its implementation within the Canadian constitutional framework, and falls short of sovereignty. In fact, its implementation "should enhance the participation of Aboriginal peoples in the Canadian federation, and ensure that Aboriginal peoples and their governments do not exist in isolation, separate and apart from the rest of Canadian society."[147] That inclusiveness requires the application of the Charter of Rights and Freedoms to Aboriginal governments.[148] From the federal perspective, the jurisdiction of Aboriginal governments will likely extend "to matters that are internal to the group, integral to its distinct Aboriginal culture, and essential to its operation as a government or institution."[149] In some areas neither integral to Aboriginal culture nor internal to the group, but where some Aboriginal jurisdiction might be negotiated, it will be subject to federal and provincial paramountcy. No deviation will be allowed "from the basic principle that those federal and provincial laws of overriding national or provincial importance will prevail over conflicting Aboriginal laws."[150] Finally, there is a lengthy list of subject matters "where there are no compelling reasons for Aboriginal governments or institutions to exercise law-making authority."[151] They include subject matters related to sovereignty, defence and external relations, and "other National Interest Powers" including management of the national economy, national law and order, health and safety, and specific federal undertakings such as aeronautics and the postal service.

The list of powers reserved to the federal government, coupled with the position of the British Columbia government help to clarify the direction in which two of the most concerned governments – Ottawa because of its Aboriginal responsibilities, and British Columbia because of the magnitude of the outstanding claims in the province – wish to take us. In neither case does the tone suggest that the government is speaking nation-to-nation to equals, nor however that it is speaking to a subset of its own citizens. Both governments speak the language of authority, stating what has to be. They are protective documents, stating the limits to self-government – this far and no farther. They are adversarial, staking out a counter-position. Further, although references to the

Charter are something of an exception, the language is that of governments, not of citizens. Even where a phrase is inclusive, such as "all British Columbians," the tone is more of rejecting difference than embracing commonality. What appears to happen in the claim/self-government negotiating process is that the federal and provincial governments impose the Canadian constraints and the Aboriginal party injects the "nation" demands for recognition.[152]

Thus both British Columbian and federal positions leave the impression that external controls and limits are to be imposed on Aboriginal governments, and that major powers are to be wielded by what, by inference, are non-Aboriginal governments. Of course, they are not. They are Canadian and provincial governments responsible to all of their residents/citizens, including Aboriginal citizens. To fail to underline this point is to reinforce the idea that the self-governing Aboriginal community is the only significant community to which its members belong. This reinforces the very isolation that the federal government claims it is seeking to end. It strengthens the false idea that self-government (and land claims) negotiations take place between bargaining agents for discrete communities – the Aboriginal nation, and federal and provincial communities. This, however, is not so. In the same way, as the resident of a province is simultaneously a Canadian citizen and a member of the pan-Canadian community, the citizen of an Aboriginal nation is also – even when land claims negotiations are under way – constitutionally a citizen of Canada and a resident of a province or territory. That is what "within Canada" means. These constitutionally based multiple civic identities are central to clear thinking, even if Aboriginal enthusiasm for Canadian citizenship is occasionally tepid, and attitudes to the provinces often even less positive.

The pressure to see the "other" as truly "other," rather than as part of oneself is likely to be reinforced by negotiating processes that engender solidarity sentiments on both sides. Such sentiments make it difficult for the Aboriginal party to see part of him- or herself in the bargaining adversary, and for the federal and provincial governments to keep in the forefront of their own minds that they are negotiating with their own citizens – who are members of the federal and provincial communities, as well as members of Aboriginal nations. Governments need to remember that they are *not* non-Aboriginal governments. Thus, although the British Columbia government states that it "represents all the citizens of British Columbia at the table,"[153] the tenor of its policy documents, no doubt influenced by the adversarial structure of the negotiating process, suggests that its major task is to represent non-Aboriginal British Columbians. The process intended to culminate in an act of recognition, pursues its goal by fostering a negotiation-produced distinction between Aboriginal and non-Aboriginal British Columbians.

The inevitable consequence of treaty lands, and of self-government jurisdictions that straddle what are otherwise federal and provincial jurisdictions, especially if self-government is constitutionalized, is to set the members of self-governing nations somewhat apart from their provincial neighbours and from standard membership in the Canadian community. This is perhaps better described not as a consequence, but as the very purpose of treaty lands, and of jurisdictional powers that draw their sustenance from the inherent right to self-government. The goal is a special self-governing sphere of authority on their own lands, which withdraws the nation's members, to the extent of their government's jurisdiction, from federal, provincial, and territorial membership. The essential constitutional task is to maximize the benefits and minimize the costs of the differentiation.

Given the momentum behind this institutional differentiation, the reinforcement of contrary tendencies is desirable. The most obvious vehicle for that reinforcement is citizenship. That requires, first, underlining the reality of simultaneous membership in Aboriginal, provincial, and Canadian communities. Second, the massive interdependence of Aboriginal and non-Aboriginal peoples in terms of culture, economy, and intermarriage needs to be kept in mind whenever images of separate societies coexisting side by side threaten to take hold of our imagination. Further, regrettably perhaps, but inescapably, the need for a flow of resources from the Canadian people, through governments, to Aboriginal nations is more likely to be met if they are seen to belong to the Canadian community, for which citizenship is the obvious symbol. All Aboriginal policy, land claims and self-government included, should be guided by the understanding that Aboriginal people are members of provincial and territorial communities and belong to the Canadian citizen community as well as to their own nations. Language that implies that Canada is a container for an international system of separate nations held together by treaty should be rejected for its lack of realism.

It would be naïve to assume that a magic wand can bring into being at the level of emotions a strong sense of citizenship belonging by Aboriginal peoples. History forbids such an outcome. We need not, however, give added momentum to the divisive legacy of history. The positive goals of the settlement of land claims and enhanced powers of self-government need to be thought of as complementary, not rivals, to a Canadian citizenship that reinforces the "oneness" that introspective diversities threaten to challenge.

The possibility of that complementarity is increased if, as is likely, a claims settlement stimulates Aboriginal pride and generates income-raising economic activity among Aboriginal peoples. Further, as a recent comparative survey of land claims settlements concluded, "indigenous peoples have used the land claims process as a basis for participating more fully in the broader economy and, typically, have become more heavily involved with the non-indigenous population as a result of the treaty."[154] This surely will enhance the status of Aboriginal peoples in the eyes of non-Aboriginal Canadians.

The long-run impact of completed comprehensive claims on conceptions of community, on how much of a "we" develops, is ambiguous. The outcome depends on the subsequent behaviour of the parties to the settlement. The likelihood of a positive outcome will surely be increased if the process leading up to it reminds the participants of the common community to which they belong. This will be especially important in British Columbia where, unlike the other modern land claims settlements in Canada, which have mostly been in remote areas, Aboriginal and non-Aboriginal people are intermingled, and third-party interests are "of vital significance."[155] Even in Manitoba, where the dismantling of the Indian Affairs branch and the transfer of its functions to First Nations is under way, a much less fundamental change than confronts British Columbia, provincial government spokespeople have queried whether the provincial government would have "any obligations to citizens of self-governing First Nations, including their off-reserve members."[156]

*Political Science and "What Will Hold Us Together?"*
Foster and Grove, discussing the tension between judges and lawyers and expert academic witnesses from disciplines other than law, observe

that "different disciplines ask different questions and seek different kinds of responses."[157] Those differences are strikingly evident between political science and law, which suggest that the monopoly of any single discipline in academic discussions of the future of a people is to be avoided. The approaches of political science and law to the future relationship of Aboriginal and non-Aboriginal peoples may be complementary. They are, however, clearly not the same.

The unasked question, which remains unanswered when the goal of autonomy crowds out togetherness, or when nationalism pushes a common citizenship to the margins of consciousness is "What will hold us together?" Is there any common "we" group to which we all belong? Is a shared geography and propinquity enough to sustain feelings of responsibility for each other that transcend the historical Aboriginal/non-Aboriginal divide that we have inherited?

These are central questions that recur in a small body of literature written mainly by political scientists.[158] Their concern is with the whole. They assume the necessity of a degree of common civic identity as one of the glues that hold the country together. They believe that the degree of concern we have for each other is a function of the strength of the common "we" group to which we belong. If the latter is weak or nonexistent, so too will be the bonds of sympathy. Further, they note that respect for and encouragement of territorially based diversity is only half the meaning of federalism. The other half is a common citizenship in a single country. Federalism, therefore, presupposes divided civic identities, as well as a division of powers. If the goal of the political élites in the 1860s had been to maximize diversity, they would have broken the United Province of Canada into its two component parts – the later Ontario and Quebec – let each go its own way, and left Atlantic Canada as four distinct colonies. Their goal, however, was very different – to reconcile and accommodate diversity in the new country whose leaders had the task of fostering a Canadian identity and pan-Canadian political nationality to sustain the common endeavours they wished Canadians of the future to undertake.

From this perspective, the landmark *Penner Report* on self-government, with its recommendation that "self-government would mean that virtually the entire range of law-making, policy, program delivery, law enforcement and adjudication powers would be available to an Indian First

Nation government within its territory"[159] would cut the links between individual Indians and the Canadian government. Gibbins and Ponting note that Indians would virtually cease to be Canadian citizens. They could not be taxed by other governments, and the *Penner Report* fails to mention electoral links with those governments. The primary link of Indian people with the federal government would be through the intermediary of their Indian governments.[160]

Gibbins and Ponting argue the inappropriateness of such a model, and propose that the Canadian government impose conditions on self-government "to protect the values of Canadian citizenship and to ensure some minimal degree of political integration of Aboriginal individuals into the Canadian political process."[161] Bryan Schwartz offers the related criticism that the report "often reads more like an advocate's brief for Indian political autonomy than a balanced appraisal of how that goal can and should be reconciled with the interests of the larger Canadian community."[162] Ponting and Gibbins also note that to confine the citizens of Aboriginal governments only to their own government is to diminish their involvement in and connection to large affairs of state – foreign policy, postsecondary education, and economic policy, for example – that will continue to be handled by federal and provincial governments.[163] Indirectly, this is a reminder of the limited capacity of Aboriginal governments, of the important policy areas that will elude even the most optimistic assessment of their jurisdiction, and accordingly that their involvement in federal and provincial politics remains fundamental to advancing their interests.[164]

Samuel LaSelva joins Gibbins and Ponting in noting the dangers in some of the rationales for and descriptions of Aboriginal self-government. Some of the justifications, he notes, overlook the factual and moral interdependence of Aboriginal and other Canadians, postulate coexisting solitudes sharing only geography, are hostile or indifferent to the divided identities of federalism and the common country-wide citizenship it assumes – the latter being an essential support for a positive response to Aboriginal claims for fiscal and other resources – and portray radically incommensurable ways of life that destroy the possibility of a common community. LaSelva also notes that the idea of treaty federalism captures only the provincial – not the Canadian – dimension of federalism. He concludes that "Aboriginal emancipation has paradoxical qualities.

Canadian Aboriginals are victims of colonization, yet their emancipation presupposes the rejection of decolonization."[165] The constitutional imperative to LaSelva, accordingly, is to recognize and respond to the legacy of colonialism, while building a positive relationship with the majority society that accommodates Aboriginal distinctiveness, and accepts the interdependence of Aboriginal and non-Aboriginal Canadians.

Similar arguments recur in writings by other political scientists, one of whose disciplinary mandates is to analyze the sources of cohesion and fragmentation in divided societies. Peter Russell's summary is apposite: "Native autonomy and integration must be treated not as choices but as parallel and interacting paths. The path of integration cannot be followed by indigenous people without positive regard for the benefits of participating in the life of the larger and newer society."[166] These arguments are not the last gasp of an imperial mentality resisting an unwelcome erosion of yesterday's complacent paternalism. They are, on the contrary, intended to channel choice in directions that will produce a better and more secure future for Aboriginal peoples. Further, they are congruent with research findings from the 1970s demonstrating that the clear preference among nine Aboriginal communities was "to develop as Aboriginal Peoples while integrating with, and within the larger Canadian society."[167]

### Interdependence and Other Realities

Jeff Spinner recently described the relation of Old Order Amish to the American state as "partial citizenship." They "opt out of mainstream [American] society ... [and] choose to forgo liberal citizenship ... [They are] a community apart from the political community in the United States, a community that wants to stay apart. The Amish are *in* the United States, but not *of* the United States."[168] The Amish are good examples of internal parallelism, of opting out; in terms of their separateness, they are a good example of the two-row wampum portrayal of coexisting societies with different goals, limited interdependence, and minimal interference with each other.

Aboriginal peoples are not Canadian counterparts of Old Order Amish. They do not seek the degree of apartness practised by the Amish. Their way of life is neither in fact nor intention insulated from the larger society. Although they seek to reinvigorate their cultures and draw nourishment from tradition, as in the selection of leaders, they are inescapably caught up in modernity and do not wish it to be otherwise. They are, therefore, unlike the Amish, both *in* Canada and *of* Canada. Their relationship to the state is best described as differentiated citizenship rather than partial citizenship. They lack the inward-looking avoidance of the larger society practised by the Amish. They also lack the latter's self-sufficiency. They are inextricably caught up in interdependent relations with Canadian society, of which they are an integral part.

The interdependence that invalidates the two-row wampum image of our present and future relationship – two societies travelling in separate vessels down the river of life, sharing the same river, but not interfering with each other's choice of direction – is a massive reality, not a rhetorical ploy. Behind the language of nation-to-nation, and the adversary process of negotiating land claims, the intertwining of our existence rebukes the thesis that we are no more than what divides us. Our interdependence is evident in the high rate of intermarriage cited above.[169] As early as the mid-1950s, nearly 37 percent of all Indian marriages in British Columbia were with non-Indians. Hawthorn et al. predicted that mixed marriages would increase, and also hypothesized that the number of individuals with "Indian racial descent living with White status in the general community" was about the same as the number "living as band members." "Racially speaking," they concluded, "the legal Indians are becoming assimilated to the general population."[170]

Australian and American data tell similar stories of extensive marital, common law, or more casual sexual relationships. In Australia, 60 percent of Aboriginal children in the past generation have had a non-Aboriginal father or mother.[171] By 1990, over 56 percent of Native Americans lived in urban areas, compared to 13 to 14 percent at mid-century and 0.4 percent in 1900. Nearly 60 percent of Native Americans are married to non-Indians.[172] Only 22 percent of individuals claiming some Indian ancestry identified themselves as Indian.[173] The overall result is a probable weakening of "the identity of Native Americans as distinctive tribal peoples tied to specific geographical areas."[174]

These trends are only the most extreme versions of what was referred to in Chapter 3 as a "modernizing Aboriginality" – an ongoing, selective, eclectic incorporation of values, behaviours, and identities with their updated Aboriginal counterparts. The context for this cultural incorporation is what Anthony Giddens describes as "de-traditionalization" brought about by "globalizing processes [which] ... bring together a diversity of newly visible worlds and ways of life. Anyone who persists with a traditional way of doing things cannot but be aware that many other life practices exist."[175] Emma La Rocque, a Plains Cree Métis, supports Giddens by noting "that we live in a contemporary world ... This means we have many worlds from which to draw with respect to ideals of human rights or healing ... Native peoples do not have only things of the past for our resources."[176]

These processes of cultural contact and change generate contradictory interpretations. Thus the Assembly of First Nations decried the Canadian Charter of Rights and Freedoms as a foreign instrument that should be rejected. The Native Women's Association of Canada credited it with the restoration of status for Indian women who had lost it by outmarriage, and insisted on its application to future self-governing Aboriginal nations as a protection against abuses of power. RCAP claimed that some of the Charter's roots could be found in Aboriginal traditions.[177]

This interdependence and mutual borrowing does not challenge the desirability of self-government. If anything, it strengthens the arguments in its favour by giving it the task of exerting some control over the process of change that, responsive to the facts of demography and power, disproportionately flows from non-Aboriginal to Aboriginal peoples.

This interdependence, however, also underlines the magnitude of the connections between Aboriginal and non-Aboriginal Canadians. The smaller societies need the support of the latter if they are to thrive. As Chief Justice Lamer said in *Delgamuukw,* "Let us face it, we are all here to stay."[178] This was an elaboration of his observation in *Gladstone* that "distinctive Aboriginal societies exist within, and are a part of a broader social, political and economic community."[179] These realities should be seen not as an unhappy fate, but as an opportunity. Fortunately, this perspective is beginning to be used by Aboriginal scholars, and practised by some Aboriginal associations.

### An Outward-Looking Aboriginality

John Borrows, an Aboriginal law professor then at the University of British Columbia, consciously departed in a recent paper from what he took to be the focus of "some who have spent a tremendous amount of time and effort developing messages of an exclusive citizenship and measured separation for Indians through a form of self-government." He went on to argue, clearly aware of his own heterodoxy, that this focus, while necessary, was insufficient and limiting. He stressed various "intercultural forces" – education, urbanization, politics, and inter-marriage – that are undermining separate spheres of existence. For Borrows, the appropriate response to these realities was full and whole-hearted participation in Canadian affairs – in politics, business, the judiciary, and other prominent arenas: "Aboriginal people must transmit and use their culture in matters beyond 'Aboriginal' affairs." Borrows denied that he was recommending assimilation, or that in some way he was violating historic treaties. He countered these accusations by denying that "Aboriginal" had a fixed meaning, or that an identity referred to a single trait. "We are traditional, modern, and post-modern people." He reinterpreted the two-row wampum as supportive of "mutuality ... interconnectedness" and of an Aboriginal conception of citizenship that could encompass non-Aboriginal peoples. To Borrows, vigorous participation in Canadian affairs is not only dictated by realism, but also by the excitement of trying to introduce Aboriginality into the majority Canadian society – its conceptions of citizenship, relations with the land, and the exercise of power.[180]

In the article just described, Borrows summed up a socio-political theory that is woven throughout his writings. An initial premise is "that we cannot ... ignore the world we live in ... In reconstructing our world we cannot just do what we want."[181] Accordingly, in his publications he engages in a constant search for a meeting ground between Aboriginal values, practices, and identities and their counterparts in the surrounding majority society. Thus, although the impact of the Charter on First Nations communities has been disruptive, on balance he welcomed its arrival. He sees considerable congruity between its precepts and First Nations values. The meeting place of the Charter's objectives and First Nations traditions constitutes a fruitful opportunity for First Nations "to recapture the strength of principles which were often eroded through government interference."[182]

Elsewhere, in an article where he identifies himself as an Anishinabe and a Canadian citizen,[183] he seeks to build bridges between traditional First Nations law and the American, English, and international regimes that have influenced the Canadian law dealing with Aboriginal peoples. His hope is that the former will become "a dynamic, relevant, and integral part of Canadian law,"[184] with the assistance of the growing number of First Nations lawyers – over 300 in 1996[185] – who can be helpful intermediaries, a role he himself plays.

In a general discussion of the utility of legal research from an Aboriginal perspective, he foresees a "'fusion of horizons' between 'western' and Native accounts of law." The result, he hopes, will be a new language of law, a synthesis drawn from "diverse cultural understandings ... [with] the potential to transform traditional legal doctrine."[186] He resists what he sees as the false dichotomy between "traditional versus adopted self-government" because the exercising of self-government "had to incorporate the connections which life together on the same continent demanded. Therefore, the argument as to whether to accept or reject Western institutions in the exercise of self-government is misleading. While the exercise of power may have its source in the inherent right of self-government, the exercise of the power transpires in a fashion that is completely new to the people employing it. The exercise of authority is neither adopted nor traditional, but is an amalgamation of the two perspectives."[187]

Other articles partake of the same spirit of bridge-building and mutuality,[188] without overlooking how the making of agreements with non-Aboriginal neighbours has difficulty accommodating "those elements of traditional native culture which encourage autonomy from modern society. This hazard occurs because the intersection of native and non-native interests occurs at a point of convergence in the values of native and non-native society which give merit to the benefits of 'western material society.'"[189]

Borrows' enterprise, as the previous cautionary note reminds us, is not assimilation. He is a passionate defender of self-government and the strengthened Aboriginality to which it can contribute. His goal, however, is more ambitious than self-government – to inject the contemporary manifestations of updated Aboriginal traditions into the law and policy of the contemporary Canadian state. In his understanding, the dignity of self-government needs to be supplemented by the dignity that comes from making contributions to the larger society. That cannot be done if Euro-Canadian society is seen as a malevolent, implacable enemy, contact with which is a kind of contamination.

Borrows' message is repeated in more prosaic, policy-oriented language by the Federation of Saskatchewan Indian Nations (FSIN) in its recently published monograph, *Saskatchewan and Aboriginal Peoples in the 21st Century: Social, Economic and Political Changes and Challenges.*[190] Without explicitly saying so, this well-researched work powerfully argues a counter-position to the RCAP *Report*. There is no dwelling on past mistreatment, no attempt to instil guilt in the majority, and no appeal to rights as the rationale for better treatment. The monograph is simply a straightforward appeal for help to fellow members of a common community, one of whose peoples is in trouble. It expresses an undifferentiated concern simultaneously for on-reserve and off-reserve Indian peoples. Its focus is the common future of all the people in Saskatchewan. Explicit, enhanced positive participation in normal provincial politics is a goal. There is no suggestion of a two-row wampum of separate paths. The goal of Aboriginal peoples is "nothing less than to re-invent Saskatchewan."[191] The then chief of the FSIN, Blaine C. Favel, refers to the "common futures" of Aboriginal and non-Aboriginal peoples.[192] Elsewhere, the report underlines the devastation caused by the historic separate existence of First Nations people that removed them from the concerns of the non-Aboriginal majority, busily engaged in province-building. That isolation is rejected as neither possible nor desirable for Aboriginal people, who will constitute nearly one-third of the Saskatchewan population by the year 2045 and are already urbanizing very rapidly.[193]

The FSIN report, as was true of Borrows' analysis, is not advocating assimilation, or rejecting self-government, or sacrificing Indianness on the altar of modernization. Its study is a response to the brutal reality that if present trends of unemployment, social exclusion, and anomic conditions continue unchecked, the results for both Aboriginal and non-Aboriginal peoples will be catastrophic. The explicit, guiding premise is that only by becoming fully involved in the Saskatchewan community will Aboriginal peoples become part of the province-wide "we" community and thus have the moral levers to engage the majority as fellow citizens in tackling poverty and social malaise. The premise is that a common citizenship is the source of empathy.

The proposals of Borrows and the FSIN are controversial, but then so are the contrary proposals of RCAP, proposals based on a traditional two-row wampum vision and all arguments that stress self-government *and* minimize citizenship connections with the majority society. My argument is that the hope for a better future for Aboriginal peoples, and the possibility of an enduring viable relationship between Aboriginal and non-Aboriginal peoples is found in the arguments of Borrows and the FSIN. They display a too rare capacity to find and occupy the middle ground.

*Empathy and Citizenship*

There is general agreement that our willingness to share with others is broadly dependent on our joint membership in a common community.[194] In a recent paper, Keith Banting notes the significance of the "prevailing sense of community" in discriminating between legitimate community members and outsiders.[195] A 1969 federal government publication outlined the importance of the "sense of Canadian community" as both the origin and consequence of income distribution among individuals and across regions.[196] Banting speculates that a weakened pan-Canadian community could only diminish our feelings of responsibility for each other.[197]

Similar arguments are voiced by Charles Taylor who, in earlier publications,[198] has advocated the recognition of "deep diversity" communities – Aboriginal and Québécois in Canada – in ways that would give their members minimal connection to the federal government as individual citizens. In a recent short piece, "Why Democracy Needs Patriotism," by contrast, he refers to the necessity in democratic societies of "strong identification on the part of their citizens," of a citizen conviction "that their political society is a common venture of considerable moment," and to contemporary states needing "a high degree of mobilization of their members, [which] occurs around common identities." Further, to reduce alienation among minorities and the disadvantaged democratic societies must implement redistributive policies that "require a high degree of mutual commitment."[199]

The American scholar John Higham concurs in his thesis that major improvements in black-white relationships require "an inclusive national community," some "larger identity, some greater loyalty, ... [some] wider solidarity" as the supportive context for a reform-oriented "partnership between blacks and an influential segment of the white population."[200] He is in broad agreement with another scholar of

Afro-American/white relationships in the United States, George M. Fredrickson, that the stress on "black power" and "black ethnic solidarity and the disavowal of integration as a primary goal of African Americans" has increased the difficulty of finding white allies.[201]

These arguments and interpretations by Canadian and American scholars can only be applied to the situation of Aboriginal peoples in Canada with a full recognition of their separate histories, the identities forged by the latter, their national status, and their realized and prospective self-governing situation. However, it seems undeniable that a considerable validity attaches to the thesis that there is some positive relationship between our willingness to help each other and the degree to which we feel ourselves to be members of a common community of citizens. This proposition may, of course, be refuted, or alternative sources of mutual commitment may be advocated with supporting evidence. To ignore the proposition, however, is irresponsible.

### Conclusion

The premises behind the analysis of this chapter, and indeed behind the larger enterprise of writing this book, are not complicated. We are at a turning point. The past treatment of Aboriginal peoples is neither a source of pride, nor a record of success. The elementary question that confronts us is which path do we follow in our search for a more fruitful relationship between Aboriginal and non-Aboriginal peoples in Canada. We do not have a clean slate. The momentum behind the drive to self-government and the support for the positive recognition of the Aboriginal presence in Canada are irresistible imperatives to which a wholehearted "Yes" is the only answer. On the other hand, the conditions that sustained the nation-to-nation relations of the early contact period have vanished. Our nation-to-nation relationship then was international. It is not so now and hence to so describe it even if only implicitly, without qualification, risks a damaging confusion.

We are locked in an inescapable interdependence. This is dramatically so in the city. The tendency for the drive to self-government to lead to scholarly, political, and governmental neglect of the growing urban Aboriginal population needs to be resisted. The city is a locale where more and more success stories will be carved out if adaptation to the urban environment can be facilitated.

We are all part of one another, although not always harmoniously so. The future of Aboriginal peoples, whether or not they have a land base that is a requisite for effective self-government, is within Canada. If that "withinness" means that Canada is to be more than a container, or a mini-international system, we need bonds of empathy so that our togetherness is moral as well as geographical. The obvious moral bond is a shared citizenship, although there may for some time be variations in allegiance to it. Constitutional policy, accordingly, should be both sensitive to Aboriginality leading to Nunavut and a third order of Aboriginal government, and supportive of a Canadian dimension of belonging. We should not so structure our institutional arrangements that every Aboriginal interaction with the state – third order, territorial, provincial, federal, municipal – has to be suffused with Aboriginality.

It is not an act of prospective cultural imperialism – assimilation in a new guise – to hope for and view positively a future in which, more than occasionally, we jointly participate in common ventures as Canadian citizens or as residents of particular provinces as well as expressing and reinforcing Aboriginality in self-governing nations. I agree with the eloquent language of Brian Slattery who, after advocating institutional arrangements – governmental and international – that sustain multiple allegiances, continued, "the human need for community can never be fully satisfied by a single, all-encompassing group, no matter how rich or pervasive its culture. Indeed, such a group would stifle the deep-seated need for a broad and varied range of communal bonds that overlap and intersect, jostling among themselves for our allegiance. In a word, community demands communities."[202]

This suggests to me that the scholarly community as a whole, in addition to the passionate and rigorous intellectual support offered in support of Aboriginal rights, including self-government, needs to shift some resources toward the issue of how a multinational people, if that is where we are heading, can be more than an aggregation of separate nations who share indifference to each other. It may be, of course, that I suffer from a failure of imagination. Possibly I am wedded to ideas of statehood and of political community that are anachronistic. Possibly a too cautious pragmatism, the product of inertia, impedes my ready acceptance of constitutional visions that focus on how we can escape from each other and too little on how to our mutual benefit we can cooperatively work together in a country that, overall, is not a discredit to those of us who live here. I do not think so. Proposals that stress what divides us in the service of a comprehensive future separateness simply misperceive where we are. Their implementation would require a disentanglement so disruptive as to be intolerable. An appropriate starting point is a pragmatic recognition that both new Aboriginal and new non-Aboriginal interests have developed since sovereignty was first exercised by European peoples over Aboriginal nations that did not believe they had given up their own sovereignty. A workable compromise should recognize that contradictory reality, but not be dominated by it.[203]

I agree with Adeno Addis that "the task of political and legal theory in the late twentieth century must be one of imagining institutions and vocabularies that will affirm multiplicity while cultivating solidarity."[204] He helpfully coined the phrase "pluralistic solidarity"[205] for arrangements that recognize and give us our own space and simultaneously bind us to each other. Both our separateness and our togetherness need to be institutionally supported if the overall Canadian community is to survive. Aboriginal nations, given their size and resources, cannot and will not opt for an independence that exceeds their governing capacity. Non-Aboriginal Canadians cannot wipe out Aboriginal difference in pursuit of an idealized homogeneity that would make governance easier. So the choices we have to make for territorially based nations are the nature and extent of Aboriginal self-government and how we organize our common life in the areas beyond the reach of self-government.

These choices should be thought of as complementary. Each supports the other. The willingness of the members of Aboriginal nations to invest their efforts in common enterprises will not be forthcoming if their self-governing aspirations are thwarted. Reciprocally, the willingness of the non-Aboriginal federal and provincial majorities to provide the assistance, financial and other, without which self-government will be more form than substance, will not be forthcoming if self-governing Aboriginal nations are thought of as strangers sending ambassadors to federal and provincial capitals rather than as Aboriginal Canadians helping to select federal, provincial, and territorial legislators to carry out the democratically selected tasks of federal, provincial, and territorial communities.

The members of Aboriginal nations will continue to have rights and duties vis-à-vis federal and provincial governments, the obvious vehicle for which is citizenship. Further, a common citizenship will facilitate the coming and going of Aboriginal individuals and families across the borders of self-governing nations. Our practical task, to rephrase Addis, is to enhance the compatibility between Aboriginal nationhood and Canadian citizenship.

# Notes

## Introduction

1 Canada, *Report of the Royal Commission on Aboriginal Peoples* (hereinafter RCAP, *Report*), vol. 1, *Looking Forward, Looking Back* (Ottawa: Canada Communication Group Publishing, 1996), 216.

2 Since these words were initially written, the federal government has responded with *Gathering Strength: Canada's Aboriginal Action Plan* (Ottawa: Minister of Indian Affairs and Northern Development, 1997). The response, virtually devoid of analytical rigour, is disappointing. It is discussed in Chapter 4.

3 See Jeremy Webber, "Relations of Force and Relations of Justice: The Emergence of Normative Community between Colonists and Aboriginal Peoples," *Osgoode Hall Law Journal* 33, 4 (1995): 623-60; and Will Kymlicka, *Multicultural Citizenship: A Liberal Theory of Minority Rights* (Oxford: Clarendon Press, 1995).

4 H.B. Hawthorn, ed., *A Survey of the Contemporary Indians of Canada*, 2 vols. (Ottawa: Queen's Printer, 1966 and 1967).

5 Canada, "Indian Self-Government in Canada," *Minutes and Proceedings of the Special Committee on Indian Self-Government*, no. 40, 12 and 20 October 1983 (hereinafter *Penner Report*).

6 Canada, *Statement of the Government of Canada on Indian Policy* (hereinafter White Paper), presented to the First Session of the Twenty-eighth Parliament by the Honourable Jean Chrétien, Minister of Indian Affairs and Northern Development (Ottawa: Department of Indian Affairs and Northern Development, 1969).

7 C. Vann Woodward, *The Strange Career of Jim Crow* (New York: Oxford University Press, 1974), 64-5, 105-6.

8 See Richard Sigurdson, "First Peoples, New Peoples and Citizenship in Canada," *International Journal of Canadian Studies* 14 (Fall 1996): 65, for recent support for a modernized version of the citizens plus concept.

9 Peter Read, "Whose Citizens? Whose Country?," in *Citizenship and Indigenous Australians: Changing Conceptions and Possibilities*, ed. Nicolas Peterson and Will Sanders (Cambridge, UK: Cambridge University Press, 1998), 172. Emphasis in original.

10 Henry Reynolds, "Sovereignty," in *Citizenship and Indigenous Australians*, ed. Peterson and Sanders, 214.

11 Manitoba Indian Brotherhood, *Wahbung: Our Tomorrows* (Winnipeg: Manitoba Indian Brotherhood, 1971), 148.

12 "New Indian Policy 'Not Acceptable,'" *Vancouver Sun*, 26 June 1969.

13 Alan C. Cairns, *Prelude to Imperialism: British Reactions to Central African Society, 1840-1890* (London: Routledge and Kegan Paul, 1965).

## Chapter 1: Empire

1 Georges Erasmus (then National Chief of the Assembly of First Nations), in Canada, Senate, *Debates*, 18 November 1987, 2201.

2 See Chapter 1 of George E. Marcus and Michael M.J. Fischer, *Anthropology as Cultural Critique* (Chicago: University of Chicago Press, 1986).

3 For the opposing views in the "Carr controversy," see Marcia Crosby, "Construction of the Imaginary Indian," in *Vancouver Anthology: The Institutional Politics of Art,* ed. Stan Douglas (Vancouver: Talon Books, 1991), 267-91; and Robert Fulford, "The Trouble with Emily," *Canadian Art,* 10, 4 (1993): 32-9.

4 Lenore Keeshig-Tobias, "Stop Stealing Native Stories," *Globe and Mail,* 26 January 1990.

5 Michael Ames, *Cannibal Tours and Glass Boxes: The Anthropology of Museums,* 2nd rev. ed. (Vancouver: UBC Press, 1992), 161.

6 Roger Gibbins and Radha Jhappan, "The State of the Art in Native Studies in Political Science," paper presented at the Tenth Biennial Canadian Ethnic Studies Association Conference, Calgary, AB, 18-21 October 1989, 24. See also Roger Gibbins, "Citizenship, Political, and Intergovernmental Problems with Indian Self-Government," in *Arduous Journey: Canadian Indians and Decolonization,* ed. J. Rick Ponting (Toronto: McClelland and Stewart, 1986), 376. Carol La Prairie, apparently speaking from experience, observes that public debate on the value of separate criminal justice systems for Aboriginal people is constrained by "'conventional wisdoms.' Even questions about or calls for evaluations of [say] ... sentencing circles, can result in accusations of being an apologist for the *status quo* or worse." Carol La Prairie, "Separate Aboriginal Justice Systems: Ultimate Solution or False Promise?" *Policy Options* 18, 2 (1997): 10.

7 Menno Boldt, *Surviving as Indians: The Challenge of Self-Government* (Toronto: University of Toronto Press, 1993), xviii.

8 See the discussion in J.R. Miller, "'I Can Only Tell What I Know': Shifting Notions of Historical Understanding in the 1990s," a presentation to the Authority and Interpretation Conference, University of Saskatchewan, Saskatoon, SK, 19 March 1994, 7. This paper is a very valuable contribution to discussion of the problems that attach to the voice appropriation controversy, silencing, and taboo.

9 F. Allan Hanson, "Empirical Anthropology, Postmodernism, and the Invention of Tradition," in *Present Is Past: Some Uses of Tradition in Native Societies,* ed. Marie Mauzé (Lanham, MD: University Press of America, 1997), 195-214.

10 Miller, "I Can Only Tell What I Know," 4.

11 In a recent lecture raising certain practical concerns about Aboriginal self-government, Ian Scott, former Ontario Attorney General, noted, but disagreed with, the suggestion his subject "is not, some will say, a matter about which non-aboriginals have a right to speak." Ian Scott, "Facing up to Aboriginal Self-Government: Three Practical Suggestions," the 1992 Laskin Lecture, York University, Toronto, ON, 11 March 1992, 14. See also Bryan Schwartz, *First Principles, Second Thoughts: Aboriginal Peoples, Constitutional Reform and Canadian Statecraft* (Montreal: Institute for Research on Public Policy, 1986), 325; and Douglas Sanders, "An Uncertain Path: The Aboriginal Constitutional Conferences," in *Litigating the Values of a Nation: The Canadian Charter of Rights and Freedoms,* ed. Joseph M. Weiler and Robin M. Elliot (Toronto: Carswell, 1986), 72-3.

12 Sir John A. Macdonald, quoted in Augie Fleras and Jean Edward Elliott, *The "Nations Within"* (Toronto: Oxford University Press, 1992), 39.

13 Evidence of D.C. Scott to the Special Committee of the House of Commons examining the Indian Act amendments of 1920, quoted in John Leslie and Ron Macguire, eds., *The Historical Development of the Indian Act,* 2nd ed. (Ottawa: Treaties and Historical Research Centre, Research Branch, Corporate Policy, Department of Indian and Northern Affairs, 1979), 114. Scott's overall view is captured by E. Brian Titley in the title of his biography, as well as in the repeated evidence confirming

its accuracy, *A Narrow Vision: Duncan Campbell Scott and the Administration of Indian Affairs in Canada* (Vancouver: UBC Press, 1986). According to Scott, Indian opponents of the assimilation policy were unwisely opposing their "ultimate destiny" (p. 116). On another occasion, he argued that the "happiest future for the Indian race is absorption into the general population, and this is the object of the policy of our government. The great forces of intermarriage and education will finally overcome the lingering traces of native custom and tradition" (p. 34).

14 Quoted in Donald B. Smith and Ian L. Getty, eds., *One Century Later: Western Canadian Reserve Indians since Treaty 7* (Vancouver: University of British Columbia Press, 1978), xi. For more on Jenness, see below, pp. 54-6. For similar views by his colleague Marius Barbeau, see Lawrence Nowry, *Man of Mana: Marius Barbeau* (Toronto: NC Press, 1995), 301-2.

15 Canada, *Report of the Royal Commission on Aboriginal Peoples* (hereinafter RCAP, *Report*), vol. 2 (2), *Restructuring the Relationship* (Ottawa: Canada Communication Group Publishing, 1996), 553. This philosophy was reiterated by Jack Pickersgill, Minister of Indian Affairs, in 1956. Peter McFarlane, *Brotherhood to Nationhood: George Manuel and the Making of the Modern Indian Movement* (Toronto: Between the Lines, 1993), 49.

16 Canada, *Statement of the Government of Canada on Indian Policy* (hereinafter White Paper), presented to the First Session of the Twenty-eighth Parliament by the Honourable Jean Chrétien, Minister of Indian Affairs and Northern Development (Ottawa: Department of Indian Affairs and Northern Development, 1969).

17 A.R.M. Lower, *Colony to Nation: A History of Canada* (Toronto: Longmans Green, 1946).

18 Canada, *Report of the Royal Commission on Bilingualism and Biculturalism*, 5 vols. (Ottawa: Queen's Printer, 1967-70).

19 Canada, *Report of the Royal Commission on the Status of Women in Canada* (Ottawa: Queen's Printer, 1970).

20 RCAP, *Report*.

21 RCAP is discussed in more detail in Chapter 4.

22 Robert A. Milen, "Canadian Representation and Aboriginal Peoples: A Survey of the Issues," in *For Seven Generations. An Information Legacy of the Royal Commission on Aboriginal Peoples, RCAP Research Reports. Governance. Project Area 2: Federalism and Intergovernmental Issues,* no. 486 [CD-ROM] (Ottawa: Libraxus, 1997).

23 Owen Carrigan, ed., *Canadian Party Platforms 1867-1968* (Toronto: Copp Clark, 1968), 24. See pp. 244, 269, 318-9, 337, and 351 for the 1962, 1965, and 1968 federal elections.

24 Richard Diubaldo, *The Government of Canada and the Inuit 1900-1967* (Ottawa: Indian and Northern Affairs Canada, 1985), 113.

25 Ibid.

26 Ibid., 2.

27 Canada, Royal Commission on Aboriginal Peoples (RCAP), *The High Arctic Relocation. A Report on the 1953-5 Relocation* (Ottawa: Canada Communication Group Publishing, 1994), 13.

28 Ibid., 157.

29 Ibid., 66.

30 Ibid., 99. Relocation had "broad support ... both within and outside government, including the churches and the Hudson's Bay Company." The failings, accordingly, "were not individual failings; they were, primarily, institutional and, more broadly, societal failings." Ibid., 100. See also p. 159. Other relocations, many of which were disasters, showed the same tendency of governments to see "Aboriginal people as

unsophisticated, poor, outside modern society and generally incapable of making the right choices." RCAP, *Report,* vol. 1, *Looking Forward, Looking Back,* 412.

31 Harry W. Daniels, ed., *The Forgotten People: Métis and Non-status Indian Land Claims* (Ottawa: Native Council of Canada, 1979), 7.

32 Dave McKay, "The Non-People," (Indian Claims Commission Collection, National Library of Canada, Ottawa, ON, 1972, mimeographed).

33 Donald Purich, *The Métis* (Toronto: James Lorimer, 1988), 140-7. For a Métis perspective on the Ewing Commission, see Murray Dobbin, *The One-and-a-Half Men: The Story of Jim Brady and Malcolm Norris, Métis Patriots of the Twentieth Century* (Vancouver: New Star Books, 1981), Chapter 6.

34 Joe Sawchuk, *The Dynamics of Native Politics: The Alberta Métis Experience* (Saskatoon: Purich Publishing, 1998), 96.

35 F. Laurie Barron, "The CCF and the Development of Métis Colonies in Southern Saskatchewan during the Premiership of T.C. Douglas, 1944-1961," *Canadian Journal of Native Studies* 10, 2 (1990): 256.

36 Roy MacGregor, *Chief: The Fearless Vision of Billy Diamond* (Markham: Viking/Penguin, 1989), 57.

37 Georges Erasmus, "We the Dene," in *Dene Nation – The Colony Within,* ed. Mel Watkins (Toronto: University of Toronto Press, 1977), 178-9.

38 H.B. Hawthorn, ed., *A Survey of the Contemporary Indians of Canada,* 2 vols. (Ottawa: Queen's Printer, 1966 and 1967).

39 See Titley, *A Narrow Vision,* Chapter 6.

40 See Maria Campbell's introduction to Dobbin's *The One-and-a-Half Men,* where she reports her difficulty in writing it. "I did not want Murray [a white man] to write about my heroes. It was none of his business. My people had already been hurt enough by the writings of white historians." However, she did so out of respect for Dobbin's honesty and admiration for the two Métis leaders whose careers he traced. Another native writer stated: "We have been redefined so many times we no longer quite know who we are." Cecil King, "Here Come the Anthros," in *Indians and Anthropologists: Vine Deloria, Jr., and the Critique of Anthropology,* ed. Thomas Biolsi and Larry J. Zimmerman (Tucson: University of Arizona Press, 1997), 117. The undignified status of being a specimen, an object, for research that enhanced academic careers but was of no benefit to those who were studied was what drew the ire of Vine Deloria, Jr., in his polemical and famous article "Anthropologists and Other Friends," Chapter 4 in Vine Deloria, Jr., *Custer Died for Your Sins: An Indian Manifesto* (Norman and London: University of Oklahoma Press, 1988 [original edition published in 1969]). In "Patriarchy and Paternalism: The Legacy of the Canadian State for First Nations Women," *Canadian Journal of Women and the Law* 6, 1 (1993): 185-6, Mary Ellen Turpel underlined the frustration of being an object in someone else's study – in this case, of the Royal Commission on the Status of Women, 1970. The Commission had no First Nations person as a commissioner, and the background study for the Commission was undertaken by two non-Aboriginal persons, and reveals "little sensitivity" to First Nation women's different cultural perspective on the Commission's mandate. In the mid-1960s, the *Hawthorn Report* noted, unhappily, that Indians were objects of research, possibly its beneficiaries, but certainly not consumers of the research that dissected their condition. Hawthorn, *A Survey of Contemporary Indians of Canada,* vol. 2, 243.

41 Hugh McDowall Clokie, *Canadian Government and Politics* (Toronto: Longmans, Green, 1944); J.A. Corry, *Democratic Government and Politics* (Toronto: University of Toronto Press, 1946); R. MacGregor Dawson, *The Government of Canada* (Toronto: University of Toronto Press, 1947); and Alexander Brady, *Democracy in*

the Dominions: A Comparative Study in Institutions (Toronto: University of Toronto Press, 1947).

42 See Douglas Cole, *Captured Heritage: The Scramble for Northwest Coast Artifacts* (Seattle: University of Washington Press, 1985).

43 Hedley Bull, "The Revolt against the West," in *The Expansion of International Society,* ed. Hedley Bull and Adam Watson (Oxford: Clarendon Press, 1984), 221.

44 See Lord Hailey, *An African Survey: Revised 1956* (London: Oxford University Press, 1957), 228-35, for Portuguese and Spanish colonies in Africa; and Lord Hailey, *An African Survey* (London: Oxford University Press, 1938), 194-201, and 212, for French and Belgian colonies in Africa.

45 V.G. Kiernan, *The Lords of Human Kind: European Attitudes to the Outside World in the Imperial Age* (Harmondsworth, Middlesex: Penguin Books, 1972). In Africa, according to Philip Curtin, in the "great age of imperialism [after 1870] racism became dominant in European thought. Few believed that any 'lower race' could actually reach the heights of Western achievement. Their salvation would have to be achieved in some other way; but meanwhile they were entitled, in their inferiority, to the paternal protection of a Western power. The idea of trusteeship gradually replaced that of conversion." Philip D. Curtin, *The Image of Africa: British Ideas and Action 1780-1850* (Madison: University of Wisconsin Press, 1964), 415.

46 Lord Lugard, *The Dual Mandate in British Tropical Africa,* 5th ed. (Hamden, CT: Archon Books, 1965).

47 Ibid., 62-3. See S. James Anaya, *Indigenous Peoples in International Law* (New York: Oxford University Press, 1996), 23-6, for a discussion of "Trusteeship Doctrine and Its 'Civilizing Mission.'"

48 Alan C. Cairns, "Aboriginal Canadians, Citizenship, and the Constitution," in *Reconfigurations: Canadian Citizenship and Constitutional Change. Selected Essays by Alan C. Cairns,* ed. Douglas E. Williams (Toronto: McClelland and Stewart, 1995), 243.

49 Lawrence Martin, *Chrétien: The Will to Win,* vol. 1 (Toronto: Lester Publishing, 1995), 191.

50 Jennifer Clark, "The 'Winds of Change' in Australia: Aborigines and the International Politics of Race, 1960-1972," *International History Review* 20, 1 (1998): 99-100, 109.

51 Duncan Campbell Scott could not visualize "the co-existence of culturally diverse peoples within the same political entity. Tolerance, after all, would have implied a residue of self-doubt, and in the heyday of an empire on which the sun supposedly never set, there was little likelihood of such ambivalence." Titley, *A Narrow Vision,* 201.

52 See Bull, "The Revolt against the West," and R.J. Vincent, "Racial Equality," in *The Expansion of International Society,* ed. Hedley Bull and Adam Watson (Oxford: Clarendon Press, 1984), 239-54.

53 George Manuel and Michael Posluns, *The Fourth World: An Indian Reality* (Don Mills, ON: Collier-Macmillan, 1974), 6. "The aboriginal peoples," argues Vine Deloria, Jr., "can only argue the morality of their case. Overwhelmed by the European peoples, they cannot look forward to the day when they regain control of their lands." Quoted in Manuel and Posluns, *The Fourth World,* xi.

54 See Paul L.A.H. Chartrand, "'Terms of Division.' Problems of 'Outside Naming' for Aboriginal Peoples in Canada," *Journal of Indigenous Studies* 2, 2 (1991): 3-22, for a discussion.

55 Canada, Special Joint Committee of the Senate and the House of Commons Appointed to Examine and Consider the Indian Act, *Minutes of Proceedings and Evidence,* no. 1, 28 and 30 May 1946, 8.

56  RCAP, *Report,* vol. 1, *Looking Forward, Looking Back,* 14, 19. The total for Inuit did not, of course, include those living in Labrador since Newfoundland was not yet part of Canada.

57  Ibid., 15.

58  Gunnar Myrdal, *An American Dilemma. The Negro Problem and Modern Democracy,* 2 vols. (New York: Harper Brothers Publishers, 1944).

59  Ibid., vol. 1, xlix. See also vol. 1, 54-5.

60  T.R.H. Davenport, *South Africa: A Modern History,* 3rd ed. (Toronto: University of Toronto Press, 1987), 340.

61  Edward A. Said, *Culture and Imperialism* (New York: Alfred A. Knopf, 1993).

62  See Bill Ashcroft, Gareth Griffiths, and Helen Tiffin, eds., *The Post-Colonial Studies Reader* (London: Routledge, 1995), for an exhaustive compendium of key writings in postcolonial theory and criticism.

63  Emma La Rocque, "The Colonization of a Native Woman Scholar," in *Women of the First Nations: Power, Wisdom, and Strength,* ed. Christine Miller and Patricia Chuchryk (Winnipeg: University of Manitoba Press, 1996), 13.

64  J.M. Blaut, *The Colonizer's Model of the World: Geographical Diffusionism and Eurocentric History* (New York: Guilford Press, 1993), 1.

65  Bruce G. Trigger, *A History of Archaeological Thought* (Cambridge, UK: Cambridge University Press, 1989), 131, 134. Trigger notes that after 1905 the professional international archaeological community "unanimously" credited the construction of Zimbabwe to the Bantu, although the white public and amateur archaeologists continued to deny its African origins. Pp. 134-5.

66  See Michael D. Coe, *Breaking the Maya Code* (London: Penguin Books, 1992).

67  See Georges E. Sioui, *For an Amerindian Autohistory* (Montreal and Kingston: McGill-Queen's University Press, 1992), xix-xx.

68  Bruce G. Trigger, *Natives and Newcomers: Canada's Heroic Age Reconsidered* (Montreal and Kingston: McGill-Queen's University Press, 1985), 4.

69  Ibid., 46.

70  John Borrows' reinterpretation of the Royal Proclamation is an excellent example of what Trigger and Washburn were looking for. In his documented reinterpretation, Borrows stressed that for First Nations the Royal Proclamation was seen as evidence of a nation-to-nation relationship, and of guarantee of self-government manifested in a treaty of peace and friendship, and not as an expression of British sovereignty. John Borrows, "Constitutional Law from a First Nation Perspective: Self-Government and the Royal Proclamation," *University of British Columbia Law Review* 28, 1 (1994): 1-47.

71  Wilcomb E. Washburn and Bruce G. Trigger, "Native Peoples in Euro-American Historiography," in *The Cambridge History of Native Peoples of the Americas,* vol. 1, part 1, *North America,* ed. Bruce G. Trigger and Wilcomb E. Washburn (Cambridge, UK: Cambridge University Press, 1996), 62, 107.

72  Canada, Royal Commission on Aboriginal Peoples (RCAP), *Partners in Confederation: Aboriginal Peoples, Self-Government and the Constitution* (Ottawa: Canada Communication Group, 1993), 36.

73  The Right Honourable Joe Clark, Minister Responsible for Constitutional Affairs (notes for a speech delivered at a luncheon hosted by the Saskatchewan Métis Assembly at the Saskatoon Inn, Saskatoon, SK, 28 September 1991), 5.

74  Canada, House of Commons, *Debates,* 10 March 1992, 7879; Canada, Senate, *Debates,* 17 March 1992, 1043.

75  Daniel N. Paul, *We Were Not the Savages: A Micmac Perspective on the Collision of European and Aboriginal Civilizations* (Halifax: Nimbus Publishing, 1993), vii.

76  Ibid., v.

77 Ibid., vii.
78 Ibid., 12. This claim is controversial. See Elisabeth Tooker, "The United States Constitution and the Iroquois League," in *The Invented Indian: Cultural Fictions and Government Policies,* ed. James A. Clifton (New Brunswick, NJ: Transaction Publishers, 1994), 107-28. See Gail Landsman, "Informant as Critic: Conducting Research on a Dispute between Iroquoianist Scholars and Traditional Iroquois," in *Indians and Anthropologists: Vine Deloria, Jr., and the Critique of Anthropology,* ed. Thomas Biolsi and Larry J. Zimmerman (Tucson: University of Arizona Press, 1997), for an analysis of the passions this debate aroused between rival schools.
79 First Nations Circle on the Constitution, *To the Source: Commissioners' Report* (Ottawa: Assembly of First Nations, 1992).
80 Ibid., 2.
81 Ibid.
82 Ibid., vi.
83 Ibid.
84 Ibid., 4.
85 Ibid., 20.
86 Ibid., 28.
87 Ibid., 59.
88 Ibid., 9, 42, 43, 46, 48, and 76.
89 Ibid., 9.
90 See ibid., 48, for the claim that "Aboriginal peoples ... the original environmentalists ... have much to teach white society about environmental practices."
91 Ibid., 77.
92 Bill Ashcroft, Gareth Griffiths, and Helen Tiffin, *The Empire Writes Back: Theory and Practice in Post-Colonial Literature* (London: Routledge, 1989).
93 For more on the Quebec Royal Commission of Inquiry on Constitutional Problems, see *The Tremblay Report,* Carleton Library no. 64, ed. David Kwavnick (Toronto: McClelland and Stewart, 1973).
94 Pierre Elliott Trudeau, "The Province of Quebec at the Time of the Strike," in *The Asbestos Strike,* ed. Pierre Elliott Trudeau, trans. James Boake (Toronto: James Lewis and Samuel, 1974), 7.
95 Thomas Flanagan's *Riel and the Rebellion: 1885 Reconsidered* (Saskatoon: Western Producer Prairie Books, 1983) was denounced by Murray Dobbin, Project Co-ordinator for the Batoche Centenary Corporation in Saskatchewan, as "so vicious and patently unfair that [it] ... very nearly becomes a diatribe." After accusing Flanagan of ignoring and distorting history, Dobbin concludes that "for pure nastiness and vengefulness it is unmatched in recent literature. It is not simply flawed, but fundamentally flawed. All in all it is a shameful and wasted effort that people would be well advised to avoid – unless, of course, they are interested in a case study of how uncomely zeal can lead a good historian to blatantly misrepresent history." Flanagan's response, headed "The Man Who Couldn't Quote Straight," asserts Dobbin is incapable of quoting correctly, getting fifteen of sixteen quotes wrong, and of engaging in a "parody of the scholarly method, [by quoting] himself and attribut[ing] it to me." He concludes that Dobbin's promulgation of a "dubious hypothesis does a disservice not only to scholarship but to the legitimate political goals of the Métis people." Dobbin's review and Flanagan's response are found in "Riel: A Criticism and a Response," *Alberta History* 32, 2 (1984): 24-8.

　　For another revealing instance of historical controversy over contested interpretations of Aboriginal/non-Aboriginal relations, which space limitations preclude more than a brief reference to, see Robin Brownlie and Mary-Ellen Kelm, "Desperately Seeking Absolution: Native Agency as Historical Alibi?," *Canadian*

*Historical Review* 75, 4 (1994): 543-56, and Douglas Cole and J.R. Miller, "Desperately Seeking Absolution: Responses and Reply," *Canadian Historical Review* 76, 4 (1995): 628-40, a controversy over works by Cole and Ira Chaikin, Miller, and Tina Loo, mainly dealing with the potlatch, residential schools, and pass laws.

The controversy over James A. Clifton, ed., *The Invented Indian,* further underlines the passions aroused by widely varying views of the (in this case American) past. The Clifton volume of essays takes issue with what the editor sees as a massive historical revisionism to strengthen American Indians "in the competition between interest groups for control of resources and for prestige" (p. 39). What Clifton calls "cultural fictions" are, in his words, "fabrications of pseudo-events and relationships, counterfeits of the past and present that suit someone's or some group's purposes in their dealing with others" (p. 44). In a passionate rejoinder, Vine Deloria, Jr., places the Clifton volume in the historical context that for most of the previous five centuries, "whites have had unrestricted power to describe Indians in any way they chose." Now that American Indians are taking control of their own past, history becomes a battleground in which Indian historians seek to overturn the harmful consequences of white domination of the historical record, and some white authors, such as Clifton, seek to recapture the intellectual monopoly they have lost. A review of the Clifton book can thus provide, argues Deloria, a "demonstration of the errors and hidden agendas ... showing that these are indeed second rate scholars on a holy mission of stopping the barbarian hordes (Indians) at the gates before they overwhelm the old citadels of comfortable fiction." Vine Deloria, Jr., "Comfortable Fictions and the Struggle for Turf: An Essay Review of *The Invented Indian: Cultural Fictions and Government Policies,*" *American Indian Quarterly* 16, 3 (1992): 398-9. Another reviewer asserts that Clifton "uses and abuses theories and scholarship as suits his political aims," and concludes that *The Invented Indian* "is the antithesis of responsible scholarship." Pauline Turner Strong, "The Invented Indian [book review]," *American Ethnologist* 21, 4 (1994): 1052-3.

96 Carole M. Gentry and Donald A. Grinde Jr., eds., *The Unheard Voices: American Indian Responses to the Columbian Quincentenary 1492-1992* (Los Angeles: American Indian Studies Center, University of California, 1994).

97 Gregory R. Campbell, "The Politics of Counting: Critical Reflections on the Depopulation Question of Native North America," in *The Unheard Voices,* ed. Gentry and Grinde Jr., 101, 107.

98 Phrases by Douglas Ubelaker, quoted in Russell Thornton, *American Indian Holocaust and Survival* (Norman and London: University of Oklahoma Press, 1987), 35.

99 Hamar Foster and Alan Grove, "Looking behind the Masks: A Land Claims Discussion Paper for Researchers, Lawyers and Their Employers," *University of British Columbia Law Review* 27, 2 (1993): 223.

100 Donald J. Bourgeois, "The Role of the Historian in the Litigation Process," *Canadian Historical Review* 67, 2 (1986): 204.

101 G.M. Dickinson and R.D. Gidney, "History and Advocacy: Some Reflections on the Historian's Role in Litigation," *Canadian Historical Review* 68, 4 (1987): 578.

102 *Delgamuukw* v. *B.C.,* [1991] 79 DLR (4th) 185.

103 *Delgamuukw* v. *B.C.,* [1997] 3 SCR 1010.

104 Julie Cruikshank, "Invention of Anthropology in British Columbia's Supreme Court: Oral Tradition as Evidence in *Delgamuukw* v. *B.C.,*" *BC Studies* 95 (Autumn 1992): 28.

105 Robin Fisher, "Judging History: Reflections on the Reasons for Judgment in *Delgamuukw* v. *B.C.,*" *BC Studies* 95 (Autumn 1992): 46-7. See also Joel R. Fortune, "Construing *Delgamuukw:* Legal Arguments, Historical Argumentation, and the Philosophy of History," *University of Toronto Faculty of Law Review* 51, 1 (1993): 80-117.

106 Michael Asch and Catherine Bell, "Definition and Interpretation of Fact in Canadian

Aboriginal Title Litigation: An Analysis of *Delgamuukw*," *Queen's Law Journal* 19, 2 (1994): 503-50, is a measured critique of the judgment coauthored by an anthropologist and a professor of law.

107 Ken MacQueen, *Vancouver Sun,* 13 July 1991, quoted in Bruce G. Miller, "Introduction," *BC Studies* 95 (Autumn 1992): 5. Before doing so, however, they should read the assessment of their colleague, Robert Paine. Paine argues that the anthropological witnesses failed to apply their anthropological skills either to understanding the complexities of McEachern's role as a judge or to "interpreting and contextualizing" the Native evidence, rather than echoing it. The "anthropologist's ire ... was directed at Judge McEachern's failure to accept *on their terms* what he heard and saw, as testimony and proof of what constitutes historical evidence *on his terms.*" Rather than "demonizing the judge" for his failings, he suggested they should reflect on their contribution to his failure. Robert Paine, "In Chief Justice McEachern's Shoes: Anthropology's Ineffectiveness in Court," *POLAR* 19, 2 (1996): 59, 60, 62. Emphasis in original.

The historical controversy over the Gitksan case was, in part, a conflict between written and oral history or the old history and the new history. The Gitksan and Wet'suwet'en tried in court "to make their claim in a way that allowed them to control the representation of their culture to the world as well as to themselves. They enacted [their songs and ceremonial regalia] as performances bound to an understanding of the relationship between human history and landscape, expressing connection to land and attachment to place. They understood these performances to be a restatement of their Declaration of Title ... By evaluating the authenticity of these oral traditions exclusively within the framework of western jurisprudence, the judge is basically denying Gitksan and Wet'suwet'en versions of how their lives have changed over the years." Cruikshank, "Invention of Anthropology," 39-40. See also RCAP, *High Arctic Relocation,* 2, 11, and 161, on oral versus written history. In general, the commissioners found oral history was a helpful supplement to written history, and indeed gave different meanings to what was in the written record. This was oral history of very recent vintage, and hence with greater reliability. Jan Vansina, *Oral Tradition as History* (Madison: University of Wisconsin Press, 1985), is a classic analysis of the reliability of oral tradition as history.

108 *Delgamuukw v. B.C.,* [1997] 3 SCR 1010. The discussion of *Delgamuukw* in this paragraph was written before I had read Dara Culhane's passionate and incisive analysis of the *Delgamuukw* cases (1991, 1993, and 1997), *The Pleasure of the Crown: Anthropology, Law and First Nations* (Burnaby: Talon Books, 1998). I very strongly recommend it.

109 For a global overview, see Talal Asad, ed., *Anthropology and the Colonial Encounter* (New York: Humanities Press, 1973).

110 Peter Kulchyski, "Anthropology in the Service of the State: Diamond Jenness and Canadian Indian Policy," *Journal of Canadian Studies* 28, 2 (1993): 21-50. Articles with such titles as Russel Lawrence Barsh's "Are Anthropologists Hazardous to Indians' Health?," *Journal of Ethnic Studies* 15, 4 (1988): 1-38, reveal the extent of the transformation in the intellectual climate in a time of reassessment.

111 See Nowry, *Man of Mana,* dedication, 108-9, 214, 235-6.

112 Clifford Geertz, *Works and Lives: The Anthropologist as Author* (Stanford: Stanford University Press, 1988), 133.

113 Ron Ignace, George Speck, and Renee Taylor, "Some Native Perspectives on Anthropology and Public Policy," in *Anthropology, Public Policy and Native Peoples in Canada,* ed. Noel Dyck and James B. Waldram (Montreal and Kingston: McGill-Queen's University Press, 1995), 166-7. See also Manuel and Posluns, *The Fourth World,* 158-60, for satirical comments about the "hordes" of anthropologists who

came in the 1960s "like vultures – pecking away at our minds, our clothes, our houses, and our graves until we threatened to shatter if they broke rhythm." The American Indian critique of anthropology was led by Vine Deloria Jr., in *Custer Died for Your Sins*. A reassessment of Deloria's 1969 analysis in 1997 accepted much of his criticism. See *Indians and Anthropologists*, ed. Biolsi and Zimmerman, and in particular see Elizabeth S. Grobsmith, "Growing Up on Deloria: The Impact of His Work on a New Generation of Anthropologists," in *Indians and Anthropologists*.

114 Noel Dyck, "'Telling It Like It Is:' Some Dilemmas of Fourth World Ethnography and Advocacy," in *Anthropology, Public Policy and Native Peoples in Canada*, ed. Dyck and Waldram, 192-212.

115 See Washburn and Trigger, "Native Peoples in Euro-American Historiography," 109, for the constraints that "native requirements" can impose on scholars whose research requires Native cooperation. See also Eduardo Duran and Bonnie Duran, *Native American Postcolonial Psychology* (Albany: State University of New York Press, 1995), 25, for the hostility of Native Americans for "the colonizing techniques of the anthropologists and other well-meaning albeit arrogant social scientists. A high level of distrust exists among Native American people to anyone asking questions, regardless of the good promised by the results of the research and often regardless of the tribal affiliations of the researcher."

116 See Ames, *Cannibal Tours and Glass Boxes*.

117 Bruce G. Trigger, "A Present of Their Past? Anthropologists, Native People, and Their Heritage," *Culture* 8, 1 (1988): 72.

118 Ibid., 75.

119 Ibid., 77. See Rennard Strickland, *Tonto's Revenge: Reflections on American Indian Culture and Policy* (Albuquerque: University of New Mexico Press, 1997), Chapter 6, "Lone Man, Walking Buffalo, and NAGPRA: Cross-Cultural Understanding and Safeguarding Human Rights, Sacred Objects, and Cultural Patrimony," for a discussion of the 1991 Native American Grave Protection and Repatriation Act from an American Indian perspective.

120 See Alan D. McMillan, *Native Peoples and Cultures of Canada: An Anthropological Overview*, 2nd ed. (Vancouver and Toronto: Douglas and McIntyre, 1995), 15, for a revealing incident of conflict between archaeologists and local Indian bands, plus the Union of Ontario Indians, when the archaeologists tried to salvage information from the cemetery of an extinct Native people, threatened by a housing development. The Union placed the archaeologist in charge under citizen's arrest.

121 See Nina Swidler et al., eds., *Native Americans and Archaeologists: Stepping Stones to Common Ground* (Walnut Creek, CA: Alta Mira Press, 1997), published in cooperation with the Society for American Archaeology.

122 In Canada, biased historical studies "have informed relationships between Aboriginal and non-Aboriginal peoples in Canada, and all peoples' sense of themselves ... the power of these historical studies continues to be formidable, and continues to haunt Aboriginal people – especially students who find themselves objectified and vilified and essentialized and homogenized and caricatured and stereotyped by written history. Or who continue to be ignored by it, their heritage neglected and nullified." Ted Chamberlin and Hugh Brody, "History: Aboriginal History: Workshop Report," RCAP, April 1993, 24.

123 Chapter 14 in Peter Novick, *That Noble Dream: The "Objectivity Question" and the American Historical Profession* (Cambridge, UK: Cambridge University Press, 1994).

124 At least ten Canadian universities have departments of Aboriginal (or Native) Studies. RCAP, *Report*, vol. 3, *Gathering Strength*, 514.

125 Anne Norton, "Ruling Memory," *Political Theory* 21, 3 (1993): 459.

126 Chamberlin and Brody, "History: Aboriginal History," 11. Emphasis in original.

127 In its own way, the RCAP *Report* is a Canadian version of a truth commission. See Chapter 4 in this book.

128 Bull, "The Revolt against the West," 223, 228.

129 Robert Jackson, "The Weight of Ideas in Decolonization: Normative Change in International Relations," in *Ideas and Foreign Policy: Beliefs, Institutions and Political Change,* ed. Judith Goldstein and Robert O. Keohane (Ithaca, NY: Cornell University Press, 1993), 121, 124.

130 Anaya, *Indigenous Peoples,* 183.

131 Bull and Vincent, "Racial Equality," 240.

132 See RCAP, *Report,* vol. 1, *Looking Forward, Looking Back,* 227-9, for "international pressure ... [for] the world-wide objective" of the cultural survival of Aboriginal peoples, and their rights to their own land and their own forms of government.

133 Edward M. Bruner, "Ethnography as Narrative," in *The Anthropology of Experience,* ed. Victor W. Turner and Edward M. Bruner (Urbana and Chicago: University of Illinois Press, 1986), 139.

134 Manuel and Posluns, *The Fourth World,* 70.

135 Bruner, "Ethnography as Narrative," 152. See also p. 149.

136 Clark, "The 'Winds of Change' in Australia," 115-6.

137 RCAP, *Report,* vol. 1, *Looking Forward, Looking Back,* 236-8.

138 RCAP, *Report,* vol. 3, *Gathering Strength,* 597-8, 602, 620-44.

139 Ibid., 586.

140 RCAP, *Report,* vol. 4, *Perspectives and Realities,* 139.

141 RCAP, *Report,* vol. 3, *Gathering Strength,* 353.

142 RCAP, *Report,* vol. 4, *Perspectives and Realities,* 128.

### Chapter 2: Assimilation

1 Charles F. Wilkinson, *American Indians, Time, and the Law: Native Societies in a Modern Constitutional Democracy* (New Haven and London: Yale University Press, 1987), 75. See also p. 13.

2 Michael W. Posluns, "Evading the Unspeakable: A Commentary on *Looking Back, Looking Forward,* Volume I of the Report of the RCAP," *Canada Watch* 5, 5 (1997), 87.

3 T.C. Pocklington, *The Government and Politics of the Alberta Métis Settlements* (Regina, SK: Canadian Plains Research Center, 1991), 18. According to Murray Dobbin, "everyone at the [Commission] hearings, [no matter what their perspective], agreed that the Métis had to be segregated, temporarily at least, from the white population." Murray Dobbin, *The One-and-a-Half Men: The Story of Jim Brady and Malcolm Norris, Métis Patriots of the Twentieth Century* (Vancouver: New Star Books, 1981), 101.

4 John Leslie and Ron Macguire, eds., *The Historical Development of the Indian Act,* 2nd ed. (Ottawa: Treaties and Historical Research Centre, Research Branch, Corporate Policy, Department of Indian and Northern Affairs, 1979), 27.

5 John Leonard Taylor, "Canadian Indian Policy during the Inter-War Years, 1918-1939," (Department of Indian Affairs and Northern Development, Ottawa, 1984, mimeographed), 143-4.

6 Ibid., 151-3.

7 With the important exception of eight Alberta Métis settlements established by the provincial government in 1938, which "constitute the only collective Métis land base in Canada." Pocklington, *Government and Politics* 39. This is a very valuable study.

8 A proposed amendment in 1924 that would have brought Inuit under the Indian Act was opposed in the House of Commons, and not proceeded with. Taylor,

"Canadian Indian Policy during the Inter-War Years," 87-8.

9 Canada, *Report of the Royal Commission on Aboriginal Peoples* (hereinafter RCAP, *Report*), vol. 3, *Gathering Strength* (Ottawa: Canada Communication Group Publishing, 1996), 435.

10 Diamond Jenness, *Eskimo Administration,* vol. 2, *Canada,* technical paper no. 14 (Montreal: Arctic Institute of North America, 1964), table of contents.

11 Richard Diubaldo, *The Government of Canada and the Inuit 1900-1967* (Ottawa: Indian and Northern Affairs Canada, 1985), 51-2.

12 "In this Act, 'aboriginal peoples of Canada' includes the Indian, Inuit and Métis peoples of Canada." Constitution Act, 1982, Schedule B to Canada Act, 1982 (UK), Part II, s. 35(2).

13 These prohibitions were extended in a 1914 Indian Act amendment prohibiting Indians in the four western provinces and the territories from participating in Indian dances off the reserve, or "in any show, exhibition, performance, stampede or pageant in aboriginal costume without the consent of the Superintendent General of Indian Affairs or his authorized Agent." Taylor, "Canadian Indian Policy during the Inter-War Years," 135.

14 "For twelve years I was taught to love my neighbour – especially if he was white – but to hate myself. I was made to feel untrustworthy, inferior, incapable, and immoral." Jane Willis, *An Indian Girlhood* (Don Mills, ON: New Press, 1973), 62-3, quoted in Jean Goodwill and Norma Sluman, *John Tootoosis* (Winnipeg: Pemmican Publications, 1984), 97. "Education," according to Brian Titley, "was to be nothing less than an instrument of cultural annihilation." E. Brian Titley, *A Narrow Vision: Duncan Campbell Scott and the Administration of Indian Affairs in Canada* (Vancouver: UBC Press, 1986), 93.

15 See RCAP, *Report,* vol. 1, *Looking Forward, Looking Back,* for devastatingly critical analyses of the Indian Act (Chapter 9) and residential schools (Chapter 11).

16 Noel Dyck, *What Is the Indian "Problem"?* (St. John's, NF: Institute of Social and Economic Research, 1991), 27.

17 Edward M. Bruner, "Ethnography as Narrative," in *The Anthropology of Experience,* ed. Victor W. Turner and Edward M. Bruner (Urbana and Chicago: University of Illinois Press, 1986), 139.

18 See Canada, *Statement of the Government of Canada on Indian Policy* (hereinafter White Paper), presented to the First Session of the Twenty-eighth Parliament by the Honourable Jean Chrétien, Minister of Indian Affairs and Northern Development (Ottawa: Department of Indian Affairs and Northern Development, 1969). The classic analysis of the White Paper episode is Sally M. Weaver, *Making Canadian Indian Policy: The Hidden Agenda 1968-1970* (Toronto: University of Toronto Press, 1981). The parallel with the American situation deserves more attention than it can be given here. A House Concurrent Resolution, passed in 1953, declared a new policy of abolishing the special federal government role as soon as possible and making Indians simply standard American citizens. President Nixon spoke against unilateral termination in 1970, and it was officially rejected by Congress in 1988. David E. Wilkins, *American Indian Sovereignty and the U.S. Supreme Court* (Austin: University of Texas Press, 1997), 166, 237. Law professor Ken Lysyk favourably quoted long extracts from President Nixon's speech in his presentation to a joint 1971 parliamentary committee on the constitution. Canada, Parliament, Special Joint Committee of the Senate and of the House of Commons on the Constitution of Canada, *Minutes of Proceedings and Evidence,* no. 59, 25 March 1971, 9-10.

19 White Paper, 5.

20 Ibid., 9.

21 Ibid., 11.

22 The Right Honourable Pierre Elliott Trudeau, remarks on Indian, Aboriginal and treaty rights, Vancouver, BC, 8 August 1969. See also White Paper, 11. Barsh and Henderson's summary of Trudeau's position is biting, but apposite. He "consistently assumes that Indians are a 'section' of Canadian society, rather than a separate commonwealth, because they are located within Canada's borders. His logic is nothing more than this: Indians are here, so they must be Canadian – being Canadian, they must be just like other Canadians." Russel Lawrence Barsh and James [sákéj] Youngblood Henderson, "Aboriginal Rights, Treaty Rights, and Human Rights: Indian Tribes and 'Constitutional Renewal,'" *Journal of Canadian Studies* 17, 2 (1982): 70.

23 The Right Honourable Pierre Elliott Trudeau, remarks made during a question and answer session at a meeting of the Don Valley Liberal Association, Don Valley, ON, 21 January 1972.

24 Ibid.

25 Chrétien explicitly rejected consultation with Indians on the final White Paper proposals, believing prior discussion would be counterproductive. He preferred to present Indians with a fait accompli. Lawrence Martin, *Chrétien: The Will to Win,* vol. 1 (Toronto: Lester Publishing, 1995), 196-7.

26 Anthony Westell, column, *Vancouver Sun,* 26 June 1969.

27 See H.B. Hawthorn, ed., *A Survey of the Contemporary Indians of Canada,* 2 vols. (Ottawa: Queen's Printer, 1966 and 1967), vol. 1, 377-8.

28 Menzies' speech was delivered in 1965, and is quoted in Bain Attwood and Andrew Markus, "Representation Matters: The 1967 Referendum and Citizenship," in *Citizenship and Indigenous Australians: Changing Conceptions and Possibilities,* ed. Nicolas Peterson and Will Sanders (Cambridge, UK: Cambridge University Press, 1998), 122.

29 C.T. Loram and T.F. McIlwraith, eds., *The North American Indian Today* (Toronto: University of Toronto Press, 1943).

30 Ibid., 5, 7, and 8.

31 Ibid., 8.

32 Ibid., 10.

33 Quoted in Geoffrey Gray, "From Nomadism to Citizenship: A.P. Elkin and Aboriginal Advancement," in *Citizenship and Indigenous Australians,* ed. Peterson and Sanders, 59.

34 Loram and McIlwraith, *The North American Indian Today,* 251-2.

35 Diamond Jenness, *The Indians of Canada,* 2nd ed., Anthropological Series no. 15, Bulletin 65 (Ottawa: National Museum of Canada, 1935), 350.

36 Canada, Special Joint Committee of the Senate and the House of Commons Appointed to Examine and Consider the Indian Act, *Minutes of Proceedings and Evidence,* no. 7, 25 March 1947, 310.

37 Ibid., 307. See also p. 309.

38 Ibid., 311.

39 Jenness, *Eskimo Administration,* vol. 2, 174-5. His overall scheme is described in Chapter 16, including in the appendix.

40 Douglas was replaced by Woodrow Lloyd in 1961.

41 James M. Pitsula, "The Saskatchewan CCF Government and Treaty Indians, 1944-64," *Canadian Historical Review* 75, 1 (1994): 49.

42 Ibid., 23. Although the Douglas government set up a number of Métis settlements, or colonies, to overcome the destitution and marginalization of the Métis, they were to function as a training program to facilitate integration. The Métis were treated as disadvantaged people disconnected from their Aboriginal status. The CCF, according to Barron, pursued a policy of integration for Métis that was driven by the party's strong egalitarian strain. Neither self-determination nor recognition

of "national or even special status for the Métis" was seriously considered. F. Laurie Barron, "The CCF and the Development of Métis Colonies in Southern Saskatchewan during the Premiership of T.C. Douglas, 1944-1961," *Canadian Journal of Native Studies* 10, 2 (1990): 261. Eventually, the colonies faded away as failed experiments.

43 See James M. Pitsula, "The Thatcher Government in Saskatchewan and Treaty Indians, 1964-1971: The Quiet Revolution," *Saskatchewan History* 48, 1 (1996).

44 Ibid., 9.

45 Ibid., 4.

46 Ibid., 5.

47 Ibid., 13, 16.

48 Ibid., 15.

49 See Ken Rasmussen, "Saskatchewan Aboriginal Relations"; Darcy A. Mitchell and Paul Tennant, "Government to Government: Aboriginal Peoples and British Columbia"; David Cameron and Jill Wherrett, "New Relationship, New Challenges: Aboriginal Peoples and the Province of Ontario"; and Kathy L. Brock, "Relations with Canadian Governments: Manitoba," in *For Seven Generations. An Information Legacy of the Royal Commission on Aboriginal Peoples, RCAP Research Reports. Governance. Project Area 8: Domestic Government Case Studies* [CD-ROM] (Ottawa: Libraxus, 1997).

50 Quebec, Commission d'étude sur l'integrité du territoire du Québec, *Rapport de la Commission d'Étude sur l'Integrité du Territoire du Québec, 4. Le Domaine Indien, 4.1 rapport des commissionaires* (Québec: Commission d'étude sur l'integrité du territoire du Québec, 1971), 365, 372, 375, 378.

51 Charles Taylor, *Multiculturalism and "The Politics of Recognition"* (Princeton, NJ: Princeton University Press, 1992).

52 See Chapter 4 for an analysis of the RCAP *Report.*

53 Loram and McIlwraith, *The North American Indian Today,* 8.

54 Jenness, *The Indians of Canada,* 306-7.

55 Canada, Special Joint Committee of the Senate and the House of Commons Appointed to Examine and Consider the Indian Act, *Minutes of Proceedings and Evidence,* no. 7, 25 March 1947, 317, referring to Gilbert Monture.

56 A. Grenfell Price, *White Settlers and Native Peoples* (Cambridge, UK: Cambridge University Press, 1949), 95-6, 98. See also p. 201.

57 H.B. Hawthorn, C.S. Belshaw, and S.M. Jamieson, *The Indians of British Columbia: A Study of Contemporary Social Adjustment* (Toronto: University of Toronto Press, 1958), 12, 39.

58 Olive Patricia Dickason, *Canada's First Nations: A History of Founding Peoples from Earliest Times* (Toronto: McClelland and Stewart, 1992), 387.

59 Menno Boldt, "Social Correlates of Nationalism: A Study of Native Indian Leaders in a Canadian Internal Colony," *Comparative Political Studies* 14, 2 (1981): 214-5. See also William I.C. Wuttunee, *Ruffled Feathers: Indians in Canadian Society* (Calgary: Bell Books, 1971), for a strong defence of the White Paper. Wuttunee, an opponent of Harold Cardinal, was barred from several reserves, including his own – the Red Pheasant Reserve, SK – for his support of the White Paper. See Peter McFarlane, *Brotherhood to Nationhood: George Manuel and the Making of the Modern Indian Movement* (Toronto: Between the Lines, 1993), for Wuttunee's support for assimilation. He was hired by the Department of Indian Affairs to "lobby reserve Indians on the government's behalf" (p. 111). Len Marchand, the first Indian member of Parliament, elected for the Liberals in 1968, initially supported the policy, but wavered as Indian opposition developed. McFarlane, *Brotherhood to Nationhood,* 110.

60 RCAP, *Report,* vol. 1, *Looking Forward, Looking Back,* 15.

61 RCAP, *Report*, vol. 4, *Perspectives and Realities*, 204.

62 Ibid., 607.

63 Howard Adams, a prominent Aboriginal activist, born as a Métis, "realized [as he grew up] that being a Métis was something very ugly, something very unpleasant and undesirable and I began to hate myself and I was very sensitive to the kind of things that people would say and do against me, particularly white people. And it became so unpleasant that I found myself wanting to move away from it as soon as possible. So immediately that I finished high school I absolutely got out and I rejected my own culture and my own people, my own parents even ... I became a white man." *The Pierre Berton Show,* with Pierre Berton (9 January 1969, mimeographed), 10. See also Howard Adams, *Prison of Grass: Canada from a Native Point of View,* rev. ed. (Saskatoon: Fifth House Publishers, 1989), Chapter 13, "The White Ideal and the Colonized Personality," for a discussion of the internalization of white attitudes by Aboriginal peoples, self-hate, and the desire to pass for white. See RCAP, *Report,* vol. 1, *Looking Forward, Looking Back,* 618, for other examples of the suppression of Métis identity.

64 Bruce G. Trigger, "The Historians' Indian: Native Americans in Canadian Historical Writing from Charlevoix to the Present," in *The Native Imprint: The Contribution of First Peoples to Canada's Character,* vol. 1, *To 1815,* ed. Olive Patricia Dickason (Lethbridge, AB: Athabaska University Educational Enterprises, 1995), 443. Barsh and Henderson report that "many tribal leaders [believe that] if life in tribal communities can be rendered sufficiently intolerable by federal supervision that stifles initiative and frustrates economic progress, the 'problem' of native peoples will simply autodestruct through emigration ... There is only one avenue of escape: leave the community and vanish into the 'Canadian mosaic' as displaced persons." Barsh and Henderson, "Aboriginal Rights, Treaty Rights, and Human Rights," 56. I have reversed the order of the preceding two sentences. See also RCAP, *Report,* vol. 4, *Perspectives and Realities,* 527-8, for examples of "passing."

65 Dobbin, *The One-and-a-Half Men,* 45. See also p. 95.

66 Andrew Markus, *Governing Savages* (Sydney: Allen and Unwin, 1990), Chapter 12. See also Maria Lane, "Indigenous Australians and the Legacy of European Conquest: Invasion and Resurgence," in *Indigenous Australians and the Law,* ed. Elliott Johnston, Martin Hinton, and Daryle Rigney (Sydney, Australia: Cavendish Publishing, 1997), 14, and Gray, 55.

67 See Canada, Senate, "The Indians and the Great War," *Sessional Papers, The Aboriginal Soldier after the Wars: Report of the Standing Senate Committee on Aboriginal Peoples,* no. 27 (1920), 13-27, which details the remarkably high voluntary recruitment record of Indians in the First World War and numerous incidents of great courage. In 1942, the Métis leader Jim Brady asserted that "our true destiny is not bound by the success or failure attendant upon Métis deliberations ... It is bound up with our continued existence as Canadians who fight [for] those liberties to which we are all devoted." Dobbin, *The One-and-a-Half Men,* 136.

68 Goodwill and Sluman, *John Tootoosis,* 115. See RCAP, *Report,* vol. 1, *Looking Forward, Looking Back,* Chapter 12, "Veterans," for an excellent analysis of Aboriginal wartime participation – in both world wars and the Korean War – their positive experience in the ranks, and their subsequent disillusion when they returned home to face discrimination and less favourable treatment from governments than non-Aboriginal veterans.

69 John Borrows, "Negotiating Treaties and Land Claims: The Impact of Diversity within First Nations Property Interests," *The Windsor Yearbook of Access to Justice* 12 (1992): 233.

70 Ibid., 206, 208.

71 Tim Rowse, "Indigenous Citizenship and Self-Determination: The Problem of Shared Responsibilities," in *Citizenship and Indigenous Australians,* ed. Peterson Sanders, 80.

72 Markus, *Governing Savages,* Chapter 3.

73 Taylor, "Canadian Indian Policy during the Inter-War Years," 2, 205.

74 Ibid., 79.

75 Ibid., 149.

76 Ibid., 205. See, in general, ibid., Chapter 12.

77 See Goodwill and Sluman, *John Tootoosis,* for the career of Tootoosis in provincial and national Indian organizations, and the government's hostility to Indian political activity, especially during the interwar years.

78 Taylor, "Canadian Indian Policy during the Inter-War Years," 210.

79 John F. Leslie, "A Historical Survey of Indian-Government Relations, 1940-1970," (Ottawa: Royal Commission Liaison Office, Department of Indian Affairs and Northern Development, 1993), 53.

80 Rennard Strickland, *Tonto's Revenge: Reflections on American Culture and Policy* (Albuquerque: University of New Mexico Press, 1997), 100.

81 Lane, "Indigenous Australians and the Law," 7.

82 Taylor, "Canadian Indian Policy during the Inter-War Years," 210.

83 The Honourable A.C. Hamilton, *Canada and Aboriginal Peoples: A New Partnership* (Ottawa: Minister of Indian Affairs and Northern Development, 1995), 11, 31.

84 Edward H. Spicer, "The Nations of a State," *Boundary 2, Special Issue: "1492-1992: American Indian Persistence and Resurgence"* 19, 3 (1992): 36-7.

85 For example, Duncan Campbell Scott, Deputy Superintendent General of Indian Affairs from 1913 to 1932, "invariably underestimated the resilience of native culture. He continued to insist, in spite of evidence to the contrary, that the Indians were a 'weird and waning race,' destined ultimately to disappear. At the end of his career, he was as stubbornly convinced of this eventuality as he had been at its inception." Titley, *A Narrow Vision,* 202.

86 Spicer, "The Nations of a State," 48.

87 See RCAP, *Report,* vol. 4, *Perspectives and Realities,* 89, 526-8, for continuing urban racism in the 1990s.

88 For example, see Goodwill and Sluman, *John Tootoosis,* for John Tootoosis, 120-1, 168-9; McFarlane, *Brotherhood to Nationhood,* 36, 37, 46, 142; Roy MacGregor, *Chief: The Fearless Vision of Billy Diamond* (Markham: Viking/Penguin, 1989), xix-xxi, 41, 47, 78; and Dobbin, *The One-and-a-Half Men,* 34, 37, 45.

89 McFarlane, *Brotherhood to Nationhood,* 40.

90 Ibid., 36.

91 Douglas Cole and Ira Chaikin, *An Iron Hand upon the People: The Law against the Potlatch on the Northwest Coast* (Vancouver and Toronto: Douglas and McIntyre, 1990), 183.

92 Aboriginal peoples hid "their [healing and other] practices and practitioners from non-Aboriginal eyes in order to protect them." Concealment was so effective that some Aboriginal people are unaware of their existence. RCAP, *Report,* vol. 3, *Gathering Strength,* 355. See also p. 362 n. 3, and RCAP, *Report,* vol. 1, *Looking Forward, Looking Back,* 190.

93 See Keith H. Basso, *Portraits of "the Whiteman." Linguistic Play and Cultural Symbols among the Western Apache* (Cambridge, UK: Cambridge University Press, 1979), for an American study.

94 See Dobbin, *The One-and-a-Half Men,* for the careers and political activity of two Métis leaders.

95 John J. Borrows, "A Genealogy of Law: Inherent Sovereignty and First Nations

Self-Government," *Osgoode Hall Law Journal* 30, 2 (1992): 294, 297-8.

96 The American situation was no different. Until recently, American Indians were "powerless," and were, with few exceptions, spoken for by others. They were the "targets" of a succession of programs aimed at the "Indian problem." "None of these programs was initiated by the Indians; [and] none enjoyed the consensual support of Indians." Murray L. Wax, "Educating an Anthro: The Influence of Vine Deloria, Jr.," in *Indians and Anthropologists: Vine Deloria, Jr., and the Critique of Anthropology*, ed. Thomas Biolsi and Larry J. Zimmerman (Tucson: University of Arizona Press, 1997), 53.

97 Aboriginal peoples are not convinced that the policy is dead. They see its survival in the continuing denial of Aboriginal rights and the failure to treat their recognition in s. 35 of the 1982 Constitution Act with sufficient seriousness. Hamilton, *Canada and Aboriginal Peoples*, 15.

98 Indian Chiefs of Alberta, *Citizens Plus: A Presentation by the Indian Chiefs of Alberta to Right Honourable P.E. Trudeau, June 1970* (Edmonton: Indian Association of Alberta, 1970).

99 "Citizens Plus," *Indian-Eskimo Association of Canada Bulletin* 11, 3 (1970): 4.

100 Rudy Platiel, "1970 in Retrospect," *Indian-Eskimo Association of Canada Bulletin* 11, 5 (1970): 1-2.

101 Indian Chiefs of Alberta, *Citizens Plus*, 1.

102 Ibid., 16.

103 Ibid., 13-4.

104 Ibid., 37.

105 Harold Cardinal, *The Unjust Society* (Edmonton: M.G. Hurtig, 1969).

106 Ibid., 12, 18, 24, 26.

107 Ibid., 12.

108 *Bulletin 201: Recent Statements by the Indians of Canada, General Synod Action 1969, Some Government Responses, Suggested Resource* (Toronto: Anglican Church of Canada, 1970), 30.

109 Manitoba Indian Brotherhood, *Wahbung: Our Tomorrows* (Winnipeg: Manitoba Indian Brotherhood, 1971), 33.

110 Ibid., 52.

111 Ibid., 74.

112 Ibid., 190-1.

113 Ibid., 99, 148.

114 *Bulletin 201*, 28.

115 C.E.S. Franks reports that Secretary of State funding for representative Aboriginal associations grew from $6 million given to twenty-four associations (from 1971 to 1973) to $13.4 million distributed among fifty-seven associations (from 1983 to 1984). C.E.S. Franks, *Public Administration Questions Relating to Aboriginal Self-Government* (Kingston, ON: Institute of Intergovernmental Relations, 1987), 24. See Canada, *Indian and Native Programs: A Study Team Report to the Task Force on Program Review* (Ottawa: Supply and Services, 1986), 491-7, for an analysis of core funding to representative Native organizations.

116 See Alan C. Cairns, "Aboriginal Canadians, Citizenship, and the Constitution," in *Reconfigurations: Canadian Citizenship and Constitutional Change. Selected Essays by Alan C. Cairns,* ed. Douglas E. Williams (Toronto: McClelland and Stewart, 1995), 245-9, for a discussion of Aboriginal gains in the 1982 Constitution Act and in the defeated Charlottetown Accord.

117 Mary Jane Morris, Don Kerr, and François Nault, "Projections of the Population with Aboriginal Identity, Canada, 1996-2016," in *For Seven Generations*, reports approximately 96,000 re-instatements from 1985 to 1994.

118 See also the section titled "A Time of Transition" in Chapter 3 of this book, and Chapters 4 and 5.

119 Canada, *Consensus Report on the Constitution, Charlottetown, August 28, 1992,* Final Text, and Draft Legal Text, 9 October 1992.

120 Ovide Mercredi and Mary Ellen Turpel, *In the Rapids: Navigating the Future of First Nations* (Toronto: Viking/Penguin, 1993), 35.

121 RCAP, *Report,* vol. 2 (2), *Restructuring the Relationship,* 614-5.

122 See Canada, *Indian and Native Programs: A Study Team Report to the Task Force on Program Review.*

123 Sally M. Weaver, "Indian Policy in the New Conservative Government, Part I: The Nielsen Task Force of 1985," *Native Studies Review* 2, 1 (1986): 15.

124 Sally M. Weaver, "Indian Policy in the New Conservative Government, Part II: The Nielsen Task Force in the Context of Recent Policy Initiatives," *Native Studies Review* 2, 2 (1986): 18.

125 Sally M. Weaver, "Indian Policy in the New Conservative Government, Part I," 19.

126 Ibid., 6.

127 Preston Manning, *The New Canada* (Toronto: Macmillan, 1992), 304.

128 Reform Party of Canada, "Aboriginal Affairs Task Force Report," 15 September 1995. It is noteworthy that Manning's brother-in-law, a Métis, "react[s] furiously" to any suggestions that Manning is personally racist. Sharpe and Braid cite several examples of Manning's behaviour that make allegations of racism difficult to believe. Sydney Sharpe and Don Braid, *Storming Babylon: Preston Manning and the Rise of the Reform Party* (Toronto: Key Porter Books, 1992), 128-30.

129 Melvin H. Smith, *Our Home or Native Land?* (Victoria: Crown Western, 1995), 264.

130 For support of Smith's analysis, see Tom McFeeley, "The Case against Affirmative Apartheid," *British Columbia Report* 6, 41 (12 June 1995): 32-7; for the quotation, see Tony Hall, "Between Jihad and McWorld: Our Home and Native Land," *Canadian Forum* 75, 850 (June 1996): 5.

131 Tim Rowse, *White Flour, White Power: From Rations to Citizenship in Central Australia* (Cambridge, UK: Cambridge University Press, 1998), 213.

132 RCAP, *Report,* vol. 3, *Gathering Strength,* 63-4; and RCAP, *Report,* vol. 4, *Perspectives and Realities,* 66.

133 See Helen Stone, "Aboriginal Women and Self-Government: A Literature Review," (Ottawa: Research and Analysis Directorate, Department of Indian and Northern Affairs, 1994).

134 Emma La Rocque, "Re-examining Culturally Appropriate Models in Criminal Justice Applications," in *Aboriginal and Treaty Rights in Canada: Essays on Law, Equality, and Respect for Difference,* ed. Michael Asch (Vancouver: UBC Press, 1997), 91-3.

135 RCAP, *Report,* vol. 3, *Gathering Strength,* 65-6; and RCAP, *Report,* vol. 4, *Perspectives and Realities,* 63, 77-8, 573-4.

136 John Borrows, "Contemporary Traditional Equality: The Effect of the Charter on First Nation Politics," *University of New Brunswick Law Journal* 43 (1994): 45.

137 Stone, "Aboriginal Women and Self-Government," 14.

138 In addition, there will be other citizens on "the nation's traditional territory, and several thousand citizens living elsewhere in Canada. The nation-government will exercise some functions for all its citizens and some only for those living on Aboriginal lands." RCAP, *Report,* vol. 5, *Renewal: A Twenty-Year Commitment,* 84 n. 9.

139 I thank an anonymous external assessor of this manuscript who cited these remarkable achievements of a people whose extensive contact with Canadian society dates from the Second World War.

140 Leslie and Macguire, eds., *Historical Development of the Indian Act*, 27.

141 Ibid., 115.

142 Martin, *Chrétien,* 197-201.

143 See the discussion in the section titled "Ancestry versus Identity" in Chapter 4. See also the section in Chapter 3 titled "An Alternative Vision: A Modernizing Aboriginality," for evidence of behaviour that formerly might have been described as assimilation, but is now redefined as a modernizing aboriginality.

### Chapter 3: Choice

1 For a discussion, see Alan C. Cairns, "Aboriginal Canadians, Citizenship, and the Constitution," in *Reconfigurations: Canadian Citizenship and Constitutional Change. Selected Essays by Alan C. Cairns,* ed. Douglas E. Williams (Toronto: McClelland and Stewart, 1995), 245.

2 Kent McNeil, "The Decolonization of Canada: Moving toward Recognition of Aboriginal Governments," *Western Legal History* 7, 1 (1994): 129. McNeil argues that "despite its rejection, the accord probably altered the relationship between the aboriginal peoples and the Canadian state in fundamental and irrevocable ways" by its recognition of an inherent right of self-government that predated "the colonization of Canada by Europeans," and by its recognition in the bargaining process that Aboriginal peoples "have a stake in the whole constitutional structure of the country" (pp. 140-1). Peter W. Hogg and Mary Ellen Turpel have made proposals for implementing Aboriginal self-government, based on elements of the Charlottetown Accord, without the necessity of a constitutional amendment. Peter W. Hogg and Mary Ellen Turpel, "Implementing Aboriginal Self-Government: Constitutional and Jurisdictional Issues," *Canadian Bar Review* 74, 2 (1995): 187-224.

3 The following points are taken from Canada, *Consensus Report on the Constitution, Charlottetown, August 28, 1992,* Final Text, and Draft Legal Text, 9 October 1992.

4 Consensus Report on the Constitution, Charlottetown, 28 August 1992, Final Text (s.41). The Consensus Report is reproduced in *The Charlottetown Accord, the Referendum and the Future of Canada,* ed. Kenneth McRoberts and Patrick Monahan (Toronto: University of Toronto Press, 1993), 279-309.

5 McNeil, "Decolonization of Canada," 132.

6 This discussion of the Charlottetown Accord is taken from Cairns, *Reconfigurations,* 247-9.

7 However, the Aboriginal voice is plural, not monolithic. See below, pp. 205-9.

8 Canada, "Indian Self-Government in Canada," *Minutes and Proceedings of the Special Committee on Indian Self-Government,* no. 40, 12 and 20 October 1983 (hereinafter *Penner Report*), 63.

9 Noel Lyon, *Aboriginal Self-Government: Rights of Citizenship and Access to Governmental Services* (Kingston, ON: Institute of Intergovernmental Relations, 1984), 5.

10 *Penner Report,* 63.

11 Quoted in Roger Gibbins and J. Rick Ponting, "An Assessment of the Probable Impact of Aboriginal Self-Government in Canada," in *The Politics of Gender, Ethnicity and Language in Canada,* ed. Alan C. Cairns and Cynthia Williams, Collected Research Studies of the Royal Commission on the Economic Union and Development Prospects for Canada, vol. 34 (Toronto: University of Toronto Press, 1986), 178.

12 Frank Cassidy and Robert L. Bish, *Indian Government: Its Meaning in Practice* (Lantzville, BC, and Halifax, NS: Oolichan Books and the Institute for Research on Public Policy, 1989), 56.

13 Anne Norton, "Ruling Memory," *Political Theory* 21, 3 (1993): 454.

14 Darlene Johnston, "First Nations and Canadian Citizenship," in *Belonging: The*

*Meaning and Future of Canadian Citizenship,* ed. William Kaplan (Montreal and Kingston: McGill-Queen's University Press, 1993), 349.

15 Tony Hall, noting the number of band governments that prevented the setting up of polling stations, stated: "This decision reflects a strong current of opinion among many First Nations people that their participation in the vote, no matter which side of the question they took, would be inconsistent with the distinct constitutional status of Indian societies in Canada." Tony Hall, "The Assembly of First Nations and the Demise of the Charlottetown Accord" (30 November 1992, mimeographed), 1.

16 J.R. Ponting, "Internationalization: Perspectives on an Emerging Direction in Aboriginal Affairs," *Canadian Ethnic Studies* 22, 3 (1990): 93. According to Cree leader Billy Diamond, his father taught him "one thing ... never, never agree with the government – no matter what. And I never have. Never." Roy MacGregor, *Chief: The Fearless Vision of Billy Diamond* (Markham: Viking/Penguin, 1989), 4.

17 With the exception being the Métis of the settlements in Alberta, discussed earlier.

18 Tim Rowse, *White Flour, White Power: From Rations to Citizenship in Central Australia* (Cambridge, UK: Cambridge University Press, 1998), 221-2.

19 James [sákéj] Youngblood Henderson, "Empowering Treaty Federalism," *Saskatchewan Law Review* 58, 2 (1994): 241-329.

20 For example, after citing the strong assertion of cultural difference by Ralph Akiwenzie, an Ojibway chief, Claude Denis stated: "This blunt affirmation of cultural difference is not a mere statement of fact, for its utterance provides part of the foundation for the political claim of aboriginal self-government, which is a centrepiece of the current Canadian constitutional debate." Claude Denis, "Rights and Spirit Dancing: Aboriginal Peoples versus the Canadian State," in *Explorations in Difference: Law, Culture and Politics,* ed. Jonathan Hart and Richard W. Bauman (Toronto: University of Toronto Press, 1996), 199.

21 Emma La Rocque, "Re-examining Culturally Appropriate Models in Criminal Justice Applications," in *Aboriginal and Treaty Rights in Canada: Essays on Law, Equality, and Respect for Difference,* ed. Michael Asch (Vancouver: UBC Press, 1997), 87-8.

22 Keith H. Basso, *Portraits of "the Whiteman." Linguistic Play and Cultural Symbols among the Western Apache* (Cambridge, UK: Cambridge University Press, 1979), 5. He was writing about the American situation.

23 John Borrows, "Negotiating Treaties and Land Claims: The Impact of Diversity within First Nations Property Interests," *The Windsor Yearbook of Access to Justice* 12 (1992): 232.

24 La Rocque, "Re-examining Culturally Appropriate Models in Criminal Justice Applications," 78-80, 82-3.

25 First Nations Circle on the Constitution, *To the Source: Commissioners' Report* (Ottawa: Assembly of First Nations, 1992), 64.

26 Joyce Green, "Constitutionalizing the Patriarchy: Aboriginal Women and Aboriginal Government," *Constitutional Forum* 4, 4 (1993): 118. See also La Rocque, "Re-examining Culturally Appropriate Models in Criminal Justice Applications," 87, 90.

27 P.A. Monture-Okanee and M.E. Turpel, "Aboriginal Peoples and Canadian Criminal Law: Rethinking Justice," *University of British Columbia Law Review,* special edition (1992): 256, 258.

28 See above, pp. 33-5.

29 La Rocque, "Re-examining Culturally Appropriate Models in Criminal Justice Applications," 90.

30 Quoted in Rennard Strickland, *Tonto's Revenge: Reflections on American Culture and Policy* (Albuquerque: University of New Mexico Press, 1997), 13. Emphasis in original.

31 La Rocque, "Re-examining Culturally Appropriate Models in Criminal Justice Applications," 88.

32 Michael Posluns criticizes the RCAP *Report* for its portrait of an Aboriginal world view defined by contrast to the "culture and perspectives ... [of] non-Aboriginal peoples." To employ "Aboriginality ... to foster a sense of negative otherness" is to fail to exploit the concept's capacity to link and unite peoples – its outward reach. Michael W. Posluns, "Evading the Unspeakable: A Comment on *Looking Back, Looking Forward,* Volume I of the Report of the RCAP," *Canada Watch* 5, 5 (1997): 87.

33 Joseph H. Carens, "Citizenship and Aboriginal Self-Government," in *For Seven Generations. An Information Legacy of the Royal Commission on Aboriginal Peoples, RCAP Research Reports. Governance. Project Area 4: Citizenship,* no. 3422-5 [CD-ROM] (Ottawa: Libraxus, 1997).

34 Patrick Macklem, "Distributing Sovereignty: Indian Nations and Equality of Peoples," *Stanford Law Review* 45, 5 (1993): 1343-4, 1359-60.

35 Stewart Clatworthy and Anthony H. Smith, *Population Implications of the 1985 Amendments to the Indian Act: Final Report* (Perth, ON: Living Dimensions, 1992), ii, a report prepared for the AFN.

36 Pierre Gauvin and Diane Fournier, "Marriages of Registered Indians: Canada and Four Selected Bands, 1967 to 1990," Technical Paper 92-1 (Ottawa: Department of Indian Affairs and Northern Development, July 1992), 8.

37 Karl Eschbach, "The Enduring and Vanishing American Indian: American Indian Population Growth and Intermarriage in 1990," *Ethnic and Racial Studies* 18 (January 1995): 91, 92, 95. According to Eschbach, in the United States slightly more than half of the children of the intermarried are identified by their parents as white. P. 97.

38 Stephen Thernstrom and Abigail Thernstrom, *America in Black and White: One Nation, Indivisible* (New York: Simon and Schuster, 1997), 526. The authors note that incomplete data suggest the estimates "may be as much as one-fifth too low."

39 First Nations Circle on the Constitution, *To the Source,* 70.

40 Colin Irwin, "Lords of the Arctic: Wards of the State, The Growing Inuit Population, Arctic Resettlement and Their Effects on Social and Economic Change," for the *Review of Demography and Its Implications for Economic and Social Policy* (Ottawa: Health and Welfare Canada, [1988]), 34, 44.

41 Carol La Prairie, "Separate Aboriginal Justice Systems: Ultimate Solution or False Promise?" *Policy Options* 18, 2 (1997): 9-10. See also Roger F. McDonnell, "Prospects for Accountability in Canadian Aboriginal Justice Systems," in *Accountability for Criminal Justice,* ed. Philip C. Stenning (Toronto: University of Toronto Press, 1995), 474.

42 Susantha Goonatilake, "The Self Wandering between Cultural Localization and Globalization," in *The Decolonization of Imagination: Culture, Knowledge and Power,* ed. Jan Nederveen and Bhikhu Parekh (London: Zed Books, 1995), 232-3.

43 Bruce G. Trigger, "The Historians' Indian: Native Americans in Canadian Historical Writing from Charlevoix to the Present," in *The Native Imprint: The Contribution of First Peoples to Canada's Character,* vol. 1, *To 1815,* ed. Olive Patricia Dickason (Lethbridge, AB: Athabaska University Educational Enterprises, 1995), 443.

44 Jeremy Webber, "Relations of Force and Relations of Justice: The Emergence of Normative Community between Colonists and Aboriginal Peoples," *Osgoode Hall Law Journal* 33, 4 (1995): 656.

45 Several sentences in the previous two paragraphs are taken from Cairns, *Reconfigurations,* 256-7. RCAP Commissioner Paul L.A.H. Chartrand observed, "It is not helpful to tell the Métis and other buffalo hunting cultures of the Plains that we have aboriginal rights to maintain that economy and that culture, which are now

gone, and to insist that the law protects only what is distinctive to a culture and not what all cultures have in common." "Opening the Door to Justice and Democratic Participation in Canada for Aboriginal Peoples," notes for a speech to the "Blueprint for the Future ... A Public Forum at the Banff Centre for Management" conference, Banff, AB, 5 March 1997, 2.

46 As Susan Strange forcefully argues in *The Retreat of the State: The Diffusion of Power in the World Economy* (Cambridge, UK: Cambridge University Press, 1996).

47 Kwame Anthony Appiah, "The Postcolonial and the Postmodern," in *The Post-Colonial Studies Reader,* ed. Bill Ashcroft, Gareth Griffiths, and Helen Tiffin (London: Routledge, 1995), 124.

48 Edward A. Said, *Culture and Imperialism* (New York: Alfred A. Knopf, 1993), xxv, 15. Emphasis in original.

49 Salman Rushdie, *Imaginary Homelands: Essays and Criticisms 1981-1991* (London: Granta Books, 1992), 394. Emphasis in original.

50 See above, pp. 42-3.

51 Sally M. Weaver, "A New Paradigm in Canadian Indian Policy for the 1990s," *Canadian Ethnic Studies* 22, 3 (1990): 12. "What is most impressive about the survival of American Indians, their success in not vanishing, is that they resist not merely by clinging to the past but by changing, accepting, even welcoming at least part of the present. Their persistence should provoke us ... to realize to what a large degree culture is transformation." Karl Kroeber, "American Indian Persistence and Resurgence," *Boundary 2,* Special Issue, *1492-1992: American Indian Persistence and Resurgence* 19, 3 (1992): 1.

52 Eric Hobsbawm and Terence Ranger, eds., *The Invention of Tradition* (Cambridge, UK: Cambridge University Press, 1983).

53 John Borrows, "A Genealogy of Law: Inherent Sovereignty and First Nations Self-Government," *Osgoode Hall Law Journal* 30, 2 (1992): 307-8.

54 Dara Culhane, "Adding Insult to Injury: Her Majesty's Loyal Anthropologist," *BC Studies* 95 (Autumn 1992): 85. Ron Ignace made the same point. Museums "don't seem to understand that we still exist as people, that we adapt and change ... while still maintaining some of our principles that were tried and true over the years ... You have two cultures. There is the open western culture that Native people live by, but there's also an underground Native culture that is not spoken about and not displayed ... [Academic anthropologists] see only the surface life-styles of a people and they don't get to understand the deeper ways and means of a people's techniques of survival under trying conditions." Ron Ignace, George Speck, and Renee Taylor, "Some Native Perspectives on Anthropology," *BC Studies* 95 (Autumn 1992): 168-9.

55 John Borrows, "Frozen Rights in Canada: Constitutional Interpretation and the Trickster," *American Indian Law Review* 22, 1 (1997): 63. Borrows' comment was part of a critique of recent Supreme Court decisions that had identified the Aboriginal rights recognized and affirmed by s. 35(1) of the 1982 Constitution Act as "the practices, traditions and customs central to the Aboriginal societies that existed in North America prior to contact with Europeans." *R. v. Van der Peet,* [1996] 2 SCR 507 at 548, para. 44. This definition, Borrows noted, made the recognized and affirmed rights irrelevant to the contemporary physical and cultural survival of indigenous peoples. Borrows, "Frozen Rights in Canada," 49, 58-9.

56 George Speck, answering the question "Where are the Indians at Alert Bay?" said: "We're the people down at the dock fixing our nets, we're the people walking down the streets drinking Coke and Slushies ... we're social workers, but we're living in a community that is not recognizable in terms of long houses, button blankets and masks ... There is very little on the surface that distinguishes us from other people.

It has far more to do with our history, our social and economic relations to the outside, and how white people and Indian people see each other and interact together." Ignace, Speck, and Taylor, "Some Native Perspectives on Anthropology," 178.

57 Canada, *Report of the Royal Commission on Aboriginal Peoples* (hereinafter RCAP, *Report*), vol. 2 (1), *Restructuring the Relationship* (Ottawa: Canada Communication Group Publishing, 1996), 117; and RCAP, *Report,* vol. 4, *Perspectives and Realities,* 158, 164, 202, 237, 395, 531, 537.

58 RCAP, *Report,* vol. 4, *Perspectives and Realities,* 407.

59 RCAP, *Report,* vol. 3, *Gathering Strength,* 188.

60 Ibid., 602.

61 Ibid., 612, 648 n. 28.

62 RCAP, *Report,* vol. 1, *Looking Forward, Looking Back,* 693.

63 Gary D. Sandefur, Ronald R. Rindfuss, and Barney Cohen, eds., "Introduction," in *Changing Numbers, Changing Needs. American Indian Demography and Public Health,* ed. Gary D. Sandefur, Ronald R. Rindfuss, and Barney Cohen (Washington, DC: National Academy Press, 1996), 4.

64 Russell Thornton, "Tribal Membership Requirements and the Demography of 'Old' and 'New' Native Americans," in *Changing Numbers,* ed. Sandefur, Rindfuss, and Cohen, 105.

65 Eugene P. Ericksen, "Problems in Sampling the Native American and Alaska Native Populations," in *Changing Numbers,* ed. Sandefur, Rindfuss, and Cohen, 114, 118, 121.

66 "A constitution," stated the Supreme Court of Canada, "may seek to ensure that vulnerable minority groups are endowed with institutions and rights necessary to maintain and promote their identities against the assimilative pressures of the majority." *Reference re Secession of Quebec* (1998), 228 NR 203 at 251, para. 74.

67 Kurt H. Wolff, ed., *The Sociology of Georg Simmel* (New York: Free Press, 1950), 30-1.

68 See Irwin, "Lords of the Arctic."

69 RCAP, *Report,* vol. 3, *Gathering Strength,* 75.

70 Ibid., 85. "Many native communities are undergoing dramatic social upheaval and disintegration ... If [they] ... are not willing to take an uncompromising stand against violence, particularly sexual violence, there may not be functioning native communities in the future. Studies show that, as young people and women have more access to urban centres, they will run from abusive or desperate environments." La Rocque, "Re-examining Culturally Appropriate Models in Criminal Justice Applications," 93.

71 RCAP, *Report,* vol. 3, *Gathering Strength,* 54-86, for a discussion of violence.

72 Ibid., 109. See also Eduardo Duran and Bonnie Duran, *Native American Postcolonial Psychology* (Albany: State University of New York Press, 1995), Chapter 3, for a discussion of the pathologies based on "acute and/or chronic reaction to colonialism" (p. 6), manifested in damaged personalities, self-hatred, low self-esteem and disorientation.

73 Carol La Prairie, "Community Justice or Just Communities? Aboriginal Communities in Search of Justice," *Canadian Journal of Criminology* 37 (October 1995): 527-9.

74 In addition to La Prairie's "Community Justice or Just Communities? Aboriginal Communities in Search of Justice," see also her articles "The 'New' Justice: Some Implications for Aboriginal Communities," *Canadian Journal of Criminology* 40 (January 1998): 61-79; "Aboriginal Crime and Justice: Explaining the Present, Exploring the Future," *Canadian Journal of Criminology* 34 (July-October 1992): 281-97; and "Separate Aboriginal Justice Systems." See also McDonnell, "Prospects for Accountability in Canadian Aboriginal Justice Systems."

75 See Clatworthy and Smith, *Population Implications of the 1985 Amendments to the Indian Act,* Chapters 3, 4, and 5.

76 See Tom Flanagan, "An Unworkable Vision of Self-Government," *Policy Options* 18, 2 (1997): 20-1, for the incentives to corruption in small communities divided by kinship where the governing élite controls extensive, externally provided funds. In "The Challenge of Indigenous Self-Determination," *University of Michigan Journal of Law Reform* 26, 2 (1993): 277-312, Russel Lawrence Barsh, a sympathetic and supportive advocate of indigenous peoples and their rights, paints an extremely bleak picture of the politics and governance of "American Indian tribes [which] are wealthier and have enjoyed greater powers of internal self-government far longer than indigenous peoples anywhere else. The rhetoric of sovereignty, antimaterialism, and traditionalism is stronger here than anywhere else" (p. 292). The results and the rhetoric are far apart.

77 Vaclav Havel, *Living in Truth* (London: Faber and Faber, 1989).

78 Basil Davidson, *The Black Man's Burden: Africa and the Curse of the Nation-State* (New York: Times Books/Random House, 1992), 298.

79 Jim Harding, "Aboriginal Self-Government and the Urban Social Crisis," in *Continuing Poundmaker and Riel's Quest,* ed. Richard Gosse, James [sákéj] Youngblood Henderson, and Roger Carter (Saskatoon: Purich Publishing, 1994), 380.

80 Wolff, ed., *Sociology of Georg Simmel*, 30.

81 McDonnell, "Prospects for Accountability in Canadian Aboriginal Justice Systems," 475.

### Chapter 4: The Constitutional Vision

1 Secondary analysis of the *Report* is limited. There are nine short articles in *Policy Options* 18, 2 (1997), nine short commentaries in *Canada Watch* 5, 5 (1997), and four, essentially critical, columns by Jeffrey Simpson in successive issues of the *Globe and Mail,* 25-28 February 1997.

2 J. Peter Meekison, notes for a speech to the "Blueprint for the Future ... A Public Forum at the Banff Centre for Management" conference, Banff, AB, 5 March 1997, 1. The publications referred to in the text are not exhaustive. See Canada, *Report of the Royal Commission on Aboriginal Peoples* (hereinafter RCAP, *Report*), vol. 5, *Renewal: A Twenty-Year Commitment* (Ottawa: Canada Communication Group Publishing, 1996), 330-2, for a complete list of the Commission's publications.

3 RCAP, *Report, vol. 1, Looking Forward, Looking Back,* 513.

4 Ibid., 430-9.

5 Ila Bussidor and Üstün Bilgen-Reinart, *Night Spirits: The Story of the Relocation of the Sayisi Dene* (Winnipeg: University of Manitoba Press, 1997).

6 RCAP, *Report,* vol. 1, *Looking Forward, Looking Back,* 354-6; and RCAP, *Report,* vol. 2 (1), *Restructuring the Relationship,* 425, 487, 552, 555-6.

7 RCAP, *Report,* vol. 1, *Looking Forward, Looking Back,* 7.

8 Ibid., 7-8. The need for healing is a recurrent theme. See RCAP, *Report,* vol. 4, *Perspectives and Realities,* 17, 57, 307, 488.

9 RCAP, *Report,* vol. 5, *Renewal: A Twenty-Year Commitment,* 141. The recommendations are summarized in ibid., 141-255.

10 Canada, *Gathering Strength: Canada's Aboriginal Action Plan* (Ottawa: Minister of Indian Affairs and Northern Development, 1997).

11 Ibid., 11.

12 Ibid., 5.

13 Patrick Macklem, "Normative Dimensions of an Aboriginal Right of Self-Government," *Queen's Law Journal* 21 (Fall 1995): 173-219; Patrick Macklem, "Distributing Sovereignty: Indian Nations and Equality of Peoples," *Stanford Law Review* 45, 5 (1993): 1311-67.

14 Reproduced in Appendix A, RCAP, *Report,* vol. 1, *Looking Forward, Looking Back,* 699-702.

15 RCAP, *Report,* vol. 3, *Gathering Strength,* 529.

16 Ibid., 664.

17 Ibid., 561.

18 RCAP, *Report,* vol. 4, *Perspectives and Realities,* 551.

19 Ibid., 552.

20 RCAP, *Report,* vol. 3, *Gathering Strength,* 501.

21 Ibid., 530. See also pp. 562 and 664.

22 With respect to Aboriginal groups living in urban areas, 80.8 percent of registered off-reserve Indian people live in urban areas, 69.3 percent of non-registered Indian people, 64.9 percent of Métis people, and 21.9 percent of Inuit. RCAP, *Report,* vol. 5, *Renewal: A Twenty-Year Commitment,* 50 n. 6.

23 RCAP, *Report,* vol. 4, *Perspectives and Realities,* 520. Table 7.6, p. 604, indicates 20 percent off-reserve rural Aboriginal population (146,100).

24 RCAP, *Report,* vol. 1, *Looking Forward, Looking Back,* 16. For the geographical definition of the south, the location of 62 percent of the registered population, see ibid., 25-6 n. 11.

25 RCAP, *Report,* vol. 4, *Perspectives and Realities,* 248.

26 Ibid., 232-3. See also pp. 245, 247, and 249.

27 Ibid., 242.

28 RCAP, *Report,* vol. 2 (2), *Restructuring the Relationship,* 425, 448, 519, 543, 557.

29 Ibid., 451.

30 Ibid., 574.

31 Ibid., 780.

32 RCAP, *Report,* vol. 4, *Perspectives and Realities,* 529.

33 Canada, Royal Commission on Aboriginal Peoples (RCAP), *Partners in Confederation: Aboriginal Peoples, Self-Government and the Constitution* (Ottawa: Canada Communication Group, 1993), 44.

34 RCAP, *Report,* vol. 2 (1), *Restructuring the Relationship,* 94-5 n. 4, which lists thirty-two studies.

35 Ibid., 15.

36 An assessment based on an analysis of the footnotes in RCAP, *Report,* vol. 4, *Perspectives and Realities,* Chapter 7, "Urban Perspectives."

37 Jeffrey Simpson, "Just What Is a 'Nation' and How Can It Work Like a Province?" *Globe and Mail,* 25 February 1997.

38 John Gray, "Absent Aboriginals: Not a Word about Natives," *Globe and Mail,* 24 May 1997.

39 The *Report* devoted 353 pages to lands and resources, 96 pages to treaties, and only 102 pages to "Urban Perspectives." Volume 2 of the *Report* is over 1,100 pages and has as its primary theme "the revitalization of Aboriginal nationhood," while admitting this excludes about half of the Aboriginal population. RCAP, *Report,* vol. 2 (1), *Restructuring the Relationship,* 10.

40 Canada, Senate Standing Committee on Aboriginal Peoples, *Minutes of Proceedings and Evidence,* 35th Parliament, 2nd Session, no. 2, 10 December 1996 (Ottawa: Queen's Printer, 1996).

41 See, for example, "Special Issue: The RCAP Report and the Future of Canada," *Canada Watch* 5, 5 (1997). Of the nine authors, only two make even passing references to Aboriginal people in cities.

42 RCAP, *Report,* vol. 4, *Perspectives and Realities,* 522. See also pp. 521-38 for a discussion of Aboriginal cultural identity.

43 Stewart Clatworthy and Anthony H. Smith, *Population Implications of the 1985*

Amendments to the Indian Act: Final Report (Perth, ON: Living Dimensions, 1992), ii.

44 RCAP, *Report,* vol. 3, *Gathering Strength,* Chapters 5 and 6; RCAP, *Report,* vol. 4, *Perspectives and Realities,* 214, 241, 571; and RCAP, *Report,* vol. 5, *Renewal: A Twenty-Year Commitment,* 608.

45 RCAP, *Report,* vol. 2 (1), *Restructuring the Relationship,* 154 ; RCAP, *Report,* vol. 4, *Perspectives and Realities,* 157, 598; and RCAP, *Report,* vol. 5, *Renewal: A Twenty-Year Commitment,* 157.

46 RCAP, *Report,* vol. 4, *Perspectives and Realities,* 605-7.

47 See Table 7.4, "Aboriginal Population by Nation of Origin, Selected Census Metropolitan Areas, 1991," RCAP, *Report,* vol. 4, *Perspectives and Realities,* 592-7, for relevant data. At least thirty-five nations are represented in Vancouver's Aboriginal population, which complicates its political mobilization. RCAP, *Report,* vol. 4, *Perspectives and Realities,* 590.

48 However, the Commission does suggest the possibility of the extraterritorial extension, in a few policy areas, of the jurisdiction of landed nation-governments to urban nation members. This is discussed, along with several other experimental approaches to bring the nations and the city together in RCAP, *Report,* vol. 4, *Perspectives and Realities,* 588-601.

49 Ibid., 561. They do, however, recommend sensitivity to Métis and treaty people in the three Prairie provinces.

50 RCAP, *Report,* vol. 1, *Looking Forward, Looking Back,* Chapter 16. See also the summary in Canada, Royal Commission on Aboriginal Peoples (RCAP), *People to People, Nation to Nation: Highlights from the Report of the Royal Commission on Aboriginal Peoples* (Ottawa: Minister of Supply and Services, 1996), 53-7.

51 RCAP, *Report,* vol. 4, *Perspectives and Realities,* 232.

52 These urban possibilities are discussed in RCAP, *Report,* vol. 2 (1), *Restructuring the Relationship,* 150-6, 272-9; and RCAP, *Report,* vol. 4, *Perspectives and Realities,* 580-601.

53 RCAP, *Report,* vol. 4, *Perspectives and Realities,* 612.

54 RCAP, *Report,* vol. 1, *Looking Forward, Looking Back,* 15.

55 RCAP, *Report,* vol. 4, *Perspectives and Realities,* 607.

56 Ibid., 204.

57 RCAP, *Report,* vol. 1, *Looking Forward, Looking Back,* 24 n. 7.

58 RCAP, *Report,* vol. 4, *Perspectives and Realities,* Chapters 7 and 2 respectively.

59 Ibid., 202.

60 Ibid., 531, 537.

61 See Clatworthy and Smith, *Population Implications of the 1985 Amendments to the Indian Act,* for a discussion.

62 There is a brief discussion of intermarriage as it relates to Bill C-31 and the new rules for inheriting legal Indian status in RCAP, *Report,* vol. 4, *Perspectives and Realities,* 37-49, and a recognition of mixed genetic heritage and varied ancestry in RCAP, *Report,* vol. 2 (1), *Restructuring the Relationship,* 177, 237-8, but contemporary intermarriage rates are neither reported, discussed, nor analyzed.

63 One senior commission interviewee asserted that the Commission never confronted this choice as such. It was a by-product of the decision to give priority to the nation as the unit of self-determination and cultural reinvigoration.

64 The preliminary findings of a research study by the Department of Indian Affairs and Northern Development's Research and Analysis Directorate employing 1991 data reported a marked advantage of off-reserve status Indians in terms of per capita income, educational attainment, and life expectancy. Per capita income was 50 percent higher, and life expectancy 4.6 years longer. See Daniel Beavon and Martin Cooke, "Measuring the Well-Being of First Nation Peoples" (2 October

1998, mimeographed). For a discussion, see Jeffrey Simpson, "Aboriginal Conundrum," *Globe and Mail*, 15 October 1998.

65 RCAP, *Report*, vol. 2 (2), *Restructuring the Relationship*, 806.

66 Ibid., 966; and RCAP, *Report*, vol. 4, *Perspectives and Realities*, 214, 610.

67 RCAP, *Report*, vol. 2 (2), *Restructuring the Relationship*, 803, 814; and RCAP, *Report*, vol. 3, *Gathering Strength*, 168, 170.

68 RCAP, *Report*, vol. 2 (2), *Restructuring the Relationship*, 966.

69 Ibid., 801. See also RCAP, *Report*, vol. 4, *Perspectives and Realities*, 212.

70 RCAP, *Report*, vol. 3, *Gathering Strength*, 121.

71 RCAP, *Report*, vol. 4, *Perspectives and Realities*, 212.

72 Ibid., 216.

73 Ibid., 214, 241, 571.

74 RCAP, *Report*, vol. 1, *Looking Forward, Looking Back*, 25 n. 10.

75 RCAP, *Report*, vol. 4, *Perspectives and Realities*, 522.

76 See, for example, RCAP, ibid., 211-2, 214, 520-1, 570, 572, 608, 609. In some cases, the contrast is between the non-reserve population and the total population.

77 RCAP, *Report*, vol. 2 (2), *Restructuring the Relationship*, 815.

78 Ibid., 1023.

79 RCAP, *Report*, vol. 4, *Perspectives and Realities*, 537. See also ibid., 158, re the bombardment of youth "with the images and sounds of the dominant society ... Non-Aboriginal culture pervades the life of Aboriginal youth, especially in the city." Contrast the views of the Australian Aboriginal academic, Maria Lane, who defends the liberal and individualist urban setting, and queries why it is that the "notion of integration [which she distinguishes from assimilation], or individual self-determination, is treated as a pariah." Maria Lane, "Indigenous Australians and the Legacy of European Conquest: Invasion and Resurgence," in *Indigenous Australians and the Law*, ed. Elliott Johnston, Martin Hinton, and Daryle Rigney (Sydney, Australia: Cavendish Publishing, 1997), 29.

80 RCAP, *Report*, vol. 4, *Perspectives and Realities*, 522.

81 Note, for example, the negative reference to "federal policy [that] emphasizes individual advancement and integration into the broader Canadian economy more than rebuilding Aboriginal economies and all that entails." RCAP, *Report*, vol. 2 (2), *Restructuring the Relationship*, 798. See also pp. 798-800.

82 This paragraph has been informed by helpful comments from Kathy Brock and David Cameron.

83 Chartrand stated that he "was especially honoured to be appointed as a member of the historic Métis nation of Western Canada. [He saw his contribution as springing from his professional background and his] life experiences in having been born and raised in an historic Métis community, one of twelve children of a Métis trapper, fisherman and carpenter." Paul L.A.H. Chartrand, "Opening the Door to Justice and Democratic Participation in Canada for Aboriginal Peoples," notes for a speech to the "Blueprint for the Future ... A Public Forum at the Banff Centre for Management" conference, Banff, AB, 5 March 1997, 1.

84 For additional criteria to ensure that Aboriginal persons' perspectives and experience-based knowledge were incorporated into the research program, see Canada, Royal Commission on Aboriginal Peoples (RCAP), "Ethical Guidelines for Research," *Integrated Research Plan* (Ottawa: Royal Commission on Aboriginal Peoples, 1993), 37-40.

85 RCAP, *Report*, vol. 2 (2), *Restructuring the Relationship*, 1015. "Aboriginal peoples are political entities that, because of their treaties, the recognition of their rights in Canada's constitution, and the nature of their social and cultural cohesion, need to be recognized as nations, negotiated with as nations, and thereby empowered

to implement their own solutions within a flexible Canadian federation." Ibid., 1016.

86 RCAP, *Report,* vol. 1, *Looking Forward, Looking Back,* xxiv. See also RCAP, *Partners in Confederation,* 31, describing Canadians as "a partial and imperfect realization of [the] ... ideal [of] ... a multinational Confederation of peoples and communities united in peace and fellowship."

87 RCAP, *Report,* vol. 1, *Looking Forward, Looking Back,* xxv.

88 RCAP, *Report,* vol. 2 (2), *Restructuring the Relationship,* 562.

89 RCAP, *Report,* vol. 1, *Looking Forward, Looking Back,* 610.

90 RCAP, *Report,* vol. 2 (1), *Restructuring the Relationship,* 21.

91 Ibid., 20, 42.

92 Ibid., 44, 47.

93 Colonialism references are ubiquitous. RCAP, *Report,* vol. 1, *Looking Forward, Looking Back,* 180, 181, 187, 188, 236, 376, 603, 608, 609, 610, 611, 612, 616; RCAP, *Report,* vol. 2 (1), *Restructuring the Relationship,* 327, 328; RCAP, *Report,* vol. 3, *Gathering Strength,* 7, 60, 73, 74, 75, 87, 96, 355, 357; and RCAP, *Report,* vol. 4, *Perspectives and Realities,* 8, 19, 57, 148, 149, 404.

94 RCAP, *Report,* vol. 5, *Renewal: A Twenty-Year Commitment,* 16.

95 RCAP, *Report,* vol. 2 (2), *Restructuring the Relationship,* 422, 570, 574-6.

96 Ibid., 572.

97 Ibid., 577.

98 RCAP, *Report,* vol. 2 (1), *Restructuring the Relationship,* 21.

99 Ibid., 18-20.

100 Ibid., 83.

101 Ibid., 2-4.

102 Ibid., 10.

103 Ibid., 17. See also p. 74.

104 Ibid., 167; RCAP, *Report,* vol. 5, *Renewal: A Twenty-Year Commitment,* 158.

105 RCAP, *Report,* vol. 2 (1), *Restructuring the Relationship,* 307; RCAP, *Report,* vol. 5, *Renewal: A Twenty-Year Commitment,* 149.

106 RCAP, *Report,* vol. 2 (1), *Restructuring the Relationship,* 52.

107 RCAP, *People to People, Nation to Nation,* 51.

108 See RCAP, *Report,* vol. 5, *Renewal: A Twenty-Year Commitment,* 148-54, for "Restructuring the Relationship" recommendations.

109 RCAP, *Report,* vol. 2 (1), *Restructuring the Relationship,* 52.

110 Ibid., 22. See also RCAP, *Partners in Confederation,* 22-7, for a defence of the compact theory, including supporting quotes from Justice Thomas-Jean-Jacques Loranger in 1883. See also RCAP, *Report,* vol. 2 (1), *Restructuring the Relationship,* 194-5, quoting Loranger, and 394-5 n 146, for references to the compact theory literature.

111 RCAP, *Report,* vol. 2 (1), *Restructuring the Relationship,* 194. In an earlier publication, *Partners in Confederation,* the Commission refers repeatedly to the "confederal" relationship between Aboriginal peoples and the Crown going back to the Royal Proclamation of 1763. See RCAP, *Partners in Confederation,* 17, 19, 23.

112 See Samuel V. LaSelva, *The Moral Foundations of Canadian Federalism* (Montreal and Kingston: McGill-Queen's University Press, 1996), for an important analysis of fraternity.

113 With one exception. In its discussion of the North, the Commission is strikingly positive about the progress toward a new relationship between Aboriginal and non-Aboriginal peoples. RCAP, *Report,* vol. 4, *Perspectives and Realities,* 396. Northerners are skilled in discussing constitutional development. RCAP, *Report,* vol. 4, *Perspectives and Realities,* 403. They now talk of "their shared history." RCAP, *Report,* vol. 4, *Perspectives and Realities,* 412. Presumably, these positive

features reflect population ratios much more favourable to Aboriginal peoples, which helps to explain the Inuit preference for public government in Nunavut, also shared by the Inuit of Nunavik in Northern Quebec and the Inuvialuit in the Western Arctic, ratios that diminish the salience of nation and cleavages. RCAP, *Report,* vol. 4, *Perspectives and Realities,* 430-4. These developments are encouraged by a degree of shared culture born of rugged conditions, and possibly by the fact that neither the Inuit nor the Métis were subjected to reserve life and the cultural assault experienced by status Indians.

114 RCAP, *Report,* vol. 5, *Renewal: A Twenty-Year Commitment,* 129. This does not appear to be an official recommendation, as the commissioners simply state that they "believe" there should be an Aboriginal member of the Court. This "proposal" is not included in the "Summary of Recommendations." RCAP, *Report,* vol. 5, *Renewal: A Twenty-Year Commitment,* 129.

115 RCAP, *Report,* vol. 2 (1), *Restructuring the Relationship,* 172.

116 Ibid., 287-8, 297-8. Section 36(2) of the Constitution Act, 1982, reads as follows: "Parliament and the government of Canada are committed to the principle of making equalization payments to ensure that provincial governments have sufficient revenues to provide reasonably comparable levels of public services at reasonably comparable levels of taxation."

117 RCAP, *Report,* vol. 2 (1), *Restructuring the Relationship,* 87-9, 166, 177-180, 234-6, 264, 278.

118 RCAP, *Report,* vol. 4, *Perspectives and Realities,* 200.

119 Ibid., 217.

120 Ibid., 203.

121 RCAP, *Report,* vol. 2 (1), *Restructuring the Relationship,* 63.

122 Ibid., 153-4, 161-2; RCAP, *Report,* vol. 4, *Perspectives and Realities,* 591, 598.

123 RCAP, *Report,* vol. 4, *Perspectives and Realities,* 249.

124 Ibid., 253.

125 RCAP, *Report,* vol. 1, *Looking Forward, Looking Back,* Appendix A, 699.

126 See RCAP, *Report,* vol. 5, *Renewal: A Twenty-Year Commitment,* 154-74.

127 Ibid., 84 n. 9. In addition to the resident population, there will be "a larger number on the nation's traditional territory, and several thousand citizens living elsewhere in Canada. The nation-government will exercise some functions for all its citizens, and some only for those living on Aboriginal lands." RCAP, *Report,* vol. 5, *Renewal: A Twenty-Year Commitment,* 84 n. 9.

128 The lower figure of 2,000 comes from the *Report*'s assessment that the Labrador identifying Métis (2,075) would probably "qualify as a nation" in terms of the *Report*'s criteria. RCAP, *Report,* vol. 4, *Perspectives and Realities,* 204-5, 207, 257.

129 "Ordinarily, an Aboriginal nation should comprise at least several thousand people, given the range of modern governmental responsibilities and the need to supply equivalent levels of services and to co-ordinate policies with other governments." RCAP, *Report,* vol. 2 (1), *Restructuring the Relationship,* 179.

130 See RCAP, *Report,* vol. 1, *Looking Forward, Looking Back,* 317-8, for a discussion.

131 Canada, Senate Standing Committee on Aboriginal Peoples, *Minutes of Proceedings and Evidence,* 35th Parliament, 2nd Session, no. 2, 10 December 1996 (Ottawa: Queen's Printer, 1996).

132 RCAP, *Report,* vol. 2 (1), *Restructuring the Relationship,* 223.

133 Ibid., 219.

134 Ibid., 326-53, for an excellent discussion of "capacity building," including human resource needs and proposals to meet them; RCAP, *Report,* vol. 2 (2), *Restructuring the Relationship,* 838, 864; and RCAP, *Report,* vol. 3, *Gathering Strength,* 540-60 ("Education for Self-Government").

135 See Tom Flanagan, "An Unworkable Vision of Self-Government," *Policy Options* 18, 2 (1997), 20. "In practice, both funding and expertise will have to be imported from the outside, and most Aboriginal nations will be self-governing in name only. This is simply a consequence of size."

136 RCAP, *Report,* vol. 2 (1), *Restructuring the Relationship,* 168, 237-40, 251-3.

137 Ibid., 253, 280, 293.

138 The preceding observations do not apply to the public government model favoured by the Inuit, which would include all residents of the territory. RCAP, *Report,* vol. 2 (1), *Restructuring the Relationship,* 247-8. Nor does it refer to community of interest arrangements, primarily in urban areas, which would exercise limited service functions. Membership of the latter would be by individual choice, and from many nations. Community of interest arrangements are not part of a third order of government. RCAP, *Report,* vol. 2 (1), *Restructuring the Relationship,* 248-9.

139 "The protection of the rights of non-aboriginal residents on settlement lands will be of critical importance for the province in treaty negotiations." British Columbia, Ministry of Aboriginal Affairs, "British Columbia's Approach to Treaty Settlements: Self-Government," 10 December 1996 update, http://www.aaf.gov.bc.ca/ aaf/pubs/s-gsumm.htm.

140 The Commission, however, proposes a Canada-wide framework agreement "to establish common principles and directions to guide the negotiation of treaties with recognized Aboriginal nations." RCAP, *Report,* vol. 2 (1), *Restructuring the Relationship,* 324-5. Presumably, this would set limits to variation.

141 RCAP, *Report,* vol. 5, *Renewal: A Twenty-Year Commitment,* 163.

142 RCAP, *Report,* vol. 1, *Looking Forward, Looking Back,* 608-10.

143 Ibid., 130-2.

144 Ibid., 137-41; RCAP, *Report,* vol. 2 (2), *Restructuring the Relationship,* 467-8, 484, 784.

145 RCAP, *Report,* vol. 1, *Looking Forward, Looking Back,* 689.

146 Ibid., 258; RCAP, *Report,* vol. 2 (2), *Restructuring the Relationship,* 527.

147 RCAP, *Report,* vol. 1, *Looking Forward, Looking Back,* 249.

148 Ibid., 608.

149 RCAP, *Report,* vol. 2 (1), *Restructuring the Relationship,* 4.

150 RCAP, *Partners in Confederation,* 36.

151 RCAP, *Report,* vol. 5, *Renewal: A Twenty-Year Commitment,* 5.

152 RCAP, *Report,* vol. 1, *Looking Forward, Looking Back,* 8.

153 RCAP, *Report,* vol. 2 (2), *Restructuring the Relationship,* 579. See also ibid., 427, on the need to redress the "power imbalance between Aboriginal governments and federal and provincial governments."

154 RCAP, *Report,* vol. 2 (2), *Restructuring the Relationship,* 675. See also ibid., 683.

155 Ibid., 1020.

156 Ibid., 589, 592-7.

157 RCAP, *Report,* vol. 5, *Renewal: A Twenty-Year Commitment,* 18-20.

158 RCAP, *Report,* vol. 1, *Looking Forward, Looking Back,* 700.

159 Kathy L. Brock, "Relations with Canadian Governments: Manitoba," in *For Seven Generations. An Information Legacy of the Royal Commission on Aboriginal Peoples, RCAP Research Reports. Governance. Project Area 8: Domestic Government Case Studies* [CD-ROM] (Ottawa: Libraxus, 1997).

160 Jonathan Malloy and Graham White, "Aboriginal Participation in Canadian Legislatures," in *Fleming's Canadian Legislatures, 1997,* 11th ed., ed. Robert J. Fleming and J.E. Glen (Toronto: University of Toronto Press, 1997), 64.

161 Ibid., 65.

162 RCAP, *Report,* vol. 1, *Looking Forward, Looking Back,* 702.

163 RCAP, *Report,* vol. 2 (1), *Restructuring the Relationship,* 374-82.

164 Ibid., 374.

165 Ibid.

166 RCAP, *People to People, Nation to Nation,* 132. Representation at the centre received negligible attention in the Commission's extensive research program. Only one piece of RCAP research devoted to representation at the centre is cited in the notes to the chapter "A Survey of the Issues." See Robert A. Milen, "Canadian Representation and Aboriginal Peoples: A Survey of the Issues," in *For Seven Generations,* cited in RCAP, *Report,* vol. 2 (1), *Restructuring the Relationship,* 410 n. 294.

167 Russel Lawrence Barsh and James [sákéj] Youngblood Henderson, *The Road: Indian Tribes and Political Liberty* (Berkeley: University of California Press, 1980), 281. See also pp. 221, 260-1.

168 James [sákéj] Youngblood Henderson, "Empowering Treaty Federalism," *Saskatchewan Law Review* 58, 2 (1994): 323.

169 RCAP, *Report,* vol. 2 (1), *Restructuring the Relationship,* 375-6.

170 Ibid., 377.

171 Ibid.

172 Ibid. "This legislation would be referred to the House of Commons for mandatory debate and voting." Ibid., 377-8.

173 Ibid., 379.

174 Ibid., 380.

175 Ibid., 380-1.

176 Ibid., 382. The analysis in this section is complicated by language use that fluctuates between referring to the relevant entities to be represented as nations or peoples, and then stressing that the governing principle of the Aboriginal parliament is its foundation on a nation-to-nation principle. RCAP, *Report,* vol. 2 (1), *Restructuring the Relationship,* 382. See also p. 377. However, Aboriginal people(s) and nation(s) are not the same. See RCAP, *Report,* vol. 1, *Looking Forward, Looking Back,* xiv, "A Note about Terminology." The note's clarification does not resolve the ambiguity springing from the shifts in terminological usage in the section "Representation in the Institutions of Canadian Federalism." RCAP, *Report,* vol. 2 (1), *Restructuring the Relationship,* 374-82.

177 It may be that the focus on the self-rule third order and the neglect of shared rule reflected an implicit theory of incorporation in stages. Self-rule recognition then becomes the prelude to subsequent shared-rule involvement. If so, the third order can be seen positively as inclusion, rather than as maximizing distance from the surrounding society. While the preceding is a plausible theory, the Commission's adherence to the idea of a staged incorporation is not evident in the published *Report.*

178 Tim Schouls, "Aboriginal Peoples and Electoral Reform in Canada: Differentiated Representation versus Voter Equality," *Canadian Journal of Political Science* 29, 4 (1996): 742. See also p. 749. See also Roger Gibbins, "Electoral Reform and Canada's Aboriginal Population: An Assessment of Aboriginal Electoral Districts," in *Aboriginal Peoples and Electoral Reform in Canada,* ed. Robert A. Milen (Toronto and Oxford: Dundurn Press, 1991), 182-3, for concerns about the weakening of citizenship ties that could result if separate Aboriginal electoral districts and self-government were instituted simultaneously.

179 RCAP, *Report,* vol. 2 (1), *Restructuring the Relationship,* 379.

180 RCAP, *Report,* vol. 2 (2), *Restructuring the Relationship,* 1017.

181 Paul Tennant, "Aboriginal Rights and the Penner Report on Indian Self-Government," in *The Quest for Justice: Aboriginal Peoples and Aboriginal Rights,* ed. Menno Boldt and J. Anthony Long (Toronto: University of Toronto Press, 1985), 327-8.

182 RCAP, *Report,* vol. 4, *Perspectives and Realities,* 547-8, 550, 552.

183 Ibid., 551.

184 RCAP, *Report*, vol. 2 (1), *Restructuring the Relationship*, 292-3; RCAP, *Report*, vol. 5, *Renewal: A Twenty-Year Commitment*, 164.

185 RCAP, *Report*, vol. 5, *Renewal: A Twenty-Year Commitment*, 164.

186 RCAP, *Report*, vol. 2 (1), *Restructuring the Relationship*, 290-2.

187 RCAP, *Report*, vol. 4, *Perspectives and Realities*, 580-4.

188 RCAP, *Report*, vol. 2 (1), *Restructuring the Relationship*, 86.

189 See the comments of Michael W. Posluns, "Evading the Unspeakable: A Commentary on *Looking Back, Looking Forward*, Volume I of the Report of the RCAP," *Canada Watch* 5, 5 (1997): 87.

190 The Commission's research program, however, produced thirteen studies of relations between federal, provincial, and territorial governments and Aboriginal peoples, one for each province and territory as well as the federal government.

191 See Gunnar Myrdal, *An American Dilemma. The Negro Problem and Modern Democracy*, 2 vols. (New York: Harper Brothers Publishers, 1944).

192 A possible defence of the Commission silence on this issue is that a Myrdal-type examination of the surrounding society in the service of reconstituting Canada was inhibited because its undertaking would have required dealing with future Quebec-Canada relations, which was out of the question.

193 RCAP, *Report*, vol. 1, *Looking Forward, Looking Back*, 688.

194 RCAP, *Report*, vol. 2 (1), *Restructuring the Relationship*, 53-4.

195 RCAP, *Report*, vol. 1, *Looking Forward, Looking Back*, 612.

196 For a rare exception referring to "Aboriginal peoples ... and their fellow citizens," see RCAP, *Report*, vol. 2 (1), *Restructuring the Relationship*, 371, and possibly p. 66.

197 Charles Taylor, *Reconciling the Solitudes: Essays on Canadian Federalism and Nationalism*, ed. Guy Laforest (Montreal and Kingston: McGill-Queen's University Press, 1993), 183.

198 RCAP, *Report*, vol. 2 (1), *Restructuring the Relationship*, 239. This is not the normal divided civic identities of federalism, but one of a primary national Aboriginal citizen identity, and a container identity as "citizens of Canada," not as separate, individual members of a Canadian nation.

199 See RCAP, *Report*, vol. 2 (2), *Restructuring the Relationship*, 1017.

200 RCAP, *Report*, vol. 3, *Gathering Strength*, 665.

201 The following comments focus on the nation-government proposal, not the proposals for representation in central government institutions, which are somewhat more inclusive.

202 RCAP, *Report*, vol. 5, *Renewal: A Twenty-Year Commitment*, 87 n. 25.

203 RCAP, *Report*, vol. 2 (1), *Restructuring the Relationship*, 63.

204 RCAP, *Report*, vol. 2 (2), *Restructuring the Relationship*, 812.

205 Dennis Guest, *The Emergence of Social Security in Canada* (Vancouver: University of British Columbia Press, 1980), 218 n. 39, 145, 222 n. 52. See H.B. Hawthorn, ed., *A Survey of the Contemporary Indians of Canada*, vol. 1 (Ottawa: Queen's Printer, 1966 and 1967), Chapter 15, "Indians and Welfare Services," for a historical analysis of the fact that "Indians have consistently received different and in most cases inferior welfare services to those provided to non-Indians" (p. 315) and the piecemeal erosion of the difference after the Second World War.

206 RCAP, *Report*, vol. 2 (2), *Restructuring the Relationship*, 788.

207 Ibid., 847.

208 Geoffrey Gray, "From Nomadism to Citizenship: A.P. Elkin and Aboriginal Advancement," in *Citizenship and Indigenous Australians: Changing Conceptions and Possibilities*, ed. Nicolas Peterson and Will Sanders (Cambridge, UK: Cambridge University Press, 1998), 64.

209 T.H. Marshall, *Class, Citizenship, and Social Development* (Westport, CT: Greenwood Press, 1976), 84.

210 Keith G. Banting, *The Welfare State and Canadian Federalism,* 2nd ed. (Montreal and Kingston: McGill-Queen's University Press, 1987), especially 118-21.

211 Thomas J. Courchene, *Equalization Payments: Past, Present, and Future* (Toronto: Ontario Economic Council, 1984), 23, 84, 89, 130, 406. See Karin Treff and David B. Perry, *1996 Finances of the Nation* (Toronto: Canadian Tax Foundation, 1997), Table 2:7 for 1995-6 and 1996-7 figures for Newfoundland.

212 Hawthorn, *A Survey of the Contemporary Indians of Canada,* vol. 1, 396.

213 RCAP, *Report,* vol. 2 (1), *Restructuring the Relationship,* 168, 226-34.

214 Ramesh Mishra, *Society and Social Policy: Theories and Practice of Welfare,* 2nd ed. (Atlantic Highlands: Humanities Press, 1981), 35-6, 55.

215 RCAP, *Report,* vol. 1, *Looking Forward, Looking Back,* 679-80.

216 RCAP, *Report,* vol. 3, *Gathering Strength,* 6. See also ibid., 52, 566, 664.

217 Ibid., 361.

218 Ibid., 351.

219 Ibid., 220.

220 Ibid., 232.

221 Ibid., 294, 363 n. 24, 442.

222 Ibid., 545, 557-8, 595, 634, 636.

223 RCAP, *Report,* vol. 2 (2), *Restructuring the Relationship,* focusing on land and resources, and economic development also underlines the need for supportive, cooperative working relations between Aboriginal governments and provincial governments, especially in areas of land use and resources, as well as with municipalities and regional bodies, and with the private sector, including banks, credit unions, and trust companies. The goal is to end the stultifying effects of isolation and exclusion.

### Chapter 5: The Choice Revisited

1 Dr. Lloyd Barber, former Indian Land Claims Commissioner, speaking in 1974, quoted in Siksika Nation Indian Government Committee, *Treaty Federalism – A Concept for the Entry of First Nations into the Canadian Federation and Commentary on the Canadian Unity Proposals* (Gleichen, AB: Siksika Nation Tribal Administration, 1992), 6-7.

2 H.B. Hawthorn, "The Survival of Small Societies," in *Pilot Not Commander: Essays in Memory of Diamond Jenness,* ed. Pat Lotz and Jim Lotz, *Anthropologica* 13, 1 and 2 (1971), Special Issue.

3 See above, pp. 54-6.

4 H.B. Hawthorn, ed., *A Survey of the Contemporary Indians of Canada,* 2 vols. (Ottawa: Queen's Printer, 1966 and 1967), vol. 1, 13.

5 H.B. Hawthorn, C.S. Belshaw, and S.M. Jamieson, *The Indians of British Columbia. A Study of Contemporary Social Adjustment* (Toronto: University of Toronto Press, 1958), 478-9.

6 Hawthorn, "The Survival of Small Societies," 63.

7 Ibid., 64, 66. This premise also informed his doctoral thesis, supervised by Bronislaw Malinowski, and published as H.B. Hawthorn, "The Maori: A Study in Acculturation," *American Anthropological Association Memoirs* 46, no. 64, part 2 (April 1944).

8 Hawthorn, "The Survival of Small Societies," 66.

9 These themes were all anticipated in the earlier volume *The Indians of British Columbia,* by Hawthorn, Belshaw, and Jamieson, although urban migration was at an earlier stage.

10 Hawthorn, *A Survey of Contemporary Indians of Canada,* vol. 2, 179.

11 Ibid., vol. 1, 279.

12 The "rights and privileges guaranteed by treaty to some Indians are insignificant in

relation to both Indian needs and the positive role played by modern governments ... The claims of a socio-economic nature founded on treaties are generally unimportant when contrasted with the role which governments have assumed for the non-Indian population." Hawthorn, *A Survey of Contemporary Indians of Canada,* vol. 1, 247.

13 See Indian Chiefs of Alberta, *Citizens Plus: A Presentation by the Indian Chiefs of Alberta to Right Honourable P.E. Trudeau, June 1970* (Edmonton: Indian Association of Alberta, 1970). The first one-third of *Citizens Plus* was reprinted in *The Only Good Indian, Essays by Canadian Indians,* ed. Waubageshig (Toronto: New Press, 1970), 5, introduced by the relevant direct quotation from the *Hawthorn Report.*

14 Indian Chiefs of Alberta, *Citizens Plus,* 19-20.

15 Ibid., 16.

16 Ibid., 37.

17 Ibid., 58.

18 Ibid., 14. Earlier in the best-selling *The Unjust Society* (Edmonton: M.G. Hurtig, 1969), Harold Cardinal, who led the Alberta "citizens plus" delegation to Ottawa, had noted how "for the most part [Indians] like to think of themselves as Canadians" (p. 18). See also pp. 12, 24. He wrote of the future contribution of Canadian Indians who wish "to work with our fellow Canadians" to add to the Canadian knowledge base (p. 13).

19 Canadian Press, "New Indian Policy 'Not Acceptable,'" *Vancouver Sun,* 26 June 1969.

20 Manitoba Indian Brotherhood, *Wahbung: Our Tomorrows* (Winnipeg: Manitoba Indian Brotherhood, 1971), xvi.

21 Ibid., 33.

22 Ibid., 52.

23 Ibid., 74.

24 Ibid., 99. See also p. 148.

25 Ibid., 190.

26 Nisga'a Tribal Council, *Citizens Plus* (New Aiyansh, BC: Nisga'a Tribal Council, 1976).

27 Ibid., 27.

28 Canada, Task Force on Canadian Unity, *A Future Together: Observations and Recommendations* (Ottawa: Minister of Supply and Services, 1979), 58. See also Alan Pratt, "Federalism in the Era of Aboriginal Self-Government," in *Aboriginal Peoples and Government Responsibility,* ed. David Hawkes (Ottawa: Carleton University Press, 1989), for an attempt to update "citizens plus," and apply it to the roles of federal and provincial governments with respect to Indian peoples. Pratt argues that the federal role is the "plus" role – to enhance and preserve "aboriginality" – and that it includes at a minimum a variety of responsibilities linked to the positive status of "aboriginal persons, communities, institutions and lands," plus specific legal protections. The provincial role is to treat all individuals, including Aboriginal, equally as citizens in terms of "equity of services." Pp. 51-3. In addition, of course, the federal government should also treat Aboriginal individuals equally with other Canadians when its "plus" role is not involved. Kathleen Jamieson implicitly contrasted the position of Indian women who lost status by marrying non-Indians, and thus became "citizens minus," with the *Hawthorn Report*'s advocacy of "citizens plus." Kathleen Jamieson, *Indian Women and the Law in Canada: Citizens Minus* (Ottawa: Advisory Council on the Status of Women, 1978).

29 See also the earlier discussion of the defeat of the White Paper in Chapter 2.

30 Roy MacGregor, *Chief: The Fearless Vision of Billy Diamond* (Markham: Viking/Penguin, 1989), 196-7.

31 Canada, House of Commons, *Debates,* 11 July 1969, 11147.

32 Joe Sawchuk, *The Dynamics of Native Politics: The Alberta Métis Experience* (Saskatoon: Purich Publishing, 1998), 117, 160.

33 Peter Kulchyski, ed., *Unjust Relations: Aboriginal Rights in Canadian Courts* (Toronto: Oxford University Press, 1994), 15.

34 The Declaration is reproduced in Mel Watkins, ed., *Dene Nation – The Colony Within* (Toronto: University of Toronto Press, 1977), 3-4.

35 Sawchuk, *Dynamics of Native Politics,* 133.

36 See Canada, "Indian Self-Government in Canada," *Minutes and Proceedings of the Special Committee on Indian Self-Government,* no. 40, 12 and 20 October 1983 (hereinafter *Penner Report*).

37 Assembly of First Nations, "Self Determination/Termination: Indian-Crown Relations at a Crossroads?" Draft #2, for discussion only (Ottawa, 7 September 1995, mimeographed), 9-10.

38 Hamar Foster and Alan Grove, "Looking behind the Masks: A Land Claims Discussion Paper for Researchers, Lawyers and Their Employers," *University of British Columbia Law Review* 27, 2 (1993): 231.

39 Joyce Green, "Options for Achieving Aboriginal Self-Determination," *Policy Options* 18, 2 (1997): 12.

40 Canada, *Report of the Royal Commission on Aboriginal Peoples* (hereinafter RCAP, *Report*), vol. 1, *Looking Forward, Looking Back* (Ottawa: Canada Communication Group Publishing, 1996), 612.

41 RCAP, *Report,* vol. 1, *Looking Forward, Looking Back,* 612.

42 Under the heading "Weaknesses," the AFN working document observed, in note form, "'Generic' approach – Aboriginal peoples – recommendations apply not only to First Nations, but also Métis, Inuit, 'non-status' ... has the effect of 'watering down' conclusions and recommendations. Would have gone much further re: self-determination, remedies, if only dealing with First Nations." Assembly of First Nations, "Royal Commission on Aboriginal Peoples' Final Report and Recommendations, Preliminary Analysis and Commentary," Draft #3, for discussion only (Ottawa, 22 February 1997, mimeographed), 13.

43 Harold Cardinal, *The Rebirth of Canada's Indians* (Edmonton: Hurtig, 1977), 137. Cardinal notes that the phrase was known in other parts of Indian country, "but even there the term was misunderstood" (p. 137).

44 Doug Sanders, "The Nishga Case," in *The Recognition of Aboriginal Rights: Case Studies I, 1996,* ed. Samuel W. Corrigan and Joe Sawchuk (Brandon, MB: Bearpaw Publishing, 1996), 89-91.

45 Cardinal, *The Rebirth of Canada's Indians,* 137.

46 Sanders, "The Nishga Case," 92.

47 Indian-Eskimo Association of Canada, *Native Rights in Canada* (Toronto: Indian-Eskimo Association of Canada, 1970).

48 Peter A. Cumming and Neil H. Mickenberg, *Native Rights in Canada,* 2nd ed. (Toronto: University of Toronto Press, 1972), vii.

49 Thomas Flanagan, "From Indian Title to Aboriginal Rights," in *Law and Justice in a New Land: Essays in Western Canadian Legal History,* ed. Louis Knafla (Toronto: Carswell, 1986), 82.

50 Ibid., 82. A colleague, who was involved in the first edition, suggests that this statement is an exaggeration.

51 This paragraph is a rephrasing of Flanagan, "From Indian Title to Aboriginal Rights," 82, supplemented by Cardinal, *Rebirth of Canada's Indians,* 136-40.

52 Cumming and Mickenberg, *Native Rights in Canada,* 3, n. 3.

53 Indian-Eskimo Association of Canada, *Native Rights in Canada,* 27.

54 See Canada, Parliament, Special Joint Committee on the Constitution of Canada

(1970-2), *Minutes of Proceedings and Evidence of the Special Joint Committee of the Senate and the House of Commons on the Constitution of Canada,* 3 March 1970-1 February 1972.

55 The Calder case and its background are lucidly discussed in Sanders, "The Nishga Case." The quote, from Justice Hall, is on 93. See also *Calder* v. *A.G.B.C.,* [1973] 1 SCR 313 at 346, Hall J.

56 The National Indian Brotherhood changed its name to the Assembly of First Nations in 1982.

57 *Penner Report,* 7.

58 Bryan Schwartz, *First Principles, Second Thoughts: Aboriginal Peoples, Constitutional Reform and Canadian Statecraft* (Montreal and Kingston: Institute for Research on Public Policy, 1986), 325.

59 The Honourable A.C. Hamilton, *Fact Finder for the Minister of Indian Affairs and Northern Development: Canada and Aboriginal Peoples: A New Partnership* (Ottawa: Department of Indian Affairs and Northern Development, 1995), 71.

60 *R.* v. *Sparrow,* [1990] 1 SCR 1075 at 1103-4.

61 Hawthorn, *A Survey of Contemporary Indians of Canada,* vol. 1, 211.

62 Peter W. Hogg, *Constitutional Law of Canada,* 4th ed., vol. 1 (Scarborough, ON: Carswell, 1997), s. 27, p. 18, n. 86.

63 Ibid., 383-90.

64 See also P. Macklem et al., eds., *Canadian Constitutional Law,* 2nd ed. (Toronto: Emond Montgomery Publications, 1997), which devoted sixty-six pages to "Aboriginal Peoples and the Constitution," 477-543.

65 Bora Laskin, *Canadian Constitutional Law,* 2nd ed. (Toronto: Carswell, 1960), 241-2.

66 See Noel Lyon and Ronald G. Atkey, eds., *Canadian Constitutional Law in a Modern Perspective* (Toronto: University of Toronto Press, 1970), and John D. Whyte and William R. Lederman, *Canadian Constitutional Law* (Toronto: Butterworths, 1975).

67 See Foster and Grove, "Looking behind the Masks," 215, and 237-46, for a discussion of remuneration.

68 See in particular the contributions of John Borrows, James [sákéj] Youngblood Henderson, and Mary Ellen Turpel (now Turpel-Lafond and now on the bench).

69 Major legal cases can be explored in any recent text on Canadian constitutional law.

70 See, for example, Brian Slattery, "Aboriginal Sovereignty and Imperial Claims," *Osgoode Hall Law Journal* 29, 4 (1991): 681-703, where he argues that "indigenous American nations had exclusive title to their territories at the time of European contact and participated actively in the formation of Canada and the United States. This fact requires us to rewrite our constitutional histories and reconsider the current status of indigenous American nations." Ibid., 681. See also Brian Slattery, "The Organic Constitution: Aboriginal Peoples and the Evolution of Canada," *Osgoode Hall Law Journal* 34, 1 (1995): 101-12.

71 The supportive role of legal academics is equally evident in the United States. "It is noteworthy," adds Ralph W. Johnson, "that the great bulk of academic legal literature on both sides of the border tends to take a pro-Indian point of view." Ralph W. Johnson, "Fragile Gains: Two Centuries of Canadian and United States Policy toward Indians," *Washington Law Review* 66, 3 (1991): 716.

72 Michael Asch is an important contributor, as was the late Sally Weaver.

73 See in particular Will Kymlicka, *Liberalism, Community, and Culture* (Oxford: Oxford University Press, 1989); *Multicultural Citizenship: A Liberal Theory of Minority Rights* (Oxford: Clarendon Press, 1995); and *Finding Our Way: Rethinking Ethnocultural Relations in Canada* (Oxford: Oxford University Press, 1998).

74 This was equally true of the United States, where "[Franz] Boas and other cultural anthropologists did not expect or desire that American society should become a

loose federation of distinctive ethnic cultures, each with equal claim to a unique value. As ethnographers, they tried to look at the peoples they studied in the South Pacific or on Indian reservations without ethnocentric preconceptions. But they usually assumed that each society had a single dominant culture and that minorities within it had to conform to the essential values of the larger society in order to survive and prosper." George M. Fredrickson, "Demonizing the American Dilemma," review of *The End of Racism: Principles for a Multiracial Society,* by Dinesh D'Souza, in *New York Review of Books,* 19 October 1995, 12.

75 Kent McNeil, "Envisaging Constitutional Space for Aboriginal Governments," *Queen's Law Journal* 19, 1 (1993): 95-136; Bruce Ryder, "The Demise and Rise of the Classical Paradigm in Canadian Federalism: Promoting Autonomy for the Provinces and First Nations," *McGill Law Journal* 36, 2 (1991): 308-81; and Patrick Macklem, "First Nations Self-Government and the Borders of the Canadian Legal Imagination," *McGill Law Journal* 36, 2 (1991): 382-456.

76 Patrick Macklem, "Distributing Sovereignty: Indian Nations and Equality of Peoples," *Stanford Law Review* 45, 5 (1993): 1366. I recognize that some readers may argue that to focus (initially) on these three articles, followed by a selective tour of other legal contributions, is to support the interpretive conclusions I reach with what a critic might view as a carefully constructed unrepresentative sample. Further, exception may be taken to singling out one or two articles by an author rather than considering that person's work as a whole. My goal, however, is not to cover and assess the relevant legal literature exhaustively – a task that would daunt a PhD student searching for a thesis topic – but to identify the orientations and implicit assumptions behind the support for Aboriginal peoples and their goals that characterize contemporary legal scholarship.

77 *Delgamuukw* v. *B.C.,* [1997] 3 SCR 1010.

78 *Delgamuukw* v. *B.C.,* [1991] 5 CNLR xiii.

79 *Delgamuukw* v. *B.C.,* [1997] 3 SCR, 1010 at 1069, para. 87.

80 Ibid., at 1084, para. 118. See Kent McNeil, "The Meaning of Aboriginal Title," in *Aboriginal and Treaty Rights in Canada: Essays on Law, Equality, and Respect for Difference,* ed. Michael Asch (Vancouver: UBC Press, 1997). McNeil's article, critiquing earlier judicial attempts to define Aboriginal title, which were typically restrictive, is an incisive argument that Aboriginal title should be defined "as an all encompassing interest which is not limited to precolonial uses of the land. This approach ... provides the Aboriginal peoples with the opportunity to develop their lands in ways that meet the contemporary needs of their communities. It is an approach which supports the self-sufficiency and growth of those communities and the preservation of Aboriginal cultures." McNeil, "The Meaning of Aboriginal Title," 154.

81 Ryder, "Demise and Rise of the Classical Paradigm in Canadian Federalism," 363.

82 McNeil, "Envisaging Constitutional Space for Aboriginal Governments," 95.

83 Macklem, "First Nations Self-Government and the Borders of the Canadian Legal Imagination," 395.

84 Ibid., 424.

85 Ibid., 390 n. 30.

86 Ibid., 387 n. 23.

87 McNeil, "Envisaging Constitutional Space for Aboriginal Governments," 134.

88 Ibid., 136.

89 Ryder, "Demise and Rise of the Classical Paradigm in Canadian Federalism," 363. Ryder does not explain how this consent is to be expressed.

90 Macklem, "First Nations Self-Government and the Borders of the Canadian Legal Imagination," 424-5, 449, 455.

91 Ryder, "Demise and Rise of the Classical Paradigm in Canadian Federalism," 368.

92 Mary Ellen Turpel, "Aboriginal Peoples and the Canadian Charter: Interpretive Monopolies, Cultural Differences," *Canadian Human Rights Yearbook* 6 (1989-90): 4, 30, 35. The "difference" theme – "we are not you" – is repeated in other writings. In "Patriarchy and Paternalism: The Legacy of the Canadian State for First Nations Women," *Canadian Journal of Women and the Law* 6, 1 (1993): 174-92, she distances herself from white feminists, and from the 1970 *Report of the Royal Commission on the Status of Women in Canada,* which addresses the latter's agenda, but not hers, and generally communicates a two-row wampum vision of the future. In another article, she describes Aboriginal peoples as "different – culturally, politically, spiritually, linguistically," and she states "this difference is profound." She does, however, deny that "Aboriginal cultures should be seen as totally separate wholes utterly apart from the dominant Canadian political and consumer culture." The paper is a plea for distinct justice institutions for Aboriginal people, but not necessarily "'separate' justice systems." Mary Ellen Turpel, "On the Question of Adapting the Canadian Criminal Justice System for Aboriginal Peoples: Don't Fence Me In," *Aboriginal Peoples and the Justice System* (Ottawa: Royal Commission on Aboriginal Peoples, 1993), 167, 169, 180.

93 Anthony Giddens, *In Defence of Sociology: Essays, Interpretations and Rejoinders* (Cambridge: Polity Press, 1996), Chapter 6, "The Future of Anthropology"; and Hans-Rudolf Wicker, "From Complex Culture to Cultural Complexity," in *Debating Cultural Hybridity,* ed. Pnina Werbner and Tariq Modood (London: Zed Books, 1997).

94 See Russel Lawrence Barsh and James [sákéj] Youngblood Henderson, *The Road: Indian Tribes and Political Liberty* (Berkeley: University of California Press, 1980), especially Chapter 23 and Conclusion; James [sákéj] Youngblood Henderson, "Empowering Treaty Federalism," *Saskatchewan Law Review* 58, 2 (1994): 241-329; Russel Lawrence Barsh and James [sákéj] Youngblood Henderson, "Aboriginal Rights, Treaty Rights, and Human Rights: Indian Tribes and 'Constitutional Renewal,'" *Journal of Canadian Studies* 17, 2 (1982): 55-81; James [sákéj] Youngblood Henderson, "Implementing the Treaty Order," in *Continuing Poundmaker and Riel's Quest,* ed. Richard Gosse, James [sákéj] Youngblood Henderson, and Roger Carter (Saskatoon: Purich Publishing, 1994), 52-62. Andrew Bear Robe, after reading Barsh and Henderson's *The Road,* advocated treaty federalism for Indian First Nations. They would enjoy "protected sovereign status," in a system of shared sovereignty, be exempted from the Charter's application, and have guaranteed representation in both the House of Commons and the Senate. The latter – parliamentary representation – does not appear to be central to Bear Robe's treaty federalism, as it is presented in the epilogue as a positive response to recommendations that emerged in other arenas. Andrew Bear Robe, "Treaty Federalism," *Constitutional Forum* 4, 1 (1992): 12, 18, 23, 25, 44-5.

95 Henderson, "Empowering Treaty Federalism," 242-5.

96 From the perspective of "the tribes ... the BNA Act empowered Canada to enforce treaties and to implement the Crown's duty of protection, but it was not an independent source of authority over tribes or their citizens." Barsh and Henderson, "Aboriginal Rights, Treaty Rights, and Human Rights," 67-8.

97 Henderson, "Empowering Treaty Federalism," 276-9; Henderson, "Implementing the Treaty Order," 55-7.

98 Henderson, "Empowering Treaty Federalism," 250.

99 "The treaty relations between the First Nations and the European Crowns are understood best as a branch of international law and as royal prerogatives in the constitutional law of Great Britain." Ibid., 246. See also pp. 270-3.

100 "The treaties united the First Nations as freely associated states of the United Kingdom, not as part of any colony, province or dominion. Consequently, treaty federalism

united independent First Nations under one Crown, *but not under one law.*" Ibid., 252. Emphasis in original. See also p. 257.

101 Ibid., 316.

102 Ibid., 324-5.

103 Ibid., 323-4.

104 Mary Ellen Turpel, "Indigenous Peoples' Rights of Political Participation and Self-Determination: Recent International Legal Developments and the Continuing Struggle for Recognition," *Cornell International Law Journal* 25, 3 (1992): 600.

105 Henderson, "Empowering Treaty Federalism," 321.

106 Ibid., 303.

107 See, however, Barsh and Henderson, *The Road,* 249, 253, which notes the tension and competition between tribal reservation Indians and urban Indians in the United States but notes that their separate goals are both legitimate.

108 Henderson, "Empowering Treaty Federalism," 245.

109 Barsh and Henderson, *The Road,* 281. See also pp. 221, 260-1.

110 Barsh and Henderson, "Aboriginal Rights, Treaty Rights, and Human Rights," 75-6.

111 The focus is overwhelmingly on the latter. For example, in his discussion of the Charlottetown Accord, Kent McNeil focuses exclusively on its self-government provisions, and fails to mention the provisions dealing with the Canadian dimension: proposals for the House of Commons, the Senate, the Supreme Court, and first ministers' conferences – the arenas where Aboriginal peoples and non-aboriginal citizens collaborate in the governing of Canada. Kent McNeil, "The Decolonization of Canada: Moving toward Recognition of Aboriginal Governments," *Western Legal History* 7, 1 (1994): 113-41. In another article, McNeil argues that, except for its gender equality provisions, the Charter of Rights and Freedoms does not apply to Aboriginal governments. As a non-lawyer, I take no exception to the rigour of the legal analysis that leads to that conclusion. However, from a political science perspective, the article notably omits any discussion of the political role of the Charter as a potent symbol of Canadian citizenship, and hence ignores the consequences of excluding Aboriginal peoples from its ambit for the assessment by non-Aboriginal Canadians of whether the former are to be included in the "we" group. That issue, which can be rephrased as whether we do or we do not feel responsible for each other, is not a concern. Kent McNeil, "Aboriginal Governments and the Canadian Charter of Rights and Freedoms," *Osgoode Hall Law Journal* 34, 1 (1996): 61-99.

112 Brian Slattery is an important exception. See Brian Slattery, "Rights, Communities, and Tradition," *University of Toronto Law Journal* 41 (1991): 447-67, and Brian Slattery, "First Nations and the Constitution: A Question of Trust," *Canadian Bar Review* 71 (June 1992): especially 274, 286, 287-93. See also the discussion of John Borrows below in this chapter in the section titled "An Outward-Looking Aboriginality."

113 Macklem, "First Nations Self-Government and the Borders of the Canadian Legal Imagination," 453-5.

114 Sawchuk, *Dynamics of Native Politics,* 170.

115 Canada, Indian and Northern Affairs Canada, *Creating Opportunity: Progress on Commitments to Aboriginal Peoples* (Ottawa: Indian and Northern Affairs Canada, 1995), 18.

116 J. Rick Ponting, *First Nations in Canada: Perspectives on Opportunity, Empowerment, and Self-Determination* (Toronto: McGraw-Hill Ryerson, 1997), 71-4.

117 Cameron W. Stout, "Nunavut: Canada's Newest Territory in 1999," *Canadian Social Trends* 44 (Spring 1997): 14.

118 See the depressing data and analysis of despair, poverty, social breakdown, low income, high unemployment, and 90 percent fiscal dependence of the Nunavut

government on Ottawa quoted in Erin Anderssen, "Nunavut to be a Welfare Case: Sweeping Social, Economic Problems Face Canada's Newest Territory," and Jeffrey Simpson, "Tough Times Lie Ahead for the New Territory of Nunavut," *Globe and Mail,* 5 June 1998.

119 The Morton-Knopff Court Party thesis is available in the following: F.L. Morton and Rainer Knopff, "The Supreme Court as the Vanguard of the Intelligentsia: The Charter Movement as Post-Materialist Politics," in *Canadian Constitutionalism: 1791-1991,* ed. Janet Ajzenstat (Ottawa: Canadian Study of Parliament Group, 1992). See pp. 72-5 for the role of law schools. See also F.L. Morton, "The Charter Revolution and the Court Party," *Osgoode Hall Law Journal* 30, 3 (1992): 641-3 for the law schools; and Rainer Knopff and F.L. Morton, "Canada's Court Party," in *Rethinking the Constitution,* ed. Anthony A. Peacock (Don Mills, ON: Oxford University Press, 1996).

120 Some of the problems of advocacy legal scholarship are thoughtfully discussed in Charles F. Abernathy, "Advocacy Scholarship and Affirmative Action," *Georgetown Law Journal* 86 (1997): 377-404. See also Foster and Grove, "Looking behind the Masks," for a general discussion of the temptations to politicize scholarship in land claims cases.

121 See, however, Schwartz, who asserts that "constitutional reform with respect to aboriginal peoples is an area where there is a need to develop structures and principles that will accommodate the just concerns of many different groups." Schwartz, *First Principles, Second Thoughts,* 326. The book as a whole, with "Canadian State-craft" in the subtitle, displays a consistent concern with the political task of how we can get along with each other.

122 Rogers M. Smith, in a critique of what he calls democratic cultural pluralism, suggests that its supporters have focused on protecting cultural minorities. However, "though they recognize some pressures for shared political identity amid the diversity they applaud, their emphasis is on finding ways to grant increased recognition for certain subgroups, not on what sorts of national political identities can and should be advanced." Smith, *Civic Ideals: Conflicting Visions of Citizenship in US History* (New Haven and London: Yale University Press, 1997), 481. Although Smith is not writing directly about legal analysis of Aboriginal futures in Canada, his observations are relevant to the Canadian setting.

123 Peter H. Russell, "Aboriginal Nationalism and Quebec Nationalism: Reconciliation through Fourth World Colonization," *Constitutional Forum* 8, 4 (1997): 113.

124 In addition to the references in subsequent notes, the following sources have been helpful: Canada, Department of Indian Affairs and Northern Development, *Comprehensive Land Claims Policy* (Ottawa: Supply and Services Canada, 1987); Department of Indian Affairs and Northern Development, *Federal Policy for the Settlement of Native Claims* (Ottawa: Supply and Services, 1993); Department of Indian Affairs and Northern Development, *Comprehensive Land Claims Policy and Status of Claims,* 21 November 1997 update, http://www.inac.gc.ca/subject/ claims/comp/Ccpol.html; Wendy Moss and Peter Niemczak, *Aboriginal Land Claims,* Background Paper for Parliamentarians, rev. ed. (Ottawa: Research Branch, Library of Parliament, 1992); John A. Olthuis and H.W. Roger Townshend, "Is Canada's Thumb on the Scales? An Analysis of Canada's Comprehensive and Specific Claims Policies and Suggested Alternatives," in *For Seven Generations. An Information Legacy of the Royal Commission on Aboriginal Peoples,* RCAP *Research Reports. Governance. Project Area 4: Treaties and Aboriginal Lands,* no. 63174-63891 [CD-ROM] (Ottawa: Libraxus, 1997).

125 The Honourable Ronald A. Irwin, Minister of Indian Affairs and Northern Development, *Executive Summary: Aboriginal Self-Government* (Ottawa: Department of Indian Affairs and Northern Development, 1995), 1. The main document is The

Honourable Ronald A. Irwin, Minister of Indian Affairs and Northern Development, *Aboriginal Self-Government: The Government of Canada's Approach to Implementation of the Inherent Right and the Negotiation of Aboriginal Self-Government* (Ottawa: Department of Indian Affairs and Northern Development, 1995).

126 Canada, Royal Commission on Aboriginal Peoples (RCAP), *Treaty Making in the Spirit of Co-existence: An Alternative to Extinguishment* (Ottawa: Canada Communication Group Publishing, 1995).

127 Canada, Royal Commission on Aboriginal Peoples (RCAP), *Partners in Confederation: Aboriginal Peoples, Self-Government and the Constitution* (Ottawa: Canada Communication Group, 1993).

128 A position underlined by A.C. Hamilton. "Aboriginal peoples believe that the surrender requirement undermines fundamental rights far beyond the land itself. They see surrender, no matter how focused or limited, as an attempt to extinguish their very identity, beliefs and ways of life. For them, in these terms, extinguishment is inconceivable." Hamilton, *Fact Finder for the Minister of Indian Affairs and Northern Development: Canada and Aboriginal Peoples: A New Partnership,* 42. See also pp. 31, 49-50.

129 *R. v. Sparrow* [1990] 1 SCR, 1075 at 1108.

130 RCAP, *Partners in Confederation,* 36. Emphasis in original.

131 Ibid., 37.

132 Ibid., 49.

133 Michael Asch and Norman Zlotkin, "Affirming Aboriginal Title: A New Basis for Comprehensive Claims Negotiations," in *Aboriginal and Treaty Rights in Canada: Essays on Law, Equality, and Respect for Difference,* ed. Michael Asch (Vancouver: UBC Press, 1997).

134 Ibid., 209.

135 Ibid., 228.

136 Ibid., 216.

137 Ibid., 218. See also p. 228.

138 Ibid., 218. See also p. 228.

139 Hamilton, *Fact Finder for the Minister of Indian Affairs and Northern Development,* 6-7, 37, 54.

140 Ibid., 6, 9-12.

141 Ibid., 11.

142 Treaty making in British Columbia occurs under the aegis of the British Columbia Treaty Commission. See Christopher McKee, *Treaty Talks in British Columbia: Negotiating a Mutually Beneficial Future* (Vancouver: UBC Press, 1996).

143 British Columbia, Ministry of Aboriginal Affairs, "British Columbia's Approach to Treaty Settlements: Self-Government," 10 December 1996 update, http://www.aaf.gov.bc.ca/aaf/pubs/s-gsumm.htm.

144 British Columbia, Ministry of Aboriginal Affairs, "Summary – Fiscal Arrangements for Treaty Negotiations in BC," 10 December 1996 update, http://www.aaf.gov.bc.ca/aaf/pubs/f-asumm.htm.

145 British Columbia, Ministry of Aboriginal Affairs, "British Columbia's Approach to Treaty Settlements: Lands and Resources," 11 December 1996 update, http://www.aaf.gov.bc.ca/aaf/pubs/context.htm.

146 See Jill Wherrett, *Aboriginal Self-Government. Current Issue Review,* Background Paper for Parliamentarians (Ottawa: Research Branch, Library of Parliament, 1996), for a discussion.

147 Irwin, *Aboriginal Self-Government,* 4.

148 Ibid.

149 Ibid., 5.

150 Ibid., 11.

151 Ibid., 6.

152 This was also the case in the Charlottetown Accord in which the legal text located "the inherent right of self-government within Canada," a restriction imposed by federal and provincial governments and opposed by some Aboriginal peoples as contradicting their nation-to-nation relationship with Canada. McNeil, "The Decolonization of Canada," 132.

153 British Columbia, Ministry of Aboriginal Affairs, "British Columbia's Approach to Treaty Settlements."

154 Ken S. Coates, *Summary Report, Social and Economic Impacts of Aboriginal Land Claims Settlements: A Case Study Analysis,* report prepared for the Ministry of Aboriginal Affairs, Province of British Columbia/Federal Treaty Negotiation Office, Government of Canada, 1995, 9.

155 Ibid., 4.

156 Kathy L. Brock, "Relations with Canadian Governments: Manitoba," in *For Seven Generations.*

157 Foster and Grove, "Looking behind the Masks," 220.

158 Charles Taylor is an important exception to the political science literature discussed in the following paragraphs. His "deep diversity" thesis, applied initially to Quebec, and by analogy to Aboriginal peoples, argues that citizens of "deep diversity" communities will not have direct individual connections to the federal government. Their link to the latter will be mediated via their membership in the Quebec or Aboriginal nation. Charles Taylor, *Reconciling the Solitudes: Essays on Canadian Federalism and Nationalism,* ed. Guy Laforest (Montreal and Kingston: McGill-Queen's University Press, 1993), 183. This lack of recognition of divided loyalties/identities means that the federal government essentially exists on sufferance, with minimal legitimacy of its own. Taylor's position, however, may have changed. See the discussion in the section titled "Empathy and Citizenship" below in this chapter.

159 *Penner Report,* 63.

160 Roger Gibbins and J. Rick Ponting, "The Paradoxical Nature of the Penner Report," *Canadian Public Policy* 10, 2 (1984): 223-4.

161 Roger Gibbins and J. Rick Ponting, "An Assessment of the Probable Impact of Aboriginal Self-Government in Canada," in *The Politics of Gender, Ethnicity and Language in Canada,* ed. Alan C. Cairns and Cynthia Williams, Collected Research Studies of the Royal Commission on the Economic Union and Development Prospects for Canada, vol. 34 (Toronto: University of Toronto Press, 1986), 233. See pp. 233-6 for a discussion.

162 Schwartz, *First Principles, Second Thoughts,* 151.

163 Gibbins and Ponting, "An Assessment of the Probable Impact of Aboriginal Self-Government in Canada," 206-9. See also Roger Gibbins, "Citizenship, Political, and Intergovernmental Problems with Indian Self-Government," in *Arduous Journey: Canadian Indians and Decolonization,* ed. J. Rick Ponting (Toronto: McClelland and Stewart, 1986), which is adapted from a Gibbins and Ponting piece in *The Politics of Gender, Ethnicity and Language in Canada,* ed. Cairns and Williams.

164 C.E.S. Franks, *Public Administration Questions Relating to Aboriginal Self-Government* (Kingston, ON: Institute of Intergovernmental Relations, 1987), especially Chapter 5.

165 Samuel V. LaSelva, *The Moral Foundations of Canadian Federalism* (Montreal and Kingston: McGill-Queen's University Press, 1996), 150.

166 Russell, "Aboriginal Nationalism and Quebec Nationalism," 116. See also Gibbins and Ponting: "Just as it can be argued that aboriginal self-government must not permit aboriginals to turn their backs on Canada, so too Canadians must not be

permitted to turn their backs on long-standing aboriginal problems that will not simply fade away in the new dawn of aboriginal self-government" ("An Assessment of the Probable Impact of Aboriginal Self-Government in Canada," 235-6). See also Alan C. Cairns, "Aboriginal Canadians, Citizenship, and the Constitution," in *Reconfigurations: Canadian Citizenship and Constitutional Change. Selected Essays by Alan C. Cairns,* ed. Douglas E. Williams (Toronto: McClelland and Stewart, 1995), 257-9; and Richard Sigurdson, "First Peoples, New Peoples and Citizenship in Canada," *International Journal of Canadian Studies* 14 (Fall 1996): 59, 68.

167 J.W. Berry and M. Wells, "Attitudes towards Aboriginal Peoples and Aboriginal Self-Government in Canada," in *Aboriginal Self-Government in Canada,* ed. John Hylton (Saskatoon: Purich Publishing, 1994), 225.

168 Jeff Spinner, *The Boundaries of Citizenship: Race, Ethnicity, and Nationality in the Liberal State* (Baltimore and London: Johns Hopkins University Press, 1994), 97-8. Emphasis in original.

169 See above, p. 100.

170 Hawthorn, Belshaw, and Jamieson, *Indians of British Columbia,* 61-2, 438-9.

171 Maria Lane, "Indigenous Australians and the Legacy of European Conquest: Invasion and Resurgence," in *Indigenous Australians and the Law,* ed. Elliott Johnston, Martin Hinton, and Daryle Rigney (Sydney, Australia: Cavendish Publishing, 1997), 15.

172 Russell Thornton, "Tribal Membership Requirements and the Demography of 'Old' and 'New' Native Americans," in *Changing Numbers, Changing Needs: American Indian Demography and Public Health,* ed. Gary D. Sandefur, Ronald R. Rindfuss, and Barney Cohen (Washington, DC: National Academy Press, 1996), 109-10.

173 Jeffrey S. Passel, "The Growing American Indian Population, 1960-1990: Beyond Demography," in *Changing Numbers,* ed. Sandefur, Rindfuss, and Cohen, 86.

174 Thornton, "Tribal Membership Requirements and the Demography of 'Old' and 'New' Native Americans," 111.

175 Giddens, *In Defence of Sociology,* 214.

176 Emma La Rocque, "Re-examining Culturally Appropriate Models in Criminal Justice Applications," in *Aboriginal and Treaty Rights in Canada: Essays on Law, Equality, and Respect for Difference,* ed. Michael Asch (Vancouver: UBC Press, 1997), 91.

177 "It should be remembered that First Peoples are no strangers to the doctrines of freedom and equality that animate the Charter ... To some extent ..., [the] principles [of the Charter] can be viewed as the product of cultural fusion, stemming from inter-societal contacts in the villages and forests of North America, with effects that rippled outward into the salons and marketplaces of pre-revolutionary Europe. In interpreting and applying the Charter, we would do well to keep in mind the complementary ideals of freedom and responsibility that have informed Aboriginal outlooks from ancient times, ideals that have continuing relevance to Canadian society today." RCAP, *Partners in Confederation,* 40.

178 *Delgamuukw* v. *B.C.,* [1997] 3 SCR 1010 at 1123-4, para. 186.

179 *R.* v. *Gladstone,* [1996] 2 SCR 723 at 774, para. 73, quoted in *Delgamuukw* v. *B.C.,* [1997] 3 SCR 1010 at 1107, para. 161.

180 John Borrows, "'Landed' Citizenship: Narratives of Aboriginal Political Participation," paper presented at the "Citizenship, Diversity and Pluralism: Comparative Perspectives" conference, University of Saskatchewan, Saskatoon, SK, 30 October-1 November 1997, 1-8. For supportive remarks see also Michael W. Posluns, "Evading the Unspeakable: A Commentary on *Looking Back, Looking Forward,* Volume I of the Report of the RCAP," *Canada Watch* 5, 5 (1997): 87.

181 John Borrows, "Contemporary Traditional Equality: The Effect of the Charter on First Nation Politics," *University of New Brunswick Law Journal* 43 (1994): 23.

182 Ibid., 21. See also p. 31.

183 John Borrows, "With You or Without You: First Nations Law (in Canada)," *McGill Law Journal* 41, 3 (1996): 664.

184 Ibid., 629.

185 Ibid., 660 n. 159.

186 John Borrows, "Constitutional Law from a First Nation Perspective: Self-Government and the Royal Proclamation," *University of British Columbia Law Review* 28, 1 (1994): 6, 9.

187 John Borrows, "A Genealogy of Law: Inherent Sovereignty and First Nations Self-Government," *Osgoode Hall Law Journal* 30, 2 (1992): 311 n. 78.

188 John Borrows, "Living between Water and Rocks: First Nations Environmental Planning and Democracy," *University of Toronto Law Journal* 47 (Fall 1997): 417-8.

189 John Borrows, "Negotiating Treaties and Land Claims: The Impact of Diversity within First Nations Property Interests," *The Windsor Yearbook of Access to Justice* 12 (1992): 182.

190 Federation of Saskatchewan Indian Nations, *Saskatchewan and Aboriginal Peoples in the 21st Century: Social, Economic and Political Changes and Challenges* (Regina, SK: Printwest Publishing Services, 1997).

191 Ibid., 9.

192 Ibid., 144.

193 Ibid., 60.

194 See Rogers M. Smith, *Civic Ideals: Conflicting Visions of Citizenship in US History* (New Haven and London: Yale University Press, 1997), 470-506, for a helpful elaboration of the argument in this section.

195 Keith G. Banting, "Social Citizenship and the Multicultural Welfare State: Social Policy and the New Politics," paper presented at the "Citizenship, Diversity, and Pluralism: Comparative Perspectives" conference, University of Saskatchewan, Saskatoon, SK, 31 October-1 November 1997, 1.

196 Ibid., 6-7.

197 Ibid., 24-5.

198 See above, this chapter, n. 158.

199 Charles Taylor, "Why Democracy Needs Patriotism," in *Debating the Limits of Patriotism, For Love of Country, Martha C. Nussbaum with Respondents,* ed. Joshua Cohen (Boston: Beacon Press, 1996), 119-20.

200 John Higham, "America's Three Reconstructions," *New York Review of Books,* 6 November 1997, 56.

201 George M. Fredrickson, "Demonizing the American Dilemma," review of *The End of Racism: Principles for a Multiracial Society,* by Dinesh D'Souza, in *New York Review of Books,* 19 October 1995, 14.

202 Brian Slattery, "The Paradoxes of National Self-Determination," *Osgoode Hall Law Journal* 32, 4 (1994): 731, 733.

203 See Patrick Macklem, "Normative Dimensions of an Aboriginal Right of Self-Government," *Queen's Law Journal* 21 (Fall 1995): 188-90, for a qualified defence of pragmatism.

204 Adeno Addis, "On Human Diversity and the Limits of Toleration," in *Ethnicity and Group Rights,* ed. Ian Shapiro and Will Kymlicka (New York and London: New York University Press, 1997), 126.

205 Ibid., 142.

# Bibliography

Abernathy, Charles F. "Advocacy Scholarship and Affirmative Action." *Georgetown Law Journal* 86 (1997): 377-404.

Adams, Howard. *Prison of Grass: Canada from a Native Point of View.* Rev. ed. Saskatoon: Fifth House Publishers, 1989.

Addis, Adeno. "On Human Diversity and the Limits of Toleration." In *Ethnicity and Group Rights,* ed. Ian Shapiro and Will Kymlicka. New York and London: New York University Press, 1997.

Ames, Michael. *Cannibal Tours and Glass Boxes: The Anthropology of Museums.* 2nd rev. ed. Vancouver: UBC Press, 1992.

Anaya, S. James. *Indigenous Peoples in International Law.* New York: Oxford University Press, 1996.

Appiah, Kwame Anthony. "The Postcolonial and the Postmodern." In *The Post-Colonial Studies Reader,* ed. Bill Ashcroft, Gareth Griffiths, and Helen Tiffin. London: Routledge, 1995.

Asad, Talal, ed. *Anthropology and the Colonial Encounter.* New York: Humanities Press, 1973.

Asch, Michael, and Catherine Bell. "Definition and Interpretation of Fact in Canadian Aboriginal Title Litigation: An Analysis of *Delgamuukw.*" *Queen's Law Journal* 19, 2 (1994): 503-50.

Asch, Michael, and Norman Zlotkin. "Affirming Aboriginal Title: A New Basis for Comprehensive Claims Negotiations." In *Aboriginal and Treaty Rights in Canada: Essays on Law, Equality, and Respect for Difference,* ed. Michael Asch. Vancouver: UBC Press, 1997.

Ashcroft, Bill, Gareth Griffiths, and Helen Tiffin. *The Empire Writes Back: Theory and Practice in Post-Colonial Literature.* London: Routledge, 1989.

—, eds. *The Post-Colonial Studies Reader.* London: Routledge, 1995.

Assembly of First Nations. "Royal Commission on Aboriginal Peoples' Final Report and Recommendations, Preliminary Analysis and Commentary." Draft #3, for discussion only. Ottawa, 22 February 1997. Mimeographed.

—. "Self Determination/Termination: Indian-Crown Relations at a Crossroads?" Draft #2, for discussion only. Ottawa, 7 September 1995. Mimeographed.

Attwood, Bain, and Andrew Markus. "Representation Matters: The 1967 Referendum and Citizenship." In *Citizenship and Indigenous Australians: Changing Conceptions and Possibilities,* ed. Nicolas Peterson and Will Sanders. Cambridge, UK: Cambridge University Press, 1998.

Banting, Keith G. "Social Citizenship and the Multicultural Welfare State: Social Policy and the New Politics." Paper presented at the "Citizenship, Diversity, and Pluralism: Comparative Perspectives" conference. University of Saskatchewan, Saskatoon, SK, 30 October-1 November 1997.

—. *The Welfare State and Canadian Federalism.* 2nd ed. Montreal and Kingston: McGill-Queen's University Press, 1987.

Barron, F. Laurie. "The CCF and the Development of Métis Colonies in Southern

Saskatchewan during the Premiership of T.C. Douglas, 1944-1961." *Canadian Journal of Native Studies* 10, 2 (1990).

Barsh, Russel Lawrence. "Are Anthropologists Hazardous to Indians' Health?" *Journal of Ethnic Studies* 15, 4 (1988): 1-38.

—. "The Challenge of Indigenous Self-Determination." *University of Michigan Journal of Law Reform* 26, 2 (1993): 277-312.

Barsh, Russel Lawrence, and James [sákéj] Youngblood Henderson. "Aboriginal Rights, Treaty Rights, and Human Rights: Indian Tribes and 'Constitutional Renewal.'" *Journal of Canadian Studies* 17, 2 (1982): 55-81.

—. *The Road: Indian Tribes and Political Liberty.* Berkeley: University of California Press, 1980.

Basso, Keith H. *Portraits of "the Whiteman." Linguistic Play and Cultural Symbols among the Western Apache.* Cambridge, UK: Cambridge University Press, 1979.

Beavon, Daniel, and Martin Cooke. "Measuring the Well-Being of First Nation Peoples." 2 October 1998. Mimeographed.

Berry, J.W., and M. Wells. "Attitudes towards Aboriginal Peoples and Aboriginal Self-Government in Canada." In *Aboriginal Self-Government in Canada,* ed. John Hylton. Saskatoon: Purich Publishing, 1994.

Blaut, J.M. *The Colonizer's Model of the World: Geographical Diffusionism and Eurocentric History.* New York: Guilford Press, 1993.

Boldt, Menno. "Social Correlates of Nationalism: A Study of Native Indian Leaders in a Canadian Internal Colony." *Comparative Political Studies* 14, 2 (1981).

—. *Surviving as Indians: The Challenge of Self-Government.* Toronto: University of Toronto Press, 1993.

Borrows, John. "Constitutional Law from a First Nation Perspective: Self-Government and the Royal Proclamation." *University of British Columbia Law Review* 28, 1 (1994): 1-47.

—. "Contemporary Traditional Equality: The Effect of the Charter on First Nation Politics." *University of New Brunswick Law Journal* 43 (1994).

—. "Frozen Rights in Canada: Constitutional Interpretation and the Trickster." *American Indian Law Review* 22, 1 (1997): 37-64.

—. "A Genealogy of Law: Inherent Sovereignty and First Nations Self-Government." *Osgoode Hall Law Journal* 30, 2 (1992): 291-353.

—. "'Landed' Citizenship: Narratives of Aboriginal Political Participation." Paper presented at the "Citizenship, Diversity and Pluralism: Comparative Perspectives" conference, University of Saskatchewan, Saskatoon, SK, 30 October-1 November 1997.

—. "Living between Water and Rocks: First Nations, Environmental Planning and Democracy." *University of Toronto Law Journal* 47 (Fall 1997): 417-68.

—. "Negotiating Treaties and Land Claims: The Impact of Diversity within First Nations Property Interests." *The Windsor Yearbook of Access to Justice* 12 (1992): 179-234.

—. "With You or Without You: First Nations Law (in Canada)." *McGill Law Journal* 41, 3 (1996): 629-65.

Bourgeois, Donald J. "The Role of the Historian in the Litigation Process." *Canadian Historical Review* 67, 2 (1986): 195-205.

Brady, Alexander. *Democracy in the Dominions: A Comparative Study in Institutions.* Toronto: University of Toronto Press, 1947.

British Columbia, Ministry of Aboriginal Affairs. "British Columbia's Approach to Treaty Settlements: Lands and Resources." 11 December 1996 update. http://www.aaf.gov.bc.ca/aaf/pubs/context.htm.

—. "British Columbia's Approach to Treaty Settlements: Self-Government." 10 December 1996 update. http://www.aaf.gov.bc.ca/aaf/pubs/s-gsumm.htm.

—. "Summary – Fiscal Arrangements for Treaty Negotiations in BC." 10 December 1996 update. http://www.aaf.gov.bc.ca/aaf/pubs/f-asumm.htm.

Brock, Kathy L. "Relations with Canadian Governments: Manitoba." In *For Seven Generations. An Information Legacy of the Royal Commission on Aboriginal Peoples, RCAP Research Reports. Governance. Project Area 8: Domestic Government Case Studies* [CD-ROM]. Ottawa: Libraxus, 1997.

Brownlie, Robin, and Mary-Ellen Kelm. "Desperately Seeking Absolution: Native Agency as Historical Alibi?" *Canadian Historical Review* 75, 4 (1994): 543-56.

Bruner, Edward M. "Ethnography as Narrative." In *The Anthropology of Experience,* ed. Victor W. Turner and Edward M. Bruner. Urbana and Chicago: University of Illinois Press, 1986.

Bull, Hedley. "The Revolt against the West." In *The Expansion of International Society,* ed. Hedley Bull and Adam Watson. Oxford: Clarendon Press, 1984.

*Bulletin 201: Recent Statements by the Indians of Canada, General Synod Action 1969, Some Government Responses, Suggested Resource.* Toronto: Anglican Church of Canada, 1970.

Bussidor, Ila, and Üstün Bilgen-Reinart. *Night Spirits: The Story of the Relocation of the Sayisi Dene.* Winnipeg: University of Manitoba Press, 1997.

Cairns, Alan C. "Aboriginal Canadians, Citizenship, and the Constitution." In *Reconfigurations: Canadian Citizenship and Constitutional Change. Selected Essays by Alan C. Cairns,* ed. Douglas E. Williams. Toronto: McClelland and Stewart, 1995.

—. *Prelude to Imperialism: British Reactions to Central African Society, 1840-1890.* London: Routledge and Kegan Paul, 1965.

Cameron, David, and Jill Wherrett. "New Relationship, New Challenges: Aboriginal Peoples and the Province of Ontario." In *For Seven Generations. An Information Legacy of the Royal Commission on Aboriginal Peoples, RCAP Research Reports. Governance. Project Area 8: Domestic Government Case Studies* [CD-ROM]. Ottawa: Libraxus, 1997.

Campbell, Gregory R. "The Politics of Counting: Critical Reflections on the Depopulation Question of Native North America." In *The Unheard Voices: American Indian Responses to the Columbian Quincentenary 1492-1992,* ed. Carole M. Gentry and Donald A. Grinde, Jr. Los Angeles: American Indian Studies Center, University of California, 1994.

Canada. *Consensus Report on the Constitution, Charlottetown, August 28, 1992.* Final Text, and Draft Legal Text. 9 October 1992.

—. *Constitution Act, 1982.*

—. *Gathering Strength: Canada's Aboriginal Action Plan.* Ottawa: Minister of Indian Affairs and Northern Development, 1997.

—. *Report of the Royal Commission on Aboriginal Peoples.* 5 vols. Ottawa: Canada Communication Group Publishing, 1996.

—. *Report of the Royal Commission on Bilingualism and Biculturalism.* 5 vols. Ottawa: Queen's Printer, 1967-70.

—. *Report of the Royal Commission on the Status of Women in Canada.* Ottawa: Queen's Printer, 1970.

—. *Indian and Native Programs: A Study Team Report to the Task Force on Program Review.* Ottawa: Supply and Services, 1986.

—. *Statement of the Government of Canada on Indian Policy.* Presented to the First Session of the Twenty-eighth Parliament by the Honourable Jean Chrétien, Minister of Indian Affairs and Northern Development. Ottawa: Department of Indian Affairs and Northern Development, 1969.

Canada. Department of Indian Affairs and Northern Development. *Comprehensive Land Claims Policy.* Ottawa: Supply and Services Canada, 1987.

—. *Comprehensive Land Claims Policy and Status of Claims.* 21 November 1997 update.

http://www.inac.gc.ca/subject/claims/comp/Ccpol.html.

—. *Federal Policy for the Settlement of Native Claims.* Ottawa: Supply and Services, 1993.

Canada. House of Commons. *Debates.*

—. "Indian Self-Government in Canada." *Minutes and Proceedings of the Special Committee on Indian Self-Government,* no. 40, 12 and 20 October 1983.

Canada. Indian and Northern Affairs Canada. *Creating Opportunity: Progress on Commitments to Aboriginal Peoples.* Ottawa: Indian and Northern Affairs Canada, 1995.

Canada. Parliament. Special Joint Committee on the Constitution of Canada (1970-2). *Minutes of Proceedings and Evidence of the Special Joint Committee of the Senate and the House of Commons on the Constitution of Canada.* 3 March 1970-1 February 1972.

Canada. Royal Commission on Aboriginal Peoples. "Ethical Guidelines for Research." *Integrated Research Plan.* Ottawa: Royal Commission on Aboriginal Peoples, 1993.

—. *The High Arctic Relocation. A Report on the 1953-5 Relocation.* Ottawa: Canada Communication Group Publishing, 1994.

—. *Partners in Confederation: Aboriginal Peoples, Self-Government and the Constitution.* Ottawa: Canada Communication Group, 1993.

—. *People to People, Nation to Nation: Highlights from the Report of the Royal Commission on Aboriginal Peoples.* Ottawa: Minister of Supply and Services, 1996.

—. *Treaty Making in the Spirit of Co-existence: An Alternative to Extinguishment.* Ottawa: Canada Communication Group Publishing, 1995.

Canada. Senate. *Debates.*

—. "The Indians and the Great War," *Sessional Papers, The Aboriginal Soldier After the Wars: Report of the Standing Senate Committee on Aboriginal Peoples,* no. 27 (1920), 13-27.

—. Senate Standing Committee on Aboriginal Peoples. *Minutes of Proceedings and Evidence.* 35th Parliament, 2nd Session, no. 2, 10 December 1996. Ottawa: Queen's Printer, 1996.

—. *Sessional Papers.*

Canada. Special Joint Committee of the Senate and the House of Commons Appointed to Examine and Consider the Indian Act. *Minutes of Proceedings and Evidence.* 28 May 1946-21 June 1948.

Canada. Task Force on Canadian Unity. *A Future Together: Observations and Recommendations.* Ottawa: Minister of Supply and Services, 1979.

Cardinal, Harold. *The Rebirth of Canada's Indians.* Edmonton: Hurtig, 1977.

—. *The Unjust Society.* Edmonton: M.G. Hurtig, 1969.

Carens, Joseph H. "Citizenship and Aboriginal Self-Government." In *For Seven Generations. An Information Legacy of the Royal Commission on Aboriginal Peoples.* RCAP *Research Reports. Governance. Project Area 4: Citizenship* [CD-ROM]. Ottawa: Libraxus, 1997.

Carrigan, Owen, ed. *Canadian Party Platforms 1867-1968.* Toronto: Copp Clark, 1968.

Cassidy, Frank, and Robert L. Bish. *Indian Government: Its Meaning in Practice.* Lantzville, BC, and Halifax, NS: Oolichan Books and the Institute for Research on Public Policy, 1989.

Chamberlin, Ted, and Hugh Brody. "History: Aboriginal History: Workshop Report." Royal Commission on Aboriginal Peoples, April 1993.

Chartrand, Paul L.A.H. "Opening the Door to Justice and Democratic Participation in Canada for Aboriginal Peoples." Notes for a speech to the "Blueprint for the Future ... A Public Forum at the Banff Centre for Management" conference, Banff, AB, 5 March 1997.

—. "'Terms of Division.' Problems of 'Outside Naming' for Aboriginal Peoples in Canada." *Journal of Indigenous Studies* 2, 2 (1991): 3-22.

"Citizens Plus." *Indian-Eskimo Association of Canada Bulletin* 11, 3 (1970).

Clark, Jennifer. "The 'Winds of Change' in Australia: Aborigines and the International Politics of Race, 1960-1972." *International History Review* 20, 1 (1998): 89-117.

Clark, The Right Honourable Joe, Minister Responsible for Constitutional Affairs. Notes for a speech delivered at a luncheon hosted by the Saskatchewan Métis Assembly at the Saskatoon Inn, Saskatoon, SK, 28 September 1991.

Clatworthy, Stewart, and Anthony H. Smith. *Population Implications of the 1985 Amendments to the Indian Act: Final Report.* Perth, ON: Living Dimensions, 1992.

Clifton, James A., ed. *The Invented Indian: Cultural Fictions and Government Policies.* New Brunswick, NJ: Transaction Publishers, 1994.

Clokie, Hugh McDowall. *Canadian Government and Politics.* Toronto: Longmans, Green, 1944.

Coates, Ken S. *Summary Report, Social and Economic Impacts of Aboriginal Land Claims Settlements: A Case Study Analysis.* Report prepared for the Ministry of Aboriginal Affairs, Province of British Columbia/Federal Treaty Negotiation Office, Government of Canada, 1995.

Coe, Michael D. *Breaking the Maya Code.* London: Penguin Books, 1992.

Cole, Douglas. *Captured Heritage: The Scramble for Northwest Coast Artifacts.* Seattle: University of Washington Press, 1985.

Cole, Douglas, and Ira Chaikin. *An Iron Hand upon the People: The Law against the Potlatch on the Northwest Coast.* Vancouver and Toronto: Douglas and McIntyre, 1990.

Cole, Douglas, and J.R. Miller. "Desperately Seeking Absolution: Responses and Reply." *Canadian Historical Review* 76, 4 (1995): 628-40.

Corry, J.A. *Democratic Government and Politics.* Toronto: University of Toronto Press, 1946.

Courchene, Thomas J. *Equalization Payments: Past, Present, and Future.* Toronto: Ontario Economic Council, 1984.

Crosby, Marcia. "Construction of the Imaginary Indian." In *Vancouver Anthology: The Institutional Politics of Art,* ed. Stan Douglas. Vancouver: Talon Books, 1991.

Cruikshank, Julie. "Invention of Anthropology in British Columbia's Supreme Court: Oral Tradition as Evidence in *Delgamuukw* v. *B.C.*" *BC Studies* 95 (Autumn 1992).

Culhane, Dara. "Adding Insult to Injury: Her Majesty's Loyal Anthropologist." *BC Studies* 95 (Autumn 1992).

—. *The Pleasure of the Crown: Anthropology, Law and First Nations.* Burnaby: Talon Books, 1998.

Cumming, Peter A., and Neil H. Mickenberg. *Native Rights in Canada.* 2nd ed. Toronto: University of Toronto Press, 1972.

Curtin, Philip D. *The Image of Africa: British Ideas and Action 1780-1850.* Madison: University of Wisconsin Press, 1964.

Daniels, Harry W., ed. *The Forgotten People: Métis and Non-status Indian Land Claims.* Ottawa, Native Council of Canada, 1979.

Davenport, T.R.H. *South Africa: A Modern History.* 3rd ed. Toronto: University of Toronto Press, 1987.

Davidson, Basil. *The Black Man's Burden: Africa and the Curse of the Nation-State.* New York: Times Books/Random House, 1992.

Dawson, R. MacGregor. *The Government of Canada* . Toronto: University of Toronto Press, 1947.

*Delgamuukw* v. *B.C.,* [1991] 79 DLR (4th) 185.

Deloria Jr., Vine. "Comfortable Fictions and the Struggle for Turf: An Essay Review of *The Invented Indian: Cultural Fictions and Government Policies.*" *American Indian Quarterly* 16, 3 (1992).

—. *Custer Died for Your Sins: An Indian Manifesto.* Norman and London: University of Oklahoma Press, 1988 [1969].

Denis, Claude. "Rights and Spirit Dancing: Aboriginal Peoples versus the Canadian State." In *Explorations in Difference: Law, Culture and Politics,* ed. Jonathan Hart and Richard W. Bauman. Toronto: University of Toronto Press, 1996.

Dickason, Olive Patricia. *Canada's First Nations: A History of Founding Peoples from Earliest Times.* Toronto: McClelland and Stewart, 1992.

Dickinson, G.M., and R.D. Gidney. "History and Advocacy: Some Reflections on the Historian's Role in Litigation." *Canadian Historical Review* 68, 4 (1987): 576-85.

Diubaldo, Richard. *The Government of Canada and the Inuit 1900-1967.* Ottawa: Indian and Northern Affairs Canada, 1985.

Dobbin, Murray. *The One-and-a-Half Men: The Story of Jim Brady and Malcolm Norris, Métis Patriots of the Twentieth Century.* Vancouver: New Star Books, 1981.

Dobbin, Murray, and Thomas Flanagan. "Riel: A Criticism and a Response." *Alberta History* 32, 2 (1984).

Duran, Eduardo, and Bonnie Duran. *Native American Postcolonial Psychology.* Albany: State University of New York Press, 1995.

Dyck, Noel. "'Telling It Like It Is:' Some Dilemmas of Fourth World Ethnography and Advocacy." In *Anthropology, Public Policy and Native Peoples in Canada,* ed. Noel Dyck and James B. Waldram. Montreal and Kingston: McGill-Queen's University Press, 1995.

—. *What Is the Indian "Problem"?* St. John's: Institute of Social and Economic Research, 1991.

Erasmus, Georges. "We The Dene." In *Dene Nation – The Colony Within,* ed. Mel Watkins. Toronto: University of Toronto Press, 1977.

Ericksen, Eugene P. "Problems in Sampling the Native American and Alaska Native Populations." In *Changing Numbers, Changing Needs. American Indian Demography and Public Health,* ed. Gary D. Sandefur, Ronald R. Rindfuss, and Barney Cohen. Washington, DC: National Academy Press, 1996.

Eschbach, Karl. "The Enduring and Vanishing American Indian: American Indian Population Growth and Intermarriage in 1990." *Ethnic and Racial Studies* 18 (January 1995).

Federation of Saskatchewan Indian Nations. *Saskatchewan and Aboriginal Peoples in the 21st Century: Social, Economic and Political Changes and Challenges.* Regina: Printwest Publishing Services, 1997.

First Nations Circle on the Constitution. *To the Source: Commissioners' Report.* Ottawa: Assembly of First Nations, 1992.

Fisher, Robin. "Judging History: Reflections on the Reasons for Judgment in *Delgamuukw* v. *B.C.*" *BC Studies* 95 (Autumn 1992).

Flanagan, Thomas. "From Indian Title to Aboriginal Rights." In *Law and Justice in a New Land: Essays in Western Canadian Legal History,* ed. Louis Knafla. Toronto: Carswell, 1986.

—. *Riel and the Rebellion: 1885 Reconsidered.* Saskatoon: Western Producer Prairie Books, 1983.

—. "An Unworkable Vision of Self-Government." *Policy Options* 18, 2 (1997).

Fleras, Augie, and Jean Edward Elliott. *The "Nations Within."* Toronto: Oxford University Press, 1992.

Fortune, Joel R. "Construing *Delgamuukw*: Legal Arguments, Historical Argumentation, and the Philosophy of History." *University of Toronto Faculty of Law Review* 51, 1 (1993): 80-117.

Foster, Hamar, and Alan Grove. "Looking behind the Masks: A Land Claims Discussion Paper for Researchers, Lawyers and their Employers." *University of British Columbia Law Review* 27, 2 (1993): 213-55.

Franks, C.E.S. *Public Administration Questions Relating to Aboriginal Self-Government.*

Kingston, ON: Institute of Intergovernmental Relations, 1987.

Fredrickson, George M. "Demonizing the American Dilemma." Review of *The End of Racism: Principles for a Multiracial Society,* by Dinesh D'Souza. In *New York Review of Books,* 19 October 1995.

Fulford, Robert. "The Trouble with Emily." *Canadian Art* 10, 4 (1993): 32-9.

Gauvin, Pierre, and Diane Fournier. "Marriages of Registered Indians: Canada and Four Selected Bands, 1967 to 1990." Technical Paper 92-1. Ottawa: Department of Indian Affairs and Northern Development, July 1992.

Geertz, Clifford. *Works and Lives: The Anthropologist as Author.* Stanford: Stanford University Press, 1988.

Gentry, Carole M., and Donald A. Grinde, Jr., eds. *The Unheard Voices: American Indian Responses to the Columbian Quincentenary 1492-1992.* Los Angeles: American Indian Studies Center, University of California, 1994.

Gibbins, Roger. "Citizenship, Political, and Intergovernmental Problems with Indian Self-Government." In *Arduous Journey: Canadian Indians and Decolonization,* ed. J. Rick Ponting. Toronto: McClelland and Stewart, 1986.

—. "Electoral Reform and Canada's Aboriginal Population: An Assessment of Aboriginal Electoral Districts." In *Aboriginal Peoples and Electoral Reform in Canada,* ed. Robert A. Milen. Toronto and Oxford: Dundurn Press, 1991.

Gibbins, Roger, and Radha Jhappan. "The State of the Art in Native Studies in Political Science." Paper presented at the Tenth Biennial Canadian Ethnic Studies Association Conference. Calgary, AB, 18-21 October 1989.

Gibbins, Roger, and J. Rick Ponting. "An Assessment of the Probable Impact of Aboriginal Self-Government in Canada." In *The Politics of Gender, Ethnicity and Language in Canada,* ed. Alan C. Cairns and Cynthia Williams. Collected Research Studies of the Royal Commission on the Economic Union and Development Prospects for Canada, vol. 34. Toronto: University of Toronto Press, 1986.

—. "The Paradoxical Nature of the Penner Report." *Canadian Public Policy* 10, 2 (1984).

Giddens, Anthony. *In Defence of Sociology: Essays, Interpretations and Rejoinders.* Cambridge: Polity Press, 1996.

Goodwill, Jean, and Norma Sluman. *John Tootoosis.* Winnipeg: Pemmican Publications, 1984.

Goonatilake, Susantha. "The Self Wandering between Cultural Localization and Globalization." In *The Decolonization of Imagination: Culture, Knowledge and Power,* ed. Jan Nederveen and Bhikhu Parekh. London: Zed Books, 1995.

Gray, Geoffrey. "From Nomadism to Citizenship: A.P. Elkin and Aboriginal Advancement." In *Citizenship and Indigenous Australians: Changing Conceptions and Possibilities,* ed. Nicolas Peterson and Will Sanders. Cambridge, UK: Cambridge University Press, 1998.

Green, Joyce. "Constitutionalizing the Patriarchy: Aboriginal Women and Aboriginal Government." *Constitutional Forum* 4, 4 (1993).

—. "Options for Achieving Aboriginal Self-Determination." *Policy Options* 18, 2 (1997).

Grobsmith, Elizabeth S. "Growing up on Deloria: The Impact of His Work on a New Generation of Anthropologists." In *Indians and Anthropologists: Vine Deloria, Jr., and the Critique of Anthropology,* ed. Thomas Biolsi and Larry J. Zimmerman. Tucson: University of Arizona Press, 1997.

Guest, Dennis. *The Emergence of Social Security in Canada.* Vancouver: University of British Columbia Press, 1980.

Hailey, Lord. *An African Survey.* London: Oxford University Press, 1938.

—. *An African Survey: Revised 1956.* London: Oxford University Press, 1957.

Hall, Tony. "The Assembly of First Nations and the Demise of the Charlottetown Accord" 30 November 1992. Mimeographed.

—. "Between Jihad and McWorld: Our Home and Native Land." *Canadian Forum* 75, 850 (June 1996): 5-7.

Hamilton, The Honourable A.C. *Canada and Aboriginal Peoples: A New Partnership.* Ottawa: Minister of Indian Affairs and Northern Development, 1995.

—. *Fact Finder for the Minister of Indian Affairs and Northern Development: Canada and Aboriginal Peoples: A New Partnership.* Ottawa: Department of Indian Affairs and Northern Development, 1995.

Hanson, F. Allan. "Empirical Anthropology, Postmodernism, and the Invention of Tradition." In *Present Is Past: Some Uses of Tradition in Native Societies,* ed. Marie Mauzé. Lanham, MD: University Press of America, 1997.

Harding, Jim. "Aboriginal Self-Government and the Urban Social Crisis." In *Continuing Poundmaker and Riel's Quest,* ed. Richard Gosse, James [sákéj] Youngblood Henderson, and Roger Carter. Saskatoon: Purich Publishing, 1994.

Havel, Vaclav. *Living in Truth.* London: Faber and Faber, 1989.

Hawthorn, H.B. "The Maori: A Study in Acculturation." *American Anthropological Association Memoirs* 46, 64, part 2 (1944).

—. "The Survival of Small Societies." In *Pilot Not Commander: Essays in Memory of Diamond Jenness,* ed. Pat Lotz and Jim Lotz. *Anthropologica* 13, 1 and 2 (1971), Special Issue.

—, ed. *A Survey of the Contemporary Indians of Canada.* 2 vols. Ottawa: Queen's Printer, 1966 and 1967.

Hawthorn, H.B., C.S. Belshaw, and S.M. Jamieson. *The Indians of British Columbia: A Study of Contemporary Social Adjustment.* Toronto: University of Toronto Press, 1958.

Henderson, James [sákéj] Youngblood. "Empowering Treaty Federalism." *Saskatchewan Law Review* 58, 2 (1994): 241-329.

—. "Implementing the Treaty Order." In *Continuing Poundmaker and Riel's Quest,* ed. Richard Gosse, James [sákéj] Youngblood Henderson, and Roger Carter. Saskatoon: Purich Publishing, 1994.

Higham, John. "America's Three Reconstructions." *New York Review of Books,* 6 November 1997.

Hobsbawm, Eric, and Terence Ranger, eds. *The Invention of Tradition.* Cambridge, UK: Cambridge University Press, 1983.

Hogg, Peter W. *Constitutional Law of Canada.* Toronto: Carswell, 1977.

—. *Constitutional Law of Canada.* 4th ed. Vol. 1. Scarborough, ON: Carswell, 1997.

Hogg, Peter W., and Mary Ellen Turpel. "Implementing Aboriginal Self-Government: Constitutional and Jurisdictional Issues." *Canadian Bar Review* 74, 2 (1995).

Ignace, Ron, George Speck, and Renee Taylor. "Some Native Perspectives on Anthropology." *BC Studies* 95 (Autumn 1992).

—. "Some Native Perspectives on Anthropology and Public Policy." In *Anthropology, Public Policy and Native Peoples in Canada,* ed. Noel Dyck and James B. Waldram. Montreal and Kingston: McGill-Queen's University Press, 1995.

Indian Chiefs of Alberta. *Citizens Plus: A Presentation by the Indian Chiefs of Alberta to Right Honourable P.E. Trudeau, June 1970.* Edmonton: Indian Association of Alberta, 1970.

Indian-Eskimo Association of Canada. *Native Rights in Canada.* Toronto: Indian-Eskimo Association of Canada, 1970.

Irwin, Colin. "Lords of the Arctic: Wards of the State, The Growing Inuit Population, Arctic Resettlement and Their Effects on Social and Economic Change." For *Review of Demography and Its Implications for Economic and Social Policy.* Ottawa: Health and Welfare Canada, [1988].

Irwin, The Honourable Ronald A., Minister of Indian Affairs and Northern Development. *Aboriginal Self-Government: The Government of Canada's Approach to*

*Implementation of the Inherent Right and the Negotiation of Aboriginal Self-Government.* Ottawa: Department of Indian Affairs and Northern Development, 1995.

—. *Executive Summary: Aboriginal Self-Government.* Ottawa: Department of Indian Affairs and Northern Development, 1995.

Jackson, Robert. "The Weight of Ideas in Decolonization: Normative Change in International Relations." In *Ideas and Foreign Policy: Beliefs, Institutions and Political Change,* ed. Judith Goldstein and Robert O. Keohane. Ithaca, NY: Cornell University Press, 1993.

Jamieson, Kathleen. *Indian Women and the Law in Canada: Citizens Minus.* Ottawa: Advisory Council on the Status of Women, 1978.

Jenness, Diamond. *Eskimo Administration.* Vol. 2, *Canada.* Technical paper no.14. Montreal: Arctic Institute of North America, 1964.

—. *The Indians of Canada.* 2nd ed. Anthropological Series no. 15, Bulletin 65. Ottawa: National Museum of Canada, 1935.

Johnson, Ralph W. "Fragile Gains: Two Centuries of Canadian and United States Policy toward Indians." *Washington Law Review* 66, 3 (1991): 643-718.

Johnston, Darlene. "First Nations and Canadian Citizenship." In *Belonging: The Meaning and Future of Canadian Citizenship,* ed. William Kaplan. Montreal and Kingston: McGill-Queen's University Press, 1993.

Kiernan, V.G. *The Lords of Human Kind: European Attitudes to the Outside World in the Imperial Age.* Harmondsworth, Middlesex: Penguin Books, 1972.

King, Cecil. "Here Come the Anthros." In *Indians and Anthropologists: Vine Deloria, Jr., and the Critique of Anthropology,* ed. Thomas Biolsi and Larry J. Zimmerman. Tucson: University of Arizona Press, 1997.

Knopff, Rainer, and F.L. Morton. "Canada's Court Party." In *Rethinking the Constitution,* ed. Anthony A. Peacock. Don Mills, ON: Oxford University Press, 1996.

Kroeber, Karl. "American Indian Persistence and Resurgence." *Boundary 2, Special Issue: 1492-1992: American Indian Persistence and Resurgence* 19, 3 (1992).

Kulchyski, Peter. "Anthropology in the Service of the State: Diamond Jenness and Canadian Indian Policy." *Journal of Canadian Studies* 28, 2 (1993).

—, ed. *Unjust Relations: Aboriginal Rights in Canadian Courts.* Toronto: Oxford University Press, 1994.

Kymlicka, Will. *Finding Our Way: Rethinking Ethnocultural Relations in Canada.* Oxford: Oxford University Press, 1998.

—. *Liberalism, Community, and Culture.* Oxford: Oxford University Press, 1989.

—. *Multicultural Citizenship: A Liberal Theory of Minority Rights.* Oxford: Clarendon Press, 1995.

Landsman, Gail. "Informant as Critic: Conducting Research on a Dispute between Iroquoianist Scholars and Traditional Iroquois." In *Indians and Anthropologists: Vine Deloria, Jr., and the Critique of Anthropology,* ed. Thomas Biolsi and Larry J. Zimmerman. Tucson: University of Arizona Press, 1997.

Lane, Maria. "Indigenous Australians and the Legacy of European Conquest: Invasion and Resurgence." In *Indigenous Australians and the Law,* ed. Elliott Johnston, Martin Hinton, and Daryle Rigney, 3-30. Sydney, Australia: Cavendish Publishing, 1997.

La Prairie, Carol. "Aboriginal Crime and Justice: Explaining the Present, Exploring the Future." *Canadian Journal of Criminology* 34 (July-October 1992): 281-97.

—. "Community Justice or Just Communities? Aboriginal Communities in Search of Justice." *Canadian Journal of Criminology* 37 (October 1995): 521-45.

—. "The 'New' Justice: Some Implications for Aboriginal Communities." *Canadian Journal of Criminology* 40 (January 1998): 61-79.

—. "Separate Aboriginal Justice Systems: Ultimate Solution or False Promise?" *Policy Options* 18, 2 (1997).

La Rocque, Emma. "The Colonization of a Native Woman Scholar." In *Women of the First Nations: Power, Wisdom, and Strength,* ed. Christine Miller and Patricia Chuchryk. Winnipeg: University of Manitoba Press, 1996.

—. "Re-examining Culturally Appropriate Models in Criminal Justice Applications." In *Aboriginal and Treaty Rights in Canada: Essays on Law, Equality, and Respect for Difference,* ed. Michael Asch. Vancouver: UBC Press, 1997.

LaSelva, Samuel V. *The Moral Foundations of Canadian Federalism.* Montreal and Kingston: McGill-Queen's University Press, 1996.

Laskin, Bora. *Canadian Constitutional Law.* 2nd ed. Toronto: Carswell, 1960.

Leslie, John F. "A Historical Survey of Indian-Government Relations, 1940-1970." Ottawa: Royal Commission Liaison Office, Department of Indian Affairs and Northern Development, 1993.

Leslie, John, and Ron Macguire, eds. *The Historical Development of the Indian Act.* 2nd ed. Ottawa: Treaties and Historical Research Centre, Research Branch, Corporate Policy, Department of Indian and Northern Affairs, 1979.

Loram, C.T., and T.F. McIlwraith, eds. *The North American Indian Today.* Toronto: University of Toronto Press, 1943.

Lower, A.R.M. *Colony to Nation: A History of Canada.* Toronto: Longmans Green, 1946.

Lugard, Lord. *The Dual Mandate in British Tropical Africa.* 5th ed. Hamden, CT: Archon Books, 1965.

Lyon, Noel. *Aboriginal Self-Government: Rights of Citizenship and Access to Governmental Services.* Kingston, ON: Institute of Intergovernmental Relations, 1984.

Lyon, Noel, and Ronald G. Atkey, eds. *Canadian Constitutional Law in a Modern Perspective.* Toronto: University of Toronto Press, 1970.

McDonnell, Roger F. "Prospects for Accountability in Canadian Aboriginal Justice Systems." In *Accountability for Criminal Justice,* ed. Philip C. Stenning, 449-77. Toronto: University of Toronto Press, 1995.

McFarlane, Peter. *Brotherhood to Nationhood: George Manuel and the Making of the Modern Indian Movement.* Toronto: Between the Lines, 1993.

McFeeley, Tom. "The Case against Affirmative Apartheid." *British Columbia Report* 6, 41 (12 June 1995): 32-7.

MacGregor, Roy. *Chief: The Fearless Vision of Billy Diamond.* Markham: Viking/Penguin, 1989.

McKay, Dave. "The Non-People." Indian Claims Commission Collection, National Library of Canada, Ottawa, ON, 1972. Mimeographed.

McKee, Christopher. *Treaty Talks in British Columbia: Negotiating a Mutually Beneficial Future.* Vancouver: UBC Press, 1996.

Macklem, Patrick. "Distributing Sovereignty: Indian Nations and Equality of Peoples." *Stanford Law Review* 45, 5 (1993): 1311-67.

—. "First Nations Self-Government and the Borders of the Canadian Legal Imagination." *McGill Law Journal* 36, 2 (1991): 382-456.

—. "Normative Dimensions of an Aboriginal Right of Self-Government." *Queen's Law Journal* 21 (Fall 1995): 173-219.

Macklem, P., K.E. Swinton, R.C.B. Risk, C.J. Robertson, L.E. Weinrib, and J.D. Whyte, eds. *Canadian Constitutional Law.* 2nd ed. Toronto: Emond Montgomery Publications, 1997.

McMillan, Alan D. *Native Peoples and Cultures of Canada: An Anthropological Overview.* 2nd ed. Vancouver and Toronto: Douglas and McIntyre, 1995.

McNeil, Kent. "Aboriginal Governments and the Canadian Charter of Rights and Freedoms." *Osgoode Hall Law Journal* 34, 1 (1996): 61-99.

—. "The Decolonization of Canada: Moving toward Recognition of Aboriginal Governments." *Western Legal History* 7, 1 (1994): 113-41.

—. "Envisaging Constitutional Space for Aboriginal Governments." *Queen's Law Journal* 19, 1 (1993): 95-136.

—. "The Meaning of Aboriginal Title." In *Aboriginal and Treaty Rights in Canada: Essays on Law, Equality, and Respect for Difference,* ed. Michael Asch. Vancouver: UBC Press, 1997.

McRoberts, Kenneth, and Patrick Monahan, eds. *The Charlottetown Accord, the Referendum and the Future of Canada.* Toronto: University of Toronto Press, 1993.

Malloy, Jonathan, and Graham White. "Aboriginal Participation in Canadian Legislatures." In *Fleming's Canadian Legislatures, 1997.* 11th ed., ed. Robert J. Fleming and J.E. Glen. Toronto: University of Toronto Press, 1997.

Manitoba Indian Brotherhood. *Wahbung: Our Tomorrows.* Winnipeg: Manitoba Indian Brotherhood, 1971.

Manning, Preston. *The New Canada.* Toronto: Macmillan, 1992.

Manuel, George, and Michael Posluns. *The Fourth World: An Indian Reality.* Don Mills, ON: Collier-Macmillan, 1974.

Marcus, George E., and Michael M.J. Fischer. *Anthropology as Cultural Critique.* Chicago: University of Chicago Press, 1986.

Markus, Andrew. *Governing Savages.* Sydney: Allen and Unwin, 1990.

Marshall, T.H. *Class, Citizenship, and Social Development.* Westport, CT: Greenwood Press, 1976.

Martin, Lawrence. *Chrétien: The Will to Win.* Vol. 1. Toronto: Lester Publishing, 1995.

Meekison, J. Peter. Notes for a speech to the "Blueprint for the Future ... A Public Forum at the Banff Centre for Management" conference, Banff, AB, 5 March 1997.

Mercredi, Ovide, and Mary Ellen Turpel. *In the Rapids: Navigating the Future of First Nations.* Toronto: Viking/Penguin, 1993.

Milen, Robert A. "Canadian Representation and Aboriginal Peoples: A Survey of the Issues." In *For Seven Generations. An Information Legacy of the Royal Commission on Aboriginal Peoples, RCAP Research Reports.* [CD-ROM]. Ottawa: Libraxus, 1997.

Miller, Bruce G. "Introduction." *BC Studies* 95 (Autumn 1992).

Miller, J.R. "'I Can Only Tell What I Know': Shifting Notions of Historical Understanding in the 1990s." Presentation to the Authority and Interpretation Conference. University of Saskatchewan, Saskatchewan, SK, 19 March 1994.

Mishra, Ramesh. *Society and Social Policy: Theories and Practice of Welfare.* 2nd ed. Atlantic Highlands: Humanities Press, 1981.

Mitchell, Darcy A., and Paul Tennant. "Government to Government: Aboriginal Peoples and British Columbia." In *For Seven Generations. An Information Legacy of the Royal Commission on Aboriginal Peoples, RCAP Research Reports. Governance. Project Area 8: Domestic Government Case Studies* [CD-ROM]. Ottawa: Libraxus, 1997.

Monture-Okanee, P.A., and M.E. Turpel. "Aboriginal Peoples and Canadian Criminal Law: Rethinking Justice." *University of British Columbia Law Review,* special edition (1992).

Morris, Mary Jane, Don Kerr, and François Nault. "Projections of the Population with Aboriginal Identity, Canada, 1996-2016." In *For Seven Generations. An Information Legacy of the Royal Commission on Aboriginal Peoples, RCAP Research Reports.* [CD-ROM]. Ottawa: Libraxus, 1997.

Morton, F.L. "The Charter Revolution and the Court Party." *Osgoode Hall Law Journal* 30, 3 (1992).

Morton, F.L., and Rainer Knopff. "The Supreme Court as the Vanguard of the Intelligentsia: The Charter Movement as Post-Materialist Politics." In *Canadian Constitutionalism: 1791-1991,* ed. Janet Ajzenstat, 57-80. Ottawa: Canadian Study of Parliament Group, 1992.

Moss, Wendy, and Peter Niemczak. *Aboriginal Land Claims.* Background Paper for Parliamentarians. Rev. ed. Ottawa: Research Branch, Library of Parliament, 1992.

Myrdal, Gunnar. *An American Dilemma. The Negro Problem and Modern Democracy.* 2 vols. New York: Harper Brothers Publishers, 1944.

Nisga'a Tribal Council. *Citizens Plus.* New Aiyansh, BC: Nisga'a Tribal Council, 1976.

Norton, Anne. "Ruling Memory." *Political Theory* 21, 3 (1993).

Novick, Peter. *That Noble Dream: The "Objectivity Question" and the American Historical Profession.* Cambridge, UK: Cambridge University Press, 1994.

Nowry, Lawrence. *Man of Mana: Marius Barbeau.* Toronto: NC Press, 1995.

Olthuis, John A., and H.W. Roger Townshend. "Is Canada's Thumb on the Scales? An Analysis of Canada's Comprehensive and Specific Claims Policies and Suggested Alternatives." In *For Seven Generations. An Information Legacy of the Royal Commission on Aboriginal Peoples. RCAP Research Reports. Governance. Project Area 4: Treaties and Aboriginal Lands* [CD-ROM]. Ottawa: Libraxus, 1997.

Paine, Robert. "In Chief Justice McEachern's Shoes: Anthropology's Ineffectiveness in Court." *POLAR* 19, 2 (1996).

Passel, Jeffrey S. "The Growing American Indian Population, 1960-1990: Beyond Demography." In *Changing Numbers, Changing Needs: American Indian Demography and Public Health,* ed. Gary D. Sandefur, Ronald R. Rindfuss, and Barney Cohen. Washington, DC: National Academy Press, 1996.

Paul, Daniel N. *We Were Not the Savages: A Micmac Perspective on the Collision of European and Aboriginal Civilizations.* Halifax, Nimbus Publishing Ltd., 1993.

*The Pierre Berton Show,* with Pierre Berton. 9 January 1969. Mimeographed.

Pitsula, James M. "The Saskatchewan CCF Government and Treaty Indians, 1944-64." *Canadian Historical Review* 75, 1 (1994).

—. "The Thatcher Government in Saskatchewan and Treaty Indians, 1964-1971: The Quiet Revolution." *Saskatchewan History* 48, 1 (1996).

Platiel, Rudy. "1970 in Retrospect." *Indian-Eskimo Association of Canada Bulletin* 11, 5 (1970).

Pocklington, T.C. *The Government and Politics of the Alberta Métis Settlements.* Regina, SK: Canadian Plains Research Center, 1991.

*Policy Options* 18, 2 (1997).

Ponting, J. Rick. *First Nations in Canada: Perspectives on Opportunity, Empowerment, and Self-Determination.* Toronto: McGraw-Hill Ryerson, 1997.

—. "Internationalization: Perspectives on an Emerging Direction in Aboriginal Affairs." *Canadian Ethnic Studies* 22, 3 (1990).

Posluns, Michael W. "Evading the Unspeakable: A Commentary on *Looking Back, Looking Forward,* Volume I of the Report of the RCAP." *Canada Watch* 5, 5 (1997).

Pratt, Alan. "Federalism in the Era of Aboriginal Self-Government." In *Aboriginal Peoples and Government Responsibility,* ed. David Hawkes. Ottawa: Carleton University Press, 1989.

Price, A. Grenfell. *White Settlers and Native Peoples.* Cambridge, UK: Cambridge University Press, 1949.

Purich, Donald. *The Métis.* Toronto: James Lorimer, 1988.

Quebec. Commission d'étude sur l'integrité du territoire du Québec. *Rapport de la Commission d'Étude sur l'Integrité du Territoire du Québec. 4. Le Domaine Indien. 4.1 rapport des commissionaires.* Québec: Commission d'étude sur l'integrité du territoire du Québec, 1971.

—. Royal Commission of Inquiry on Constitutional Problems. *The Tremblay Report.* Carleton Library no. 64, ed. David Kwavnick. Toronto: McClelland and Stewart, 1973.

Rasmussen, Ken. "Saskatchewan Aboriginal Relations." In *For Seven Generations. An Information Legacy of the Royal Commission on Aboriginal Peoples, RCAP Research*

Reports. Governance. Project Area 8: Domestic Government Case Studies [CD-ROM]. Ottawa: Libraxus, 1997.

Read, Peter. "Whose Citizens? Whose Country?" In *Citizenship and Indigenous Australians: Changing Conceptions and Possibilities,* ed. Nicolas Peterson and Will Sanders. Cambridge, UK: Cambridge University Press, 1998.

Reform Party of Canada. "Aboriginal Affairs Task Force Report." 15 September 1995.

Reynolds, Henry. "Sovereignty." In *Citizenship and Indigenous Australians: Changing Conceptions and Possibilities,* ed. Nicolas Peterson and Will Sanders. Cambridge, UK: Cambridge University Press, 1998.

Robe, Andrew Bear. "Treaty Federalism." *Constitutional Forum* 4, 1 (1992).

Rowse, Tim. "Indigenous Citizenship and Self-Determination: The Problem of Shared Responsibilities." In *Citizenship and Indigenous Australians: Changing Conceptions and Possibilities,* ed. Nicolas Peterson and Will Sanders. Cambridge, UK: Cambridge University Press, 1998.

—. *White Flour, White Power: From Rations to Citizenship in Central Australia.* Cambridge, UK: Cambridge University Press, 1998.

Rushdie, Salman. *Imaginary Homelands: Essays and Criticisms 1981-1991.* London: Granta Books, 1992.

Russell, Peter H. "Aboriginal Nationalism and Quebec Nationalism: Reconciliation through Fourth World Colonization." *Constitutional Forum* 8, 4 (1997).

Ryder, Bruce. "The Demise and Rise of the Classical Paradigm in Canadian Federalism: Promoting Autonomy for the Provinces and First Nations." *McGill Law Journal* 36, 2 (1991): 308-81.

Said, Edward A. *Culture and Imperialism.* New York: Alfred A. Knopf, 1993.

Sandefur, Gary D., Ronald R. Rindfuss, and Barney Cohen, eds. "Introduction." In *Changing Numbers, Changing Needs. American Indian Demography and Public Health,* ed. Gary D. Sandefur, Ronald R. Rindfuss, and Barney Cohen. Washington, DC: National Academy Press, 1996.

Sanders, Douglas. "The Nishga Case." In *The Recognition of Aboriginal Rights: Case Studies I, 1996,* ed. Samuel W. Corrigan and Joe Sawchuk. Brandon, MB: Bearpaw Publishing, 1996.

—. "An Uncertain Path: The Aboriginal Constitutional Conferences." In *Litigating the Values of a Nation: The Canadian Charter of Rights and Freedoms,* ed. Joseph M. Weiler and Robin M. Elliot. Toronto: Carswell, 1986.

Sawchuk, Joe. *The Dynamics of Native Politics: The Alberta Métis Experience.* Saskatoon: Purich Publishing, 1998.

Schouls, Tim. "Aboriginal Peoples and Electoral Reform in Canada: Differentiated Representation versus Voter Equality." *Canadian Journal of Political Science* 29, 4 (1996): 729-49.

Schwartz, Bryan. *First Principles, Second Thoughts: Aboriginal Peoples, Constitutional Reform and Canadian Statecraft.* Montreal: Institute for Research on Public Policy, 1986.

Scott, Ian. "Facing up to Aboriginal Self-Government: Three Practical Suggestions." The 1992 Laskin Lecture. York University, Toronto, ON, 11 March 1992.

Sharpe, Sydney, and Don Braid. *Storming Babylon: Preston Manning and the Rise of the Reform Party.* Toronto: Key Porter Books, 1992.

Sigurdson, Richard. "First Peoples, New Peoples and Citizenship in Canada." *International Journal of Canadian Studies* 14 (Fall 1996).

Siksika Nation Indian Government Committee. *Treaty Federalism – A Concept for the Entry of First Nations into the Canadian Federation and Commentary on the Canadian Unity Proposals.* Gleichen, AB: Siksika Nation Tribal Administration, 1992.

Sioui, Georges E. *For an Amerindian Autohistory.* Montreal and Kingston: McGill-Queen's University Press, 1992.

Slattery, Brian. "Aboriginal Sovereignty and Imperial Claims." *Osgoode Hall Law Journal* 29, 4 (1991): 681-703.
—. "First Nations and the Constitution: A Question of Trust." *Canadian Bar Review* 71 (June 1992): 261-93.
—. "The Organic Constitution: Aboriginal Peoples and the Evolution of Canada." *Osgoode Hall Law Journal* 34, 1 (1995): 101-12.
—. "The Paradoxes of National Self-Determination." *Osgoode Hall Law Journal* 32, 4 (1994): 703-33.
—. "Rights, Communities, and Tradition." *University of Toronto Law Journal* 41 (1991): 447-67.
Smith, Donald B., and Ian L. Getty, eds. *One Century Later: Western Canadian Reserve Indians since Treaty 7.* Vancouver, University of British Columbia Press, 1978.
Smith, Melvin H. *Our Home or Native Land?* Victoria: Crown Western, 1995.
Smith, Rogers M. *Civic Ideals: Conflicting Visions of Citizenship in US History.* New Haven and London: Yale University Press, 1997.
"Special Issue: The RCAP Report and the Future of Canada." *Canada Watch* 5, 5 (1997).
Spicer, Edward H. "The Nations of a State." *Boundary 2, Special Issue: "1492-1992: American Indian Persistence and Resurgence"* 19, 3 (1992).
Spinner, Jeff. *The Boundaries of Citizenship: Race, Ethnicity, and Nationality in the Liberal State.* Baltimore and London: Johns Hopkins University Press, 1994.
Stone, Helen. "Aboriginal Women and Self-Government: A Literature Review." Ottawa: Research and Analysis Directorate, Department of Indian and Northern Affairs, 1994.
Stout, Cameron W. "Nunavut: Canada's Newest Territory in 1999." *Canadian Social Trends* 44 (Spring 1997).
Strange, Susan. *The Retreat of the State: The Diffusion of Power in the World Economy.* Cambridge, UK: Cambridge University Press, 1996.
Strickland, Rennard. *Tonto's Revenge: Reflections on American Indian Culture and Policy.* Albuquerque: University of New Mexico Press, 1997.
Strong, Pauline Turner. "The Invented Indian [book review]." *American Ethnologist* 21, 4 (1994).
Supreme Court of Canada. *Calder* v. *A.G.B.C.,* [1973] 1 SCR.
—. *Delgamuukw* v. *B.C.,* [1997] 3 SCR.
—. *Reference re Secession of Quebec* (1998), 228 NR.
—. *R.* v. *Gladstone,* [1996] 2 SCR.
—. *R.* v. *Sparrow,* [1990] 1 SCR.
—. *R.* v. *Van der Peet,* [1996] 2 SCR.
Swidler, Nina, Kurt E. Dongoske, Roger Anyon, and Alan S. Downer, eds. *Native Americans and Archaeologists: Stepping Stones to Common Ground.* Walnut Creek, CA: Alta Mira Press, 1997.
Taylor, Charles. *Multiculturalism and "The Politics of Recognition."* Princeton, NJ: Princeton University Press, 1992.
—. *Reconciling the Solitudes: Essays on Canadian Federalism and Nationalism,* ed. Guy Laforest. Montreal and Kingston: McGill-Queen's University Press, 1993.
—. "Why Democracy Needs Patriotism." In *Debating the Limits of Patriotism, For Love of Country, Martha C. Nussbaum with Respondents,* ed. Joshua Cohen. Boston: Beacon Press, 1996.
Taylor, John Leonard. "Canadian Indian Policy during the Inter-War Years, 1918-1939." Ottawa: Department of Indian Affairs and Northern Development, 1984. Mimeographed.
Tennant, Paul. "Aboriginal Rights and the Penner Report on Indian Self-Government." In *The Quest for Justice: Aboriginal Peoples and Aboriginal Rights,* ed. Menno Boldt and J. Anthony Long. Toronto: University of Toronto Press, 1985.

Thernstrom, Stephen, and Abigail Thernstrom. *America in Black and White: One Nation, Indivisible.* New York: Simon and Schuster, 1997.

Thornton, Russell. *American Indian Holocaust and Survival.* Norman and London: University of Oklahoma Press, 1987.

—. "Tribal Membership Requirements and the Demography of 'Old' and 'New' Native Americans." In *Changing Numbers, Changing Needs. American Indian Demography and Public Health,* ed. Gary D. Sandefur, Ronald R. Rindfuss, and Barney Cohen. Washington, DC: National Academy Press, 1996.

Titley, E. Brian. *A Narrow Vision: Duncan Campbell Scott and the Administration of Indian Affairs in Canada.* Vancouver: UBC Press, 1986.

Tooker, Elisabeth. "The United States Constitution and the Iroquois League." In *The Invented Indian: Cultural Fictions and Government Policies,* ed. James A. Clifton. New Brunswick, NJ: Transaction Publishers, 1994.

Treff, Karin, and David B. Perry. *1996 Finances of the Nation.* Toronto: Canadian Tax Foundation, 1997.

Trigger, Bruce G. "The Historians' Indian: Native Americans in Canadian Historical Writing from Charlevoix to the Present." In *The Native Imprint: The Contribution of First Peoples to Canada's Character.* Vol. 1, *To 1815,* ed. Olive Patricia Dickason. Lethbridge, AB: Athabaska University Educational Enterprises, 1995.

—. *A History of Archaeological Thought.* Cambridge, UK: Cambridge University Press, 1989.

—. *Natives and Newcomers: Canada's Heroic Age Reconsidered.* Montreal and Kingston: McGill-Queen's University Press, 1985.

—. "A Present of Their Past? Anthropologists, Native People, and Their Heritage." *Culture* 8, 1 (1988).

Trudeau, Pierre Elliott. "The Province of Quebec at the Time of the Strike." In *The Asbestos Strike,* ed. Pierre Elliott Trudeau, trans. James Boake. Toronto: James Lewis and Samuel, 1974.

—. Remarks made during a question and answer session at a meeting of the Don Valley Liberal Association. Don Valley, ON, 21 January 1972.

—. Remarks on Indian, Aboriginal, and treaty rights. Vancouver, BC, 8 August 1969.

Turpel, Mary Ellen. "Aboriginal Peoples and the Canadian Charter: Interpretive Monopolies, Cultural Differences." *Canadian Human Rights Yearbook* 6 (1989-90): 3-45.

—. "Indigenous Peoples' Rights of Political Participation and Self-Determination: Recent International Legal Developments and the Continuing Struggle for Recognition." *Cornell International Law Journal* 25, 3 (1992): 579-602.

—. "On the Question of Adapting the Canadian Criminal Justice System for Aboriginal Peoples: Don't Fence Me In." *Aboriginal Peoples and the Justice System,* 161-83. Ottawa: Royal Commission on Aboriginal Peoples, 1993.

—. "Patriarchy and Paternalism: The Legacy of the Canadian State for First Nations Women." *Canadian Journal of Women and the Law* 6, 1 (1993): 174-92.

Vansina, Jan. *Oral Tradition as History.* Madison: University of Wisconsin Press, 1985.

Vincent, R.J. "Racial Equality." In *The Expansion of International Society,* ed. Hedley Bull and Adam Watson. Oxford: Clarendon Press, 1984.

Washburn, Wilcomb E., and Bruce G. Trigger. "Native Peoples in Euro-American Historiography." In *The Cambridge History of Native Peoples of the Americas.* Vol. I, part 1, *North America,* ed. Bruce G. Trigger and Wilcomb E. Washburn. Cambridge, UK: Cambridge University Press, 1996.

Watkins, Mel, ed. *Dene Nation – The Colony Within.* Toronto: University of Toronto Press, 1977.

Waubageshig, ed. *The Only Good Indian, Essays by Canadian Indians.* Toronto: New Press, 1970.

Wax, Murray L. "Educating an Anthro: The Influence of Vine Deloria, Jr." In *Indians and Anthropologists: Vine Deloria, Jr., and the Critique of Anthropology,* ed. Thomas Biolsi and Larry J. Zimmerman. Tucson: University of Arizona Press, 1997.

Weaver, Sally M. "Indian Policy in the New Conservative Government, Part I: The Nielsen Task Force of 1985." *Native Studies Review* 2, 1 (1986).

—. "Indian Policy in the New Conservative Government, Part II: The Nielsen Task Force in the Context of Recent Policy Initiatives." *Native Studies Review* 2, 2 (1986).

—. *Making Canadian Indian Policy: The Hidden Agenda 1968-1970.* Toronto: University of Toronto Press, 1981.

—. "A New Paradigm in Canadian Indian Policy for the 1990s." *Canadian Ethnic Studies* 22, 3 (1990).

Webber, Jeremy. "Relations of Force and Relations of Justice: The Emergence of Normative Community between Colonists and Aboriginal Peoples." *Osgoode Hall Law Journal* 33, 4 (1995): 623-60.

Wherrett, Jill. *Aboriginal Self-Government. Current Issue Review.* Background Paper for Parliamentarians. Ottawa: Research Branch, Library of Parliament, 1996.

Whyte, John D., and William R. Lederman. *Canadian Constitutional Law.* Toronto: Butterworths, 1975.

Wicker, Hans-Rudolf. "From Complex Culture to Cultural Complexity." In *Debating Cultural Hybridity,* ed. Pnina Werbner and Tariq Modood. London: Zed Books, 1997.

Wilkins, David E. *American Indian Sovereignty and the U.S. Supreme Court.* Austin: University of Texas Press, 1997.

Wilkinson, Charles F. *American Indians, Time, and the Law: Native Societies in a Modern Constitutional Democracy.* New Haven and London: Yale University Press, 1987.

Willis, Jane. *An Indian Girlhood.* Don Mills, ON: New Press, 1973.

Wolff, Kurt H., ed. *The Sociology of Georg Simmel.* New York: Free Press, 1950.

Woodward, C. Vann. *The Strange Career of Jim Crow.* New York: Oxford University Press, 1974.

Wuttunee, William I.C. *Ruffled Feathers: Indians in Canadian Society.* Calgary: Bell Books, 1971.

# Index

organizations, 88; rehabilitation of Louis Riel, 32-3; rivalry with status Indians for federal attention, 28; settlements, in Alberta, 21, 48; settlements, in Saskatchewan, 22; urban, in RCAP, 125

Mickenberg, Neil H., 169

Micmac people, 196

Military service, by Aboriginal people, 60

Ministry of Aboriginal Affairs (BC), 196

*Modernizing Aboriginality,* 97, 102-6, 204

Museums, and confiscated Aboriginal artifacts, 23-4, 38. *See also* Anthropologists

Myrdal, Gunnar, 29, 152

Naskapi, and self-government in Quebec, 196

"Nation," Aboriginal: as central to viewpoint of RCAP, 132-6; and citizenship, 8, 94-5, 167-8; disappearance of conditions for, 142-3; in *Penner Report,* 167; significance of, 7, 28-9, 32-5, 70, 93-5, 171; term, emergence of, 170, 171-2. *See also* Self-government, Aboriginal; Treaties

National Indian Brotherhood, 67, 169

Native people. *See* Aboriginal people

*Native Rights in Canada,* 169-70

Native Women's Association of Canada (NWAC), 74, 205

*The New Canada,* 72

New Zealand, Maori "voice" appropriation, 16

Newhouse, David, 124

Nielsen Task Force, 71-2

*Night Spirits,* 117

Nisga'a Aboriginal title decision (Calder case), 170-1, 188

*The North American Indian Today* conference, 53-4, 58

Northwest Territories: Aboriginal majority in legislature, 146; comprehensive land claims, 171, 188-9

Norton, Anne, 39

Nunavut: emergence of, 110; as form of Inuit self-government, 76; Inuit representatives in legislature of, 146. *See also* Inuit people

Office of the Commissioner of Official Languages, 145

Old Age Pension Act, 155

Old Age Security Act, 155

Old Order Amish, 203

Ontario, enfranchisement of Aboriginal people, 57

*Our Home or Native Land?* 72-3

Parallelism: and Aboriginal-government relations, 91, 93-4, 95, 149-50; and Aboriginal "nations," 93-5; versus assimilation, 91-7; and Charlottetown Accord, 83-4; contrast, discourse of, 97-102; cri-

tique of, 95-6, 115, 149-50; as goal of Aboriginal organizations, 48, 70, 78, 93; ideology of, 98; objectives of, 92-3; in philosophy of RCAP, 70-1, 117, 132; separatism, Aboriginal, 6. *See also* "Nation," Aboriginal; Reserves; Two-wampum policy

*Partners in Confederation: Aboriginal Peoples, Self-Government and the Constitution* (RCAP), 32, 124, 190, 191-2

Paul, Daniel N., 33

*Penner Report*: and Aboriginal constitutional conferences, 172; and Aboriginal relations with federal government, 201-2; focus on land-based bands, 167, 183; inattentive to governing capacity of Aboriginal nations, 186; support for Aboriginal self-government, 8, 84, 150; and two-row wampum policy, 166; use of "Indian First Nations" phrase, 172. *See also* House of Commons Special Committee on Indian Self-Government

*People to People, Nation to Nation* (RCAP), 135

Pitsula, James M., 56

Ponting, J. Rick, 87, 202

Posluns, Michael, 27, 43, 48

Potlatch, banning of, 50, 66

Price, A. Grenfell, 58-9

Provincial government: Aboriginal distrust of, 90

Quebec: comprehensive land claims, 171, 189; and Constitution of Canada, 7; constitutional crisis, 69; and Meech Lake Accord, 84; nationalist movement, and legal scholarship, 176, 184; nationhood, compared with Aboriginal nationhood, 94-5; possibility of independent society, 100; Quiet Revolution, as model for cultural evolution, 106; referendum, anticipated, 85; use of notwithstanding clause to protect language rights, 156

RCAP. *See Report of the Royal Commission on Aboriginal Peoples;* Royal Commission on Aboriginal Peoples

Red Paper (1970), 67-8

Reform Party: opposed to special status for Aboriginal people, 72, 89; support of assimilation policy for Aboriginal people, 6, 79

*Report of the Royal Commission on Aboriginal Peoples:* and Aboriginal identity, importance of, 126-32; and Aboriginal "nation," centrality of, 122, 132-6, 137, 142; constitutional vision of, 120, 121, 122-36; cultural survival, emphasis on, 128-32; federal government lack of response to, 5, 121; and federalism, 132-3, 135, 136, 142-3; importance of land-based Aboriginal "nations," 123, 129; language of, 4-5; on

Strickland, Rennard, 63
Sturdy, J.H., 56
Supreme Court of Canada: Calder decision
(Nisga'a Aboriginal title), 170-1, 188;
*Delgamuukw* v. *B.C.*, 176-7, 205; in RCAP,
absence of, 136
"The Survival of Small Societies," 161, 162

Taxes: exemption from, phased out by BC
after treaty settlement, 196; and self-
governing Aboriginal nations, 141, 151
Taylor, Charles, 153, 208
Thatcher, Ross, 56-7
*To the Source*, 33-5, 98-9, 101
Tomlinson Commission (South Africa),
29-30
Tootoosis, John, 63
Treaties: contemporary, in context of federal
system, 193; existing, supported by Constitution Act (1982), s. 35(1), 189; in
*Hawthorn Report*, 163; as "nation-to-
nation" agreements, 179-80; objection to,
by Reform Party, 72; in RCAP, 144-5, 160;
unique to each Aboriginal nation, 141
Treaty federalism: and Aboriginal represen-
tation, 180-2; and concept of Aboriginal
"nation," 70, 93-4, 132-42, 179-80, 183;
historical basis for, 181; implications of, 7,
179-83; objection to "citizens plus" concept, 182; in RCAP, 135
*Treaty Making in the Spirit of Co-existence*
(RCAP), 190-1, 192
Treaty of Waitangi (1841), 16
*Tremblay Report*, 35
Trigger, Bruce, 32, 101-2
Trudeau, Pierre: on the *Tremblay Report*, 35;
and White Paper (1969), 18, 52, 78
Turpel, Mary Ellen, 71, 179, 180
Two-row wampum policy, 5, 7, 9, 71, 92,
95, 115, 158, 166, 203, 204, 206. *See also*
Parallelism

United Nations: effect of international envi-
ronment on Canadian Indian policy, 26;
Resolution 1514, Declaration on the
Granting of Independence to Colonial
Countries and Peoples, 41
United States: assimilation policy, 47, 53, 61;
Constitution and Bill of Rights, alleged
Aboriginal models for, 33; intermarriage,
100, 204; Native American population
growth, 108, 204; race relations, 9, 29,
152, 210
*The Unjust Society*, 68
Urban Aboriginal people: acculturation of,
59, 97, 99, 100, 102, 125, 162; economic
benefits of urban life, 128, 162-2, 185; and
intermarriage, 97, 100, 125; lack of scholarly interest in, 184-5; limited opportunity for self-government, 28, 75, 89, 113,
154; and loss of culture, 124, 125, 129-31;

as percentage of Aboriginal population,
8, 73, 123, 154; in RCAP, 122, 123-6, 128-32;
social services for, 113. *See also* Aboriginal
identity

"Voice," Aboriginal: accusations of appropriation of, 14-6, 39; end of government
appropriation of, 165; as plural, 6

*Wahbung: Our Tomorrows*, 164
Washburn, Wilcomb, 32
*We Were Not the Savages*, 33
Weaver, Sally, 104
Webber, Jeremy, 102
White Paper (1969): assimilationist policy
of, 9, 18, 26, 51-3; defeat of, 65-70, 78, 165;
opposition to, 43, 65-70, 74; premises,
51-3; reflected in Nielsen Task Force, 72.
*See also* Assimilation policy
"Why Democracy Needs Patriotism," 209
Wilson, Bertha, 132
Women, Aboriginal: apprehension about
Aboriginal self-government, 74, 111-2; and
Bill C-31, 69-70, 74; mothers' allowance,
155; in political institutions, ignored by
RCAP, 147; reinstatement of Indian status
of, 69-70, 74, 127, 157, 205; and removal of
Indian Act, s. 12(1)(b), 157; status in, "tra-
ditional" Aboriginal society, 34; support
for Charter of Rights and Freedoms, 74,
98, 101, 157, 205; violence against, in Abo-
riginal communities, 74, 111-2
Woodward, C. Vann, 9

Yukon, comprehensive land claims, 171, 188-9

Zlotkin, Norman, 193